PREFERENTIAL
LIBERALIZ

Preferential Services Liberalization offers the first, comprehensive analysis of the conditions that the WTO sets for preferential trade agreements (PTAs) in the area of services. Johanna Jacobsson provides an in-depth analysis of the relevant GATS rules, puts forward a practical method to analyze services PTAs, and applies the method to services agreements concluded by the EU. The result is a detailed examination of the legal criteria for services PTAs and methods to study them, combined with a better understanding of the level of liberalization reached by the EU and its member states. This book does go beyond the EU in analyzing the implications that multi-level governance has for international services liberalization. It proposes a new approach to study services commitments of any federal state and argues that lower levels of government should receive more attention in international negotiations over services trade.

Johanna Jacobsson is Assistant Professor at IE University (Madrid, Spain). Her main fields of research are international trade law and the EU's internal market law and external trade relations. Professor Jacobsson holds a Ph.D. from European University Institute, Florence and an LL. B., LL.M. and B.A. from University of Helsinki.

CAMBRIDGE INTERNATIONAL TRADE AND ECONOMIC LAW

Series editors

Dr Lorand Bartels, *University of Cambridge*
Professor Thomas Cottier, *University of Berne*
Professor William Davey, *University of Illinois*

As the processes of regionalisation and globalization have intensified, there have been accompanying increases in the regulations of international trade and economic law at the levels of international, regional and national laws.

The subject matter of this series is international economic law. Its core is the regulation of international trade, investment and cognate areas such as intellectual property and competition policy. The series publishes books on related regulatory areas, in particular human rights, labour, environment and culture, as well as sustainable development. These areas are vertically linked at the international, regional and national level, and the series extends to the implementation of these rules at these different levels. The series also includes works on governance, dealing with the structure and operation of related international organisations in the field of international economic law, and the way they interact with other subjects of international and national law.

Books in the series

Emerging Powers in International Economic Law
Sonia E. Rolland and David M. Trubek

Commitments and Flexibilities in the WTO Agreement on Subsidies and Countervailing Measures
Jose Guilherme Moreno Caiado

The Return of the Home State to Investor-State Disputes: Bringing Back Diplomatic Protection?
Rodrigo Polanco

The Public International Law of Trade in Legal Services
David Collins

Industrial Policy and the World Trade Organization: Between Legal Constraints and Flexibilities
Sherzod Shadikhodjaev

The Prudential Carve-Out for Financial Services: Rationale and Practice in the GATS and Preferential Trade Agreements
Carlo Maria Cantore

Judicial Acts and Investment Treaty Arbitration
Berk Demirkol

Domestic Judicial Review of Trade Remedies: Experiences of the Most Active WTO Members
Edited by Müslüm Yilmaz

The Relevant Market in International Economic Law: A Comparative Antitrust and GATT Analysis
Christian A. Melischek

International Organizations in WTO Dispute Settlement: How Much Institutional Sensitivity?
Marina Foltea

Public Services and International Trade Liberalization: Human Rights and Gender Implications
Barnali Choudhury

The Law and Politics of WTO Waivers: Stability and Flexibility in Public International Law
Isabel Feichtner

African Regional Trade Agreements as Legal Regimes
James Thuo Gathii

Liberalizing International Trade after Doha: Multilateral, Plurilateral, Regional, and Unilateral Initiatives
David A. Gantz

Processes and Production Methods (PPMs) in WTO Law: Interfacing Trade and Social Goals
Christiane R. Conrad

Non-Discrimination in International Trade in Services: 'Likeness' in WTO/ GATS
Nicolas F. Diebold

The Law, Economics and Politics of Retaliation in WTO Dispute Settlement
Edited by Chad P. Bown and Joost Pauwelyn

The Multilateralization of International Investment Law
Stephan W. Schill

Trade Policy Flexibility and Enforcement in the WTO: A Law and Economics Analysis
Simon A. B. Schropp

PREFERENTIAL SERVICES LIBERALIZATION

The Case of the European Union and Federal States

JOHANNA JACOBSSON

IE University, Madrid, Spain

This book has been published with a financial subsidy from the European University Institute.

CAMBRIDGE
UNIVERSITY PRESS

University Printing House, Cambridge CB2 8BS, United Kingdom

One Liberty Plaza, 20th Floor, New York, NY 10006, USA

477 Williamstown Road, Port Melbourne, VIC 3207, Australia

314-321, 3rd Floor, Plot 3, Splendor Forum, Jasola District Centre, New Delhi - 110025, India

103 Penang Road, #05-06/07, Visioncrest Commercial, Singapore 238467

Cambridge University Press is part of the University of Cambridge.

It furthers the University's mission by disseminating knowledge in the pursuit of education, learning and research at the highest international levels of excellence.

www.cambridge.org
Information on this title: www.cambridge.org/9781108469937
DOI: 10.1017/9781316998120

© Johanna Jacobsson 2020

First published 2020
First paperback edition 2022

A catalogue record for this publication is available from the British Library

ISBN 978-1-108-47616-4 Hardback
ISBN 978-1-108-46993-7 Paperback

CONTENTS

TABLES

FOREWORD

Johanna Jacobsson has accomplished no small feat. She has managed to bring together, under one roof, a very comprehensive analysis of one of the thorniest issues not only in trade in services, but in trade in general: how should we understand preferential agreements within a context where protection (an elusive notion in and of itself) is afforded through non-tariff barriers only (i.e. measures aiming, in principle, to address market failures, and hence presumably non-discriminatory)?

To do this, she has laid down two axes: practice, illustrative practice, since an exhaustive analysis of all preferential schemes would require considerably more space; and a high-ebb benchmark, federalism, a process as far-reaching as one can imagine. By doing that, she attracts the attention of the reader to the span, the realistic span that one needs to keep as backdrop when approaching the question of preferential integration in the realm of services trade.

Her methodology is invaluable for various reasons, and it is this aspect of her work I want to insist upon, since, in my view, this is her main doctrinal contribution. For one, terms that look like empty shells when they appear in Article V of GATS, suddenly come to life. 'Substantial sectoral coverage', 'prohibition of discriminatory measures' are hardly self-interpreting terms. Johanna walks us through a very representative sample of preferential agreements, and offers an understanding of the terms in the real world. Second, thanks to this work, we are in a better position to evaluate not simply the legal consistency of various agreements with the overarching statutory provisions, but further, to appreciate the depth of preferential integration, and the wedge that emerges between preferential and MFN integration.

And, even more importantly, we have a better picture about how much we can achieve at the MFN level. In that, her work sensitized me at least, to the limits of MFN when we discuss non-tariff barriers. It is one thing to exchange tariff concessions at the six-digit level, a level uninformed by regulatory concerns. It is a different game to discuss statutory requirements for lawful supply of service in any given market. Since a very substantial number of services are either experience or credence goods, and hence, the need to regulate is present, integration will ultimately be the function of regulatory rapprochement. This is easier done across like-minded players, than otherwise.

And here we touch on the most sensitive integration issues associated with the current shape and functioning of the WTO. Can the WTO continue to operate observing the 'single undertaking' approach? Is it time to formally endorse variable geometry?

Going through the pages of this book, this thought emerged first as a nudge, and then was reincarnated as necessity. Johanna's work offers a precious platform to entertain this, in my view the most important, issue regarding not simply trade integration, but the (continued) relevance of the WTO. Anyone thinking about, or working on a (the) WTO 2.0 will have a lot to learn when going through her analysis in this respect.

Johanna thus, by addressing her research question in the manner that she has decided to address it, is offering not simply a very comprehensive discussion of preferential integration in the realm of trade in services. She is offering much more, much much more. Her work will be discussed by all those entrusted with the shaping of world trade relations, and the appropriate institutional vehicle to do that. At times of crisis of confidence in the machinery promoting trade integration, this is no small feat, by any reasonable benchmark.

Petros C. Mavroidis
Edwin B. Parker Professor of Law
Columbia Law School, New York City, New York

ACKNOWLEDGEMENTS

This book is to a large extent based on a PhD project carried out at the European University Institute in Florence and defended in December 2016. The resulting thesis focused on the criteria that the WTO's General Agreements on Trade in Services (GATS) sets for preferential services agreements. It also included the methodology that is presented in this book to analyze services agreements in light of the GATS criteria and especially in light of the EU's practice. The present book, however, goes further and sets this discussion in a wider context – that of federalism. The relevance of federalism has in the last couple of years become evident in international trade negotiations. Sub-central levels of government were in a key role both in the TTIP negotiations with the United States and in the CETA negotiations with Canada. In Europe, the Wallonian saga in the CETA context showed the impact that some EU Member State's own regions can have for the EU's trade negotiation capacity. As the power of regions and even cities is becoming more recognized, it can be predicted that the role of sub-central levels of government is set to grow further in international trade negotiations.

The completion of this book would not have been possible without the support and participation of several people and institutions. I wholeheartedly thank the European University Institute and the Academy of Finland for making it possible for me to pursue doctoral studies in the field of international trade law. It is hard to imagine a more inspiring place to work and study than the EUI. I also thank Judge Allan Rosas from the Court of Justice of the European Union for offering me the chance to work in his cabinet for a year during my PhD. I wholeheartedly thank also the Finnish Institute of International Affairs for welcoming me as a visiting researcher during a year of my research and providing me with a wonderful working environment. The book was finalized at IE University, Madrid, where I have the pleasure to work as Assistant Professor in a truly international and innovative environment.

Discussions with many academics and practitioners have helped me to understand what services trade is really about – even if I still have much to learn. I would particularly like to mention and thank Prof. Bernard Hoekman, Hamid Mamdouh, Martin Roy, Antonia Carzaniga, Juan Marchetti, Rolf Adlung, Pierre Sauvé, Prof. Markus Krajewski, Amelia Porges and Prof. Jukka Snell. I also thank Prof. Robert Wolfe, Judge Allan Rosas and Prof. Bernard Hoekman for their very helpful comments as members of jury at my doctoral defence.

Finally, I would like to sincerely thank my PhD supervisor, Professor Petros C. Mavroidis, who not only helped me to enter and understand the world of trade law but also opened my eyes to the possibilities of approaching legal research from less traditional angles. His support and encouragement was crucial also for the conclusion of the present book. My sincere thanks also to the anonymous reviewers of the book proposal. Their comments encouraged me to go deeper in the issue of federalism and the implications that multi-level governance has for international services liberalization.

The balancing act between research and 'normal life' is not always easy to handle. For helping me to keep my act together I thank my dear friends and family. I would not have completed this book without your support. That is even more so with my parents, Leena and Jarmo. I have relied, and I keep relying, on your support, love and wisdom. This book is dedicated to you. Y a ti Rafa, gracias por todo cariño.

ABBREVIATIONS

AA	Association Agreement
AB	Appellate Body (WTO)
BV	Business visitor
CCP	Common Commercial Policy (EU)
CETA	Comprehensive Economic and Trade Agreement (EU-Canada)
CJEU	Court of Justice of the European Union
CRTA	Committee on Regional Trade Agreements
CSS	Contractual service supplier
CU	Customs union
DCFTA	Deep and Comprehensive Free Trade Area
EC	European Communities
EEA	European Economic Area
EEC	European Economic Community
EFTA	European Free Trade Association
ENT	Economic Needs Test
EPA	Economic Partnership Agreement
EU	European Union
FTA	Free trade agreement
GATS	General Agreement on Trade in Services
GATT	General Agreement on Tariffs and Trade
GDP	Gross domestic product
GSP	Generalized System of Preferences
EIA	Economic Integration Agreement
ICT	Intra-company transferee
IP	Independent professional
JEEPA	Japan–European Union Economic Partnership Agreement
ICJ	International Court of Justice
ILC	International Law Commission
MA	Market access
MFN	Most-favoured nation principle
NAFTA	North American Free Trade Agreement
NT	National treatment
PTA	Preferential trade agreement

RTA	Regional trade agreement
SC	Sectoral coverage
TCN	Third-country national
TEU	Treaty on European Union
TFEU	Treaty on the Functioning of the European Union
TiSA	Trade in Services Agreement
TRIPS	Agreement on Trade-Related Aspects of Intellectual Property Rights
USA	United States of America
USTR	United States Trade Representative
USCMA	United States Mexico Canada Agreement
WTO	World Trade Organization

CITED TREATIES AND EU LEGISLATION

GATT/World Trade Organization

Agreement on Technical Barriers to Trade (TBT Agreement II), April 15, 1994, 1868 U.N.T.S. 120, LT/UR/A-1A/10 (1994)

General Agreement on Tariffs and Trade, April 15, 1994, Marrakesh Agreement Establishing the World Trade Organization, Annex 1A, The legal texts: the Results of the Uruguay Round of Multilateral Trade Negotiations (1999), 1867 U.N.T.S. 187, 33 I.L.M. 1153 (1994)

General Agreement on Trade in Services, 15 April 1994, Marrakesh Agreement Establishing the World Trade Organization, Annex 1B, The legal texts: the Results of the Uruguay Round of Multilateral Trade Negotiations 284 (1999), 1869 U.N.T.S. 183, 33 I.L.M. 1167 (1994)

Differential and More Favourable Treatment, Reciprocity and Fuller Participation of Developing Countries, Decision of 28 November 1979 by Signatories to the General Agreement on Tariffs and Trade, L/4903

Transparency Mechanism for Regional Trade Agreements, General Council, Decision of 14 December 2006, WT/L/671, 18 December 2006

Preferential Treatment to Services and Services Suppliers of Least-Developed Countries, Ministerial Conference Decision of 17 December 2011, WT/L/847, 19 December 2011

Understanding on Rules and Procedures Governing the Settlement of Disputes, Marrakesh Agreement Establishing the World Trade Organization, Annex 2, 1869 U.N.T.S. 401, 33 I.L.M. 1226 (1994)

European Union

International Treaties

Comprehensive Economic and Trade Agreement (CETA) between Canada, of the one part, and the European Union and its Member States, of the other part, Official Journal of the European Union L 11 of 14 January 2017

Convention on the law applicable to contractual obligations opened for signature in Rome on 19 June 1980, Official Journal of the European Union L 266 of 9 October 1980

Economic Partnership Agreement between the CARIFORUM States, of the one part, and the European Community and its Member States, of the other part, Official Journal of the European Union L 289 of 30 October 2008

Free Trade Agreement between the European Union and its Member States, of the one part, and the Republic of Korea, of the other part, Official Journal of the European Union L 127 of 14 May 2011

Agreement Establishing an Association between Central America, on the one hand, and the European Community and its Member States, on the other, Official Journal of the European Union L 346 of 15 December 2012

Association Agreement between the European Union and the European Atomic Energy Community and their Member States, of the one part, and Georgia, of the other part, Official Journal of the European Union L 261 of 30 August 2014

Primary Legislation

Consolidated versions of the Treaty on European Union and of the Treaty establishing the European Community, OJ C 321E, 29.12.2006, p. 1–186

Secondary Legislation

Directive 96/71/EC of the European Parliament and of the Council of 16 December 1996 concerning the posting of workers in the framework of the provision of services, OJ L 18, 21.1.1997, p. 1–6

Directive 2005/36/EC of the European Parliament and of the Council of 7 September 2005 on the recognition of professional qualifications, OJ L 255, 30.9.2005, p. 22–142

Directive 2006/123/EC of the European Parliament and of the Council of 12 December 2006 on services in the internal market, OJ L 376, 27.12.2006, p. 36–68

Directive 2008/104/EC of the European Parliament and of the Council of 19 November 2008 on Temporary Agency Work, OJ L 327, 5.12.2008, p. 9–14

Directive 2011/98/EU of the European Parliament and of the Council of 13 December 2011 on a single application procedure for a single permit for third-country nationals to reside and work in the territory of a Member State and on a common set of rights for third-country workers legally residing in a Member State, OJ L 343, 23.12.2011, p. 1–9

Directive 2014/36/EU of the European Parliament and of the Council of 26 February 2014, on the conditions of entry and stay of third-country nationals for the purpose of employment as seasonal workers, OJ L 94, 28.3.2014, p. 375–390

Directive 2014/66/EU of the European Parliament and of the Council of 15 May 2014 on the conditions of entry and residence of third-country nationals in the framework of an intra-corporate transfer, OJ L 157, 27.5.2014, p. 1–22

CITED CASES

International Court of Justice

LaGrand (Germany *v.* United States of America), 1999 I.C.J. 9 (Order of Mar. 3) and Judgment, I.C.J. Reports 2001, p. 466

Avena and Other Mexican Nationals (Mex. *v.* U.S.), Judgment, 2004 I.C.J. Rep. 12 (Mar. 31)

GATT/WTO Dispute Settlement Body

European Community - Tariff Treatment on Imports of Citrus Products from Certain Countries in the Mediterranean Region, L/5776, 7 February 1985, GATT Panel Report, unadopted

Canada - Measures Affecting the Sale of Gold Coins, L/5863, 17 September 1985, GATT Panel Report, unadopted

Canada - Alcoholic Drinks, DS17/R – 39S/27, 18 February 1992, GATT Panel Report

United States - Malt Beverages, DS23/R, 16 March 1992, GATT Panel Report

Japan - Taxes on Alcoholic Beverages, WT/DS8/AB/R, WT/DS10/AB/R, WT/DS11/AB/R, Report of the Appellate Body, circulated 4 October 1996

European Communities - Regime for the Importation, Sale and Distribution of Bananas, Report of the Appellate Body, WT/DS27/AB/R, circulated 9 September 1997

United States - Import Prohibition of Certain Shrimp and Shrimp Products, Report of the Appellate Body, WT/DS58/AB/R, circulated 12 October 1998

Turkey - Restrictions on Imports of Textile and Clothing Products, WT/DS34/R, Report of the Panel, circulated 31 May 1999

Turkey - Restrictions on Imports of Textile and Clothing Products, WT/DS34/AB/R, Report of the Appellate Body, circulated 22 October 1999

Canada - Certain Measures Affecting the Automotive Industry, WT/DS139/R, WT/DS142/R, Report of the Panel, circulated 11 February 2000

United States - Definitive Safeguard Measures on Imports of Circular Welded Carbon Quality Line Pipe from Korea, WT/DS202/AB/R, Report of the Appellate Body, circulated 15 February 2002

Mexico - Measures Affecting Telecommunications Services, Report of the Panel, WT/DS204/R, circulated 2 April 2004

United States – Measures Affecting the Cross-Border Supply of Gambling and Betting Services, Report of the Appellate Body, WT/DS285/AB/R, circulated 7 April 2005
China – Measures Affecting Trading Rights and Distribution Services for Certain Publications and Audiovisual Products, WT/DS363/R, Report of the Panel, circulated 12 August 2009
China – Measures Affecting Trading Rights and Distribution Services for Certain Publication and Audiovisual Entertainment Products, WT/DS363/AB/R, Report of the Appellate Body, circulated 21 December 2009
China – Electronic Payment Services, WT/DS413/R, Report of the Panel, circulated 16 July 2012
Argentina – Measures Relating to Trade in Goods and Services, WT/DS453/AB/R, Report of the Appellate Body, circulated 14 April 2016

The Court of Justice of the European Union

Case 22/70, Commission *v.* Council [1971] ECR 263
Case 804/79, Commission *v.* United Kingdom [1981] ECR 1045
C-113/89, Rush Portuguesa Ld^a *v.* Office national d'immigration [1990] ECR I-1417
C-43/93, Raymond Vander Elst *v.* Office des migrations Internationales [1994] ECR I-3803
Joined cases C-49/98, C-50/98, C-52/98 to C-54/98 and C-68/98 to C-71/98, Finalarte Sociedade de Construção Civil Ld^a (C-49/98), Portugaia Construções Ld^a (C-70/98) and Engil Sociedade de Construção Civil SA (C-71/98) v Urlaubs- und Lohnausgleichskasse der Bauwirtschaft and Urlaubs- und Lohnausgleichskasse der Bauwirtschaft *v.* Amilcar Oliveira Rocha (C-50/98), Tudor Stone Ltd (C-52/98), Tecnamb-Tecnologia do Ambiante Ld^a (C-53/98), Turiprata Construções Civil Ld^a (C-54/98), Duarte dos Santos Sousa (C-68/98) and Santos & Kewitz Construções Ld^a (C-69/98) [2001] ECR I-7831
C-445/03 Commission *v.* Luxembourg [2004] ECR I-10191
C-341/05, Laval un Partneri Ltd *v.* Svenska Byggnadsarbetareförbundet, Svenska Byggnadsarbetareförbundets avdelning 1, Byggettan and Svenska Elektrikerförbundet [2007] ECR I-11767
Joined cases C-307/09 to C-309/09, Vicoplus SC PUH (C-307/09), BAM Vermeer Contracting sp. zoo (C-308/09) and Olbek Industrial Services sp. zoo (C-309/09) *v.* Minister van Sociale Zaken en Werkgelegenheid [2011] ECR I-00453
C-414/11, Daiichi Sankyo Co. Ltd, Sanofi-Aventis Deutschland GmbH *v.* DEMO Anonimos Viomikhaniki kai Emporiki Etairia Farmakon [2013] EU:C:2013:520
C-137/12, Commission *v.* Council (Conditional Access Services) [2013] EU:C:2013:675
C-28/12, European Commission *v.* Council of the European Union [2015] EU:C:2015:282
Opinion 1/75, Opinion of the Court of 11 November 1975 given pursuant to Article 228 of the EEC Treaty [1975] ECR 01355

~

Introduction

I WTO and Preferential Services Liberalization

The purpose of the book is threefold. First, it examines the rules of the World Trade Organization (WTO) on economic integration agreements (EIAs), which are preferential trade agreements (PTAs) concluded in the field of services.[1] Second, it presents the results of an empirical analysis of international trade agreements concluded by the European Union (EU) and including liberalization of trade in services.[2] Drawing on the interpretation of the relevant WTO rules, the book analyzes the level of liberalization reached by the EU in those agreements. Particular attention

---

[1] EIAs are PTAs focusing on the liberalization of services. The term EIA is employed in Art. V of the WTO's General Agreement on Trade in Services (GATS).

[2] 'Empirical' in the present book refers to the nature of our method which is to go through the EU's services schedules in four chosen EIAs. Even though it concerns interpretation of legal text and thus corresponds to the traditional method of conducting legal research, we refer to our analysis as empirical in order to distinguish it from the interpretation of the proper texts of the agreements. Instead of engaging in an extensive interpretation of the EU's schedules in accordance with the customary rules of interpretation, we give numerical values to the EU's sector-specific commitments based on placing the commitments in simple categories. Our choice of vocabulary is therefore meant to take some distance to a traditional legal analysis. However, 'empirical' in this book does not mean information gained by experience, observation or experiment – even though experience and repeated observations are definitely useful in order to understand the complex nature of services schedules and the way in which services commitments are formulated. The scheduled services commitments are part of the overall agreement but each party provides its own commitments. They are typically vaguer and practically oriented than the actual chapters of the agreement. That makes the interpretation of services schedules somewhat special and, arguably, especially challenging.

1

is paid to the federal-type structure of the EU, which is reflected in the multi-level liberalization of services in the Union. Third and finally, the conclusions on the application of the WTO rules on EIAs are extended outside the EU to all states with constitutionally divided powers in services regulation. Typically, such states are federations.

The book contributes to the growing amount of research on preferential trade agreements (PTAs). Such research has become topical with the vast increase in the numbers of PTAs globally. Whereas earlier research used to be focused on PTAs in the field of goods, there is now a significant number of trade lawyers, social scientists and economists working on preferentialism in the field of services too. At the moment almost all new PTAs, especially among developed countries, include provisions on the liberalization of services. Moreover, a subset of WTO Members (including the EU) has embarked on a so-called plurilateral initiative to liberalize services through a new international agreement – the Trade in Services Agreement (TiSA).[3] Considering that tariffs on goods, especially preferential ones, are already relatively low, many countries have turned their attention to services. This is a logical development also in light of new technologies that enable services to become more globally tradable. It is also widely understood that services play a key role in infrastructure as well as global supply chains. Thus the dismantling of barriers in services trade often leads to productivity gains also in other sectors of the economy.

The first part of the book focuses on the theory of preferentialism in services, taking into account the law as well as the special characteristics of services trade as compared to trade in goods. The starting point of this analysis is Art. V of the WTO's General Agreement on Trade in Services (GATS).[4] Art. V lays down the discipline for EIAs, which are PTAs including liberalization of trade in services.[5] In principle, all EIAs

---

[3] The negotiations, however, came to a halt in 2016. For information on the negotiations that took place until then, see e.g. the webpages of the European Commission and the United States Trade Representative: http://ec.europa.eu/trade/policy/in-focus/tisa/ and https://ustr.gov/TiSA (last accessed on 1 February 2019).

[4] General Agreement on Trade in Services, 15 Apr. 1994, Marrakesh Agreement Establishing the World Trade Organization, Annex 1B, The legal texts: the Results of the Uruguay Round of Multilateral Trade Negotiations 284 (1999), 1869 U.N.T.S. 183, 33 I.L. M. 1167 (1994) (hereinafter GATS).

[5] In the following, the acronym PTA is used when referred to preferential trade agreements in general sense. Such agreements may include liberalization of goods, services or both. Several commentators, as well as the WTO Secretariat, prefer to use the term Regional

concluded by WTO Members[6] with each other or non-members should abide by its provisions. In practice, however, compliance with the Art. V rules is questionable to the least. There are numerous reasons behind the lack of respect for the legal discipline, but they can, in essence, be summarized in two: the rules are vague and they have proved hard to enforce.

So far, the legal content of Art. V GATS has attracted relatively little attention. Compared to the existing literature on Art. XXIV of the General Agreement on Tariffs and Trade (GATT),[7] research on Art. V is modest in amount. Preferentialism in the field of goods has been the object of economic and policy-oriented research already for decades. However, notwithstanding the large interest, the exact conditions that Art. XXIV GATT sets for free-trade agreements (FTAs) and customs unions (CUs) also remain unclear due to the open-endedness in the wording of the conditions. No significant clarification has been attained due to the extremely low number of PTA-related disputes brought under the GATT/WTO dispute settlement procedure. The Members lack enthusiasm in enforcing Art. XXIV through multilateral control of PTAs. In practice, the legal disciplines of both Art. XXIV GATT and Art. V GATS have given up to the highly political nature of preferential trade.

The rules of Art. V are arguably even vaguer than those of Art. XXIV GATT, which is part of a much older agreement. The essence of Art. V is that it allows a limited derogation from the cornerstone of WTO law, the most-favoured nation principle.[8] The main requirements for GATS-consistent EIAs are that, first, they have substantial sectoral coverage and, second, that they provide for the absence or elimination of

---

Trade Agreements (RTAs). The term PTA is here considered more appropriate since the most essential feature of such agreements is their preferentiality in the relations of the participating countries. Moreover, many of today's PTAs are not limited to any specific region. See Bhagwati, J. (2008) *Termites in the Trading System: How Preferential Agreements Undermine Free Trade*. Oxford; New York: Oxford University Press, XI. When referring especially to the service part of a specific PTA or specific PTAs, the book refers to EIA(s). This clarifies that the purpose is to refer solely to the service elements of the agreement(s).

[6] Hereinafter referred to only as Members.

[7] General Agreement on Tariffs and Trade 1994, Apr. 15, 1994, Marrakesh Agreement Establishing the World Trade Organization, Annex 1A, The legal texts: the Results of the Uruguay Round of Multilateral Trade Negotiations (1999), 1867 U.N.T.S. 187, 33 I.L.M. 1153 (1994) (hereinafter GATT).

[8] In case a PTA regulates trade in goods in addition to trade in services, its WTO-consistency is determined also under Art. XXIV GATT.

substantially all discrimination in the sectors covered by the agreement.[9] In addition, the so-called internal and external trade requirements should be fulfilled. According to these requirements, an EIA should, on the one hand, be designed to facilitate trade between the parties to the agreement (the internal requirement) and, on the other hand, not raise the overall level of barriers to trade in services with regard to any Member outside the agreement (the external requirement). So far, we have no clear understanding of any of these requirements due to the open-ended nature of definitions such as 'substantial', and because of methodological difficulties in calculating the effects of barriers to services trade. At least so far, Members have been reluctant to challenge each other's PTAs and the GATT/WTO dispute settlement has so far not given much guidance on the relevant rules.

In the absence of effective control over PTAs, it is up to the Members party to such agreements to make sure that they are complying with their obligations towards other Members. However, due to the ambiguous nature of Art. V, it is unclear what is the degree of integration that Members should follow. Thus, Members inevitably face a challenge in structuring their EIAs in a WTO-consistent fashion. Due to non-enforcement, they also lack sufficient incentive to do so. Because of the uncertainty surrounding the WTO rules on PTAs, the WTO-consistency of PTAs already in force is naturally also covered by uncertainty.[10]

Economists and lawyers have already for long worried about the systemic consequence of PTAs to the multilateral trading system. So far, the debate on whether PTAs should be seen as building blocks or stumbling blocks to multilateralism has been mostly confined to the liberalization of trade in goods.[11] One of the main observations of the book is that due to inherent differences between trade in goods and

---

[9] This is to be done through elimination of existing discriminatory measures, and/or prohibition of new or more discriminatory measures, 'either at the entry into force of the agreement or on the basis of a reasonable time-frame, except for measures permitted under Articles XI, XII, XIV and XIV bis'. Discrimination is specified to be understood 'in the sense of' Art. XVII GATS (national treatment).

[10] Mitchell, A. D. & Lockhart, N. J. S. (2009) Legal Requirements for PTAs under the WTO, in Lester, S. N. & Mercurio, B. (eds.), *Bilateral and Regional Trade Agreements: Commentary and Analysis.* Cambridge; New York: Cambridge University Press, 81–113, at 113.

[11] Fink, C. & Jansen, M. (2009) Services Provisions in Regional Trade Agreements: Stumbling Blocks or Building Blocks for Multilateral Liberalization?, in Baldwin, R. & Low, P. (eds.), *Multilateralizing Regionalism: Challenges for the Global Trading System.* Cambridge: Cambridge University Press, at 222; Bhagwati, J. & Panagariya, A. (1996) *The Economics of Preferential Trade Agreements.* Washington, DC: AEI Press.

services, preferentialism in services is fundamentally different from pre-ferentialism in goods. Another important observation is that preferenti-alism in services is potentially less dangerous than in the field of goods but it should still be carefully analyzed and to at least some extent controlled as to prevent increase in the forms of integration that have most harmful discriminatory effects on outsiders and, in many cases, to those inside the agreement as well.

Whereas in goods trade, the central element of a PTA is a preferential tariff reduction vis-à-vis a WTO Member's multilateral tariff binding, in EIAs the central element is the heightened elimination of discrimination towards one's preferential partner. The difference is reflected in the legal disciplines. Unlike Art. XXIV GATT that focuses on elimination of tariffs and thus on enhanced market access for goods of preferential origin, Art. V GATS does not include any market access ('MA') discipline but is focused on the elimination of discrimination between the parties to the agreement. We argue that the difference stems from the basic features of services trade. Whereas altering the conditions for MA through tariffs is easily done with regard to goods, in the field of services the application of different sets of MA conditions to different partners is often unpractical and, in some cases, close to impossible. Instead of focusing on mostly quantitative MA limitations, Art. V requires extensive elimination of discrimination. It is proposed in the book that the emphasis on non-discrimination alleviates concern over growing preferentialism in ser-vices. Unlike the elimination of tariffs that takes place in goods PTAs, the elimination of discrimination through EIAs is more likely to benefit outsiders as well and thus makes EIAs less susceptible of creating trade diversion. This effect is coupled with the generous rules of origin that are required from EIAs by Art. V. Such rules are often implemented also in practice.[12]

As all PTAs, EIAs are capable of creating negative effects especially for outsiders. Art. V aims at reducing such effects but it suffers from the same problem as Art. XXIV. The problem is the general ambiguity in the rules. So far there is no general understanding of the level and type of liberalization EIAs must adopt in order to satisfy the Art.

---

[12] As Miroudot et al. (2010) note, liberal rules of origin for service suppliers play an important role in minimizing the distortions introduced by EIAs as companies from third-countries can benefit from the preferential treatment of EIAs through commercial presence in the territory of the parties. See Miroudot, S., Sauvage, J. & Sudreau, M. (2010) Multilateralising Regionalism: How Preferential Are Services Commitments in Regional Trade Agreements?, *OECD Trade Policy Working Papers*, No. 106, at 27.

V requirements.[13] Neither the WTO's dispute settlement mechanism nor the Members themselves have been able to provide guidance on the issue. The WTO's Committee on Regional Trade Agreements (the CRTA), the official review body of all PTAs, is now mainly an enforcer of transparency.[14] At the same time, however, there seems to be a general agreement on the urgent need to clarify what is required from PTAs. Without such clarification, PTAs continue to be undisciplined and MFN will be reduced to 'LFN'.[15]

II   Structure of the Book

The book consists of four parts. The first part presents and develops WTO law regarding preferentialism in services. It starts by exploring the historic background of regional and preferential trade agreements and the reasons for their significant increase especially during the last two decades. It then provides a substantive analysis and interpretation of Art. V GATS that includes the detailed rules on services PTAs. The aim of the first part is to provide a theoretical framework for a legal analysis of individual services agreements. The book focuses on the so-called internal requirement for EIAs included in the first paragraph of Art. V,[16] as well as on the possibility to give consideration to the relationship of the agreement to a wider process

---

[13] The same problem applies to the interpretation of Art. XXIV of the GATT. It is, however, claimed that the GATS rules on EIAs are even more open-ended than those of Art. XXIV GATT on free trade areas and custom unions.

[14] On 14 December 2006, the General Council established on a provisional basis a new transparency mechanism for all PTAs. The transparency mechanism provides for early announcement of any PTA and notification to the WTO. Members will consider the notified PTAs on the basis of a factual presentation by the WTO Secretariat. In contrast to the previous review procedure, there is, however, no longer review of the consistency (from a legal perspective) of the notified PTA with the WTO rules. See Mavroidis, P. C. (2011) Always Look on the Bright Side of Non-Delivery: WTO and Preferential Trade Agreements, Yesterday and Today. *World Trade Review*, 10(3), 375–87, at 377, as well as Mavroidis, P. C. (2015), *The Regulation of International Trade: Volume 1: GATT*, Cambridge: MIT Press, at 310–11.

[15] Mavroidis, P. C. (2005) *The General Agreement on Tariffs and Trade: A Commentary.* Oxford: Oxford University Press, at 246. See Bhagwati who refers to LFN, 'least favoured nation', as a demonstration of the increasing proportion of non-MFN trade in the overall volume of world trade: Bhagwati (2008), at 14.

[16] The first paragraph of Art. V requires that EIAs provide for 'substantial sectoral coverage' and for the absence or elimination of substantially all discrimination, in the sense of Art. XVII of the GATS (national treatment), between or among the parties, in the substantially covered sectors.

of economic integration or trade liberalization among the countries concerned (paragraph 2 of Art. V). On the contrary, the external requirement of Art. V:4, which concerns the requirement not to raise the overall level of barriers in respect of any Member outside the agreement, is not explored to the same length. That is because the book aims at providing a framework for analyzing the internal liberalization levels of EIAs. The possible tools for assessing the fulfilment of the external requirement differ from the analysis of EIAs under the internal requirement and the provisions of Art. V:2. Such tools, which largely remain to be developed, would be challenging to integrate into a textual analysis of services agreements and commitments.

The second part of the book addresses a particularly timely question which is the approach that should be adopted to services regulation, and especially services trade barriers, applied by non-central levels of government. Some of the most powerful nations, such as the United States (USA) and Canada, have divided competencies over services regulation. Arguably some of the most significant economic advantages would be realized if sub-central entities (states, regions and municipalities) engaged in deeper liberalization of services. In this regard, the EU is in the book treated as a federal entity as due to the EU's common trade policy its behaviour in its external trade relations can be compared to federal states.

To explain the particularities that relate to the liberalization of services by the EU, Chapter 4, the first chapter of Part II, reviews the key legal issues in the EU's trade policy in the field of services. The development of the EU's competences in the field of services is analyzed in light of the jurisprudence of the Court of Justice of the EU ('the Court'). In particular, we concentrate on the consequences of the unfinished nature of the EU's internal services market on its external liberalization of services.

The third and fourth parts of the book look into practice. The third part provides a new methodology that can be used to analyze EIAs in light of the criteria of GATS Art. V:1. The method is particularly suitable for coding services liberalization undertaken by federal entities. The fourth part provides an analysis of four EIAs concluded by the EU. As a result, the book provides an evaluation of the EU's services commitments in light of the GATS Art. V:1 discipline on EIAs. The method consists of a textual analysis of the EU's EIAs, particularly the sector-specific services commitments, and of coding those commitments based on the existence of discrimination.

Only the EU side's commitments are analyzed: the purpose is to find out the approximate level of liberalization reached by the EU, as well as to assess how the EU's method of liberalization corresponds to the Art. V criteria. Thus, no conclusions can be drawn on the agreements in their entirety. Since the EU has concluded EIAs with very different types of countries from several regions, the agreements are useful material for an analysis under the various elements of Art. V. Yet considering that all EU Member States are highly developed countries and advanced economies, the flexibility that Art. V GATS provides for developing countries does not apply to the EU side. Whereas the overall purpose of the agreement can be taken into account in the analysis under Art. V, it is argued that the EU side's level of liberalization should always correspond to the strict requirement of 'substantiality' in terms of sectoral coverage and elimination of discrimination.

In the interpretation of the results in light of the WTO rules, particularly Art. V GATS, specific attention is paid to the EU's commitments under Mode 4. We assess how the EU understands Mode 4 and to what extent the EU's position matches the requirements of the GATS. As with the other modes, we also try to evaluate how the liberalization level in the EU's Mode 4 commitments corresponds to the criteria of Art. V.[17] In contrast to the other modes, the scope of Mode 4 is particularly open to different interpretations as it is not clear what categories of natural persons should be covered by it.

III　Federalism and Services Liberalization: The EU and Beyond

In the WTO the EU has been one of the most active proponents of service trade liberalization. This is logical considering that the EU is the world's biggest exporter of commercial services.[18] During the past

---

[17] The GATS differentiates between four modes of supply: 1) from the territory of one Member into the territory of any other Member (cross-border trade); 2) in the territory of one Member to the service consumer of any other Member (consumption abroad); 3) by a service supplier of one Member, through commercial presence in the territory of any other Member (commercial presence, or investment) and 4) by a service supplier of one Member, through presence of natural persons of a Member in the territory of any other Member (Art. I:2(d) GATS).

[18] World Trade Statistical Review 2018, p. 16, available at www.wto.org/english/res_e/statis_e/wts2018_e/wts2018_e.pdf (last accessed on 20 February 2019). If one were to take into account the share of individual countries, the biggest exporter of commercial services would be the United States. In the EU, the single biggest exporters are United Kingdom, Germany and France.

decade the EU has become active in liberalizing services trade also through PTAs with third countries. Especially in the most recent, so-called deep and comprehensive free trade areas (DCFTAs), new market opening in services is one of the main goals of the negotiations.[19] Detailed commitments on the liberalization of services can also be found in many other types of agreements concluded by the EU with third countries. The empirical analysis conducted for the purposes of the book covers four agreements belonging to three different groups of agreements (two Association Agreements, a Free Trade Agreement and an Economic Partnership Agreement).[20] The choice of the agreements was based on an assumption that liberalization levels would vary based on the different goals of the agreements. The results partly do reflect differences in these three types of agreements.[21] However, overall, and maybe surprisingly, the differences in the level of non-discrimination provided by the EU to the partner countries are revealed to be modest.

The methodological choices are adapted to take into account the special circumstances of services trade liberalization by the EU towards third countries, especially the fact that regulation of services, unlike goods, is not uniform throughout the Union. However, the key understanding is that such special circumstances are relevant not only in the study of the EU, but in the study of all WTO Members with constitutionally divided powers in the regulation of service activities.[22] Similar circumstances are likely to rise also with regard to any other existing or future free trade area that would start

---

[19] The first such 'deep and comprehensive' FTAs aimed at more market opportunities were the EU–South Korea Free Trade Agreement of 2011 and the EU–Singapore Free Trade Agreement of 2013.

[20] See the reviewed agreements in Appendix 2.

[21] For detailed results, see Appendix 3 and Part IV of the book.

[22] 'Regulation' in this book is understood as a broad, general political and legal concept that includes all governmental policies and measures that are aimed at influencing, controlling and guiding all private activities with impacts on others. See Krajewski, M. (2003) *National Regulation and Trade Liberalization in Services: The Legal Impact of the General Agreement on Trade in Services (GATS) on National Regulatory Autonomy*. The Hague: Kluwer Law International, 4. Reference can also be made to Reagan who defines regulation as 'a process or activity in which government requires or proscribes certain activities or behaviour on the part of individuals and institutions, mostly private, but sometimes public'. See Reagan, M. (1987) *Regulation – The Politics of Policy*. Boston and Toronto: Little, Brown and Company, at 15. Regulation can take place on all levels of a state, as well as on supranational and international level.

concluding services agreements independently in its own name, similarly to the EU.[23]

The challenges that the EU as a multi-state actor faces in concluding services trade agreements are often similar especially to such countries that have a federal structure. Trade liberalization by the EU reflects the combination of supranational and national jurisdiction over trade negotiation areas. Within the field of services, as in goods, the competence to conclude agreements with third parties is within the powers of the Union.[24] However, due to the lack of internal harmonization of services regulations within the EU, the EU Member States keep scheduling their own national reservations to the common EU services schedule in EIAs. In this sense, there are similarities to countries with de-centralized regulation of services. In the case of many federal states, however, such non-central measures are not often explained in detail in the country's services schedule. A prominent example of a federal state with regional powers in the field of services is the USA. The USA has recently begun including an illustrative list of non-conforming measures ('NCMs') in the field of services for state level restrictions.[25] However, the NCMs

[23] So far, to our knowledge, the EU is the only free trade/common market area that is clearly concluding trade agreements in its own name in addition to its Member States (and thus binding itself legally too). It is also the only organization that is a Member of the WTO in its own right, in addition to its Member States. This might, however, change, as more regions are engaging in deeper integration. The EU, for its own part, is interested in agreements with other free-trade areas or common markets. Negotiations for an Association Agreement are ongoing with Mercosur. Mercosur appears as the contracting party or negotiating party to several trade agreements but it is the individual Member States rather than Mercosur that are the formal contracting parties to those agreements. The EU has also had as a goal to one day integrate its separate deals/negotiations with certain Southeast Asian countries and conclude a region-to-region trade agreement with the Association of Southeast Asian Nations (ASEAN). See European Commission's memo 'Overview of FTA and Other Trade Negotiations', updated 15 February 2018, available at http://trade.ec.europa.eu/doclib/docs/2006/december/tradoc_118238.pdf, last accessed on 20 February 2019. Whether any future agreement would bind the ASEAN as an organization naturally depends on the level of integration and legal structure that ASEAN countries are willing to adopt for the organization. According to its Charter, ASEAN has been accorded legal personality as well as an explicit international treaty-making power. In most cases, however, all Member States of the ASEAN are listed as parties to the agreement. See Cremona, M., Kleimann, D., Larik, J., Lee, R. & Vennesson, P. (2015) *ASEAN's External Agreements: Law, Practice and the Quest for Collective Action.* Cambridge: Cambridge University Press, at 84–7.

[24] For a review of the development of EU's competences in trade, see Chapter 4 of Part II of the book.

[25] NCMs are reservations that are put forward to existing and/or future measures applied by the government in case such measures are in violation of the agreement's services disciplines, such as the market access and the national treatment disciplines.

illustrated at the state and local level are provided for transparency purposes only and are not bound by the services provisions of these EIAs.[26]

In the Comprehensive Economic and Trade Agreement (CETA) between the EU and Canada, Canada has for the first time in its PTA history included a binding list of provincial and territorial non-conforming measures in the field of services and investments. In the currently stalled negotiations on the Transatlantic Trade and Investment Partnership (TTIP), on the other hand, addressing the sub-federal government both in the area of services and public procurement was one of the negotiating objectives of the EU.[27] Both negotiations are part of an important development, considering that Canada and the USA have previously addressed the regional and local levels of government only to a very limited extent in their trade agreements. In some other PTAs, countries list their sub-central reservations, while in others they simply refer to existing reservations of sub-central governments without listing them.

The book does not address the liability of local government for breaches of international law but focuses on the liability of the central state to enforce its WTO law obligations across its territory. The local liability rules, however, are a related and a highly interesting area of study. In the most comprehensive treatment of the topic, Timothy Meyer notes how the choice among various liability rules is the most important front in efforts to reconcile a robust federalism with the increasing importance of local governments to international affairs.[28] The participation of lower levels of government in international agreements, and especially in international economic agreements, is an ongoing battle in the USA, the EU and other federal nations. The example of the role that the Belgian region of Wallonia played in the CETA negotiations is a primary example of that. The same issue is in the forefront of the Brexit negotiations as the constituent parts of the United

---

[26] See p. 12 of KORUS, Annex I, the schedule of the United States and Appendix I-A to the same schedule. Page 12 includes the following statement: 'For purposes of transparency, Appendix I-A sets out an illustrative, non-binding list of non-conforming measures maintained at the regional level of government'.

[27] See Press Release 'European Union and United States to launch negotiations for a Transatlantic Trade and Investment Partnership', available http://trade.ec.europa.eu/doclib/press/index.cfm?id=869, 13 February 2013 (last accessed on 20 February 2019).

[28] Timothy, M. (2017) Local Liability in International Economic Law. *North Carolina Law Review*, 95(2), 261–338, at 262.

Kingdom have their own preferences and conditions for the future legal relationship between the UK and the EU.

The analysis of how the EU is able to fulfil GATS Art. V requirements despite not yet having fully liberalized services markets within the EU is a highly relevant issue for the future of the EU's trade policy in services. To understand how the EU behaves externally, one needs to first understand how the EU behaves internally. However, sometimes the external can teach us something about the internal. The study of the EU's external services commitments shows the incomplete nature of the EU's internal market in services and challenges one to question whether the EU can really have a common commercial policy in services. Within the Union, EU service suppliers benefit from the protection given by the EU Treaties as part of the free movement of services. Towards third-country service suppliers such a freedom does not apply and instead any third-country supplier is ultimately left to deal with a vast number of national regulations.

IV   A New Methodology to Study Services Agreements

Earlier research on the level of liberalization of EIAs has demonstrated that the services commitments in the EU's EIAs go further than the EU's multilateral commitments under the GATS and the EU's latest GATS offer of 2005.[29] Earlier studies have also studied the various policy areas covered by EIAs.[30] So far, there is, however, only limited empirical research that would consider specific EIAs in light of the criteria of Art. V GATS.[31] Most studies focus only on certain modes of delivery, most

---

[29] See; Roy, M., Marchetti, J. & Lim, H. (2007) Services Liberalization in the New Generation of Preferential Trade Agreements (PTAs): How Much Further than the GATS? *World Trade Review*, 6(2), 155–92, Marchetti, J. A. & Roy, M. (2008) *Opening Markets for Trade in Services: Countries and Sectors in Bilateral and WTO Negotiations*. Cambridge; New York: Cambridge University Press and Roy, M. (2011) Services Commitments in Preferential Trade Agreements: An Expanded Dataset. *WTO Staff Working Paper* (ERSD-2011–18). The dataset in Roy et al. (2007) and Marchetti and Roy (2008) covers thirty-seven Members in forty PTAs, and the extended dataset in Roy 2011 covers fifty-three Members in sixty-seven Agreements. The studies focus on Mode 1 and Mode 3. The dataset has been made available on the WTO website: www.wto.org/english/tratop_e/serv_e/dataset_e/dataset_e.htm. Roy et al. also analyze to what extent EIA commitments go beyond services offers in the Doha Development Agenda.

[30] Horn, H., Mavroidis, P. C. & Sapir, A. (2010) Beyond the WTO? An Anatomy of EU and US Preferential Trade Agreements. *The World Economy*, 33(11), 1565–88.

[31] Fink, C. & Molinuevo, M. (2008) East Asian Preferential Trade Agreements in Services: Liberalization Content and WTO Rules. *World Trade Review*, 7(4), 641–73 analyze the liberalization content of twenty-five East Asian EIAs and their compliance with WTO

often on Modes 1 and 3. Their point of departure is not Art. V but rather the level of liberalization set by the chosen Members GATS commitments. Most studies also do not differentiate between 'MA' and national treatment ('NT') limitations but group them together. In such an analysis, every improvement or deterioration of a commitment under either field leads to a higher or lower value in the index.[32] This is in contrast to the present study that codes limitations to NT only. Since Art. V GATS requires the elimination of existing discriminatory measures and/or prohibition of new or more discriminatory measures, any commitment falling short of full NT (whether no commitment at all or a partial commitment) brings in this study the value for that specific commitment to zero. Naturally, it can be argued that partial commitments are better

rules on regional integration. Their point of departure is, however, different than in this study as they define trade-restrictive measures as all measures that are inconsistent with GATS-style market access and national treatment disciplines. They look at all the four modes of supply but merge market access and national treatment commitments. Moreover, their study is limited to East Asian agreements. The present study focuses only on sectoral coverage and the level of non-discrimination since it is argued here that Art. V does not impose any discipline on market access. At least two studies have adopted an approach that makes a separate comparison of MA and NT commitments possible. Wang, H. (2012) The Interpretation of GATS Disciplines on Economic Integration: GATS Commitments as a Threshold? *Journal of World Trade*, 46(2), 397–438 takes China's eight EIAs as test cases for interpreting GATS Art. V in light of their sectoral coverage and level of non-discrimination. However, he does not engage in a detailed empirical analysis of China's EIAs in this respect. Miroudot et al. (2010) follows Hoekman (1995; see footnote below), Roy et al. (2007), Marchetti and Roy (2008) and Fink and Molinuevo (2008) but go further by providing the information for each signatory of the EIA, by sub-sector and by mode of supply, for both market access and national treatment commitments. Additionally, they break down partial commitments into nine categories accounting for different types of trade restrictive measures. A more detailed overview of previous empirical studies is included in Chapter 7 of Part III of the book.

[32] Several studies adopt the restrictivity index developed by Hoekman for the assessment of Members GATS commitments. See Hoekman, B. (1995) Tentative First Steps: An Assessment of the Uruguay Round Agreement on Services, Volume 1, *World Bank Policy Research Working Paper* (No. 1455). Hoekman covers all four modes of supply and distinguishes between market access and national treatment commitments. His study assessed GATS schedules only but can be used to analyze EIAs as well. In Hoekman's index the content of GATS schedules emerging from the Uruguay Round is assessed by giving, for each sub-sector and mode of supply, a score of 1 for a full commitment (without limitations), 0.5 for partial commitments, and 0 for the absence of commitments. In Roy et al. (2007), the Hoekman index is adapted so as to allow the comparison of a Member's partial commitments in different PTAs. The index gives a higher score for each improvement in a Member's partial commitments: for each step, half the difference between the score for a full commitment (1) and the score of the partial commitment being improved is added.

than nothing but since the book applies the Art. V criteria, arguably only commitments providing for full non-discrimination should pass the test of compliance with the GATS discipline on EIAs.

Even if the present method is less sophisticated than the methods based on Hoekman (1995), our approach makes it relatively easy and straightforward to compare EIAs to the Art. V criteria and also to each other.[33] The methodology adopted here lacks the value judgment that is present in studies that index improvements in commitments by giving them values between zero and one. Our method follows the way that MA and NT limitations are scheduled under the GATS but it is compatible to analyze commitments also in so-called negative-list agreements modelled after NAFTA.[34] In the case of negative scheduling, the analysis is, however, more challenging to carry out as our approach is built on going systematically through the 155 sub-sectors of the WTO's Services Sectoral Classification List.[35] In an analysis of a negatively scheduled agreement, one needs to engage in the burdensome exercise of picking each discriminatory reservation and placing it in the correct place in the sectoral classification list. Our analysis includes one agreement (the EU–Georgia EIA) that has negatively scheduled commitments under Mode 3. Otherwise, our results are based on analyzing positively scheduled commitments.

To conclude, the empirical method used in the present book is designed in a way that allows an EIA's direct comparison with the principal requirements of Art. V:1 GATS (substantial sectoral coverage and elimination of discrimination). The work does not neglect any of the

---

[33] Naturally, the comparison is rougher than comparisons based on more sophisticated analyses of differences in commitments. For comparing the degree of preferentialism between different EIAs, the method applied by Miroudot et al. (2010) is especially useful.

[34] There are two principal methods to schedule services commitments: the so-called positive and negative scheduling, often referred to as the 'top-down' (negative) and 'bottom-up' (positive) approach. In negative listing, a country covers all services except those listed, while in positive listing a country covers only listed services. The most famous example of a top-down agreement is NAFTA, whereas the GATS is a positively listed agreement. The issue is taken up in more detail further in the book.

[35] We employ a sectoral classification list prepared by the WTO Secretariat. It is a comprehensive list of services sectors and sub-sectors and it is typically used by the Members to schedule their commitments under the GATS and often also in EIAs. It was compiled by the WTO in July 1991 and its purpose was to facilitate the Uruguay Round negotiations, ensuring cross-country comparability and consistency of the commitments undertaken. The 160 sub-sectors are defined as aggregate of the more detailed categories contained in the United Nations provisional Central Product Classification (CPC). Services sectoral classification list, Note by the Secretariat, WTO document MTN.GNS/W/120, 10 July 1991.

so-called GATS 'modes of delivery' but, in fact, presents a new possible way to approach Mode 4 and adapts the methodology to include this specific mode as well. In addition, the empirical study takes into account the special structure of the EU, which is a free trade area itself but does not have uniform service regulations across its territory. As will be shown, a common characteristic of the EU's EIAs is the varying degree of asymmetry in the Member States' services commitments. How well the EU does in respect of sectoral coverage and non-discrimination depends on how well it manages to bring its Member States' commitments over the threshold of substantiality as a whole. The EU has a highly integrated commercial policy, known as the Common Commercial Policy (CCP), under which the Union enjoys exclusive competence to conclude trade agreements on behalf of all of its Member States. Notwithstanding this exclusive competence and centralized negotiation authority, the EU's schedules of services commitments are not unified: EU Member States still set out their own services commitments and limitations to the common EU schedule. This is an interesting phenomenon that has implications outside the EU as well. Several Members have internally divided competences on the regulation of services. In case there are discrepancies between the depths of liberalization on different levels of government, the relevant question is how to determine the GATS-consistency of their EIAs. In case the extent of liberalization varies between regions (or Member States, as in the case of the EU), the relevant question is how the coverage and degree of non-discrimination of an EIA by such a contracting party should be assessed. What is the salient unit in such an analysis? Should only state-level measures be analyzed or are sub-central measures as relevant? The book analyzes this problem in light of the EU example but expands the normative conclusions to federal states at large.

Federations and federal-type structures will generally be referred to as 'federal entities' across the book. This includes the EU, which is here considered to represent a 'federal-type structure'.[36] Measures taken on different national (domestic) levels of these WTO Members will be referred to as 'sub-central measures'. An alternative way to name them would be 'sub-national measures' but because of the complexity in the Members' internal constitutional structures, and especially in the case of the EU, the term sub-central measures has been adopted instead. This is

---

[36] See usage in Schütze, R. (2009) *From Dual to Cooperative Federalism: The Changing Structure of European Law*. Oxford: Oxford University Press, 287–343.

because the EU Member States, in their position towards the Union, are contrasted with sub-national entities in a single country's domestic legal order (i.e. Canadian provinces and territories and the US states). In the case of the EU, the individual services commitments of such Member States that themselves are federal states (Germany, Austria, Belgium) are also relevant. The term 'sub-central measures' is therefore considered to cover divergence both on domestic level (between different constituent parts of an individual EU Member State) and on the Union level (between different EU Member States). In the case of the USA and Canada, it covers all their internal sub-national (sub-federal) levels of government.

The measures covered by the term 'sub-central measures' are understood to cover all measures taken by other than central authorities, mainly by any regional or local governments and authorities. This is in line with the definition given in GATS Art. I:3(a)(i) to 'measures by Members'. Similarly, also measures taken by non-governmental bodies are considered covered as long as they are taken in the exercise of powers delegated by central, regional or local governments or authorities (GATS Art. I:3(a)(ii)).

PART I

Preferentialism in the WTO and in the GATS

1

Preferential Trade Agreements in the WTO

I The Historical Background of Preferential Trade

Preferential trade is not a new phenomenon. Trade relations between selected countries have been secured through various preferential arrangements throughout modern history – from colonial preferences to bilateral commercial treaties and broader regional arrangements. The most-favoured nation (MFN) clause was regularly applied in bilateral treaties of friendship, commerce and navigation in the nineteenth century. These agreements contributed to a network of interlinked agreements that preceded the formation of a proper multilateral system after the Second World War.[1]

In the field of goods, preferential trade agreements (PTAs) were concluded in modest numbers until the 1990s. The inclusion of services in PTAs is a later phenomenon. According to the DESTA database,[2] the first agreement mentioning services trade liberalization as a goal is the Treaty Establishing the European Economic Community (Treaty of Rome, 1957), while the first agreement that actually includes commitments in services trade liberalization is the Yaoundé Convention of 1969 more than ten years later.[3] Since the early 1990s, the number of EIAs has,

---

[1] Cottier, T. & Oesch, M. (2011) Direct and Indirect Discrimination in WTO Law and EU Law. NCCR *Trade Regulation Working Paper*, No. 2011/16, 3.

[2] 'Design of Trade Agreements (DESTA) Database', available at www.designoftradeagreements.org/ (last accessed on 15 January 2019).

[3] The Yaoundé Convention was a treaty signed in the city of Yaoundé, Cameroon, between the European Economic Community (EEC) and the AASM (Associated African States and Madagascar) for the first time in 1963. The second convention was signed in 1969. The

however, grown very fast. Starting from 1994, some 180 PTAs including rules on services trade have come into existence, compared with only thirty-eight in the previous forty years. Of the cumulative total of all PTAs including services, over 40 per cent have come into existence since 2000.[4] Overall the numbers of PTAs have greatly multiplied since the early 1990s. The vast increase in the numbers of PTAs can for good reasons be labelled as 'proliferation'.[5]

In the 1960s and 1970s, elements of services trade were included mostly in the so-called North–South and South–South agreements, concluded between developed and developing countries (N–S), and developing countries (S–S) respectively.[6] In the 1980s the first North–North agreements were concluded. The period of the GATS negotiations marked the beginning for a trend towards the conclusion of PTAs with a service component.[7] Their number is steadily growing and is currently at about 150 agreements in force.[8] The most active participants to EIAs have been industrialized countries with strong service industries,

---

treaties governed relations between the EEC and the EEC Member States' overseas countries and territories. See Sieber-Gasser, C. (2016) *Developing Countries and Preferential Services Trade.* Cambridge: Cambridge University Press, 63.

[4] The agreements typically include rules on both services and investment. See Heydon, K. & Woolcock, S. (2009) *The Rise of Bilateralism: Comparing American, European and Asian Approaches to Preferential Trade Agreements.* Tokyo, New York, Paris: United Nations University Press, 90.

[5] See Fiorentino, R. V., Verdeja, L. & Toqueboeuf, C. (2007) The Changing Landscape of Regional Trade Agreements: 2006 Update. *WTO Discussion Paper* No. 12, 2. Dür et al. identified a total of 733 PTAs signed between 1945 and 2009 (including concrete steps towards the preferential liberalization of trade in goods and/or services). At the same time, a list maintained by the WTO included 356 of those agreements. See Dür, A., Baccini, L. & Elsig, M. (2014) The Design of International Trade Agreements: Introducing a New Dataset. *The Review of International Organizations*, 9(3), 353–75.

[6] For N–S, e.g. agreements between the European Communities and partner countries, such as Yaoundé I (1969), Arusha Agreement II (1969), Lomé I (1975) and Lomé II (1979). For S–S agreements, e.g. Andean Group Cartagena Agreement (1969) and CARICOM (1973). See Sieber-Gasser (2016), 63.

[7] As noted by Sieber-Gasser (2016), little experience with services trade regulation was collected before the GATS. Deep services liberalization was mainly limited to the European integration and NAFTA (and the US–Canada FTA of 1987, predating NAFTA). The parallel bilateral and regional services negotiations of the EU and USA had a strong impact on the final design of services trade regulation in the GATS.

[8] In February 2019, the number of EIAs that were notified to the WTO as being in force was 151 (without accessions). The overall number of notified PTAs was 293. EIAs are usually always part of goods PTAs. Only the European Economic Area (EEA) was notified as a services only agreement in 1996. See the WTO's Regional Trade Agreements Information System available at http://rtais.wto.org/UI/PublicMaintainRTAHome.aspx (last accessed on 25 February 2019).

especially the EU and the USA, but since the 1990s developing countries have been rapidly catching up.[9]

Preferential trade was disciplined for the first time in the original GATT agreement of 1947. Art. XXIV GATT set the rules for the formation of customs unions (CUs) and free-trade areas. The rigid classification of regional integration into these two formations can be seen as the result of the historic context of the GATT. Two customs unions participated in the negotiation of the GATT: the Benelux and the Syrian-Lebanese customs union. The GATT negotiators were therefore presented with a *fait accompli*. FTAs, on the contrary, were included only in the last draft of the GATT; the seven drafts prepared before that included CUs only. According to Chase, the US negotiators played a leading role in designing the FTA provision to accommodate a secret trade agreement that the USA was planning with Canada.[10]

The text of Art. XXIV GATT has remained unchanged since then. In 1994, the provision was clarified with an Understanding agreed upon by the Members during the Uruguay Round.[11] From the beginning, the contracting parties, and later the Members of the WTO, have been under an obligation to notify every PTA they conclude. During the GATT years, the examination of PTAs was conducted in working parties established individually for that purpose. In 1996 a new body, the Committee on Regional Trade Agreements (CRTA), was created to

---

[9] Sieber-Gasser (2016), 66.

[10] Chase, K. (2006) Multilateralism Compromised: The Mysterious Origins of GATT Article XXIV. *World Trade Review*, 5(1), 1–30, 10–15. The USA had a significant role in the formulation of the FTA provision notwithstanding its commitment to multilateralism. According to Chase, the evidence shows that the US position on preferential arrangements changed because the USA wanted to accommodate a possible FTA with Canada. At the end of 1947, Canada asked the USA for tariff cuts on its key exports but was not willing to enter into a CU with the USA. The USA then came up with the idea of free trade without a common tariff system. As the USA did not want to present the idea itself because of likely public relations problems, it planted the proposal with the Lebanese and Syrian representatives. In the process, the US representatives had three goals. First, they wanted interim agreements to be accommodated. Second, they came up with the elimination of tariffs on 'substantially all trade' – not 'all trade' – so that protection for sensitive items could be retained. And third, they wanted to ensure that clauses banning tariff increases against third countries applied only at the time an FTA was formed, and did not operate indefinitely. Consequently, neither the Havana Charter nor the US–Canada FTA became law. However, the rules on CUs and FTAs survived as part of the GATT and remain in force today.

[11] Understanding on the Interpretation of Art. XXIV of the General Agreement on Tariffs and Trade (Uruguay Round Agreement). The Understanding is so far the only legislative clarification of the text of Art. XXIV GATT.

consider individual PTAs, the relationships between them and their systemic implications for the multilateral trading system.

In addition to Art. XXIV GATT, another, limited, possibility for preferential arraignments in goods trade was created by the 1979 Enabling Clause.[12] Adopted under the GATT, it enables developed Members to give differential and more favourable treatment to developing countries. This takes place under the so-called Generalized System of Preferences (GSP) through which developed countries offer non-reciprocal preferential treatment to products originating in developing countries. The Enabling Clause is also the legal basis for regional arrangements among developing countries. Moreover, it provides for the Global System of Trade Preferences (GSTP), under which a number of developing countries exchange trade concessions among themselves. According to Paragraph 4 of the Enabling Clause, Members pursuing arrangements under it must notify the other Members and furnish them with all the information they deem appropriate. The provision also provides for consultations with a view to reaching solutions that are satisfactory to all Members. Notifications under the Enabling Clause are made to the Committee on Trade and Development (CTD). A debate is held at a CTD meeting but generally the CTD requires no in-depth examination by the CRTA.

Besides Art. XXIV GATT, Art. V GATS is the other WTO provision that creates a legal basis for PTAs in the strict sense.[13] The GATS rules concerning the notification and control of EIAs are less strict than those of the GATT. Art. V:7(a) GATS requires parties to an EIA to promptly notify such an agreement and any enlargement or any significant modification of the agreement to the Council for Trade in Services (CTS). In addition, Art. V:7(b) includes the obligation of periodic reporting with regard to EIAs that are implemented on the basis of a time-frame. The CTS may pass a notified agreement to the CRTA for examination. Unlike PTAs that are notified under Art. XXIV GATT, the examination of EIAs by the CRTA is optional.

We will now turn to the issue of how PTAs are controlled in the WTO. There are two possible mechanisms: the multilateral review and dispute

---

[12] Decision of 28 November 1979 on Differential and More Favourable Treatment, Reciprocity and Fuller Participation of Developing Countries, GATT Document L/4903 (Enabling Clause).

[13] There is no separate 'Enabling Clause' for services PTAs. However, Art. V.3 GATS creates a less rigid setting for EIAs involving developing countries. According to the provision, flexibility shall be provided for where developing countries are parties to an EIA in accordance with the level of development of the countries concerned.

settlement. As we will explain, neither mechanism has proved successful in putting the GATT and GATS disciplines on PTAs into practice.

II   The Control of PTAs under WTO Law

i   The Multilateral Review of PTAs

The multilateral track for the control of PTAs concerns the review of PTAs by the Members themselves. As no panel has ever pronounced on the GATT/WTO-consistency of any PTA, it can be considered that the main responsibility over the examination of PTAs belongs to the Members.[14] Examination was first carried out in individual working parties but since the establishment of the Committee on Regional Trade Agreements (CRTA) by a decision of the WTO's General Council in February 1996, it has been the task of the CRTA. The original CRTA procedure is explained very briefly as the nature of the review mechanism has changed with the introduction of the Transparency Mechanism in 2006.

The rules for the examination of PTAs are included in Art. XXIV GATT and Art. V GATS. Art. XXIV GATT gives Contracting Parties/Members wide powers to examine notified PTAs. That is especially evident in Art. XXIV.7(b) that deals with interim agreements leading to PTAs:

> If ... the CONTRACTING PARTIES find that such agreement is not likely to result in the formation of a customs union or of a free-trade area within the period contemplated by the parties to the agreement or that such period is not a reasonable one, the CONTRACTING PARTIES shall make recommendations to the parties to the agreement. The parties shall not maintain or put into force, as the case may be, such agreement if they are not prepared to modify it in accordance with these recommendations.

Mavroidis notes that the provisions give the impression of a multilateral review system designed as an institution akin to a modern merger authority: PTAs would not be consummated unless cleared through the process established.[15] In reality, however, the Contracting Parties/Members have never lived up to their institutional promise of

---

[14] Panels are not likely to do so either in the future. See Mavroidis, P. C. (2006) If I Don't Do It, Somebody Else Will (Or Won't). *Journal of World Trade*, 40(1), 187–214.

[15] Mavroidis, P. C. (2011), Always Look on the Bright Side of Non-Delivery: WTO and Preferential Trade Agreements, Yesterday and Today. *World Trade Review*, 10(3), 375–387, at 376.

a genuine multilateral review. Prior to the establishment of the WTO, Working Party reports on PTAs notified under Art. XXIV GATT were usually adopted even though Members had divergent views on the end result. Consensus on consistency hardly existed: only on five occasions were the Contracting Parties able to agree that a PTA satisfied the requirements of Art. XXIV GATT.[16] The Contracting Parties never reached a decision on a notified PTA's inconsistency with the GATT.[17]

The review mechanism under Art. V GATS is less rigid. According to Art. V:7(a), EIAs are to be notified to the Council for Trade in Services. The Council *may* then establish a working party to examine such an agreement or enlargement or modification of that agreement and to report to the Council on its consistency with Art. V. Under Art. V:7(b), Members that are parties to EIAs implemented on the basis of a time-frame shall report periodically to the Council on the implementation. The Council may establish a working party to examine such reports if it deems such a working party necessary. Under Art. V:7(c), the Council may, based on the reports of the working parties, make recommendations to the parties as it deems appropriate.

Since the establishment of the CRTA, the Council has passed a number of EIAs to the CRTA for examination (typically examined together with the goods component of the agreement). But in contrast to PTAs notified under Art. XXIV GATT, such examination of EIAs is optional, not mandatory. Moreover, unlike Art. XXIV.7(b) GATT, Art. V GATS does not preclude the enforcement of agreements that are in conflict with working party recommendations; it simply allows for recommendations to be made to the parties of the agreement. In practice, however, the difference has been inconsequential as no PTAs have been considered inconsistent under either procedure.

---

[16] Schott, J. (1989) More Free Trade Areas?, in Schott, J. (ed.), *Free Trade Areas and US Trade Policy*. Washington, DC: Institute of International Economics, 1–58, at 25, mentions four decisions where the PTA was considered broadly consistent with the GATT. Since then, consensus has been reached only once: the report on the 1993 CU between the Czech Republic and the Slovak Republic states clearly that the PTA is fully compatible with the GATT rules. See Mavroidis (2011), at 376.

[17] WTO Committee on Regional Trade Agreements, *Synopsis of 'systemic' issues related to regional trade agreements*, Note by the Secretariat, WT/REG/W/37, 2 March 2000, and Mavroidis, P. C. (2006). See also Mitchell, A. D. & Lockhart, N. J. S. (2009) Legal Requirements for PTAs under the WTO, in Lester, S. N. & Mercurio, B. (eds.), *Bilateral and Regional Trade Agreements: Commentary and Analysis*. Cambridge; New York: Cambridge University Press, 81–113, at 112.

The CRTA conducts its examination based on information provided by the parties to the PTA. Other material includes written replies to written questions posed by other Members and discussions at CRTA meetings. Prior to 2006, the factual examination was followed by an examination report drawn by the WTO Secretariat. Once the report was accepted by the CRTA, it was to be submitted for adoption by the Members. The difficulty in reaching consensus over the consistency of PTAs with the GATT and GATS rules, however, led to a situation where no report was finalized since 1995.[18]

As a response to this deadlock, a new mechanism was adopted in 2006. The procedure to control the WTO-consistency of PTAs went through a drastic change with the General Council's adoption of a decision concerning the *Transparency Mechanism for Regional Trade Agreements*.[19] The Transparency Mechanism *de facto* replaced the existing multilateral review system of PTAs. The practical consequence of the resolution is that the consistency of PTAs responding to Art. XXIV GATT, Art. V GATS or the Enabling Clause is actually no longer checked multilaterally.[20] The new mechanism is implemented by the CRTA with regard to PTAs falling under Art. XXIV GATT and Art. V GATS. The Committee on Trade and Development is responsible for the implementation with regard to agreements falling under paragraph 2(c) of the Enabling Clause.

Under the Transparency Mechanism the WTO Secretariat prepares a factual presentation of each notified PTA. The factual presentation is distributed to the Members at least eight weeks in advance of the meeting devoted to the consideration of the PTA. The parties to the agreement must circulate answers to questions sent by other Members at least three working days before the corresponding meeting. In addition, there is a written record of the meeting devoted to the consideration of each notified agreement. The Members' questions and the parties' responses as well as a record of the discussion are available on a WTO database. The decision on the Transparency Mechanism also requires that at the end of

---

[18] The WTO website on the CRTA, available at: www.wto.org/english/tratop_e/region_e/regcom_e.htm (last accessed on 25 February 2019).

[19] Transparency Mechanism for Regional Trade Agreements, General Council, Decision of 14 December 2006, WTO Document WT/L/671 of 18 December 2006. The transparency mechanism was negotiated in the Negotiating Group on Rules and is implemented on a provisional basis. The purpose is that Members replace it by a permanent mechanism to be adopted as part of the overall results of the Doha Round.

[20] Mavroidis (2011), at 377.

the PTA's implementation period, the parties submit to the WTO a short written report on the realization of the liberalization commitments in the PTA as originally notified. However, there is no longer need to prepare a final report for adoption by the Members.[21]

In fact, the introduction of the Transparency Mechanism has normalized a practice that is to ignore the Members' treaty-based responsibilities to enforce the rules on PTAs. The enforcement of the rules has proved too hard to accomplish in a situation where, first, there is no general understanding of the exact contents of the substantive rules on PTAs, and, second, where there is not enough political willingness to tackle the issue.

From a legal point of view, it is clear that partial trade deals are allowed for Members only if they meet the requirements of Art. XXIV GATT, Art. V GATS or the Enabling Clause. Only such PTAs that fall within one of these exceptions are valid under WTO law. Thus, any Member entering a PTA should ensure that the agreement complies with the conditions of the relevant WTO exception. Otherwise, the Member risks acting inconsistently with its WTO obligations.[22] No one claims that the vast majority of the well over 200 PTAs that have been notified since the establishment of the WTO are 'customs unions'. Since most of the agreements involve liberalization of trade in goods and are not concluded solely for development purposes, they must be 'free-trade areas' within the meaning of Art. XXIV.8(b) of the GATT. However, no one knows what a free trade area really is – or really wants to know. The GATT/WTO trading system has thrived for more than half a century without knowing the answer to this question.[23] As to understanding what exactly is 'economic integration' under the criteria of Art. V:1 GATS, we are not any more enlightened.

Clearly, the main reason for the lack of comprehension of the rules on PTAs is the obscurity of the rules. Naturally, there is the possibility for the Members to provide for more legal clarity and detail to the rules. The

[21] The Decision on the Transparency Mechanism and the WTO website on the Transparency Mechanism, available at: www.wto.org/english/tratop_e/region_e/trans_mecha_e.htm (last accessed on 15 September 2018). The WTO database with reports on the agreements is available at http://rtais.wto.org.

[22] Mitchell, A. D. & Lockhart, N. (2015) Legal Requirements for PTAs under the WTO, in Lester, S., Mercurio, B. & Bartels, L. (eds.), *Bilateral and Regional Trade Agreements: Commentary and Analysis (Volume 1)*. Cambridge: Cambridge University Press, 81–114, at 82.

[23] Foreword by James Bacchus, Former Chair of the WTO Appellate Body in Lester, S., Mercurio, B. & Bartels, L. (2015) *Bilateral and Regional Trade Agreements: Commentary and Analysis (Volume 1)*. Cambridge: Cambridge University Press, at xiv.

former Director-General of the WTO, Pascal Lamy, has brought up this possibility by pointing out that it is for the governments to determine whether they need greater legal certainty in this domain.[24] This option is, however, undermined by the fact that years of effort before and during the Doha Round to address the multilateral provisions on PTAs have not proved successful.[25] New rules, therefore, seem highly unlikely.

A politics of tolerance towards PTAs has been practised already for decades. According to Snape, the formation of the EEC marked a significant start in this regard. Political considerations affected the GATT Contracting Parties in their decision not to scrutinize the deal too heavily. The Community's six original Member States had made sufficiently clear that they could withdraw from the GATT were the Contracting Parties to find that the EEC Treaty violated Art. XXIV GATT. Given that the EEC of the 1950s most likely did not meet the requirements of Art. XXIV, a precedent was created and it has been subsequently followed.[26]

The Members seem divided on all significant aspects of the WTO disciplines on PTAs. In addition, there does not seem to be enough political willingness to tackle the issue. The obscurity of the provisions is potentially damaging but it is also in the benefit of many. As noted by Mavroidis, it is actually counter-intuitive why Members would be willing to enforce the so-called internal requirement of the rules on PTAs. That is because the less trade liberalization exists among parties to a PTA, the less trade diversion is likely to take place.[27] It is maybe more understandable why Members would be willing to enforce the external trade requirement which under both Art. XXIV GATT and Art. V GATS requires that trade barriers towards outsiders must not be raised as a whole.

---

[24] WTO, *World Trade Report 2011 – The WTO and Preferential Trade Agreements: From Co-Existence to Coherence*, available at www.wto.org/english/res_e/booksp_e/anrep_e/world_trade_report11_e.pdf (last accessed 18 September 2018).

[25] In the beginning of the Doha Round, Members agreed to clarify and improve the disciplines and procedures for PTAs. See Doha Ministerial Declaration, WT/MIN(01)/DEC/1, adopted 14 November 2001, para. 29 and Negotiating Group on Rules, Compendium of Issues related to Regional Trade Agreements, TN/RL/W/8/Rev. 1, 1 August 2002.

[26] See Hoekman, B. & Sauvé, P. (1994) Liberalizing Trade in Services. *World Bank Discussion Papers*, WDP243, at 61, and the references therein, especially Snape, R. (1993) History and Economics of GATT's Article XXIV, in Anderson, K. & Blackhurst, R. (eds.), *Regional Integration and the Global Trading System*. London: Harvester-Wheatsheaf.

[27] Mavroidis (2006), at 210–11. The internal requirement concerns the criteria on the liberalization of 'substantial' amount of trade in the case of both goods and services.

However, the economic consequences of PTAs for outsiders are complex and depend on a variety of factors. Moreover, we do not have a straightforward answer to the question of whether preferentialism in general is detrimental to multilateralism or more of a catalyst for further trade liberalization. Economic consequences matter but it is important to keep in mind that PTAs are not only about GDP. The Members' reluctance to clarify and enforce the rules may also relate to the understanding that PTAs do not serve economic motives only. The WTO rules on PTAs are built on mainly economic criteria but the Members use PTAs to address various types of issues. Even if the GATT rules do not acknowledge the variety of policy reasons for CUs and FTAs, PTAs are in practice largely used also for non-economic aims.[28] The rise of the so-called mega-regionals, referring especially to Trans-Pacific Partnership (TPP) and the currently halted negotiations for a Transatlantic Trade and Investment Partnership (TTIP) between the EU and USA, as well as some initiatives by China and Russia in their geographic proximity, shows the growing importance of geo-politics as a driving factor for preferentialism.[29]

In this sense, Art. V GATS may provide more room for agreements having wider motivations than Art. XXIV GATT since its second paragraph allows consideration to be given to the 'wider process of economic integration' between the participating countries. It is, however, unclear what the provision means in practice. There is no more consensus on the meaning of Art. V:2 GATS than on the meaning of any other WTO provisions on PTAs. With so many partly conflicting interests involved, any particular interpretation of the rules is unlikely to gather the support of all Members.

---

[28] Damro lists seven big themes behind the preference to pursue PTAs: 1) marginalization syndrome ('the fear of being left out'); 2) security via economic means' 3) 'new security needs' (e.g. environmental damage, illegal migration, drug smuggling); 4) increase in negotiating leverage; 5) lock-in domestic reforms; 6) accommodate domestic constituents; and 7) practical ease. See Damro, C. (2006) The Political Economy of Regional Trade Agreements, in Bartels, L. & Ortino, F. (eds.), *Regional Trade Agreements and the WTO Legal System*. Oxford; New York: Oxford University Press, 23–42, at 29–30.

[29] The geo-political motivations of PTAs were present already during the negotiations on the International Trade Organization in the 1940s. Chase notes that despite its hatred of colonial preferences and dedication to MFN rules, the USA came to regard FTAs as instruments to promote economic and political unity against the Soviet threat and achieve broader trade liberalization than was possible multilaterally. Chase, K. (2006) Multilateralism Compromised: The Mysterious Origins of GATT Article XXIV. *World Trade Review*, 5(1), 1–30, at 22.

It seems fair to conclude that the Members are clearly not fulfilling their supervisory role over PTAs. Considering that the CRTA is now close to a pure enforcer of transparency, the legal status of current and new PTAs is set to remain unclear. Even if the primary responsibility over the enforcement of the rules on PTAs has been considered to belong to the Members, any solution one way or the other seems now possible through litigation only. However, as it will be explained in the next section, GATT/WTO panels have so far been very reluctant to interpret the rules on PTAs.

ii   PTAs in GATT/WTO Dispute Settlement

Considering the importance of PTAs to the world trade today, one could expect that GATT/WTO panels had been involved in a legal review of at least some of the agreements. However, the panels and the Appellate Body (AB) have not yet got fully engaged in the interpretation and enforcement of the rules on PTAs. The reasons arguably lie both with the Members and the panels/AB themselves. First, legal challenges are not likely. One of the most convincing explanations behind this lies in strategic reasons: all Members are now parties to PTAs and many of them do not want to limit their options or to risk their own PTAs being subjected to legal review.[30] Therefore, a situation of certain 'co-operative equilibrium' has developed: in order to avoid being challenged, Members do not challenge each other's PTAs.[31] Mavroidis also mentions such reasons as collective action problems, the benefits of non-enforcement (reduced trade diversion) and the institutional design of panels (mistrust of amateur judges).[32]

Second, Panels and the AB themselves do not seem willing to engage in a 'complex undertaking which involves consideration by the CRTA, from the economic, legal and political perspectives of different Members, of the numerous facets of a regional trade agreement in relation to the

---

[30] Following Mongolia's decision to join the Asia-Pacific Trade Agreement (APTA), all WTO members are now members of one or more PTAs (some belonging to as many as thirty). See the WTO website www.wto.org/english/thewto_e/minist_e/mc9_e/brief_rta_e.htm (last accessed on 10 May 2018).

[31] Matsushita, M., Schoenbaum, T. J. & Mavroidis, P. C. (2006) *The World Trade Organization: Law, Practice, and Policy*, 2nd ed. Oxford; New York: Oxford University Press, at 585.

[32] Mavroidis, P. C. (2010) WTO and PTAs: A Preference for Multilateralism? (or, the Dog That Tried to Stop the Bus). *Journal of World Trade*, 44(5), 1145–54, at 1150.

provisions of the WTO'.[33] The adjudicating organs of the GATT/WTO have been extremely sparing in their rulings concerning PTAs and seem to prefer to leave the consistency issues of PTAs to the Members themselves. The following statement of the former chair of the AB, James Bacchus, is revealing:

> More ominously, no one knows what a 'free-trade area' is within the meaning of Article XXIV.8(b) of the GATT – or really wants to know. The GATT/WTO trading system has thrived for more than half a century without knowing the answer to this question. As I have often said, and not entirely in jest, one of my greatest accomplishments as a Member for eight years of the Appellate Body of the WTO was that I was able to get out of Geneva alive without having to answer this question.[34]

So far, the only case that has dealt, in a limited manner, with Art. V GATS has been *Canada–Autos*.[35] However, the arguments used by the Panels or the AB with regard to Art. XXIV GATT or the Enabling Clause may be considered relevant also for the analysis of EIAs under the GATS. Since Art. V is the service trade equivalent of Art. XXIV GATT, the considerations reached in the GATT/WTO dispute settlement with regard to CUs and FTAs may be of relevance also in the interpretation of Art. V GATS.[36]

Unfortunately, the substantive guidance on the provisions of Art. XXIV is also almost non-existent. There have been several disputes that have dealt with or touched upon Art. XXIV but the panels have refrained from targeting PTAs directly. Instead, they have taken a piecemeal approach and focused on particular measures that have followed from the agreements. At least so far, panels and the AB have not been explicitly asked to rule on the validity of a specific PTA. In *US–Line Pipe Safeguards*, the evidence submitted by the USA on the NAFTA's compliance with Art. XXIV:8(b) led the Panel to conclude that the USA had established a *prima facie* case that the criteria of an FTA were met.

---

[33] A quote from the Panel Report in *EC–Citrus*, para. 9.52. See *European Community – Tariff Treatment on Imports of Citrus Products from Certain Countries in the Mediterranean Region*, L/5776, GATT Panel Report, 7 February 1985 (unadopted).

[34] Foreword by James Bacchus, Former Chair of the WTO Appellate Body in Lester, S., Mercurio, B. & Bartels, L. (2015) *Bilateral and Regional Trade Agreements: Commentary and Analysis (Volume 1)*. Cambridge: Cambridge University Press, at xiv.

[35] *Canada – Certain Measures Affecting the Automotive Industry*, WT/DS139/R, WT/DS142/R, Report of the Panel, circulated 11 February 2000.

[36] The GATS does not distinguish between FTAs and CUs as the GATT does. However, EIAs appear to be closest to FTAs. See Mitchell & Lockhart (2009), at 110.

However, the AB did not consider it necessary to address this finding and declared it to be of no legal effect.[37]

The only substantive issue has been taken up by the AB in the case *Turkey–Textiles*. The case concerned the Turkey–EC Association Council Decision of 1/95 setting out certain modalities for the completion of a CU between the EC and Turkey. The decision required the elimination of customs duties, alignment of the common customs tariff, and provisions to harmonize certain other policies.[38] The dispute arose between Turkey and India, towards which Turkey, upon the formation of the CU with the EC, began to apply a series of restrictive quantitative measures similar to those already applied by the EC. The unilateral measures were put in place for textiles and clothing products originating from a total of twenty-eight countries, India among them.

In its ruling, the AB introduced the so-called necessity test for CU measures that are inconsistent not just with the MFN obligation but also with some other GATT provisions (in this case with Articles XI and XIII GATT on quantitative restrictions). According to the AB, Art. XXIV justifies such measures only if the party to a CU demonstrates that the formation of the CU would be prevented if it were not allowed to introduce the measure at issue. In addition, the party must demonstrate that the measure is introduced upon the formation of a CU that fully meets the requirements of Art. XXIV GATT.[39] The AB concluded that Turkey had failed to demonstrate the necessity of violating Articles XI and XIII as other means were available to accommodate the internal trade requirement of Art. XXIV:8, for example through the adoption of rules of origin with certificates of movement.[40]

As the case was focused on analyzing the legality of a particular measure applied upon the completion of the CU, the AB did not engage in scrutinizing the CU itself. However, it established that a CU formed in

---

[37] Appellate Body Report, *US–Line Pipe Safeguards*, paras. 198–9. The USA had submitted evidence that NAFTA eliminated duties on 97 per cent of the Parties' tariff lines, representing more than 99 per cent of the trade among them in terms of volume. See *United States – Definitive Safeguard Measures on Imports of Circular Welded Carbon Quality Line Pipe from Korea*, WT/DS202/AB/R, Report of the Appellate Body, circulated 15 February 2002.

[38] Mathis, J. H. (2002) *Regional Trade Agreements in the GATT-WTO: Article XXIV and the Internal Trade Requirement*. The Hague: T.M.C. Asser Press, at 195.

[39] *Turkey – Restrictions on Imports of Textile and Clothing Products*, WT/DS34/AB/R, Appellate Body Report, circulated 22 October 1999, para. 58. For a detailed account of the case law on Art. XXIV GATT, see ibid.

[40] *Turkey–Textiles*, Appellate Body Report, para. 62.

accordance with the criteria of Art. XXIV can work as a type of 'defence' for CU parties to violate certain other GATT provisions. Two conditions would need to be demonstrated in this regard:

> First, the party claiming the benefit of this defence must demonstrate that the measure at issue is introduced upon the formation of a customs union that fully meets the requirements of sub-paragraphs 8(a) and 5(a) of Article XXIV. And, second, that party must demonstrate that the formation of that customs union would be prevented if it were not allowed to introduce the measure at issue. Again, *both* these conditions must be met to have the benefit of the defence under Article XXIV.[41]

In addition to the necessity test, the AB thus established that the party claiming the benefit of the defence must coincidentally demonstrate that the CU fully meets the requirements of Art. XXIV. As to the requirements themselves, the AB noted that 'neither the GATT Contracting Parties nor the WTO Members have ever reached an agreement on the interpretation of the term "substantially" in this provision'. It then went further and stated that 'substantially all the trade' as mentioned under Art. XXIV:8 is clearly 'something considerably more than merely *some* of the trade'. At the same time, however, the members of a CU were allowed to maintain, in their internal trade, certain restrictive regulations of commerce. According to the AB, the terms of Art. XXIV thus offer 'some flexibility' to the constituent members of a CU when they liberalize their internal trade. Yet, the AB cautioned that the degree of 'flexibility' is limited by the requirement that 'duties and other restrictive regulations of commerce' be 'eliminated with respect to substantially all' internal trade.[42]

The ruling in *Turkey–Textiles* was welcome as it made it clear that the rules on PTAs are to be taken seriously. At the same time, it did not bring much assistance to the interpretation of Art. XXIV. The central conclusion would seem rather obvious: 'substantially all' is more than some.

The only case that has dealt with Art. V GATS is *Canada–Autos*. In that dispute, Canada had accorded duty-free treatment to motor vehicles imported by certain manufacturers producing cars in Canada. The Panel found that the Canadian regime favoured products of certain origins and concluded that Canada did not accord the advantage on equal terms to like products of different origin. Canada tried to invoke Art. V as a defence to its breach of the MFN obligation but the Panel rejected it.

---

[41] *Turkey–Textiles*, Appellate Body Report, para. 58.
[42] Ibid., Appellate Body Report, para. 48 (original emphasis).

The Panel noted that the Canadian measure did not grant more favourable treatment to all services and service suppliers from the NAFTA member countries. In practice, only a small number of US and Mexican manufacturers/wholesalers enjoyed the more favourable treatment. According to the Panel, the requirement of Art. V:1(b) was to provide non-discrimination in the sense of NT. Once that was fulfilled, it would also ensure non-discrimination between all service suppliers of other parties to the EIA. The Panel also stated as its view that the object and purpose of the provision of Art. V:1(b) was to eliminate 'all discrimination among services and service suppliers of parties to an economic integration agreement, including discrimination between suppliers of other parties to an economic integration agreement'.[43] The Panel did not advance any further on Art. V and its conclusions on Art. V were not appealed.

Thus, not much light was shed on the internal requirement of Art. V apart from the obligation to eliminate discrimination between all services and suppliers originating in Members of the EIA. The following clarifying statement was, nevertheless, made, along the lines of *Turkey–Textiles*:

> Moreover, it is worth recalling that Article V provides legal coverage for measures taken pursuant to economic integration agreements, which would otherwise be inconsistent with the MFN obligation in Article II. Paragraph 1 of Article V refers to "an agreement liberalizing trade in services". Such economic integration agreements typically aim at achieving higher levels of liberalization between or among their parties than that achieved among WTO Members. Article V:1 further prescribes a certain minimum level of liberalization which such agreements must attain in order to qualify for the exemption from the general MFN obligation of Article II. In this respect, the purpose of Article V is to allow for ambitious liberalization to take place at a regional level, while at the same time guarding against undermining the MFN obligation by engaging in minor preferential arrangements.[44]

With the proliferation of PTAs, it may be only a question of time before a panel is forced to take a stand on the legality of a specific PTA. It may not be asked about the legality directly, but getting around the issue may,

---

[43] *Canada–Autos*, Report of the Panel, para. 10.270, and Ortino, F. (2008) The Principle of Non-Discrimination and Its Exception in GATS: Selected Legal Issues, in Alexander, K. & Andenæs, M. T. (eds.), *The World Trade Organization and Trade in Services*. Leiden: Brill, 173–204, at 202–3.

[44] *Canada–Autos*, Report of the Panel, *Canada – Certain Measures Affecting the Automotive Industry*, WT/DS139/R, circulated 11 February 2000, para. 10.271.

under the right conditions, become close to impossible. WTO panels are in a growing manner being engaged also in disputes having their origin in PTAs. Some case law at least is, therefore, likely to develop. Mitchell and Lockhart point out that it would, however, be unrealistic and even inappropriate to expect panels or the AB to develop a refined definition of 'substantially all the trade' under Art. XXIV:8 GATT. How would a panel find a textual basis for a finding that a precise threshold of exactly 95 per cent, for example, would be 'substantial' but 90 per cent never is?[45] The same expectation, or lack of expectation, applies also to Art. V:1(a) GATS. Under the GATS, reaching a precise threshold on textual grounds is likely to be even harder due to the open-endedness of such definitions as a 'wider process of economic integration' (Art. V:2). Nevertheless, in spite of these difficulties it is now settled that panels have a right (or an obligation) to review the quality of PTAs when raised on a defence.[46] With a growing number of agreements, we are likely to witness many more PTA-related cases in the future. If and when PTAs are invoked as a defence to violations of WTO law, panels will find themselves facing a task which they would rather avoid, but which someone will need to tackle, sooner or later.

III   The Implications of Proliferating Preferential Trade

The growing number of PTAs has now become a constant feature of international trade. In the past, PTAs were more common between trading partners in geographic proximity. During the past two decades, an increasing number of PTAs has been concluded between partners a large distance apart; some of them are located in different continents. This is also true for services PTAs: trading services from one side of the world to the other is made possible by globalization, improved means of international transportation and technological developments.[47]

---

[45] Mitchell and Lockhart present that if the clarification of the notion is left to panels and the AB, it is likely that they will adopt a flexible test based on the specific facts at issue. They consider that the test is likely to be premised on the word 'substantial', which indicates the need to eliminate internal restrictions covering a very considerable proportion of the trade between the parties. Mitchell & Lockhart (2009), at 96.

[46] Mathis, J. H. (2011) The 'Legalization' of GATT Article XXIV – Can Foes Become Friends?, in Bagwell, K. & Mavroidis, P. C. (eds.), *Preferential Trade Agreements: A Law and Economics analysis*. New York: Cambridge University Press, 31–9, at 39.

[47] Munin, N. (2010) *Legal Guide to GATS*. Alphen aan den Rijn: Kluwer Law International, at 217.

The causes to the proliferation of PTAs are complex. One of the most significant underlying reasons is the crisis in multilateralism in general. The world is becoming increasingly complex and trade policies are highly politicized. The post–Second World War momentum that enabled the integration of world trade is, to a certain extent, gone. Trade is no longer limited to manufacturing and its meaningful liberalization necessitates regulation that reaches deep behind the borders. This means that trade is not an area free from politics and expression of societal values, whether regional, cultural or religious values. The expansion of the demand for democracy coincides with the emergence of important developing nations that express restraint in submitting to rules and values determined by the established economies. The attainment of a consensus is an enormous challenge in the expanding and pluralistic organization that the WTO has become. This can be seen as the principal reason behind the failure of the Doha Round. While the multilateral trade negotiations are at a stalemate, economic growth is pursued elsewhere. Countries are turning to like-minded countries in the search of companions for trade agreements that could go deeper than simple tariff liberalization.[48]

The possible negative effects of PTAs are well known and are not dealt with in detail here. It suffices to say that PTAs, while creating trade, may also create diversion and thus lead to overall welfare losses.[49] However, there are also more political and principled arguments against PTAs. One of the most outspoken critics of preferentialism, Jagdish Bhagwati, sees the new mega-regional projects as hegemonic templates that strong countries use to take advantage of weaker economies. He is advocating

---

[48] Various governments are openly advocating PTAs as an engine for much-needed economic growth. For instance, the European Commission promoted the TTIP agreement as a project that would generate jobs and growth across the EU. In the course of the TTIP negotiations, the Commission often cited an economic impact assessment (CEPR) released in the beginning of the TTIP negotiations and has let it become widely understood that a European family of four would see their annual disposable income increase by an average of €545 per year as a result of the agreement. See the Commission's brochure 'The Transatlantic Trade and Investment Partnership: the Economic Analysis Explained', available at http://trade.ec.europa.eu/doclib/docs/2013/september/tra doc_151787.pdf (last accessed on 1 July 2018). The economic impact assessment of the Centre for Economic Policy Research (CEPR), commissioned by the Commission's Directorate General for Trade, is available at http://cepr.org/content/independent-study-outlines-benefits-eu-us-trade-agreement (last accessed on 1 July 2018).

[49] For a discussion of the evolving economic analysis regarding PTAs, see the volume edited by Bagwell, K. & Mavroidis, P. C. (2011) *Preferential Trade Agreements: A Law and Economics analysis.* New York: Cambridge University Press. They explore recent empirical research that casts doubt on the traditional 'trade diversion' school.

for 'garbage-free' PTAs that would adhere to trade objectives and discard what special-interest lobbies in the USA and Europe seek to foist on PTAs.[50]

An often-raised concern is that PTAs erode multilaterally negotiated concessions, which is especially detrimental for developing countries. However, at the same time developing countries are suffering from the formalistic requirement to reach the level of 'substantial' liberalization in their negotiations with the developed countries. As Bartels et al. point out, the attainment of very high liberalization levels leads to perverse outcomes especially for the least-developed countries. They argue that different levels of development should be taken better into account under Art. XXIV GATT and Art. V GATS for development-oriented PTAs to be genuinely development-oriented without artificial and harmful formalism.[51]

Realpolitik arguments suggest that MFN liberalization is not the appropriate counterfactual to preferences among PTA partners. The willingness of countries to participate in the WTO agreements might be different were they deprived of the possibility to conclude agreements on a preferential basis.[52] The banning of PTAs might, thus, have led to less satisfactory results on the multilateral level. Along this argumentation, the non-rigorous interpretation and non-enforcement of WTO rules on PTAs tell us that the Members understand this: PTAs are inevitably part of the reality in which they all live.

Mavroidis points out that the rigorous enforcement of the rules on PTAs is actually not likely to be to the benefit of the Members outside a specific PTA. The crucial criterion for PTAs under both the GATT and the GATS relates to the requirement of substantiality: PTAs must cover substantially all the trade in products or they must have substantial

---

[50] Bhagwati, Jagdish: 'The Broken Legs of Global Trade', Project Syndicate, 29 May 2012. Available at www.project-syndicate.org/commentary/the-broken-legs-of-global-trade, accessed 5 July 2018. See also Bhagwati, J. (2008) *Termites in the Trading System: How Preferential Agreements Undermine Free Trade*. Oxford; New York: Oxford University Press.

[51] Bartels, L., Silva, S., Hijazi, H., Schloemann, H. & Cottier, T. (2013) Re-Thinking Reciprocity: A New Framework for WTO Disciplines on North–South Regional Trade Agreements. *NCCR Trade Regulation Working Paper*, No. 2013/20.

[52] Mavroidis (2011), at 380. Mathis points out that Art. XXIV itself acknowledges the desirability of increasing freedom of trade through the voluntary agreements of closer integration between regional parties. This is thus the essence of what the GATT and now WTO Members have settled on – irrespective of the welfare implications of such agreements. See Mathis (2011), at 38–9.

sectoral coverage in the case of services. However, the classic Vinerian analysis suggests that wide PTAs covering a substantial amount of tariff lines also lead to a substantial trade diversion. Therefore, quite understandably, Members lack the incentive to urge a very strict interpretation of the rules on PTAs. Taking into account the economic theory on trade diversion, the poor enforcement of the rules on PTAs should thus maybe not be considered a one-sided misfortune.[53] Keeping in mind the necessity in guarding the principal rules of Art. XXIV and Art. V to prevent at least the worst types of cherry picking to the detriment of multilateral commitments, the *de facto* approach between the requirement of full implementation of the rules and complete latitude may be a well-placed compromise.

This book does not attempt to answer the question of whether PTAs should be shunned or embraced but rather to bring more focus on what is happening in practice. The book gives a picture of the level of liberalization reached in a sample of EIAs. Even if the Art. V requirements are too ambiguous to give strict guidelines as to the exact content and liberalization level of EIAs, they do point us towards a certain direction. The rules call for a substantial sectoral coverage and elimination of substantially all discrimination. These are therefore the two starting points for our empirical analysis. We argue that each EIA can, and should be, scrutinized with these two criteria in mind. Whereas no concrete values for 'substantial' can be set, Art. V makes clear that real, cross-the-border liberalization is required. In a world where trade liberalization is currently happening mostly through PTAs, the requirement for wide and deep liberalization is more necessary than ever to avoid a complex web of narrow agreements focusing on selected areas only.

Pascal Lamy has pointed out that the provisional establishment of the Transparency Mechanism 'may pave the way for non-litigious deliberations that could build confidence and understanding among members regarding the motives, contents and policy approaches underpinning regional initiatives, leading over time to a shared vision and reinforced legal provisions'.[54] The kind of deliberation referred to by the former Director-General requires in-depth information of the content and coverage of PTAs. This book provides some useful tools for such deliberation with regard to EIAs.

---

[53] See Mavroidis (2010).
[54] WTO, *World Trade Report 2011 – The WTO and Preferential Trade Agreements: From Co-Existence to Coherence*, at 4.

IV   Preferentialism in Services: Are Services Special?

i   Particularities of Going Preferential in Services

The share of trade in services in global cross-border trade is approximately 20 per cent. This is in stark contrast to the importance of the service sector in national economies.[55] The discrepancy reflects the difficulties in trading services across borders.[56] It is noteworthy that Mode 3 (commercial presence) covers approximately 50 per cent of international trade in services.[57] Trade in services is therefore, in practice, much about foreign investment. As pointed out by Fink and Jansen, this is one of the reasons why the perceived wisdom about regional integration coming from traditional trade literature does not necessarily apply to preferentialism in services.[58]

In general, the study of services liberalization can be considered more challenging than the study of trade in goods. Whereas goods trade is liberalized primarily through tariff cuts and elimination of goods-specific regulatory barriers, deep liberalization of services involves a scrutiny of the entire national regulatory framework. Given the broad modal coverage of the GATS, which extends, *inter alia*, to factor movements, i.e. capital and labour, services trade touches upon more complicated issues than goods trade. This complexity is reflected in the lack of coherent theory of services trade liberalization in academic research.

Trade diversion is usually considered to be significant if participating countries have had a high level of external protection prior to the establishment of a PTA. For PTAs concerning goods this concern has become less topical in the post-Uruguay Round era when the level of duties has, for most products, been reduced to low levels.[59] For trade in services, however, the concern is still very valid. The level of liberalization reached since the conclusion of the GATS in 1995 is modest and the barriers to trade in services are still high. There are big differences between the different modes under which services are traded. Therefore, the motivations of

---

[55] Services represent about two-thirds of global GDP and over 70 per cent of GDP in most developed countries. World Bank data on services, available at http://data.worldbank.org /indicator/NV.SRV.TETC.ZS (last accessed on 15 July 2018).

[56] Fink, C. & Jansen, M. (2009), at 224.

[57] Magdeleine, J. & Maurer, A. (2008) Measuring GATS Mode 4 Trade Flows. *WTO Staff Working Paper*, ERSD-2008-05.

[58] Fink & Jansen (2009), at 224.

[59] Mavroidis, P. C., Bermann, G. A. & Wu, M. (2013) *The Law of the World Trade Organization (WTO): Documents, Cases & Analysis.* St. Paul, MN: Thomson/West, at 155–6.

countries to liberalize services trade also vary between the modes. Incentives to grant better access to foreign investment under Mode 3 are not necessarily similar to the incentives that an enhanced movement of service suppliers under Mode 4 may offer, or a better access for online services for example. Moreover, the applicable regulations tend to vary greatly depending on the mode of delivery.

Many scholars and practitioners consider that preferentialism in the field of services is likely to be less harmful than in the field of goods. Fink and Molinuevo summarize three basic reasons for this. First, there is the issue of domestic stocktaking. Second, services regulations are often applied in a non-discriminatory manner. The third reason is the liberal rules of origin that are set out in Art. V GATS and also typically applied in EIAs.[60]

The first reason, domestic stocktaking, refers to the positive spillover effects from PTA to WTO negotiations. According to Fink and Molinuevo, such effects may be more important in services than in goods. Services negotiations require a resource-intensive stock-take of all such domestic laws and regulations that might be considered to affect trade in services. Governments that have carried out a comprehensive analysis of their domestic regulatory framework may be better prepared for services negotiations also in other contexts, particularly in the WTO. EIAs may therefore 'play a useful role in overcoming "informational" obstacles to further multilateral integration'.[61]

The second reason behind the less dangerous character of service preferentialism lies in the way regulations are typically applied in practice. Behind-the-border regulations are relevant in goods and services trade alike. In the field of services, however, regulations are the only form of protection. The lack of tariffs means that a central, discriminatory means of protection is completely absent in trade in services. This has important implications for the liberalization of services considering that origin-based discrimination is often hard or at least unpractical to implement through domestic regulation. Adapting one's internal service-related regulation depending on the origin of the service supplier is more difficult to accomplish and can be welfare-reducing as a whole.[62]

---

[60] Fink & Molinuevo (2008), East Asian Preferential Trade Agreements in Services: Liberalization Content and WTO Rules. *World Trade Review*, 7(4), 641–673, at 641–73.

[61] Ibid., at 668.

[62] With this type of legislation we mean all generally applicable regulation that applies to service suppliers in the territory of a country (to nationals and foreigners alike). Whereas MA limitations are quantitative, this type of regulation is qualitative in nature. Generally,

As is noted by Miroudot et al., such a practice can create economic distortions that can further translate into productivity losses.[63] Miroudot and Shepherd note that overall the concept of preferences is not easy to tackle in the context of services trade considering that many service-related measures are not really prone to discrimination between domestic and foreign suppliers. They give the examples of market regulations introducing rules on prices, access to networks or increasing the powers of a competition authority. Such regulations equally benefit domestic and foreign services suppliers. As they note, it is not possible to create a more competitive market for domestic suppliers only. Foreign suppliers would have to be totally excluded from such a market.[64]

Countries therefore often apply the same rules to services and service suppliers of all countries without differentiating between their MFN and PTA partners.[65] Naturally, domestic suppliers may be treated more favourably *de jure* or *de facto* as many service-related rules require nationality, residency or country-specific qualifications. For foreign service suppliers, they often prove equally burdensome for all of them.

Nevertheless, discriminatory application of domestic regulation to service suppliers of different origins is not impossible. Even if governments typically abstain from applying different sets of regulation depending on the origin of the service supplier, some of the most restrictive measures are applied on a preferential basis only. Such restrictive preferential measures

genuine liberalization of internal service-related regulation often happens through unilateral reforms and not through trade negotiations. The preferential treatment of service suppliers of any specific country is thus not usually in a central role when new service-related regulations and reforms are put in place. See Bosworth, M. & Trewin, R. (2008) The Domestic Dynamics of Preferential Services Liberalization: The Experience of Australia and Thailand, in Marchetti, J. & Roy, M. (eds.), *Opening Markets for Trade in Services: Countries and Sectors in Bilateral and WTO Negotiations*. Cambridge: Cambridge University Press, at 633–66.

[63] See Miroudot, S., Sauvage, J. & Sudreau, M. (2010) Multilateralising Regionalism: How Preferential Are Services Commitments in Regional Trade Agreements?, *OECD Trade Policy Papers*, No. 106, 6 December 2010, OECD Publishing, Paris. http://dx.doi.org/10.1787/5km362n24t8n-en, at 9. As an example they mention the promotion of a competitive market in telecoms where the facilitation of new entrants through regulation will benefit all companies.

[64] Miroudot, S. & Shepherd, B. (2014) The Paradox of 'Preferences': Regional Trade Agreements and Trade Costs in Services. *The World Economy*, 37(12), 1751–72, at 16.

[65] This is different under the so-called Mode 4 of the GATS, which involves the cross-border movement of natural persons supplying services. Different conditions are generally applied to nationals of different states. The analysis of liberalization of Mode 4 requires methods somewhat different from other modes of delivery under the GATS. Chapter 8 in Part III (methodology) deals with this problem.

are most easily applied under Modes 3 and 4. Miroudot and Shepherd note that discriminatory measures usually appear in the form of foreign equity restrictions, labour market tests for the entry of natural persons and the recognition of qualifications. But, as they note, even in these areas, not all countries introduce discriminatory measures.[66]

Undertakings originating in EIA partners may sometimes be allowed to benefit from preferential, and often earlier, access to the market. In such a case, preferential liberalization may exert more durable effects on competition than in the case of goods. For instance, if second-best suppliers obtain a first-mover advantage, it may result in the country being stuck with such suppliers even if liberalization was subsequently carried out on an MFN basis. The establishment of preferences may thus result in entry by inferior suppliers.[67] As noted by Sauvé and Shingal, in the field of services, the sequence of liberalization matters more than in goods.[68]

EIAs sometimes include certain harmonization or coordination of regulatory measures, which may benefit their service suppliers in comparison to service suppliers originating in countries with differing regulatory standards. However, regulatory coordination between EIA partners may have positive effects as well. Sometimes regulatory changes may create schemes that benefit not just the preferential partners but all foreign suppliers.[69]

In addition to the benefits of domestic stocktaking and the non-discriminatory application of services regulation, the third essential element in the less-risky character of EIAs are the liberal rules of origin. Such rules are necessitated by Art. V:6 GATS that requires service suppliers also from countries outside the EIA to benefit from the agreement as long as they are established in one of the parties and engage in substantive business operations in their territories.[70] Rules of origin

[66] Miroudot & Shepherd (2014), at 16.
[67] Winters, A. L. (2008) Preferential Liberalization of Services Trade: Economic Considerations, in Mattoo, A., Stern, R. M. & Zanini, G. (eds.), *A Handbook of International Trade in Services*, Oxford University Press, Oxford and New York, at 223–4. For economic considerations on services preferentialism, see especially Mattoo, A. & Fink, C. (2004) *Journal of Economic Integration*, 19(4), 742–79 and Hoekman, B. & Sauvé, P. (1994) Regional and Multilateral Liberalization of Service Markets: Complements or Substitutes? *Journal of Common Market Studies*, 32(3), 283–318.
[68] Sauvé, P. & Shingal, A. (2011) Reflections on the Preferential Liberalization of Services Trade. *Journal of World Trade*, 45(5), 953–63, at 954.
[69] WTO, *World Trade Report 2011 – The WTO and Preferential Trade Agreements: From Co-Existence to Coherence*, at 54.
[70] In accordance with Art. V:6 GATS, service suppliers of other Members constituted as juridical persons under the laws of a party to an EIA must be entitled to treatment granted

formed in accordance with Art. V:6 help to attenuate the so-called 'stumbling block' effect of PTAs.[71]

In the case of goods trade, rules of origin are typically based on a value-added criterion. Only goods which have sufficient value added within a specific territory (thus are sufficiently transformed) are eligible for preferential treatment. The design of rules of origin for services trade is essentially different. Instead of targeting the service and its transformation within the relevant territory, they focus on the characteristics of the service supplier. Jansen points at two reasons behind the differences in rules of origin in manufacturing and services. First, the nature of services trade significantly differs from goods trade and thus the rules of origin for services make references to issues such as place of incorporation, particular ownership or control and the level of business operations within a specific territory. Value-added rules are inappropriate for services where only under Mode 1 the service alone is crossing the border. Secondly, the rules of origin in manufacturing and services do not always serve the same purpose. In services, rules of origin similarly delimit the extent to which non-members may benefit from the EIA but they also pursue goals that are more related to regulatory issues than economic interests. Therefore, rules of origin are sometimes constructed in a way that allows for more regulatory oversight within the EIA or domestically.[72]

ii   The Lack of Market Access Discipline in Art. V GATS

EIAs tend to follow the disciplines of the GATS in their design: they generally include provisions similar to at least Art. II (MFN), Art. III (Transparency), Art. VI (Domestic regulation), Art. XVI (MA), Art. XVII (NT) and Art. XIV and XIV bis (general and security exceptions)

---

under such agreement, provided that they engage in substantive business operations in the territory of the parties to such agreement.

[71] Fink & Jansen (2009), at 248.

[72] Jansen, M. (2008) Comment: Is Services Trade Like or Unlike Manufacturing Trade?, in Panizzon, M., Pohl, N. & Sauvé, P. (eds.), *GATS and the Regulation of International Trade in Services*. Cambridge; New York: Cambridge University Press, 139–42, at 139–40. Jansen notes that in a number of sectors, such as the financial sector and telecommunications, regulation plays a crucial role in guaranteeing the efficient functioning of the markets. The policy-makers must therefore make sure that trade liberalization does not jeopardize the regulation of relevant markets. In some cases, rules of origin are designed for protectionist purposes. For example, the condition that owners or managers of foreign companies are domestic may reflect the intention to ensure that their decisions reflect the interest of the domestic establishment and not those of holding companies situated outside the EIA territory.

of the GATS. Similarly to the GATS, Members typically undertake their EIA commitments in respect of both MA and NT. It is, however, noteworthy that Art. V GATS does not include any MA discipline: it does not require any specific level of liberalization as regards the various, mostly quantitative, limitations included in Art. XVI GATS.

This is reflected in the wording of Art. V that places the emphasis in a specific EIA's analysis to the level of non-discrimination granted to one's partners. Requiring MA commitments from EIA partners would not be desirable, as countries would in that case be incentivized to apply different MA conditions to different trading partners. Relaxed quotas and other quantitative limitations in EIAs could lead to a more restrictive trading environment towards countries outside the EIA. Service suppliers from EIA partner countries would have less restrained access to each other's markets whereas outsiders would be subject to stricter requirements in the form of a higher number of discriminatory quotas and other quantitative restrictions. As a consequence, service suppliers from MFN countries would suffer while EIA service suppliers would enjoy a more favourable operating environment through more open MA conditions.

As Fink and Jansen note, preferential liberalization of services may create a long-term trade diversion effect.[73] In service markets, high location-specific sunk costs and network externalities can give first-movers a durable advantage. Second-best service suppliers may thus take over the market and will not be replaced by first-best suppliers from outside the EIA when trade is eventually liberalized on an MFN basis. Even short-term preferences can thus be detrimental as they have long-term effects.[74]

Preferential MA conditions can take the form of bigger quotas and more relaxed conditions as to the types of legal entities. They may also waive otherwise applicable economic needs tests. Also, a limited number of licences may be made more easily available to preferential partners and the numbers of their personnel may be unlimited.[75] The creation of

---

[73] 'Trade diversion' is a term originally coined by Jacob Viner. In his groundbreaking work of 1950 Viner analyzed the effects of PTA on economic welfare. He labelled those conflicting forces as 'trade creation' and 'trade diversion'. See Viner, J. (1950) *The Customs Union Issue*. New York: Carnegie Endowment for International Peace.

[74] Fink & Jansen (2009), at 230. The authors point out that the potential for trade diversion effects greatly depends on the rules of origin adopted by an EIA.

[75] Especially self-regulated industries tend to have *numerus fixus* constraints on new entry (certain professions). See Hoekman, B. (1995) Tentative First Steps: An Assessment of the Uruguay Round Agreement on Services, Volume 1. *World Bank Policy Research Working Paper*, No. 1455, at 30.

preferential MA conditions can thus significantly alter the conditions of competition to the benefit of service suppliers from an EIA partner country as others may in practice be blocked from the market due to later arrival. The problems relating to preferential MA conditions makes us propose that Art. V deliberately omits the requirement to address MA limitations.

In contrast, the requirement of elimination of discrimination towards one's EIA partner is potentially less harmful as it is more likely to benefit also those service suppliers who come from countries outside the EIA. Differentiation among foreign suppliers is more easily carried out with regard to MA conditions as various limitations on the number of services suppliers, economic needs tests and other MA requirements usually involve some type of case-specific discretion.

Considering that MA limitations tend to be the most harmful types of limitations, it can nevertheless be asked why Art. V does not include any discipline on MA at all. If the discipline existed, it could require the elimination of substantially all MA limitations (in addition to the requirement to eliminate substantially all discrimination). Such a requirement could be seen as a counterpart to the requirement of elimination of duties with respect to substantially all the trade between parties to CUs and FTAs under Art. XXIV:8 GATT. The negotiation background of Art. V does not reveal any specific reason for this – actually, we have not identified any clear reason for the neglect of an MA discipline in Art. V either in literature or through various discussions with specialists who were observing the GATS negotiations. As to the MA discipline in Art. XVI of the GATS, there is a wide array of opinions as to its reach and dimensions, especially as a result of the *US–Gambling* dispute.[76]

A close observer of the GATS negotiations has noted that, in his view, one of the underlying and also explicit purposes of Art. XVI was to reform domestic service markets. At least for such countries that were expecting the GATS to induce domestic liberalization, and not just trade liberalization, Art. XVI clearly covered not only discriminatory but also non-discriminatory MA measures.[77]

---

[76] *United States – Measures Affecting the Cross-Border Supply of Gambling and Betting Services*, Report of the Appellate Body, WT/DS285/AB/R, circulated 7 April 2005. For a discussion on the scope of Art. XVI GATS (the GATS discipline on MA), see Pauwelyn, J. (2005) Rien ne Va Plus? Distinguishing Domestic Regulation from Market Access in GATT and GATS. *World Trade Review*, 4(2), 131–70, and Mavroidis, P. C. (2007) Highway XVI ReVisited: The Road from Non-Discrimination to Market Access in GATS. *World Trade Review*, 6(1), 1–23.

[77] Interview with Hamid Mamdouh, Director, Trade in Service Division, WTO Secretariat, 31 January 2013.

One option is thus to consider whether the lack of an MA discipline in Art. V is related to the perceived function of Art. XVI as a vehicle of domestic liberalization. In such a case there would be less reason to include an MA discipline in the rules on EIAs, which are primarily targeted to ensure a high level of non-discrimination between the participating countries. As we already proposed above, an explicit encouragement towards taking commitments on quantitative limitations in the form of an MA discipline could lead to quotas and other numerical limitations being taken on a preferential basis. That type of preferentialism can be considered especially harmful in the field of services.

Due to the absence of a specific MA discipline in Art. V, Members appear free to include MA limitations in their EIAs. They are, however, restricted by the requirement to eliminate discrimination in the sense of NT as that requirement applies to such MA limitations that are prescribed or implemented in a discriminatory manner.[78] Already this has a restrictive effect on the use of MA limitations, as Members may be reluctant to formulate MA limitations that they would have to extend also to their own service suppliers.[79]

Some commentators have argued that Art. XVI should encompass discriminatory MA limitations only.[80] If this was the case, the reason for the lack of a MA discipline in Art. V could be quite straightforward: since Art. V requires the elimination of discrimination there would be no reason for it to include specific rules for the scheduling of discriminatory MA limitations. The majority opinion, however, appears to be that Art. XVI covers discriminatory and non-discriminatory measures alike. This is also the WTO Secretariat's view[81] and, most importantly, it has been

---

[78] It should be noted that subsection (f) of Art. XVI:2 refers to limitations that are by their nature discriminatory (limitations on the participation of foreign capital in terms of maximum percentage limit on foreign shareholding or the total value of individual or aggregate foreign investment).

[79] In light of the US–Gambling, Art. XVI covers also non-discriminatory measures that are in conflict with a Member's MA commitments. A Member may, however, choose to formulate its commitments in a discriminatory way or leave a specific sector completely unbound. Under Art. V, however, Members are restricted as the EIA should have a wide sectoral coverage and eliminate 'substantially all' discrimination.

[80] See especially Mavroidis (2007).

[81] See page 4 of the 2001 Scheduling Guidelines (S/L/92, 28 March 2001). The guidelines have been prepared by the WTO Secretariat and adopted by the Council on Trade in Services.

confirmed by the result in *US–Gambling*.[82] However, when the negotiation history of Art. V is considered, it cannot be ruled out that some Members might have understood Art. XVI to cover discriminatory measures only.

The following chapter analyzes the core requirements of Art. V GATS. The purpose is to address the lack of comprehension over the rules on PTAs and provide a legal interpretation of the GATS rules in light of the wider understanding of preferentialism in services that has been introduced in this chapter. The interpretation is then used as the basis for the empirical analysis of EIAs, covering Parts III and IV of the book. The underlying idea is that new proposals for the interpretation and analysis of PTAs should actively be put forward to avoid a situation where the international trade community simply stops caring about the WTO rules and their enforcement altogether. The move to the so-called 'mega-regionals' is already a reality. Even if the risks relating to preferential treatment in services are lower than in the field of goods, it is still important to keep track of the current developments and analyze to what extent new agreements open up trade in services. One of the key areas worth tracking is services regulation applied by sub-central levels of government in federal countries and free trade areas such as the EU. The issue of federalism in services regulation and liberalization is dealt with in Part II.

---

[82] The AB did not deal with this question explicitly but since the zero-quota was applied also to domestic service suppliers, the AB must have considered Art. XVI to cover non-discriminatory measures as well. The issue of discrimination came up only under the analysis of the availability of general exceptions (Art. XIV GATS).

2

The GATS Rules on Economic Integration Agreements (EIAs)

I Background of Art. V GATS

The international regulation of services trade was not born at the advent of the GATS. Rule-setting on services had started on a bilateral and a regional level already prior to the initiation of the talks on a multilateral services agreement, the GATS, during the Uruguay Round. In addition to the EU,[1] where detailed provisions on regional services liberalization existed since the EEC Treaty, the USA pioneered by including specific service disciplines in its FTA with Canada, concluded in 1987. The US–Canada FTA contained provisions on trade and investment in services and even covered temporary movement of business persons.[2]

In addition to bilateral and regional initiatives, industry-specific standard setting contributed to the increasing service flows already prior to the GATS. For example, the International Telecommunications Union, the Basel Committee on Banking Supervision and the International Aviation Organization established standards and administered agreements concerning the services provision in their respective fields. Moreover, specific schemes existed with respect to certain services. The USA, for example, had been active in concluding treaties of Friendship, Commerce and Navigation (FCN) that regulated, among other issues, aviation, shipping and communications services.[3]

---

[1] The term EU refers to all historical denominations (EEC, EC) of the European integration process.
[2] Marchetti, J. A. & Mavroidis, P. C. (2011) The Genesis of the GATS (General Agreement on Trade in Services). *European Journal of International Law*, 22(3), 689–721, at 690.
[3] Ibid.

The Uruguay Round, however, marked the debut of comprehensive trade negotiations across a wide spectrum of services sectors. Since then, trade in services has become an indispensable element of bilateral, regional and multilateral efforts of trade liberalization.[4] A significant phenomenon in the development of world trade since the establishment of the WTO in the mid-1990s is that the number of PTAs has rapidly multiplied. Today, the majority of PTAs include rules on services.[5] The stalled state of multilateral trade negotiations has driven countries to seek further opening of goods and services trade also through more innovative arrangements. In the area of services, the negotiations for a plurilateral services agreement, the TiSA, started in 2013. If a critical mass of participants is achieved, TiSA will possibly be applied on an MFN-basis.[6] At the moment the negotiations are, however, at a halt. The increasing number of EIAs, as well as the TiSA project, nevertheless show the willingness of WTO Members to engage in the liberalization of services where very little has happened in the multilateral scene since the first commitments taken upon the entry into force of the GATS in 1995.

Whereas the US demand was crucial in putting services on the multilateral negotiation agenda, the EU's role was instrumental in shaping the final agreement.[7] The EU's own example was also essential in the

---

[4] Marchetti, J. A. & Roy, M. (2008) *Opening Markets for Trade in Services: Countries and Sectors in Bilateral and WTO Negotiations.* Cambridge; New York: Cambridge University Press, at 1.

[5] According to the WTO's RTA database, over 150 EIAs (based on Art. V GATS) and over 290 PTAs (based on Art. XXIV GATT, Art. V GATS and/or the enabling clause) in total were notified and in force as of 31 January 2019. See www.wto.org/english/tratop_e/region_e/region_e.htm (last accessed on 10 February 2019). The numbers do not include accessions to existing PTAs.

[6] The economic case for a plurilateral agreement on services is clear. Lee-Makiyama notes that neither is such an idea a novelty. The GATS itself started as a plurilateral agreement that was created by a group of countries that chipped in their commitments until the collective offer was good enough to be extended to all members of the WTO on the principle of MFN. See Lee-Makiyama, H. (2012) The International Services Agreement (ISA) – from the European Vantage Point. *ECIPE Policy Brief*, No 3/2012, at 3. For possible alternatives for the final legal form of TiSA, see Giødesen Thystrup, A., *Legal Forms of Negotiated Trade in Services Agreement (TiSA) Outcomes – Perspectives on Trade Integration and an Incrementalist Approach to Quasi-Multilateralization*, CTEI Working Papers, CTEI-2016-03, 29 September 2016.

[7] According to Marchetti and Mavroidis, the USA conditioned its participation in the Uruguay Round upon the inclusion of services trade in the negotiation agenda. The EU's priority was to defend its Common Agricultural Policy and only gradually it became a key participant in the services liberalization and drafting of the GATS. See Marchetti & Mavroidis (2011), at 694–5 and 716.

formulation of the GATS rules on EIAs. The EEC Member States had detailed provisions for the liberalization of services trade in place; they needed to be taken into account in the formulation of the GATS provisions. Since preferential liberalization of trade in services was already a reality during the negotiations of the GATS, the agreement had to provide a possibility for their existence. According to Stephenson, during the Uruguay Round negotiations, a draft provision on preferential trade for services was introduced by the EU and supported by Switzerland, Australia and New Zealand. The proposed draft was included in the 'Dunkel text' of December 1991. At the end of 1991, the footnote to Art. V:1(a) was added. The final version of Art. V found in the GATS is almost identical to that set out in the Dunkel draft.[8]

The GATS allows the conclusion of EIAs that ensure comprehensive trade liberalization in trade in services. In contrast to the two strict forms of PTAs allowed under the GATT (CUs and FTAs), the drafters of the GATS opted for a broader term of 'economic integration'. The more open-ended formulation made it possible to abstain from specifying the exact type of liberalization required from EIAs.[9] Nevertheless, Art. V GATS includes a set of legal criteria that all EIAs should respect.

Since few border measures are applied in the field of services, the concept of discrimination, or rather non-discrimination, forms the core of services liberalization. As will be shown in this chapter, the requirement of non-discrimination with respect to domestic policies is the very essence of Art. V GATS.

Assessing the level of elimination of discriminatory measures is necessarily more qualitative in nature than assessing the level of duties. Notwithstanding the most blatant violations of MFN and NT, determining what constitutes discrimination requires discretion. This normally involves a value judgement. If one is to avoid empirical results being skewed by personal judgement, one has to take a relatively restrictive approach to the concept of discrimination or at least be very clear in defining one's methodology and its consistent application the deeper to the sphere of *de facto* discrimination one is willing to venture.

---

[8] Stephenson, S. (2000) Regional Agreements on Services in Multilateral Disciplines: Interpreting and Applying GATS Art. V, in Stephenson, S. (ed.), *Services Trade in the Western Hemisphere: Liberalization, Integration and Reform*. Washington, DC: Brookings Institution Press and Organization of American States, 86–104, at 88.

[9] Munin, N. (2010) *Legal Guide to GATS*. Alphen aan den Rijn: Kluwer Law International, at 26.

The present chapter interprets the various elements of Art. V. The methodology for the empirical analysis of EIAs (Part III) is designed based on the understanding of Art. V proposed here. As we argue that the rules on EIAs cannot be interpreted in a vacuum, an overall understanding of Art. V must necessarily be inspired by empirical findings. Any empirical analysis of existing agreements shows the challenges and limitations present in a legal interpretation of the GATS rules on EIAs, and in the interpretation of the EIAs themselves.

As the external effects of EIAs are outside the scope of this book and its empirical analysis, our interpretation of Art. V is focused on the first two paragraphs of Art. V: the so-called internal trade requirement and the possibility to take into account a wider process of economic integration or trade liberalization between the EIA partners. The concept of non-discrimination is dealt with in detail, as it is the fundamental building block of Art. V:1. In addition to engaging with the fundamental criterion of non-discrimination, the book provides new tools to analyze services commitments of federal entities. In addressing federal entities' commitments, we also pay attention to the internal differentiation in a specific Member's (in our empirical analysis the EU's) services commitments and argue that such differentiation, which is due to the Member's regional subdivision, must be considered under the Art. V criteria.

II The Legal Criteria for EIAs

i The Main Ingredients of Art. V

The GATS discipline on EIAs is almost five decades younger than the corresponding discipline for CUs and FTAs under the GATT. However, the two disciplines share common elements. Similarly to Art. XXIV GATT, Art. V GATS includes an internal requirement (facilitation of trade between the parties to the EIA), an external requirement (prohibition to raise the level of barriers applicable to outsiders) and a notification requirement.[10] In addition, Art. V includes features that are specific to EIAs only. This is arguably due to the different nature of preferentialism

---

[10] Since the CRTA has *de facto* been restricted to a mere transparency exercise, the notification requirement now mainly serves for transparency purposes. Those who believe that the requirements of Art. V have not been met, have the possibility to challenge the consistency of the notified EIA with the multilateral rules before a WTO Panel. Mavroidis, P. C., Bermann, G. A. & Wu, M. (2013) *The Law of the World Trade Organization (WTO): Documents, Cases & Analysis.* St. Paul: Thomson/West, at 781.

in goods and services, as well as to changes in Members' opinions towards PTAs in general. When the GATS was negotiated, PTAs were already part of the everyday practice of the Members. This was likely to call for more flexibility in the design of the discipline. In addition, as viewed in the previous chapter, services preferentialism can be considered less harmful than preferentialism in the field of goods. This may have encouraged a looser attitude to be reflected in Art. V GATS.

The flexibility is especially present in the provision of Art. V:2, which allows the EIA's contribution to the wider economic integration between its participants to be taken into account. Even more leeway is available to developing countries. Under the provision of Art. V:3, in EIAs involving developing countries, the condition regarding the elimination of discrimination is more flexible in accordance with the level of development of the countries concerned, both overall and in individual sectors and subsectors.[11]

Unlike Art. XXIV GATT, Art. V also includes a specific rule regarding the origin of the service suppliers. Suppliers originating in Members outside the agreement will still benefit from the EIA if they have substantive business operations within the territory of one of the members to the agreement. As discussed in the previous chapter, this potentially greatly extends the field of application of EIAs.

The entire provision of our centre of focus, Art. V:1 (including footnote (1)), reads as follows:

Art. V: Economic Integration
1. This Agreement shall not prevent any of its Members from being a party to or entering into an agreement liberalizing trade in services between or among the parties to such an agreement, provided that such an agreement:
(a) has substantial sectoral coverage (1), and
(b) provides for the absence or elimination of substantially all discrimination, in the sense of Art. XVII, between or among the parties, in the sectors covered under subparagraph (a), through:
(i) elimination of existing discriminatory measures, and/or
(ii) prohibition of new or more discriminatory measures,
either at the entry into force of that agreement or on the basis of a reasonable time-frame, except for measures permitted under Arts. XI, XII, XIV and XIV bis.

---

[11] For a detailed discussion of the nature and degree of flexibilities given to developing countries in Art. V, see Sieber-Gasser, C. (2016) *Developing Countries and Preferential Services Trade*. Cambridge: Cambridge University Press.

(1) This condition is understood in terms of number of sectors, volume of trade affected and modes of supply. In order to meet this condition, agreements should not provide for the a priori exclusion of any mode of supply.

The first paragraph, the *chapeau* of Art. V, gives reason to conclude that EIAs may take the form of either a bilateral or a plurilateral trade agreement between two or more countries and within one or more regions. The same provision implies that Art. V applies to both current and future EIAs. Further, the reference to 'parties' as participants to the agreements implies that the scope of the provision is not limited to agreements between Members but applies also to agreements between Members and non-Members.

To qualify as an EIA under Art. V, the agreement must satisfy three main requirements.[12] First, an EIA must have substantial sectoral coverage (paragraph 1(a)). Second, it must provide for the absence or elimination of substantially all discrimination between or among the parties and in the sectors covered under the first requirement (paragraph 1(b)). Finally, in addition to these two requirements designed to facilitate trade between the parties to the agreement (often referred to as the 'internal requirement'), an EIA must satisfy an external requirement (paragraph 4): it must not raise the overall level of barriers to trade in services with regard to any Member outside the agreement.

It is sometimes proposed that in order to be in line with Art. V, EIA commitments should go further (deeper) than the same parties' GATS commitments. However, the language of Art. V does not appear to support this interpretation. In practical terms, such an expectation is of course reasonable considering that the general level of liberalization in the original GATS commitments is low. But strictly legally we can more securely say that the respective concessions in EIAs must be at least at the level of the parties' GATS commitments. As pointed out by Adlung, it is hardly conceivable that an agreement aimed at 'liberalizing trade in services', and required to provide for 'the absence or elimination of substantially all discrimination' between its parties, would allow for the introduction of new discriminatory measures at the regional level.[13]

---

[12] EIAs liberalizing trade in services are admitted 'provided that' the conditions of the first paragraph are met. The language makes clear that the conditions are mandatory. Cottier, T. & Molinuevo, M. (2008) Article V GATS, in Wolfrum, R., Stoll, P.-T. & Feinäugle, C. (eds.), *WTO - Trade in Services*. Leiden; Boston: Martinus Nijhoff Publishers, 125–64, at 130.

[13] In practice, this however happens. See Adlung, R. (2015) The Trade in Services Agreement (TISA) and Its Compatibility with GATS: An Assessment Based on Current Evidence, *World Trade Review*, 14(4), 617–41.

The AB has not yet had the occasion, or desire, to interpret Art. V. The only reference to Art. V so far has been in the Panel Report of *Canada–Autos*. The case dealt mostly with measures relating to trade in goods, but the Panel concluded that a specific measure was inconsistent also under Art. V:1(b) since it accorded an advantage to US firms and excluded other firms in another party to the EIA.[14]

In *Turkey–Textiles*, the AB indicated that the words 'shall not prevent' in the opening paragraph of Art. XXIV:5 GATT mean that the GATT does not make impossible the formation of a customs union. The same, presumably, applies to FTAs under Art. XXIV GATT. It is noteworthy that Art. V GATS employs the same words 'shall not prevent' in its *chapeau*. Since the context of Art. XXIV GATT and Art. V GATS is identical (both provisions justify an exception to certain WTO obligations for Members engaged in deep economic integration with their preferential trading partners), one may assume that the AB's reasoning in *Turkey–Textiles* is in this respect applicable also to EIAs concluded under Art. V GATS.

There is, however, a certain difference between Art. XXIV GATT and Art. V GATS regarding the legal effects of a PTA. Both disciplines include a notification requirement, but Art. XXIV contains stronger language than Art. V on the 'conditionality' attached to the time-frame for implementation. If a Working Party were to find that the plan or schedule for an interim agreement for a PTA is not likely to result in a GATT-consistent CU or FTA, its members 'shall not maintain or put into force [an] agreement if they are not prepared to modify it in accordance with . . . the recommendations'. No such provision exists in Article V.[15] This difference has, however, become redundant as practically no multilateral control of PTAs exists any longer. The formal discussions on legal consistency of PTAs have been replaced by the Transparency Mechanism of 14 December 2006.

There are commentaries on Art. V in a number of textbooks and articles dealing with services trade. Their analysis, however, typically stays on a relatively general level. A deeper discussion is provided by Cottier and Molinuevo who go through possible interpretations for each provision of Art. V.[16] Also Stephenson and Sieber-Gasser provide useful

---

[14] Panel Report in *Canada–Automotive Industry, Canada – Certain Measures Affecting the Automotive Industry*, WT/DS139/R, circulated 11 February 2000, paras. 10.265–10.272.

[15] Hoekman, B. & Sauvé, P. (1994) Liberalizing Trade in Services. *World Bank Discussion Papers*, WDP243, at 60.

[16] Cottier, T. & Molinuevo, M. (2008) Article V GATS, in Wolfrum, R., Stoll, P.-T. & Feinäugle, C. (eds.), *WTO – Trade in Services*. Leiden; Boston: Martinus Nijhoff Publishers, 125–64.

analyses and point out a number of challenges in effectively applying these disciplines.[17]

Art. V is explored at some length also in Hoekman and Sauvé. They consider Art. V conditions to be weaker than those applying in the GATT context and stress that the weakness of the discipline on EIAs implies only a limited constraint on 'strategic' violations of the MFN obligation.[18]

We will now proceed to a more detailed analysis of the two core requirements of Art. V:1: the requirement of 'substantial sectoral coverage' and the elimination of 'substantially all discrimination'. In addition, we will shortly go through the other principal criteria of Art. V: the possibility to pay attention to 'a wider process of economic integration or trade liberalization' (Art. V:2), the flexibility provided for developing countries (Art. V:3), the external requirement (Art. V:4) and the criteria for rules of origin in EIAs (Art. V:6). Even if the focus in the book and especially in the empirical analysis is on the first paragraph of Art. V, these other criteria are essential elements in services preferentialism and they inform the overall interpretation of Art. V.[19] Art. V:5 (renegotiation of commitments) and Art. V:8 (lack of compensation for trade benefits accruing from the EIA to non-parties) are not dealt with as they are not essential elements in a compliance analysis. Art. V:7 (notification and examination procedure) has been taken up in the previous chapter.

ii Substantial Sectoral Coverage (Art. V:1(a))

The term 'substantial' in Art. V defines sufficient coverage in terms of sectors covered as well as non-discrimination provided. It appears in two different forms: 'substantial' (Art. V:1(a)) and 'substantially' (Art. V:1(b)).

According to Art. V:1(a), an EIA must have substantial sectoral coverage. The requirement is designed to prevent the conclusion of numerous sector-specific agreements that would pick and choose from areas of mutual interest. The goal is trade promotion while containing trade

---

[17] Stephenson (2000). See also Stephenson, S. M. (2000) GATS and Regional Integration, in Sauvé, P. & Stern, R. M. (eds.), *GATS 2000: New Directions in Services Trade Liberalization*. Washington, DC: Center for Business and Government Brookings Institution Press, 509–29, and Sieber-Gasser (2016).

[18] Hoekman & Sauvé (1994), at 71.

[19] The basic parameters for the empirical analysis are built on Art. V:1. However, elements arguably belonging under 'a wider process of economic integration' in line with Art. V:2 are also included in the analysis.

diversion to which randomly concluded sectoral agreements are likely to contribute.[20]

The use of the word 'substantial' gives reason to conclude that EIA partners are never under an obligation to liberalize trade in all service sectors. The requirement can be compared to Art. XXIV:8 GATT. In that context, in *Turkey-Textiles*, the AB noted that 'substantially all the trade' as mentioned under Art. XXIV:8 GATT is 'something considerably more than merely *some* of the trade'.[21] Mitchell and Lockhart conclude that the relevant amount of trade must, therefore, fall somewhere between *some* and *all* trade among the parties to the PTA. However, since there is no clear definition or agreement about the meaning of the word 'substantial' under the GATT, the practice under the GATT does not shed light on the word's definition either in the context of the GATS.[22]

Similarly to Art. XXIV:8 GATT, Art. V:1(a) GATS focuses on the level of liberalization rather than the type of trade affected.[23] Unlike paragraph 8 of Art. XXIV, Art. V:1(a) GATS, nevertheless, gives some further guidance for its interpretation. It includes the following footnote:

> This condition is understood in terms of number of sectors, volume of trade affected and modes of supply. In order to meet this condition, agreements should not provide for the a priori exclusion of any mode of supply.

However, the precise application of these additional elements remains unclear. Fink and Molinuevo point out several essential questions. First, how to understand 'volume' of services trade. Is it opposed to the 'value' of such trade? At what level of disaggregation should the count of sectors

---

[20] Cottier & Molinuevo (2008), at 132. Ortino and Sheppard cite the WTO Secretariat and conclude that the 'substantial sectoral coverage' appears to have been designed to prevent Members from using the Art. V exception for economic agreements that are limited to one specific mode of supply, such as cross-border services (Mode 1) or foreign direct investment (Mode 3). See Sheppard, A. & Ortino, F. (2006) International Agreements Covering Foreign Investment in Services: Patterns and Linkages, in Bartels, L. & Ortino, F. (eds.), *Regional Trade Agreements and the WTO Legal System*. Oxford; New York: Oxford University Press, 201–14, at 211. On governments' incentives to exclude certain economic sectors from liberalization in FTAs, see Grossman, G. M. & Helpman, E. (1995) The Politics of Free-Trade Agreements. *The American Economic Review*, 85(4), 667–90.

[21] *Turkey – Restrictions on Imports of Textile and Clothing Products*, WT/DS34/AB/R, Report of the Appellate Body, circulated 22 October 1999, para. 48 (original emphasis).

[22] Mitchell, A. D. & Lockhart, N. J. S. (2009), Legal Requirements for PTAs under the WTO. in Lester, S. & Mercurio, B. (eds.), *Bilateral and Regional Trade Agreements: Commentary and Analysis*. Cambridge and New York: Cambridge University Press, 96 and 111.

[23] Ibid., 89.

be made? And, moreover, can entire sectors be excluded from the agreement? If so, at which point would an exclusion of a sector reduce the volume of trade to a non-substantial level? As noted by the authors, the lack of sufficiently disaggregated data on trade in services further complicates the determination of volumes and value of trade covered by a specific EIA.[24]

Under the GATT, various suggestions regarding 'substantially all the trade' have been made, also among the Members. According to one of such propositions, a threshold could be set at 95 per cent of all tariff lines at the six-digit level. That starting point could then be complemented by an assessment of trade flows at various stages of the implementation of the PTA.[25] The proposal did not receive enough support.[26]

With regard to Art. V, there has been a variety of opinions regarding the scope of 'substantial sectoral coverage' among the Members. Because of the wording 'number of sectors' in the footnote to paragraph 1(a), it has been suggested that not all sectors need to be covered under an EIA to meet this criterion. Otherwise the text would have clarified that all, and not a 'number of', sectors had to be covered.[27] Some Members have argued that the exclusion of certain sectors and volume of trade would be permissible, given that the footnote to Article V.1(a) only condemns the *a priori* exclusion of a mode of supply, not specific sectors. Some have emphasized that the number of exclusions to the sectoral coverage must be restricted and not further limited by the volume of affected trade and the modes of supply.[28]

According to another line of argumentation, the word 'substantial' does not allow any, or at least any essential, sector to be excluded from an EIA. If a major sector were excluded, it would need to be considered in conjunction with the modes of supply and the volume of trade involved.[29]

---

[24] Fink, C. & Molinuevo, M. (2008), East Asian Preferential Trade Agreements in Services: Liberalization Content and WTO Rules. *World Trade Review*, 7(4), 641–673, at 660.

[25] Australia, WT/REG/W/22/Add.1, paras. 9–10.

[26] For the Members' views regarding the 'substantially all the trade' (SAT) requirement in Art. XXIV GATT, see Mavroidis, P. C. (2016) *The Regulation of International Trade: GATT*. Cambridge: MIT Press, at 302–3.

[27] EC, WT/REG50-52/M/2, para. 16; New Zealand, WT/REG/W/22, para. 17. The opinions presented here have been expressed within the Committee on Regional Trade Agreements. A synopsis of such systemic issues is included in WTO Committee on Regional Trade Agreements, *Synopsis of 'systemic' issues related to regional trade agreements*, Note by the Secretariat, WT/REG/W/37, 2 March 2000.

[28] New Zealand, WT/REG/M/22, para. 17.

[29] Argentina, WT/REG/M/22, para. 16.

Other issues brought up by the Members include the degree of detail in the examination of EIAs and the coverage of modes of supply. The first issue relates to the correct level of examination: it can be done either sector-by-sector, sub-sector-by-sub-sector or on a disaggregated basis. The coverage in terms of modes is seen to relate especially to Modes 3 and 4. For some Members, both investment and the movement of natural persons need to be included. At least one delegation has proposed that certain aspects exempted from the GATS through the GATS Annex on Movement of Natural Persons Supplying Services under the Agreement[30] need to be included in an EIA for consistency with the GATS.[31]

Whereas certain rough or approximate values for 'substantial' may be given, it is hard to see how to settle on any specific value. Such a set value may be even harder to conceive in respect of sectoral coverage than in respect of elimination of discrimination. The requirement to achieve substantial sectoral coverage presumes that we know the overall number of service sectors that exist. This is not really the case.

The GATS does not impose any specific set or list of sectors on the Members but they are free to use their own categorizations. Most Members have opted to use the WTO's Sectoral Classification List that is used as a basis of our empirical analysis.[32] However, they are not required to do so. And even if the Members typically do use the recommended list, they sometimes combine or divide certain sectors or sub-sectors to their own choosing. As witnessed by our analysis, also the EU Member States do this in certain instances even though generally they tend to follow the Secretariat's list.

Another issue relates to the emergence of new services sectors. Technological progress brings about challenges in the classification of new services. Should completely new services, or services that used to be delivered under a specific mode only, count towards the overall number of sectors towards which the 'substantial' sectoral coverage of a specific EIA should be compared? In this respect EIAs following the so-called negative listing model do better as they automatically extend all relevant

---

[30] Art. XXIX GATS provides that the Annexes, including the mentioned Annex, are an integral part of the Agreement. The said Annex provides, among other things, that the GATS 'shall not apply to measures affecting natural persons seeking access to the employment market of a Member, nor shall it apply to measures regarding citizenship, residence or employment on a permanent basis'.

[31] Japan, WT/REG/M/22, para. 18.

[32] Services sectoral classification list, Note by the Secretariat, WTO document MTN.GNS/W/120, 10 July 1991.

disciplines to new services that were not yet developed or commercialized at the time of the conclusion of the agreement. Only such current or future measures or policy areas that have been specifically excluded from liberalization would remain outside the scope of liberalization in such new services sectors.[33]

In the present book the EU's EIAs are analyzed on the basis of the Sectoral Classification List. This makes it possible to compare the EU's EIA commitments to most other Members' commitments as the majority of them use the same list both in their EIAs as well as under the GATS. However, it should be kept in mind that the overall number of sectors may, and is likely, to rise in the future and methodologies should be adapted to take them into account. The methodological challenges relating to different organization of sectors, and modes, are addressed in Chapter 9 of Part III of the book.

iii   *Absence or Elimination of Substantially All Discrimination (Art. V:1b)*

The second sub-paragraph of Art. V:1 requires that an EIA provides for the absence or elimination of substantially all discrimination in the sectors covered by the agreement. This is to be attained either through '(i) elimination of existing discriminatory measures, and/or (ii) through prohibition of new or more discriminatory measures'. There are two interlinked issues that complicate the interpretation of the provision.

First, there is no common understanding of the link between 'substantial sectoral coverage' (sub-paragraph 1(a)) and 'substantially all discrimination' (sub-paragraph 1(b)). One view is that a sector would not be considered covered unless it satisfied also the requirements under Art. V:1(b). Another view holds that the two tests need to be distinguished. According to this view, the requirement of substantial sectoral coverage merely determines the proportion of sectors or sub-sectors subject to liberalization. Art. V:1(b), on the other hand, would apply as a separate requirement by determining the general degree of discrimination that is allowed in the liberalized sectors. It would seek to determine

---

[33] Robert, M. & Stephenson, S. (2008) Opening Services Markets at the Regional Level under the CAFTA-DR: The Cases of Costa Rica and the Dominican Republic, in Marchetti, J. & Roy, M. (eds.), *Opening Markets for Trade in Services: Countries and Sectors in Bilateral and WTO Negotiations*. Cambridge; New York: Cambridge University Press, 537–72, at 562.

to what extent policy measures retaining a degree of discrimination in the liberalized sectors and modes are acceptable.[34]

The fact that Art. V:1(b) calls for the absence or elimination of discrimination in the sectors covered under sub-paragraph (a), would give reason to conclude that a sector should be considered covered only if it provides for full non-discrimination. However, in light of the Member's practice where hardly any service sector in any EIA provides for full (or even close to full) non-discrimination, we suggest that the two requirements could be treated separately. At least such an approach would be more informative than disregarding each sector where discrimination is not eliminated. Thus, each EIA could be given two separate scores under Art. V:1: one for sectoral coverage and another one for the level of non-discrimination (in the sectors covered). This is the approach in our empirical analysis on the EU's EIAs. Each sector and sub-sector gets two scores: one for being included with at least some level of commitments (coverage) and another one for the elimination of discrimination.[35] Both scores are expressed as percentage values depending on how many EU Member States have bound themselves.

The second challenge of interpretation relates to the question of whether the parties to an EIA must indeed eliminate substantially all discrimination or whether a mere standstill agreement could be considered sufficient. Hoekman and Sauvé have argued that a standstill is enough. They consider that the drafting of such a minimalistic requirement was linked to the outcome of the 1989 Canada–US FTA which largely consisted of a standstill agreement applied to a finite list of covered services.[36]

Cottier and Molinuevo, on the other hand, argue that the answer should be 'no', because the introductory sentence of Art. V:1(b) specifically calls for the 'absence or elimination' of discrimination between the EIA parties. The options of (i) and (ii) are informed by this main obligation and need to be construed accordingly. In order to live up to the obligation, EIAs must abolish discriminatory measures where they exist and prohibit the future introduction of discriminatory policies in

---

[34] WTO Committee on Regional Trade Agreements, *Synopsis of 'systemic' issues related to regional trade agreements*, Note by the Secretariat, WT/REG/W/37, 2 March 2000, at 20.

[35] See the review sheets in Appendix 3. The types of discrimination counted for in the analysis are explained later in this chapter. A detailed explanation of the methods of the empirical study is provided in Part III.

[36] Hoekman & Sauvé (1994), at 62.

those sectors or sub-sectors where no discriminatory policies are maintained at the time of the conclusion of the EIA.[37]

We agree with the interpretation of Cottier and Molinuevo and consider that Art. V goes beyond a standstill and requires EIA parties to achieve a sufficient degree of rollback of protective measures. The provision of Art. V:1(b) needs to be read as a whole and in light of its opening sentence that sets the required degree of liberalization, which is the *absence* or *elimination* of substantially all discrimination. We consider that the conjunction 'or' has been inserted in Art. V:1(b)(i) for such cases where parties have already prior to the EIA eliminated substantially all discrimination between them at least in certain sectors. In such a case, the parties are requested not to introduce any new or more discriminatory measures. As noted by Cottier and Molinuevo, the standstill obligation also ensures that the absence of discrimination will be maintained in sectors and modes that have previously been subject to unilateral liberalization.[38]

The absence of substantially all discrimination does not need to be provided at once. Art. V:b includes the possibility of eliminating discrimination on the basis of a reasonable time-frame. Therefore, discrimination does not have to be eliminated on day one but a time-frame must be set. In the discussions of the CRTA, Members have suggested periods ranging from five to ten years.[39] In any case, we consider that keeping in mind the purpose of Art. V:1, any open-ended undertaking to eliminate discrimination at a later stage should not suffice but a specific, 'reasonable' time-frame should be set.

---

[37] Cottier & Molinuevo (2008), at 136. In general, the majority view in literature does not seem to support the existence of a mere standstill obligation. With regard to NAFTA, there was an interesting debate on this issue between the EU, USA and Mexico. The USA supports the view of Hoekman and Sauvé (1994) while the EU is behind the view put forward in here. Mexico appears to aim at a compromise by suggesting that the EU and US delegations were speaking about the same thing – 'that the result of the negotiations was to comply with the requirements of Art. XVII in substantially all the sectors'. See 'Examination of the North American Free Trade Agreement', Note on the meeting of 24 February 1997, WT/REG4/M/4, CRTA, 16 April 1997, paras. 19–23.

[38] Ibid., 137. But even if one were to adopt the interpretation proposed by Hoekman and Sauvé, Art. V would create the obligation to 'freeze' the situation across services sectors. Thus, a 'standstill' would need to have substantial sectoral coverage.

[39] WTO Committee on Regional Trade Agreements, *Synopsis of 'systemic' issues related to regional trade agreements*, Note by the Secretariat, WT/REG/W/37, 2 March 2000, para. 84. Some Members have supported a ten-year period since it would coincide with that provided for integration in the area of goods set out in Art. XXIV:5 and as explained in paragraph 3 of the Understanding on the Interpretation of Art. XXIV GATT 1994. Para. 3 of the Understanding specifies that the period should exceed ten years only in exceptional cases and subject to the provision of full explanation to the Council for Trade in Goods.

In addition to these more technical issues, a central element in Art:1(b) relates to the meaning of 'discrimination'. Discrimination in WTO law covers two concepts: MFN treatment and national treatment (NT). With regard to the first, it is unclear what type of MFN treatment is required by the provision. Does the provision allow for an EIA to include a conditional MFN provision or different degrees of MFN treatment depending on the parties? Is gradual implementation of MFN treatment possible?[40] As an example, in the EU–CARIFORUM Economic Partnership Agreement ('EPA'), the commitments related to the presence of natural persons are not covered by the MFN clause at all. Compulsory provision of MFN could mitigate the possible harmful effects of proliferating PTAs. However, since Art. V requires the elimination of discrimination in the sense of NT only, we conclude that MFN as regards other EIAs is not expected from partners to an EIA. The existence of a general MFN discipline in the EU's EIAs is nevertheless noted in our empirical analysis as it tells about the overall depth of integration between the partners to the agreement.

With regard to the second aspect of discrimination, or rather non-discrimination, Art. V is clearer. It makes an explicit reference to the NT discipline of Art. XVII. Even though one could argue that it is not entirely clear whether exactly similar treatment is required under both provisions, such an argument is in our opinion far-fetched. There could hardly be any clearer indication of equivalence in interpretation than the specification that the discrimination should be eliminated 'in the sense of' Art. XVII.

Art. XVII requires that subject to any conditions and qualifications set in a Member's Schedule, 'each Member shall accord to services and service suppliers of any other Member, in respect of all measures affecting the supply of services, treatment no less favourable than that it accords to its own like services and service suppliers'. The second paragraph specifies that the requirement may be met by according either formally identical or formally different treatment to that accorded to the Member's own like services and service suppliers. This implies prohibition of both de jure as well as de facto discrimination.[41]

---

[40] Munin (2010), at 231.

[41] Ibid., 160. The coverage of de facto discrimination was confirmed by the AB in EC–Bananas III. See European Communities – Regime for the Importation, Sale and Distribution of Bananas, Report of the Appellate Body, WT/DS27/AB/R, 9 September 1997. Defining de facto discrimination is challenging, as well as understanding what type of measures count as de facto discrimination. This issue is taken up below as well as in Chapter 8 of Part III on methodology.

Some EIAs go beyond the obligations entailed in Art. XVII and engage in deeper forms of economic integration. The objective of deeper liberalization of services trade can be advanced through various regulatory cooperation instruments such as agreements on mutual recognition (MRAs) and harmonization.[42] Since the liberalization of services is primarily concerned with regulatory issues, the deeper the integration, the more issues there are that tend to fall outside NT and instead enter the sphere of non-discriminatory domestic regulation. Deep regulatory cooperation typically ends up eliminating discrimination but may, in addition, lead into an acceptance of certain parts of the service supplier's domestic regulatory framework as sufficiently adequate for the receiving Member's regulatory purposes. Our view is that because of the direct reference to Art. XVII, Art. V does not require more than elimination of discrimination in the sense of NT. Art V. nevertheless duly recognizes deeper integration: the second paragraph gives the possibility to take a wider process of economic integration into account in the analysis of EIAs. However, since the possibility is tied to evaluating whether the conditions under paragraph 1(b) are met, it would seem that Art. V:2 is recognizing elements that fall *short* of non-discrimination, not elements that go *further* than the provision of NT. The provision is thus giving leeway to EIAs that do *not* eliminate discrimination as extensively as required by Art. V:1.

A possible interpretation is that Art. V:2 simply recognizes the overall aim of deeper economic integration in a specific EIA. While such an agreement may contain regulatory elements of deep, non-discriminatory integration in certain sectors (e.g. through MRAs or even through harmonization), the agreement may still fall short of NT in some other sectors. Therefore, we consider that the mapping of instruments of

---

[42] As Trachtman notes, for mutual recognition to succeed, a satisfactory level of essential harmonization must have already taken place. Only then can countries agree on a minimum level of regulation. See Trachtman, J. P. (2014) Mutual Recognition of Services Regulation at the WTO, in Lim, A. H. & De Meester, B. (eds.), *WTO Domestic Regulation and Services Trade: Putting Principles into Practice*. New York: Cambridge University Press, at 110. Instead of mutual recognition, we can also talk about mutual acceptance of 'equivalence'. A MRA or mutual acceptance of 'equivalence' may be possible without straightforward harmonization but such outcomes are possible only once the parties are satisfied that at least the minimum requirements of domestic regulation are fulfilled, in a different but equivalent way, by the other party's regulation. Beviglia-Zampetti, A. (2000) Mutual Recognition in the Transatlantic Context: Some Reflections on Future Negotiations, in Cottier, T., Mavroidis, P. C. & Blatter, P. (eds.), *Regulatory Barriers and the Principle of Non-Discrimination in World Trade Law*. Ann Arbor: University of Michigan Press, 303–28, at 308.

deep economic integration, such as MRAs and harmonization that go beyond the requirement of non-discrimination, is in any case relevant as they might affect the overall discrimination analysis of an EIA.[43]

An EIA that does not reach the threshold of 'substantiality' may still be considered to respect the requirements of Art. V if its overall purpose is to engage in a deeper economic integration over time. Therefore, Art. V:2 must necessarily allow for a certain time-frame during which the wider process of economic integration or trade liberalization can take place. The possibility for a 'time-frame' is mentioned also under Art. V:1. The elimination of substantially all discrimination should take place either at the entry into force of that agreement or on the basis of 'a reasonable time-frame'. Since Art. V:2 allows for additional elements to be taken into account in evaluating the fulfilment of conditions under Art. V:1, the 'wider process' should be interpreted to allow for economic integration or trade liberalization to take place over a time period that is more extensive than 'a reasonable time-frame' that is available already under the conditions of Art. V:1.

Another unclear issue relates to the list of exceptions included in Art. V:1(b). Measures permitted under Articles XI, XII, XIV and XIV bis are excluded from the requirement of elimination and prohibition of discriminatory measures. Emergency safeguard measures (Art. X), on the contrary, are not mentioned in the list. A question often put forward thus is whether EIA partners retain the right to maintain them.[44] As these provisions act as exceptions, a Member is exempted from its obligations under a specific commitment in case it successfully invokes one of the provisions.

Let us assume that a Member in an EIA with another Member has prescribed a specific commitment in the field of professional services,

---

[43] A separate issue is whether MRAs concluded in the context of EIAs should still be notified to the WTO in accordance with the procedure of Art. VII and whether they should provide adequate opportunity to any other Member to indicate their interest in participating in the arrangement. Since Art. V does not require Members to engage in any MRAs or other deep regulatory instruments, a possible interpretation is that the independent obligations under Art. VII still apply. As noted by Mathis, to the extent that Art. V notifications incorporate recognition instruments falling within the meaning of Art. VII, it is up to the Members affected by them to bring cases to dispute settlement accordingly. See Mathis, J. H. (2006) Regional Trade Agreements and Domestic Regulation: What Reach for 'Other Restrictive Regulations of Commerce'?, in Bartels, L. & Ortino, F. (eds.), *Regional Trade Agreements and the WTO Legal System*. Oxford; New York: Oxford University Press, 79–108, at 98.

[44] See similar discussion on Art. XXIV:8 GATT in Mitchell & Lockhart (2009), at 98–9.

more specifically concerning medical doctors. In the commitment, in respect of Modes 3 and 4, the Member has included a language require-ment (complete fluency in the local language). In such a scenario it could possibly be argued that such a strict language requirement should be considered as a measure that is *de facto* discriminatory (at least if applic-able across the board with no possibility for exemptions) and thus subject to elimination under the criteria of Art. V. However, in this specific case, the Member might be able to invoke Art. XIV lit. b and claim that the language requirement is necessary to protect human health since patients must be able to communicate with their doctor in their own language. An additional justifying argument could be that doctors must be able to effortlessly communicate with pharmacies and medical authorities. Assuming that the Member's claim was considered legitimate and it would satisfy all the requirements under one of the justifications of Art. XIV, and the *chapeau*, the language requirement would, in that specific case, not affect the Member's compliance with Art. V:1(b).[45]

The obvious problem is that an abstract, *ex ante* analysis cannot take such situations into account. The general exceptions, as well as security excep-tions and restrictions to safeguard the balance of payments, are available as exceptions and thus do not need to be anticipated in one's schedule. Certain commitments falling short of NT may thus lower the 'compliance score' of the EIA even if they were in an *ex poste* situation (in dispute settlement) considered justified under one of the general exceptions. Since the consid-eration of EIA commitments in this light is purely speculative, any com-pliance analysis is necessarily somewhat skewed in this regard.[46]

Munin argues that Art. XVI (market access) restrictions are not cov-ered by the requirement to eliminate substantially all discrimination since Art. V:1(b) requires elimination in the sense of Art. XVII only. Therefore, according to this interpretation, the depth of MA concessions

---

[45] In order to comply with the requirements of Art. XIV, the measure would have to satisfy the necessity test, which requires, among other criteria, the Member to demonstrate that no other reasonably available alternative measure were at the Member's disposal. In this specific example of a language requirement for medical doctors, a possible alternative, less trade-restrictive measure could be cooperation with local doctors or the requirement of intermediate language skills instead of complete fluency. On the criteria of Art. XIV GATS, see Cottier, T., Delimatsis, P. & Diebold, N. (2008) Article XIV GATS General Exceptions, in Wolfrum, R., Stoll, P.-T. & Feinäugle, C. (eds.), *WTO – Trade in Services*. Leiden; Boston: Martinus Nijhoff Publishers, 287–328.

[46] The same applies to Art. XXIV:8 GATT since duties and other restrictive regulations of commerce must be eliminated *except*, where necessary, those permitted under Articles XI, XII, XIII, XIV, XV and XX.

is left to the discretion of the parties and only a wide scope of coverage of an EIA in terms of sectors is required. As has already been discussed above, we share this opinion and argue that Art. V is only concerned with the elimination of discrimination. This issue, however, invokes an important interpretative question relating to certain MA limitations: should discriminatory measures listed under Art. XVI:2 (joint venture requirements and foreign equity ceilings) be considered as measures 'in the sense of Art. XVII' to which the provision applies?[47] In our opinion, that should definitely be the case considering that in addition to being MA limitations, such measures clearly discriminate against foreign services suppliers when they limit the amount of foreign investment (but not domestic investment) and impose an obligation of cooperation with local companies (when they, on the contrary, can operate freely).

Among the Members, the central issue with regard to Art. V:1(b) has been the extent to which discriminatory measures are allowed. Most remarks have been made on the scope of the list of exceptions included in the provision. At least three Members have argued that the list is not exhaustive.[48] Divergent views have been expressed especially on safeguard measures. Some Members have argued that they can be applied on an MFN basis also between parties to an EIA, whereas some consider that safeguard measures should not be applied at all. A relevant question is also what other discriminatory measures, besides those falling under the enumerated Articles, should be allowed under an EIA.[49]

Some Members have paid attention to the difficulty of developing elaborate interpretations or formulas to clarify the requirements relating to EIAs, referring especially to the difficulty in arriving at a percentage-type test for quantitatively measuring 'substantially all discrimination', similar to the test used in defining 'substantially all the trade' in goods PTAs. As a result, it has been suggested that each EIA needs to be examined on its own merit.[50]

---

[47] Munin (2010), at 233.
[48] Argentina, Japan and Korea, WT/REG/M/22, paras. 16, 18 and 20.
[49] Hong Kong, China, non-paper entitled Systemic Issues arising from Article V of the GATS, Section 2.
[50] New Zealand, WT/REG/M/22, para. 17 and WTO Committee on Regional Trade Agreements, *Synopsis of 'systemic' issues related to regional trade agreements*, Note by the Secretariat, WT/REG/W/37, 2 March 2000, at 34.

iv   Wider Process of Economic Integration (Art. V:2)

According to Art. V:2, the relationship of the EIA to a wider process of economic integration or trade liberalization may be considered. The provision allows for an overall assessment of the agreement. One could consider a situation where a new Member State joins the EU. Under Art. V:2, the final result and the essence of the economic integration could possibly be taken into account.[51] It is important to note that such a wider process may only be considered in evaluating whether the EIA provides for the absence or elimination of substantially all discrimination, but not in regard to the requirement of substantial sectoral coverage.

The Members themselves have proposed the 'wider process of economic integration' could be construed as one involving the elimination of barriers also in goods; the drafting history of this paragraph is said to support such an argument. The harmonization of domestic regulation among parties to an EIA could also contribute to such a process.[52] The meaning of the provision has been also been perceived as relating to the interpretation of 'substantially all the trade' under Art. XXIV GATT and that of a 'reasonable time-frame' in prohibiting new or more discriminatory measures under Art. V:1(b).[53]

As already discussed above with regard to the requirement of elimination of discrimination, the provision of paragraph 2 may allow for consideration to be given to economic integration going beyond non-discrimination. One example of such deeper integration is recognition agreements, which we consider to be one demonstration of a wider process of economic integration to be taking place and thus relevant for the analysis of an EIA under Art. V. A different angle to this question is possible as well. Trachtman considers that Art. V does not provide an exception for agreements on equivalence or harmonization from other GATS requirements. He argues that in light of the *Turkey–Textiles* case, the exception of Art. V is, similarly to the exception of Art. XXIV GATT, only available with respect to measures that are *necessary* in order to form an EIA, or a FTA/CU.[54] On the other hand, as argued by Klamert, the

---

[51] Munin (2010), at 235.
[52] WTO (2000) Committee on Regional Trade Agreements, *Synopsis of 'systemic' issues related to regional trade agreements*, para. 11; Japan, WT/REG/M/23, para. 31; EC, WT/REG/W/35, para. 11.
[53] Korea, WT/REG/M/21, para. 20.
[54] Trachtman (2014), at 122. A similar view with regard to recognition agreements is put forward by Marchetti, J. & Mavroidis, P. C. (2012) I Now Recognize You (and Only You) as Equal: An Anatomy of (Mutual) Recognition Agreements in the GATS, in Lianos, I. &

broad wording of Art. V supports a more extensive interpretation of this provision than Art. XXIV that was at issue in *Turkey–Textiles*. Art. V is not limited to any specific integration model but seems to encourage flexibility in the design of EIAs through the provision of Art. V:2. We agree with Klamert who considers that the strict standard applicable to CUs and FTAs would not make much sense under Art. V as it would have the effect of blocking many measures under deep EIAs from the start.[55] Thus, MRAs and harmonization should be possible through an EIA even if such arrangements were not strictly necessary for the formation of the EIA. In our view, the notification requirement (together or separately with the EIA), as well as the offering of adequate opportunity to outsiders to participate to any recognition measures under Art. VII still apply. In this sense, we agree with Marchetti and Mavroidis who argue that the establishment of an EIA cannot provide legal shelter from requests of extension of recognition agreements from Members outside the EIA.[56]

v Special and Differential Treatment (Art. V:3)

In the GATS, developing countries do not benefit from an 'enabling clause' but are subject to the same requirements under Art. V as developed countries. However, Art. V:3 allows for flexibility in the application of the substantive liberalization requirements when developing countries are parties to EIAs, 'in accordance with the level of development of the countries concerned, both overall and in individual sectors and subsectors'. Unlike the flexibility provision of Art. V:2, flexibility for developing

---

Odudu, O. (eds.), *Regulating Trade in Services in the EU and the WTO*. Cambridge: Cambridge University Press, 415–43, at 425–7.

[55] Klamert, M. (2015) *Services Liberalization in the EU and the WTO: Concepts, Standards and Regulatory Approaches*. Cambridge: Cambridge University Press, at 62. It should be noted that the 'necessity' test formulated in *Turkey–Textiles* to determine the legitimacy of a CU/FTA still requires further clarification. The language and approach of the AB are strongly reminiscent of the more famous necessity test under Art. XX GATT. However, as noted by Bartels, any analogy to the Art. XX necessity test includes various complications in the application of the Art. XXIV defence. The most striking complication is the absence of any catalogue of objectives for the achievement of which a trade measure taken in the context of forming a PTA might be 'necessary'. In *Turkey–Textiles*, the AB assumed that it was permissible for the European Communities to seek to avoid trade diversion while concluding a PTA with Turkey but the AB did not explain why precisely this objective was considered legitimate. See Bartels, L. (2004) WTO Dispute Settlement Practice on Article XXIV of the GATT, in Ortino, F. & Petersmann, E.-U. (eds), *The WTO Dispute Settlement System, 1995–2003*. The Hague; New York: Kluwer Law International, 263–74, at 269.

[56] Marchetti & Mavroidis (2012), at 427.

countries is allowed also in regard to sectoral coverage. However, it could be argued that there is a higher degree of flexibility available towards Art. V:1(b) than Art. V:1(a) since Art. V:3(a) states that 'flexibility shall be provided . . . particularly with reference to subparagraph b'.

In addition, Art. V:3(b) allows developing countries concluding EIAs among themselves to give more favourable treatment to firms that originate in parties to the agreement. It therefore allows for discrimination against undertakings originating in countries outside the agreement, even if they were established within the territory of one of the parties.

Unlike under the Enabling Clause, Art. V:3 is not limited to EIAs among developing countries. Flexibility also applies to EIAs between developed and developing countries and operates as a limitation on the principle of reciprocity present in Art. V:1(b).[57]

vi   The External Requirement (Art. V:4)

The so-called external requirement of Art. V is set in paragraph 4. It provides that EIAs must not 'raise the overall level of barriers' to trade in services with respect to third parties. The assessment is made in comparison to the level applicable prior to such an agreement and in respect of each sector and sub-sector covered by the agreement. The provision builds upon the tradition of Art. XXIV:5 GATT and aims to prevent parties from embarking on so-called 'fortress' economic integration.[58] The coverage of 'barriers' is not defined and it is therefore unclear whether the provision covers measures subject to the general disciplines of the GATS (e.g. MFN, domestic regulation and transparency), or merely specific commitments under Articles XVI and XVII.[59]

The interpretation of the external requirement includes similar challenges to the quantification of the internal requirement. As noted by Stephenson, the difficulty of calculating the overall level of barriers to

---

[57] Cottier & Molinuevo (2008), at 141. The authors remark that some Members have suggested that the flexibility would extend to developed countries too when they participate in EIAs with developing countries. As the authors note, such an interpretation would lead to the awkward result that developed countries were required to provide for greater liberalization in agreements among themselves and maintain more restrictions towards their developing EIA partners. For an extensive treatment of special and differential treatment under Art. V, see Sieber-Gasser (2016).

[58] Cottier & Molinuevo (2008), at 144. In 'fortress' integration, countries liberalize their internal trade but do so to the detriment of third parties by raising compensatory protection in relation to services/service suppliers from countries outside the EIA.

[59] Ibid.

services trade in effect before and after the formation of an EIA makes it almost impossible to translate this requirement in practice.[60] Therefore, other approaches would need to be developed. Among the Members, there has been a proposition to require that an EIA did not reduce either the level, or growth, of trade in any sector or sub-sector below a historical trend.[61]

One way to analyze at least perceived changes to the overall level of barriers towards third parties is to review how many negotiations based on Art. XXI ('Modification of schedules') have been initiated between third parties and the EIA parties. The modification of schedules has been topical between the EU and third countries after the accessions of new Member States to the Union.[62]

vii   Rules of Origin (Art. V:6)

Art. V:6 includes the requirement to establish a liberal rule of origin for EIAs. The benefits of the EIA must be extended to any service supplier of any Member that is a 'juridical person constituted under the laws of a party', provided that such a service supplier 'engages in substantive business operations in the territory of the parties to such agreement'. As has already been discussed in Chapter 1, this feature of Art. V is unparalleled in the area of goods trade and is one of the reasons why preferentialism in services is potentially less harmful for outsiders than preferentialism in goods.

However, rules of origin are by no means clear in the area of services. Actually, the origin rules of services, particularly those for Mode 3, are one of the most complicated issues in the GATS.[63] Moreover, while rules of origin for goods have been thoroughly discussed, much less attention has been attached to the increasingly important issue of rules of origin in services. Rules of origin in services can be distilled from Art. XXVIII GATS ('Definitions'), but arguably in a defective way. The GATS-based

---

[60] Stephenson, S. (2000) Regional Agreements on Services in Multilateral Disciplines: Interpreting and Applying GATS Art. V, at 96.

[61] Hong Kong, WT/REG/W/34, para. 13.

[62] See e.g. the Commission proposal COM/2013/0689/final where the Commission explains the changes relating to the modification of commitments in the schedules of the Republic of Bulgaria and Romania in the course of their accession to the European Union and asks the Council to authorize agreements in the form of an Exchange of Letters between the European Union and third countries who had submitted claims of interest.

[63] Zdouc, W. (1999) WTO Dispute Settlement Practice Relating to the GATS, *Journal of International Economic Law*, 2(2), 295–346.

origin rules tend to consider only the legal criteria (e.g. place of incorporation) rather than economic ones (e.g. where value is added). Most EIAs follow the same approach as the one developed in GATS with the same defects and limitations.[64]

The combined criteria of Art. V:6 – constitution of a juridical person and substantive business operations – would at first sight appear relatively clear.[65] However, also there the question of what exactly constitutes a 'substantive' business operation is open to many interpretations, especially in light of today's commercial realities where services, and not only goods, are built along complicated value chains.[66]

III What Benchmark for EIAs?

The internal and external requirements set out the principal intent behind Art. V. They express the desirability of increasing trade by voluntary agreements between willing partners. Similarly to Art. XXIV GATT, they recognize that the purpose of an EIA should be to facilitate trade between the parties and not to raise barriers towards those remaining outside the agreement.[67] As in Art. XXIV, there is, however, a clear tension between the two requirements: the deeper the integration, the more dramatic are typically the effects on outsiders. This seeming irrationality was already brought up by Viner who noted the paradox of demanding a 100 per cent preference, 'which suddenly turns to a maximum evil at 99 per cent . . . ' In Viner's view, a completed customs union was still preferable since in that case the removal of duties is non-

---

[64] Gomez-Altamirano, D., Re-Thinking Rules of Origin in Services: Moving from a Legal Definition to an Economic One through a Determination of Value Addition in Global Value Chains (a paper presented at the conference of the Society of International Economic Law, 13 July 2018, Washington, DC). See also Wang, H. (2010) WTO Origin Rules for Services and the Defects: Substantial Input Test as One Way Out, *Journal of World Trade*, 44(5), 1083–108, at 1083.

[65] On both criteria, see Cottier & Molinuevo (2008), at 146–8.

[66] Moreover, services are an important part of value chains in manufacturing. Cernat and Kutlina-Dimitrova have drawn attention to the growing importance of services inputs in manufacturing sectors' exports. They argue that the existing four modes of supply of the GATS do not adequately cover this type of indirect services value-added trade. Hence, theoretically, they make the case for a new indirect mode of services supply – 'Mode 5'. See Cernat L. and Kutlina-Dimitrova, Z., Thinking in a Box: a 'Mode 5' Approach to Services Trade, Chief Economist Note, European Commission, Issue 1, March 2014. Available at: http://trade.ec.europa.eu/doclib/docs/2014/march/tradoc_152237.pdf (last accessed on 15 September 2018).

[67] Mathis (2006), at 79–80.

selective by its very nature and the 'beneficial preferences are established along with the injurious ones, the trade-creating ones along with the trade-diverting ones'.[68]

This very tension is maybe behind what has become a systemic disregard of the basic principles of Art. XXIV GATT and Art. V GATS. Moreover, it is now practically impossible to know how far or close PTAs come to fulfilling the requirements, as there is no longer any comprehensive multilateral review system. There has also been a shift in the analysis of PTAs in literature. Today, most studies focus on systemic issues stemming from PTAs as well as on reviewing the so-called WTO+ elements included in them. Even when presenting observations on a specific PTA's consistency with the WTO criteria, scholars avoid drawing any dramatic conclusions based on such observations.

Especially in the context of EIAs this is understandable considering the vagueness of the terms 'substantial' and 'substantially', as well as the complex modalities of liberalizing services. We lack a clear benchmark as to the level of liberalization that EIAs are required to attain. In addition, an objective analysis is close-to an impossible task to carry out. Because of difficulties in measuring services liberalization, assessing the fulfilment of the Art. V criteria necessarily includes a great deal of subjectivity.[69] Another challenge is that Art. V gives some room to the so-called 'living agreements'. First, the absence/elimination of discrimination can be attained on the basis of a reasonable time-frame and second, Art. V:2 allows consideration to be given to a wider process of integration. In deep economic integration projects, such as the EU, higher level of liberalization is being attained in a continuous, slow process with occasional setbacks.[70]

To propose some structure to the legal analysis of EIAs, we propose to concentrate on the first paragraph of GATS Art. V. That provision puts

---

[68] Viner, J. (1950) *The Customs Union Issue*. New York: Carnegie Endowment for International Peace, at 44 and 51.

[69] The USA has argued that since there is no objective data to base conclusion on, an assessment requires looking at 'the sum of the parts'. According to the view expressed by its representative in one of the meetings of the CRTA, we should not wait for more numbers, but rather draw some subjective conclusions according to the elements of Art. V. See 'Examination of the North American Free Trade Agreement', Note on the meeting of 24 February 1997, WT/REG4/M/4, CRTA, 16 April 1997, para. 18.

[70] In the NAFTA debate the representative of Mexico claimed that NAFTA was planned as a living agreement; it did not represent the end of a process of negotiations, but rather was an instrument moving all elements towards greater liberalization. The representative added that the EC, too, had developed in this manner. Ibid., para. 20.

forward the clearest requirement which is to eliminate, or at least aim at eliminating, substantially all discrimination across a substantial number of service sectors. Even if Art. V allows for other aspects in an EIA to be taken into account, the starting point should be in analyzing the extent of non-discrimination provided. This is the key requirement that we study in more detail in the chapter that follows.

3

Elimination of Discrimination in EIAs

I   Non-Discrimination in EIAs

i   The Key Obligation: Non-Discrimination

The essence of Art. V is the requirement of elimination of discrimination.[1] This is in contrast to the multilateral liberalization of services under the GATS. The Preamble to the GATS does not mention elimination of discrimination but merely calls, among other objectives, for progressive liberalization of services trade. The framework for such liberalization to take place over time is provided in Part IV of the GATS: under Art. XIX GATS, Members should enter into successive rounds of negotiations of specific commitments with a view to achieving a progressively higher level of liberalization. The GATS Preamble can be compared to the Preamble of the GATT 1994, which calls for the 'elimination of discriminatory treatment in international commerce'. Elimination of discrimination is thus one of the GATT's long-term objectives but a similar statement is lacking in the GATS.

There is thus a principal difference in the way multilateral and bilateral services negotiations should be conducted. The fact that non-discrimination has a key role to play in the GATS discipline on EIAs may give reason to suspect that GATS-compliant EIAs are possible between very trusting partners only. At least a certain level of similarity in cultural, political and economic backgrounds of the participating

---

[1] Similarly, Cottier, T., Delimatsis, P. & Diebold, N. (2008), Article XIV GATS (General Exceptions), in Wolfrum, W., Stoll, P.–T. & Feinäugle, C. (eds.) *WTO – Trade in Services.* Leiden: Martinus Nijhoff Publishers, at 317–18.

countries seems to contribute to a deeper integration in the field of services.[2]

The obligation to provide for a high level of non-discrimination (a 'substantial' level) brings with itself a certain challenge for any compliance analysis. Under the GATS, discrimination can exist only in a situation where the services and/or service suppliers under comparison are 'like'. The determination of the existence of discrimination thus requires a comparison of specific services and/or service suppliers to each other. This cannot be done in an abstract analysis of an EIA, and thus no completely accurate compliance analysis under Art. V can be concluded.

The question of likeness is only the first step in a discrimination analysis under Art. XXIV GATS. The finding of discrimination also requires a finding of 'a treatment no less favourable' than that accorded to one's own like services and/or service suppliers. The question of treatment, however, becomes topical only after likeness has been established.[3] In the field of services, the establishment of likeness and less favourable treatment can be a daunting task because governments can always invoke difference in treatment due to various regulatory distinctions. In the lack of any real-life service or service suppliers, we lack the means to carry out a full discrimination analysis. In the following sub-section, we explain how to approach this problem in an abstract, legal analysis of EIAs.

ii   Discrimination Analysis in the EIA Context

Non-discrimination entails the idea of a level playing field between domestic and foreign like products and services. The legal framework for the creation

---

[2] On the relevance of the 'trust theory of economic integration' in the EU and the WTO, see Lianos, I. & Odudu, O. (2012) *Regulating Trade in Services in the EU and the WTO: Trust, Distrust and Economic Integration.* Cambridge: Cambridge University Press. One form of economic integration are mutual recognition agreements (MRAs). Marchetti and Mavroidis argue that MRAs in the WTO are frequently concluded between countries having a similar cultural background. Moreover, the majority have so far been signed across geographically proximate partners who usually also share the same language. See Marchetti, J. & Mavroidis, P. C. (2012) I Now Recognize You (and Only You) as Equal: An Anatomy of (Mutual) Recognition Agreements in the GATS, in Lianos, I. & Odudu O. (eds.), *Regulating Trade in Services in the EU and the WTO,* Cambridge: Cambridge University Press, 415–443.

[3] For an analysis of the 'less favourable treatment' obligation, see Ortino, F. (2008) The Principle of Non-Discrimination and Its Exception in GATS: Selected Legal Issues, in Alexander, K. & Andenæs, M. T. (eds.), *The World Trade Organization and Trade in Services.* Leiden: Brill, 173–204, at 174 and onwards. See also Krajewski, M. & Engelke, M. (2008) Article XVII GATS, in Wolfrum, R., Stoll, P.-T. & Feinäugle, C. (eds.), *WTO – Trade in Services.* Leiden; Boston: Martinus Nijhoff Publishers, 396–420, at 409–16.

of such a playing field is set in Art. XVII GATS. Based on the rulings of the Panel and the AB in *EC–Bananas III*, we know that the following four cumulative elements need to be present in a successful NT violation claim:

1) First, there needs to be a specific commitment in the relevant sector and mode of supply;
2) Second, there must be a measure *affecting* the supply of services in the sector and mode of supply concerned;
3) Third, the measure is applied to foreign and domestic *like* services and/or service suppliers; and
4) Fourth, the measure accords to foreign services and/or service suppliers *treatment less favourable* than that accorded to their domestic counterpart.

There is thus a four-prong test to establish inconsistency of a particular measure with Art. XVII GATS.[4] The existence of a specific commitment in a given sector is a factual issue. Even though interpretative problems are always present, in an *ex ante* analysis of services commitments we have to take the existence of a commitment as taken. We also have to assume that the scheduled measure is meant to affect the supply of services in the sector and mode concerned. If that were not the purpose, the measure would not have been prescribed. The two final elements, however, pose more difficulties for an abstract analysis of services commitments. We do not have any real-life services/service suppliers to compare to each other and we typically have very few details on the measure to estimate whether it accords less favourable treatment or not. This is a genuine problem because a conclusion one way or another may result in a false finding of discrimination or non-discrimination.[5]

As noted by Mattoo, the narrower the definition of likeness, the more likely is the possibility that measures will escape the Article XVII net.[6]

---

[4] Mavroidis, P. C., Bermann, G. A. & Wu, M. (2013) *The Law of the World Trade Organization (WTO): Documents, Cases & Analysis*. St. Paul: Thomson/West, at 829.

[5] The establishment of likeness and less favourable treatment require a case-by-case analysis. In *Japan–Alcoholic Beverages II*, regarding Art. III:2 GATT, the AB came to the conclusion that 'the interpretation of the term [likeness] should be examined on a case-by-case basis'. According to the AB, this allows a fair assessment in each case of the different elements that constitute a 'similar' product. See *Japan – Taxes on Alcoholic Beverages*, WT/DS8/AB/R, WT/DS10/AB/R, WT/DS11/AB/R, Report of the Appellate Body, circulated 4 October 1996.

[6] Mattoo, A. (1997) National Treatment in the GATS: Corner-Stone or Pandora's Box? *Journal of World Trade*, 31(1), 107–35, at 122, and Mattoo, A. (2000) MFN and the GATS, in Cottier, T., Mavroidis, P. C. & Blatter, P. (eds.), *Regulatory Barriers and the Principle of Non-Discrimination in World Trade Law*. Ann Arbor: University of Michigan Press, at 55.

This issue was dealt with in a recent WTO dispute settlement case concerning services, in the case *Argentina – Financial Services*. The dispute concerned eight financial, taxation, foreign exchange and registration measures imposed by Argentina mostly on services and service suppliers from jurisdictions that did not, at the time, exchange information with Argentina for the purposes of fiscal transparency. In its ruling, the Panel found that the relevant services and service suppliers were 'like' under both Art. II:1 and Art. XVII of the GATS, because the eight challenged measures provided for differential treatment on the basis of the origin of the services and service suppliers at issue. The AB, in its ruling, pointed out that likeness may indeed be presumed where a measure provides for differential treatment based exclusively on the origin of the services and service suppliers concerned. The AB, however, found that in its analysis under Art. II:1, the Panel did not make a finding that the distinction between cooperative and non-cooperative countries in the measures at issue was based exclusively on origin, and that the Panel erred in finding likeness 'by reason of origin' in the absence of such a finding. Instead, the Panel should have undertaken an analysis of likeness on the basis of various criteria relevant for an assessment of the competitive relationship of the services and service suppliers of cooperative and non-cooperative countries. Because the Panel's finding of likeness under Art. XVII was based on its finding of likeness under Art. II:1, the AB found that the Panel erred also in its analysis under Art. XVII. Consequently, the Panel's findings of likeness of the services and service suppliers at issue under Articles II:1 and XVII of the GATS were reversed.[7]

Because the AB did not draw any conclusions on the question of whether the services and service suppliers of cooperative and non-cooperative countries were like or not, it was left unclear to what extent

---

For a comprehensive analysis in the literature, see Diebold, N. F. (2010) *Non-Discrimination in International Trade in Services: 'Likeness' in WTO/GATS.* Cambridge; New York: Cambridge University Press.

[7] *Argentina – Measures Relating to Trade in Goods and Services*, WT/DS453/AB/R, Report of the Appellate Body, circulated 14 April 2016. In the same report, the AB concluded that, where a measure is inconsistent with the non-discrimination provisions of the GATS, regulatory aspects or concerns that could potentially justify such a measure are more appropriately addressed in the context of the relevant exceptions and not in the context of the analysis of 'treatment no less favourable' under Art. II:1 and Art. XVII. Likeness in the services context has also been dealt with in *EC–Bananas III* (para. 7.322) and *China–Publications and Audiovisual Products* (paras. 7.975–7.976). See *China – Measures Affecting Trading Rights and Distribution Services for Certain Publication and Audiovisual Entertainment Products*, WT/DS363/AB/R, Report of the Appellate Body, circulated 21 December 2009.

a country's cooperation with other countries on tax matters may affect the position of its services and service suppliers in a discrimination analysis. What the AB said was that the differing treatment between cooperative and non-cooperative countries inherent in the eight measures at issue was origin-related; however, it is not origin in itself that determines which countries are on the 'cooperative' list but rather those countries' respective regulatory frameworks. The AB thus left the door open to the possibility of taking certain regulations, or rather the lack of such regulations, of the country of origin into account in the determination of 'likeness'. In this case, such regulations did not even relate to the quality of the services or the service suppliers but rather to their operating environment. However, the AB abstained from explaining how 'likeness' should be defined.[8]

As a result of differences between goods and services, WTO-compliant, unilateral and extra territorial application of one's regulations may be more feasible in the field of services than in the field of goods. One could, for example, ask if two service suppliers are like if one of them respects the rules of the core ILO Conventions with respect to employed personnel supplying services and the other one does not.[9] Could the service supplier in another Member be considered 'unlike' to one's domestic supplier if the foreign supplier's employees had working

---

[8] The AB and panels have abstained from taking a clear stand on 'likeness' in the services context also in earlier instances. In *EC-Bananas III*, the panel accepted that foreign and domestic services and services suppliers were like without justifying its decision in detail. Its restraint is obvious in its infamous conclusion of likeness according to which '. . . to the extent that entities provide these like services, they are like service suppliers' (Panel Report, para. 7.322). In *Canada-Autos* the same conclusion (this time with respect to Art. II GATS) was repeated with the addition that it was applied for 'the purpose of the case' (*Canada – Certain Measures Affecting the Automotive Industry*, WT/DS139/R, WT/DS142/R, Report of the Panel, circulated 11 February 2000, para. 10.248). In the same case, the Panel also introduced the concept of 'likeness across modes' (Panel Report, para. 10.307). The Panel also found that in the absence of 'like' domestic service suppliers, a measure by Canada could not be found to be inconsistent with the NT obligation (Panel Report, paras. 10.283–10.289). The Panel thus seemed to assume that the absence of like suppliers implied the absence of like services. The correlation between the likeness of services and service suppliers is one of the key questions in the likeness analysis. In general it appears that the determination of likeness, as well as the application of the NT principle as a whole, gives rise to a wider range of questions and uncertainties under the GATS than under the GATT. See Cossy, M. (2006) Determining 'Likeness' under the GATS: Squaring the Circle? *WTO Staff Working Paper* (ERSD-2006–08), at 2.

[9] The question addresses a situation where the foreign service supplier's employees do not access the employment market of the other Member. In such a situation, the employment laws of the home state usually apply. Under Mode 4, the receiving state may in certain cases require the application of its core labor laws to the employees of a foreign service supplier (especially in the case of contractual service suppliers).

conditions considered degrading in the other Member? One may also ask to what extent the 'method' of achieving one's professional capacity, such as the quality of one's educational institute, may affect the evaluation of 'likeness'.[10]

The liberalization of services has an important particularity. In contrast to the GATT whose disciplines are confined to the cross-border flow of goods, the GATS extends to measures affecting both the services (i.e. the product) and the service supplier (i.e. the producer). The extension of coverage to service suppliers is significant considering that many typically national regulations, such as quality standards, are based on the characteristics of the supplier.[11] This is in contrast to goods where the AB has, at least so far, drawn a line between the methods of production and the product itself. In simple terms, the basic method of differentiation has been that only such methods of production that leave a trace on the product can be taken into account in the discrimination analysis.[12] In the field of services, the competence and the performance of the 'producer',

---

[10] There is discussion of more meaning to be given to non-product related production methods and to the production environment also in the field of goods. For example, Cottier and Oesch argue that it is only a matter of time before human rights will inform the basis of definition for a like product, and 'thus will relevantly and explicitly shape the operation of non-discriminatory treatment'. See Cottier, T. & Oesch, M. (2011) Direct and Indirect Discrimination in WTO Law and EU Law. *NCCR Trade Regulation Working Paper*, No. 2011/16, at 12.

[11] Lim, A. H. & De Meester, B. (2014) *WTO Domestic Regulation and Services Trade: Putting Principles into Practice.* New York: Cambridge University Press, at 1–2. See also Cossy (2006).

[12] So far, the AB has considered that the method of production cannot affect the analysis of 'likeness', unless the method affects the product itself. However, the placement of import controls on products produced according to a specific method of production may be allowed if justified under one of the general exceptions of Art. XX GATT. In *US–Shrimp/ Turtle* the AB made clear that Members have the right to take trade action to protect the environment (in particular, relating to the conservation of exhaustible natural resources). According to the ruling, measures relating to the method of harvesting sea turtles could be considered legitimate under Art. XX(g). The USA, however, lost the case, not because it sought to protect the environment but because it discriminated between Members by violating the chapeau of Art. XX. See *United States – Import Prohibition of Certain Shrimp and Shrimp Products*, Report of the Appellate Body, WT/DS58/AB/R, circulated 12 October 1998. On the notions of non-product related and product related processes and production methods ('PPMs'), see Joshi, M. (2004) Are Eco-Labels Consistent with World Trade Organization Agreements? *Journal of World Trade*, 38(1), 69–92, at 69 and 73–4. Joshi defines non-product related PPMs as 'measures that relate to processes that do not impart any distinguishing characteristics to the final product'. See also Kudryavtsev, A. (2013) The TBT Agreement in context, in Epps, T. & Trebilcock, M. J. (eds.), *Research Handbook on the WTO and Technical Barriers to Trade*. Cheltehnham; Northampton: Edward Elgar, 17–80, at 40–7.

the service supplier, are inherently linked with the result of the 'production' – the service. This means that there is possibly a wide scope for differentiation of like services and service suppliers based on characteristics attributable to the service supplier and the methods that the supplier employs while supplying the traded service.[13]

Mattoo explains the great role played by regulatory distinctions.[14] Even if cross-price elasticity, consumer choice and other case law-established factors would point towards likeness, nothing prevents a government from intervening and imposing a regulatory component on a given service or service supplier and thus differentiating the foreign supplier from a domestic one. Moreover, likeness is of course not the sole ground for regulatory distinction; 'less favourable treatment' is the other one. The finding of discrimination between like services/service suppliers similarly requires a case-by-case analysis of the treatment granted.[15] In addition, as we have discussed above, there is also the possibility of recourse to one of the justifications under Articles XI, XII, XIV and XIV bis. No matter where the burden of proof is placed, getting a final answer in an unclear situation is possible through dispute settlement only.[16]

iii   Analyzing Discriminatory Measures in Specific Commitments

Because of the above-mentioned problems in an abstract, empirical analysis of EIAs, we consider that the most legitimate way to conduct

---

[13] According to Krajewski, the extension of the NT obligation to service suppliers can be interpreted as allowing for a certain degree of differentiation according to the production process methods (PPMs) of the service in regulatory measures. See Krajewski, M. (2003) *National Regulation and Trade Liberalization in Services: The Legal Impact of the General Agreement on Trade in Services (GATS) on National Regulatory Autonomy.* The Hague: Kluwer Law International, at 97.

[14] Mattoo (2000), at 73–5. Mattoo writes on likeness in the context of Art. II (MFN) but similar conclusions on likeness can be drawn under Art. XVII. See also Mavroidis, Bermann & Wu (2013), at 833–4.

[15] In this regard, Mattoo notes that the sequential procedure of first determining likeness and then less favourable treatment is actually not ideal in the services context but leads into a legal cul-de-sac. Instead, he proposes simultaneous consideration of the degree of unlikeness and differences in treatment. See Mattoo (2000), at 73.

[16] Discussing likeness under Art. II (MFN), Mattoo argues that in case a Member refuses access to another Member's service or service supplier the burden of proof should be placed on that Member. The Member would thus be requested to demonstrate why the foreign and domestic services/service suppliers are not like. See Mattoo (2000), at 75. As to seeking clarity through dispute settlement, a certain reservation is warranted. As the scant case law (most recently in *Argentina – Financial Services*) on 'likeness' under the GATS demonstrates, the meaning and scope of the concept remains largely unresolved.

such an analysis is to focus on explicitly discriminatory measures only.[17] Measures constituting *de facto* discrimination have to be largely omitted in an *ex ante* analysis of an EIA. Instead, the focus must be on the most detrimental types of discrimination, those constituting direct (or nearly direct) discrimination.[18] For the analysis to be possible, a likeness between foreign and domestic services and/or service suppliers in the scheduled commitments must be assumed. We consider this reasonable as otherwise no discrimination analysis is possible to carry out. In any case, legal analyses of commitments under trade agreements always include a certain margin of error since they remain on an abstract level.

In this type of abstract discrimination analysis, we divide the clearest, most explicit types of discriminatory measures in services trade into four different groups. These four groups consist of the type of measures that are taken into account in our empirical analysis.[19]

---

[17] Other methodologies are, of course, available, in other types of approaches (e.g. econometric analyses). However, since our approach is legal and our intention is to analyze EIA commitments directly in light of the Art. V criteria, a strict methodology is required.

[18] This can be equated to *de jure* discrimination. A measure that openly links a difference in treatment to the origin of the service or services and therefore modifies the conditions of competition in favour of domestic services and services suppliers is generally considered *de jure* discrimination. See Krajewski & Engelke, at 410. As for *de facto* discrimination, there is no positive concept for its determination and various views have been put forward in the literature. However, it can be considered to cover measures which do not distinguish services/services suppliers based on their origin but which with respect to a 'neutral' criterion modify the conditions of competition in favour of domestic services and/or service suppliers. Ibid., at 411. See also Krajewski (2003), at 113, where he argues that only those measures which can at least theoretically be scheduled should be seen as discriminatory. This is because the possibility to schedule a *de facto* discriminatory measure only exists if the adverse effect on foreign services/service suppliers is foreseeable or can reasonably be expected.

[19] Our analysis of the types of measures to be considered as limitations to national treatment is close to that of Miroudot and Shepherd (2014). In their analysis of existing EIAs, they map commitments that are either 'full' (no limitation), 'partial' (some limitations listed), or 'unbound' (no commitment). 'Partial' commitments are broken down into nine different types of trade restrictive measures, four for market access and five for national treatments. See the 'Typology of Limitations in Partial Market Access and National Treatment Commitments' in Miroudot, S. & Shepherd, B. (2014) The Paradox of 'Preferences': Regional Trade Agreements and Trade Costs in Services. *The World Economy*, 37(12), 1751–72, at 1770. The authors use a database developed at the OECD that covers all services agreements where an OECD economy, China or India is a party (Miroudot, S., Sauvage, J. & Sudreau, M. (2010) Multilateralising Regionalism: How Preferential Are Services Commitments in Regional Trade Agreements?, *OECD Trade Policy Working Papers*, No. 106.). The database includes a similar analysis for commitments taken under the GATS. See also the illustrative list of frequently occurring limitations to the NT obligation published by the WTO Secretariat. It is included as Attachment 1 in the Scheduling Guidelines (S/L/92, 28 March 2001). The list gives examples of

The first group covers all commitments that prescribe an 'unbound' in a specific sector or sub-sector. In substance, an 'unbound' means that the Member takes no commitment at all. It is the most straightforward limitation to NT as it entails the widest possible scope of discretion in the treatment of foreign services and service suppliers. Outside the general obligations that may apply across the sectors even when no specific commitments are undertaken, specific commitments that are left 'unbound' do not grant any guarantee of non-discrimination. Such 'empty' commitments are thus always considered discriminatory.

The second group consists of measures that are discriminatory in the clearest sense of the word: they are applied to foreigners only. This category of measures is directly discriminatory as the basis for the application of the measures lies solely in the foreign origin of the service supplier. Naturally, measures that grant more positive treatment to foreigners than to one's own nationals are not of relevance here but only the type of measures that restrict trade in services.[20] Typical measures under this first category are discriminatory market access restrictions such as the requirement of a specific legal entity, limitations to numbers of foreign services suppliers and such economic needs tests (ENTs) that are applied to foreigners only. Other clearly discriminatory measures are foreigners' non-eligibility for subsidies, prohibition to acquire real estate, discriminatory taxes and discriminatory licensing and qualification requirements. With the last types of requirements, we refer to cases where licensing is required from foreigners only and cases where foreigners are required to have higher qualifications than one's own nationals.

The third group covers measures that relate to nationality. Such measures are also based on one's origin and can thus be seen as a sub-group of the second category of measures. However, they differ from the second group in the sense that they concern measures, which are not applied only to foreigners, but include a requirement concerning one's nationality. For example, a specific commitment under professional services may prescribe that companies acting in the field of auditing services must have in their board at least one person with the nationality of the Member in question. In contrast to the second group of measures,

---

measures Members consider as possible violations of NT. Some of the measures discriminate overtly, while others appear to amount to *de facto* discrimination.

[20] Essentially, states have a sovereign right to treat their own products and nationals less favourably than imported products and foreign nationals (reverse discrimination, discrimination à rebours). See Cottier & Oesch (2011), at 8.

the measures belonging to this category are applied indistinctively to all service suppliers, but since they are based on nationality, they are clearly discriminatory.

The fourth group of considered NT limitations forms an exception to our otherwise strict approach. It consists of measures concerning one's residency. In trade law, residency requirements are typically considered to form a type of indirect, or covert, discrimination as they are not directly based on one's nationality.[21] However, because of how the GATS is structured, we consider residency requirements to be discriminatory but *only* with regard to Modes 1, 2 and 4. This is because the essence of these three modes is in that they enable the supply of services *without* residency. The requirement of residency would thus often strip a commitment under any of these three modes of its liberalization content. Although the measure does not formally distinguish service suppliers on the basis of national origin, it *de facto* offers less favourable treatment to foreign service suppliers because they are less likely to be able to meet a prior residency requirement than like service suppliers of national origin.[22] With regard to this group of measures, our analysis includes a certain margin of error but we consider that the margin of error would be more significant if residency requirements under Modes 1, 2 and 4 were not taken into account.

We do not take note of residency requirements under Mode 3 even if such requirements could potentially be considered discriminatory at least when they do not apply to the legal entity but to its personnel. For example, foreign companies established in the receiving Member may have board members or members of personnel that have their permanent residence in their country of origin. Requiring such persons to change their residence to the receiving Member may thus be seen as a restriction to the supply of services under Mode 3. However, if a similar residency requirement is applied also to legal entities of national origin, it is not directly based on the origin/nationality of the service supplier. Even though such requirement may potentially constitute a violation of the NT obligation (in case the requirement modifies the conditions of competition in favour of services or service suppliers of the Member compared to like services or service

---

[21] Klamert, M. (2015) *Services Liberalization in the EU and the WTO: Concepts, Standards and Regulatory Approaches.* Cambridge: Cambridge University Press, at 274–5.

[22] See the WTO Secretariat's Scheduling Guidelines, S/L/92, at 6. In the Scheduling Guidelines it is explained that the need to schedule residency requirements should be decided on a case-by-case basis, and in relation to the activity concerned. For example, a residency requirement may be considered discriminatory when there is no justified need to live in the country as opposed to having a bare mailing address in the country.

suppliers of any other Member), such a conclusion is not straightforward and arguably based on a case-specific analysis. Under Mode 3, the service supplier has a commercial presence in the receiving Member and, therefore, the local regulatory framework typically applies in its entirety (in the case of juridical person constituted under local laws) or at least to a larger degree than in respect of the other modes (in the case of branches and representative offices).[23] Thus, there is more leeway for residency-based measures under Mode 3 than under the other modes.

Notwithstanding the residency requirements (which are arguably a form of *de facto* discrimination), our analysis is thus limited to *de jure* discrimination. These types of discrimination can be considered to constitute the clearest violations of the NT obligation. Outside such direct forms of discrimination, we enter a far less certain ground. The more hidden types of discrimination are revealed only when reviewed in the context of a specific case.[24] Taking the example of qualification requirements, the requirement of a local qualification (such as a professional degree in the receiving state) may be considered discriminatory or non-discriminatory depending on whether service suppliers with and without the qualification can be considered like. In addition, the qualification requirement must modify the conditions of competition in favour of the Member's own services or service suppliers.[25]

---

[23] We advance the argument that one constitutive element of service supply under Mode 4 is that the service supplier (a natural or a juridical person) remains largely subject to the regulatory framework of the state of origin. Under Mode 3, the establishment of a commercial presence in the receiving state brings the service supplier deeper, or completely (depending on the legislation that is applied to different types of commercial presence), within the regulatory framework of the receiving state. Nevertheless, the discrimination analysis of residency requirements needs to be case-specific. Certain services may be practically impossible to provide without residence (e.g. daily postal delivery services), whereas certain others may require no residency or residency of a certain type of personnel only. In addition, in many occasions public policy concerns may justify the need of a local representative. Since it is often not possible to conclude whether such justified concerns are present in a residency requirement under a specific commitment, we have opted to disregard all residency requirements under Mode 3 (unless it is obvious that they are applied on a discriminatory basis).

[24] The situation can be contrasted to an analysis of a goods agreement in light of Art. XXIV GATT. Even though Art. XXIV requires the elimination of duties and other restrictive regulations of commerce on substantially all the trade between the parties, the analysis is, in practice, to a large extent limited to the elimination of duties. If there is an extensive amount of restrictive regulations of commerce left in place, such a situation is typically revealed only in practice.

[25] Members sometimes include in their schedules also measures that cannot easily be considered discriminatory. This is probably a sign of lack of clarity over the borderlines between national treatment and domestic regulation. However, such over-scheduling

The problems relating to the analysis of discriminatory measures in a schedule of specific commitments are taken up in more detail in Part II of the book concerning the methodology to study EIAs.

Finally, it should be noted that the absence of 'substantially' all discrimination depends not only on sectoral commitments but also on crosscutting horizontal commitments. They pose an additional challenge for any empirical analysis as they often include discriminatory limitations that are applied to all or a significant part of services sectors (e.g. subsidies available only to one's own nationals). This issue is taken up in more detail in Chapter 8 of Part III concerning the methodology of the empirical study.

II   The Level of Non-Discrimination Required by GATS Art. V

The biggest challenge in the analysis of EIAs under the Art. V criteria is that we do not have a clear benchmark for the requirements of sectoral coverage and elimination of discrimination. There is no unequivocal answer to the question of what 'substantial' and 'substantially' really mean. This forces one to ask whether the negotiators' purpose has been to avoid any clear-cut interpretations from being made. The diversity in the Members' positions as to the correct interpretation of 'substantiality' confirms that no common understanding exists.

In addition, an empirical analysis of the level of discrimination in EIAs includes two other significant challenges. First, because only the most blatant forms of discrimination can be taken into account, the results of an abstract empirical analysis (to which we also refer as *ex ante* analysis) are likely to show less discrimination than the agreement in reality entails. The second challenge, on the other hand, relates to the possible event of finding discrimination there where it could potentially be permitted under Articles XI, XII, XIV and XIV bis.

The measurement and assessment of 'substantial coverage' and 'substantially all discrimination' in quantitative and qualitative terms inevitably entails a case-by-case analysis on the level of specific commitments under each sector. However, the review procedure under the Transparency Mechanism of 2006 is limited to the preparation of

may also be a smart policy as some of the measures that do not at first glance appear discriminatory between domestic and foreign service suppliers can be that in practice, depending on the way they are applied. Therefore the inclusion of such measures in a schedule releases the Member from its responsibility and gives it more leeway in the application of the measure.

a simple factual presentation that only gives an overall assessment of the agreement. A more specific examination may only take place in dispute settlement where Panels and the AB would be called upon to examine the WTO-compatibility of a specific domestic measure based upon an EIA. In such a case, the compatibility of the agreement with Art. V may be examined as a preliminary matter.[26]

Dispute settlement on PTA-related issues is extremely rare and we are not likely to receive much clarity on the WTO-compliance of EIAs through that route. While the number of PTAs is growing, it would, however, be important to keep some track of their relationship to the legal discipline. Due to the modesty of the Transparency Mechanism, it is mainly left to scholars to propose alternative methods for the analysis of PTAs and to inform decision-makers of the results of such analyses. In this book, we propose one approach that pays due respect to the flexibility and complexity depicted in the discipline while providing concrete means to assess EIAs and compare them to each other.

The emphasis is on analyzing the EU's EIAs in light of the internal requirement of Art. V:1. The aim is to show how far the EU comes in eliminating discrimination across the services sectors. The purpose is not to reach a conclusion on the legality of the EU's EIAs. Some suggestions on their compliance with Art. V can, however, be made. They are made on two different grounds. First, it is suggested that if an EIA provides for non-discrimination in less than 50 per cent of the coverage of the agreement, an *a priori* assumption of the agreement falling short of Art. V requirements can be made. That is because under no circumstances can 'substantial' be considered to be less than 50 per cent of coverage. Such a low level of liberalization cannot, in our view, be saved even by the possibility of taking any wider process of integration into account. In the case of the EU, our results do not show the overall level of coverage but the percentage of Member States providing for non-discrimination. The implications of this are discussed in Chapter 12 in Part IV of the book.

The second ground for conclusions as to the liberalization level of a specific EIA in relation to the Art. V criteria relates to the Members' practice. Considering the intentional flexibility built in Art. V, the Members' practice becomes more relevant than in a situation where a clear interpretation of the wording of Art. V was available. We do not

---

[26] Cottier, T. & Molinuevo, M. (2008), Article V GATS, in Wolfrum, W., Stoll, P.-T. & Feinäugle, C. (eds.), *WTO – Trade in Services*. Leiden: Martinus Nijhoff Publishers, 138–9.

suggest the establishment of subsequent practice in the sense of Art. 31:3 (b) of the Vienna Convention on the Law of Treaties as that would require going through a much bigger sample (if not all) of EIAs with a rigorous methodology. Such a methodology is hardly available for the analysis of EIAs. Instead, we suggest a more modest comparison of the Members' EIAs to each other. In such a comparison, the overall purpose of the agreement should be taken into account. An EIA aiming to create a common market should be viewed somewhat differently from an EIA aiming at simple commercial market opening. Such comparisons should be made also between the different agreements of any single Member. The average level of liberalization in both types of comparison gives us some scope of realistic expectations to be made about the liberalization levels of various EIAs.

In the present book, the EU's EIAs are compared to each other keeping this purpose in mind. Each agreement's numerical scores on sectoral coverage and non-discrimination provide the tool for comparison, between the agreements themselves as well as to the criteria of Art. V:1. In addition, the scores show the internal differences that are present in the services commitments of individual EU Member States. The detailed methodology is applied to the EU agreements only but for the purpose of comparing the EU's EIAs with agreements made by other federal entities, the US and Canadian commitments in CETA and NAFTA are reviewed. So far, EIAs concluded by federal states have been left to little attention even though federal states are among the most active states in preferential services liberalization. Part II of the book aims to fill this gap in literature by focusing on federalism in the international liberalization of services.

PART II

Federalism and Liberalization of Services Trade

4

Services Regulation by Federal States

I Introduction

This part of the book explores the issue of federalism in the international liberalization of services. It asks how to address a regional subdivision of a WTO Member and the consequences that such a subdivision has on that Member's services commitments. The issue has so far been largely neglected by research. It is, however, a topic of considerable practical and economic significance considering that several WTO Members have constitutional structures that give powers to states, regions or other local entities in the regulation of various economic activities. In the area of services such local measures are particularly abundant and many rules concerning the quality of a specific service, the number of authorized service suppliers or the professional qualifications of service suppliers depend on sub-central regulation. Such lower level regulation can have important commercial implications in cases where it includes directly discriminatory elements or otherwise aims to protect domestic services and service suppliers.

Regional and local regulation is particularly abundant in sectors such as education, healthcare and environment. For example, in Canada the provincial governments and parliaments are responsible for various policy areas including health care, education and public works. In certain areas the powers are shared between the provinces and the federal government, including agriculture and immigration.[1] It is interesting to

---

[1] Beaudoin, Gérald A. Distribution of Powers, The Canadian Encyclopedia, last edited 23 October 2015, available at www.thecanadianencyclopedia.ca/en/article/distribution-of-powers#ProvincialPowers (last accessed on 15 December 2018).

note that the Canadian internal market itself is governed by a free trade agreement. The Agreement on Internal Trade (AIT) was an intergovernmental trade agreement signed by the Canadian First Ministers (premiers of the federation, provinces and territories). The agreement came into force in 1995. In 2017, the AIT was replaced by a new trade agreement, the Canadian Free Trade Agreement (CFTA). One of the reasons behind the modernization of the AIT was to ensure that Canadian firms secure the same access to Canada's market as that secured by firms from Canada's international trading partners, especially after the entry into force of CETA. The CFTA largely resembles an FTA that is concluded between countries. The CFTA enhances the flow of goods and services, investment and labour mobility, eliminates technical barriers to trade, expands procurement coverage and promotes regulatory cooperation within Canada. As in Canada's EIAs, Annexes I and II of the CFTA include existing and future trade affecting measures of the federation and the provinces.[2]

In the USA, the states have large powers over health, education and welfare as well as some authority over areas of justice, energy, environment and immigration.[3] As in the case of Canada, the internal market of the USA is based on a combination of federal and state-level rules and obstacles to interstate commerce remain.[4]

The biggest federal state in Europe is Germany. In Germany, the bulk of legislation is enacted at the federal level, but the German Länder have important powers in areas such as education, environmental protection,

---

[2] See www.cfta-alec.ca/canadian-free-trade-agreement/ (last accessed on 15 January 2019). One of the key changes brought by the two agreements to the Canadian provinces is a new procurement regime. The CFTA aligns it with CETA. See 'CETA Is in Effect (Mostly): What You Need to Know', Erin Brown, Norton Rose Fulbright, September 2017, available at: www.nortonrosefulbright.com/files/ca-ceta-is-in-effect-mostly-what-you-need-to-know-156391.pdf (last accessed on 15 January 2019).

[3] See the references in Walker J., Negotiation of Trade Agreements in Federal Countries, SPICe Briefing, The Scottish Parliament, 17 November 2017. Available at https://digitalpublications.parliament.scot/ResearchBriefings/Report/2017/11/17/Negotiation-of-Trade-Agreements-in-Federal-Countries# (last accessed on 15 December 2018).

[4] Michelle P. Egan provides a detailed account of economic integration in the USA and compares it to the internal market building in Europe. She notes how the American courts played a crucial role in striking down many legislative barriers of the states in light of the Commerce Clause of the US Constitution. Basic principles of free trade and the state-federal relationship thus became primarily a product of judicial elaboration. See Egan, M. P. (2015) *Single Markets: Economic Integration in Europe and the United States*. New York: Oxford University Press, at 87–93. For a comparison with the EU, see also Menon, A. & Schain, M. (2006) *Comparative Federalism: The European Union and the United States in Comparative Perspective*. Oxford; New York: Oxford University Press.

culture and broadcasting. Federal and regional powers sometimes overlap in areas such as justice, social welfare, civil law, criminal law, labour
law and economic law.[5] The German federalist system is sometimes
described as 'unitary federalism'. There is more centralization of legislation and other matters in Germany than in the United States. Moreover,
'unitary' refers to various policies, ideas and constitutional provisions
that lead to a relatively high degree of uniformity in public policy
making.[6] In the area of internal commerce, the conditions are more
uniform than in the USA and Canada.[7] However, some policy diversion
exists also between the German Länder.[8]

Another powerful example of sub-central regulatory powers are the
public procurement rules in certain federal countries. Public procurement affects both service suppliers and manufacturers of certain goods.
In the USA, roughly 65 per cent of procurement is conducted at the state/
municipality level, as compared to around 35 per cent in the EU.[9]
Moreover, most US states have bespoke 'Buy American' legislation that
governs state level procurements. In comparison, in the EU the procurement framework is exceptionally coherent as the Member States have

[5] 'Division of Powers, a portal supported by the European Committee of the Regions:
Germany', available at: https://portal.cor.europa.eu/divisionpowers/countries/
MembersLP/Germany/Pages/default.aspx (last accessed on 15 December 2018). The portal provides an overview of levels of institutional and fiscal decentralization in all EU
countries and includes a tool to compare the legislative powers of sub-national levels of
government in EU countries, as well as in the EU's candidate countries and Eastern and
Southern partnership countries.

[6] Gunlicks, A. (2003) *The Länder and German Federalism*. Manchester: Manchester
University Press, at 388. For an institutional comparison between Germany, Canada and
a few other federal states, see Broschek, J. & Goff, P. (2018) Federalism and International
Trade Policy: The Canadian Provinces in Comparative Perspective. *IRPP Insight*, No. 23.
Available at: http://irpp.org/research-studies/federalism-and-international-trade-policy/
(last accessed 15 December 2018). The authors note that the German Länder are often
in charge of implementing federal legislation and have a rather limited number of
exclusive jurisdictions. In Canada, on the other hand, there is primarily an exclusive
allocation between federal and provincial levels of government (at p. 7).

[7] In the area of services, the relative uniformity of the German market shows in the GATS
commitments of Germany (as described in the GATS schedule of the European
Communities and their Member States of 1994). There are very few limitations subscribed
on behalf of the German Länder. The Canadian and the US GATS schedules, on the other
hand, reveal a much higher number of sub-central measures.

[8] On the policy diversion, see Schmidt, M. G. (2016) Conclusion: Policy Diversity in
Germany's Federalism. *German Politics*, 25(2), 301–14.

[9] Alina Harastasanu, How Buy American Is Jeopardizing TTIP, *Global Risk Insights*,
18 July 2016, http://globalriskinsights.com/2016/07/buy-american-jeopardizing-ttip/.
Most US states have bespoke 'Buy American' legislation that governs state level
procurements.

progressively harmonized their domestic regulation of procurement
activities above specific thresholds, thus adopting the same regulatory
procurement instruments covering supply, services and work
contracts.[10] A comparable level of harmonization does not exist in the
USA. As noted by Corvaglia, the fifty US states each have their own
public procurement regulations in place. Moreover, the inclusion of the
US sub-central government entities under the WTO's Government
Procurement Agreement (GPA) is very limited: only thirty-seven US
states are bound by GPA commitments and only in their executive
branch agencies or specific state departments. Further sectoral exclusions
and restrictions apply, such as the 'Buy American' requirements imposed
on transit infrastructure funded by federal grants.[11]

Whereas there is a strong body of literature on federalism and its
impact on federal states' foreign relations, far less has been written on
specific areas of trade liberalization.[12] Research on services liberalization
particularly has so far largely neglected the question of how to address
a regional subdivision of a Member and the consequences it possibly has
on that Members' services commitments. It is noteworthy considering
that several Members have constitutional structures that give powers to
states, regions or other local entities in the regulation of services.[13] It is

[10] Corvaglia, M. A. (2018) TTIP Negotiations and Public Procurement: Internal Federalist
Tensions and External Risks of Marginalisation. *Journal of World Investment & Trade*, 19
(3), 392–414, at 401. See also Woolcock, S. & Grier, J. H. (2015) Public Procurement in the
Transatlantic Trade and Investment Partnership Negotiations, *CEPS Special Report*,
No. 100.

[11] Corvaglia, ibid. See the references at 401–2.

[12] For the role of sub-central actors in international relations, see the references in De
Baere, G. & Gutman, K. (2012) Federalism and International Relations in the European
Union and the United States: A Comparative Outlook, in Cloots, E., De Baere, G. &
Sottiaux, S. (eds.), *Federalism in the European Union*. Oxford; Portland: Hart Publishing.
In the area of trade negotiations, work by Kukucha should particularly be mentioned:
Kukucha, C. J. (2015) Federalism Matters: Evaluating the Impact of Sub-Federal
Governments in Canadian and American Foreign Trade Policy. *Canadian Foreign
Policy Journal*, 21(3), 224–37. Omiunu's work on sub-national actors, particularly the
Canadian provinces in CETA, is another rare example of research in this area:
Omiunu, O. (2017) The Evolving Role of Sub-National Actors in International
Economic Relations: A Case Study of the Canada–European Union CETA, in
Amtenbrink, F., Prévost, D. & Wessel, R. (eds.), *Shifting Forms and Levels of
Cooperation in International Economic Law: Structural Developments in Trade,
Investment and Financial Regulation*, Netherlands Yearbook of International Law, Vol.
48, Den Haag: T.M.C. Asser Press.

[13] Three-level government (federal, state/provincial and local government) is common to all
federal systems; however, there are varieties in the place and role of local government. The
issue is particularly relevant in the case of federal states but may arise also in the case of

therefore not surprising that trade negotiators are increasingly starting to press for the inclusion of regulatory measures imposed on services not only on the level of the central government but also on regional levels. The issue has entered into the spotlight especially in the context of the EU–Canada trade and investment agreement, the CETA. In that agreement, Canada has for the first time in its PTA history included a list of provincial and territorial non-conforming measures in the field of services and investments. In addition to providing binding lists of both existing and future measures, the Canadian provinces and territories have committed to providing to the EU the benefits of autonomous liberalization in a number of important services sectors.[14] In the currently stalled TTIP negotiations, on the other hand, addressing the sub-federal government both in the area of services and public procurement was one of the negotiating objectives of the EU.[15] Both negotiations are part of an important development, considering that Canada and the USA have previously addressed the regional and local levels of government only to a very limited extent in their trade agreements.

The issue is relevant in the case of any federal, or quasi-federal, state, such as Australia, Argentina, Brazil, Ethiopia, India, Mexico, Nigeria, Russia, Switzerland and many more. The division of powers in federal states that are part of the EU (Austria, Belgium and Germany) is similarly relevant. Moreover, the EU itself can be contrasted to or compared with a federation.[16]

---

unitary states where certain regulatory powers are given to local levels of government. For an overview of the role of local government in federal states, see Steytler, N. C. (ed.) (2005) The Place and Role of Local Government in Federal Systems, Konrad-Adenauer Stiftung, Occasional Papers, November 2005.

[14] See 'Technical Summary of Final Negotiated Outcomes', Government of Canada, available at https://international.gc.ca/trade-commerce/assets/pdfs/ceta-technicalsummary.pdf. The document summarizes the key negotiated outcomes of the CETA as of 18 October 2013 (last accessed 15 December 2018).

[15] See Press Release 'European Union and United States to launch negotiations for a Transatlantic Trade and Investment Partnership', available http://trade.ec.europa.eu/doclib/press/index.cfm?id=869, 13 February 2013 (last accessed 15 December 2018).

[16] There is plenty of literature on the question of the extent to which the EU can be compared with federations. The fragmented polity of the EU has often been viewed as exceptional in terms of political development. That distinction, however, is increasingly challenged by scholars who choose to focus on systematic comparison between the EU and federal states. An increasing amount of research spanning across comparative politics, public and constitutional law and international relations no longer treats the EU as *sui generis*. See references in Egan (2015), at 3. See also Schütze, R. (2009) On 'Federal' Ground: The European Union as an (Inter)national Phenomenon, *Common Market Law Review*, 46(4), 1069–105, at 1091. On the EU as a federal-type polity, see also

In accordance with the approach adopted in the present book, the EU's services commitments are considered comparable to those of federal states. Such an approach may not be as functional in many other areas of the EU's external relations as the EU Member States remain in charge of their own foreign policy, in addition to their participation in the EU's foreign policy actions and instruments.[17] However, in the area of trade such a comparison can be made, at least for practical purposes. The EU has an exclusive competence in trade and negotiates its trade, and nowadays also investment, agreements as a block. The EU institutions make laws on trade matters, negotiate and conclude international trade agreements. In the area of goods, third country products are in free circulation inside the EU once they have crossed an external border of the Union.[18] In services the situation is, however, more complex. Prior to establishment in one of the Member States, third country service suppliers cannot enjoy the free movement of services with the EU. Moreover, rules for service activities remain poorly harmonized. As our results on the study of the EU's EIAs show, the liberalization levels largely vary between different Member States. As is discussed in the last section of this chapter, the EU is nevertheless aiming at more coherence in the area of services and aspires to be more united towards its trading partners. Also, trade agreements are always negotiated and concluded on the level of the Union as a whole and the Member States do not have the possibility to enter into services agreements individually with third countries.

Regional powers are applied across various economic activities, not only in the area of services. For example, both in the EU and the USA, technical regulations on products and processes to protect health, safety, consumers and the environment are set on federal, state, regional and even on local agency level. In the USA, state regulation often coexists with

Schütze, R. (2009) *From Dual to Cooperative Federalism: The Changing Structure of European Law*. Oxford: Oxford University Press, and Cloots, E., De Baere, G. & Sottiaux, S. (2012) *Federalism in the European Union*. Oxford and Oregon, Portland: Hart Publishing. Much of the research compares the EU and the USA. See e.g. Menon, A. & Schain, M. (2006) *Comparative Federalism: The European Union and the United States in Comparative Perspective*. Oxford; New York: Oxford University Press.

[17] For analyses of EU's foreign policy and division of competences within the Union, see e.g. Eeckhout, P. (2011) *EU External Relations Law*. Oxford: Oxford University Press, and Van Vooren, B. & Wessel, R. A. (2014) *EU External Relations Law: Text, Cases and Materials*. Cambridge: Cambridge University Press. For a comprehensive overview of the EU's and its Member States engagement with various international organizations, see Wesssel, R. & Odermatt, J. (eds.) *Research Handbook on the EU's Engagement with International Organisations*. Cheltenham; Northampton: Edward Elgar (forthcoming).

[18] Articles 28 and 29 TFEU.

federal regulation and thus imposes a double layer of regulatory require-ments with a significant economic impact on business. In the EU, national (and several layers of sub-national) regulations are abundant, especially in the non-harmonized sectors.[19] Considering the various policy preferences and regulatory goals that are at play in various eco-nomic activities, there can be significant differences in the ways they are regulated on different levels of government. This is especially true in the provision of services, where government intervention is more prevalent than in manufacturing. The rationale is that of consumer protection since the intangible nature of services makes it more difficult to assess safety and quality than is the case with physical products.[20]

This part of the book focuses on the role that sub-central measures play in international trade agreements and especially in EIAs. It uses the examples of the USA and Canada in analyzing the question of EIAs' compatibility with Art. V GATS. The key argument is that no matter how sub-federal, or any sub-central measures, are listed, from a legal point of view, they can in excessive amounts be against the Article V discipline. That is because any other conclusion would seriously undermine the criterion of substantiality in the case of countries that have constitution-ally divided powers in their internal regulation of service activities.

II   The Impact of Federalism on Trade Liberalization

One of the most often mentioned goals of modern trade agreements is to go deeper in services liberalization. In the area of services, liberalization necessarily means tackling regulation. That regulation is often not lim-ited to central levels of government but reaches regional levels which may be states, territories, provinces, areas or even more local levels such as municipalities. As the supply of services, and especially professional services, is often dependent on such lower-level regulation, liberalization commitments made only by central authorities may fall short of creating the big gains that relate to truly open markets in services. However, quite surprisingly, there is so far very little literature on sub-central measures in services liberalization. Research has so far largely neglected the ques-tion of how to address an internal subdivision of a WTO Member and the

---

[19] Beviglia-Zampetti, A. (2000) Mutual Recognition in the Transatlantic Context: Some Reflections on Future Negotiations, in Cottier, T., Mavroidis, P. C. & Blatter, P. (eds.), *Regulatory Barriers and the Principle of Non-Discrimination in World Trade Law.* Ann Arbor: University of Michigan Press, 303–28, at 315.

[20] Egan (2015), at 160.

consequences it possibly has on that Members' services commitments. This is striking considering the significant economic impact that such measures can have on trade. The role of regions and even cities is likely to only grow in the future and more focus should be directed beyond the central government.[21]

A large variety, and especially divergence, in the internal regulations of a country, or a trading block in the case of the EU, can clearly be a hindrance to trade in services. Therefore, one of the explicit aims of the EU's new generation trade agreements has become to include in the services schedules regulatory measures imposed on services not only on the level of the central government but also on regional levels of the other party.[22]

In CETA between the EU and Canada, the latter has for the first time in its PTA history included a list of provincial and territorial non-conforming measures (NCMs) in the field of services and investments.[23] The Canadian provinces and territories are bound to regulatory status quo and have committed to providing to the EU the

---

[21] From climate change and renewable energy to international trade, sub-national governments are increasingly active in tackling matters of international concern. Meyer notes that 41 per cent of the claims brought under the investor–state dispute settlement ('ISDS') provisions of NAFTA have challenged sub-national government action (which is not excluded from the ISDS provisions of NAFTA). Canada, the most frequent respondent under NAFTA chapter 11, also has the highest percentage of claims involving local action. Twenty-two of its thirty-eight claims involve local action, a remarkable 58 per cent of claims. The WTO has also seen its share of claims challenging local action. Out of 502 cases filed to date, at least forty-one have challenged sub-national action (including claims against EU Member States) – a bit more than 8 per cent of cases. Timothy, M. (2017) Local Liability in International Economic Law. *North Carolina Law Review*, 95(2), 261–338, at 276–7.

[22] See e.g. the European Commission's negotiation mandates for both the CETA and TTIP agreements. In the CETA negotiation directives it is stated that 'The Agreement shall include substantial, explicit and binding commitments in all those areas under negotiation which fall, wholly or in part, under the jurisdiction of Canadian Provinces and Territories'. Moreover, 'the Agreement shall enter into force only upon the completion of the necessary procedures to bind the Canadian Provinces and Territories in all those areas under negotiation which fall wholly or in part under their jurisdiction'. See Annex 1 of the partially declassified 2008 negotiation directives, available at http://data.consilium.europa .eu/doc/document/ST-9036-2009-EXT-2/en/pdf (last accessed on 5 June 2018).

[23] 'Technical Summary of Final Negotiated Outcomes, Agreement-in-principle, documents summarizing the important negotiated outcomes of the Canada–European Union Comprehensive Economic and Trade Agreement as of October 18, 2013', The Government of Canada, p. 13, available at www.international.gc.ca/trade-agreements-accords-commerciaux/assets/pdfs/ceta-aecg/ceta-technicalsummary.pdf (last accessed on 5 June 2018). The CETA has not yet been signed nor ratified by the Parties. It is therefore not included in the empirical part of the present book.

benefits of autonomous liberalization in a number of important service sectors (architectural, engineering, foreign legal consultancy, urban planning, tourism, business services).[24]

The USA, on the other hand, has recently begun including an illustrative list of existing NCMs in the field of services for state level restrictions. However, the NCMs illustrated at the state and local level are provided for transparency purposes only and do not bind the USA nor the US states.[25] And no real liberalization of state level measures seems to be involved as all US EIAs done according to a negative listing include a reservation regarding *all* existing NCMs of all US states, as well as the District of Columbia and Puerto Rico.[26] There is no indication of any market access opening having been done to state level measures in the course of the negotiations for the EIAs. On the contrary, in its GATS schedule, the USA has specified also state-level measures. Art. I of the GATS specifies 'measures by Members' meaning measures taken by central, regional or local governments and authorities alike. Any

[24] Ibid. Another area of major commercial interest is government procurement. Enhanced access to the Canadian public procurement market, including in particular access to the sub-federal levels of procurement, was a major negotiating aim of the EU in CETA. The final (not ratified) agreement provides full coverage of Canadian procurement, covering federal, provincial and municipal procurement, with relatively few explicit exceptions. See 'EU–Canada Comprehensive Economic and Trade Agreement (CETA)', European Parliament, Directorate-General for External Policies, Policy Department, EP/EXPO/B/INTA/FWC/2013-08/Lot7/02-03, December 2015, available at www.europarl.europa.eu/RegData/etudes/IDAN/2015/535016/EXPO_IDA(2015)535016_EN.pdf (last accessed on 30 November 2018). The EU is pushing for an enhanced sub-federal market access in services and in government procurement also in the TTIP negotiations. See 'The Beauty of Public Procurement in TTIP' by Patrick Messerlin, ECIPE Bulletin No. 1/2016, available at http://ecipe.org/publications/the-beauty-of-public-procurement-in-ttip/ (last accessed on 30 November 2018).

[25] See p. 12 of KORUS, Annex I, the schedule of the United States and Appendix I-A to the same schedule. Page 12 includes the following statement: 'For purposes of transparency, Appendix I-A sets out an illustrative, non-binding list of non-conforming measures maintained at the regional level of government'. After KORUS, the same Appendix was included in the TPP, from which the USA later withdrew. The new US–Canada–Mexico agreement signed in November 2018 does not include such an appendix, at least not in the version that has been published on the website of the United States Trade Representative (USTR).

[26] See p. 12 of KORUS, Annex I, the schedule of the United States. The exempted measures are: 'All existing non-conforming measures of all states of the United States, the District of Columbia, and Puerto Rico'. In addition to the KORUS, a similar exemption is present in all US EIAs that have been concluded in accordance with negative listing (all agreements have been concluded after the entry into force of the GATS). The service schedule of the US–Jordan FTA of 2010 is the only US EIA that follows a positive listing model and appears to reflect the US GATS commitments to a large extent.

measures could, subject to negotiations, be left unbound in a Member's schedule under the GATS but such an outright exclusion of all sub-central measures was not exercised by the USA. This may have been hard to negotiate in the multilateral setting. Moreover, the GATS commitments are so shallow that there was likely to be less diversion between central and regional measures than in later EIAs.[27] Also, the positive listing under the GATS allows the WTO Member to choose which sectors and sub-sectors to liberalize, whereas in negative listing (followed by most of US EIAs) all service sectors are covered and each measure going against the agreement's disciplines has to be specifically exempted. Even in areas where regional and local measures are abundant, it would thus be necessary to enlist each restrictive measure.[28] Under the GATS, the Members were able to decide the level of precision with which the commitment was formulated and leave certain areas simply 'unbound'. Moreover, in positive listing, a commitment of a multi-level actor such as the USA or the EU can be built in accordance with the 'lowest common denominator'.[29] This may lead to a weaker commitment than necessary in light of the applicable regulations in some regions of the Member, but it makes for a more coherent schedule of commitments.

In the course of the TTIP negotiations, it was reported that the EU was pushing for the inclusion of sub-central measures in the US services schedule. According to one news report, the USA was offering to follow the same approach as in its recent agreement with South Korea (KORUS), thus merely providing an illustrative list of state-level NCMs instead of specifying them individually. At the same time, the USA was pushing to formulate the services schedules in accordance with the negative list approach. The EU, which until the CETA followed a 'positive-list' approach, reportedly communicated that it was willing

---

[27] About the poor level of liberalization in the WTO Members' GATS commitments, see e.g. Adlung, R. & Roy, M. (2005) Turning Hills into Mountains? Current commitments under the GATS. *Journal of World Trade*, 39(6), 1161–94. Regarding EIA provisions that fall short of the same countries' GATS commitments, see Adlung, R. & Morrison, P. (2010) Less than the GATS: 'Negative Preferences' in Regional Services Agreements. *Journal of International Economic Law*, 13(4), 1103–43.

[28] All post-GATS US EIAs define a 'measure' close to identical to GATS Art. I. The texts of the agreements are available on the webpage of the USTR: https://ustr.gov/trade-agreements/free-trade-agreements (last accessed on 20 January 2019).

[29] Meaning that the commitment is put forward in accordance with the least liberal regulations even if some regions of the Member would have more open market access conditions in that specific service sector. The issue is taken up in more detail in the following section of this chapter (analyzed in relation to the EU's scheduling practice).

to consider a negative list, but only if the USA provided a detailed list of all restrictions on services trade maintained by states and local entities. The EU argued that this was necessary in order to fully assess the value of the US services offer because it would show the exact extent of the market access that EU service suppliers would gain. This was unlikely to happen as the USA had thus far refused to engage in such an endeavour arguing that the mapping of state-level services barriers would be a Herculean task and could take 'two years to complete'.[30]

The relevance of the lower levels of government for services liberalization has gone surprisingly unnoticed, even if the practical consequences for market access can be significant. This may have to do with the generally low level of liberalization reached in the area of services, especially in the multilateral context. However, not much more attention has been paid to sub-central measures in preferential services agreements either.

The most prominent treatment is provided by Meyer who analyzes the liability of local government for breaches of international economic law. He focuses on the Trans-Pacific Partnership (TPP) agreement and notes the treaty practice that is familiar also from other EIAs concluded by the USA: 'unnoticed among the TPP's thirty chapters, schedules, and annexes, are provisions that exempt state, provincial, and local measures from compliance with many of the agreement's nondiscrimination rules'. He further notes that under the TPP, sub-national governments such as California or Ontario – governments with substantial regulatory authority over regional economies that are much larger than many national economies – may continue to discriminate against foreign investors or foreign service providers indefinitely. Meyer points out that the exemptions provided in TPP represent the multilateralization of a trend that has been underway for a number of years in US treaty practice: 'efforts to reduce the federal government's liability for sub-national action that the federal government often cannot control and of which it is frequently unaware'.[31] He also notes that countries that most frequently push to

[30] Jutta Hennig, 'Under Pressure to Show TTIP Progress, U.S., EU Focus on Market Access', Inside U.S. Trade – 04/18/2014, Vol. 32, No. 16 (posted 17 April 2014). According to the news piece, an EU source signalled that the list demanded by the EU also served a tactical reason: once the USA had admitted not being able to provide the list, it would give Brussels a free pass to push back on US demands. At that point, the negotiations could begin on services, the source had said.
[31] Meyer, T. (2017) Local Liability in International Economic Law. *North Carolina Law Review*, Vol. 95, 261–338, at 261.

exclude local measures from their international economic agreements are wealthy and powerful federal states such as the USA, Canada, Mexico and Australia. Meanwhile, many weaker developing nations are centralized and thus do not benefit from immunity for discriminatory regional acts.[32]

In empirical literature, Marchetti and Roy have paid some attention to sub-central measures. They have noted that a number of agreements using a negative-list approach do not include in their 'List of existing non-conforming measures' such measures that are applied by sub-central entities, either at the state/provincial level or local level. Even if the measures of such entities are not listed, the existing level of access provided by them is nevertheless bound and cannot be made more restrictive. Given the importance of state/provincial entities in federal states, the authors have in their empirical study considered as 'partial commitments' – as opposed to 'full commitments' with a score of one – situations where a country had not prescribed any limitations in a given sector but where state/provincial level measures were not listed. These were only scored as 'full commitments' in view of information suggesting that non-conforming measures were not applied (e.g. where a commitment in another negotiating context revealed that no such measures were in existence).[33]

In general, sub-central measures are typically not completely excluded from PTAs; they are often bound at existing levels (i.e. grandfathered), but they are not listed. However, the blanket inclusion of all sub-central measures among non-conforming measures (reservations) in practice equals to a complete exclusion from the key service disciplines, and most importantly from NT. That is why the listing of sub-central mea-sures in CETA is a big step forward. It should also be noted that with countries that do not list their sub-central measures, it is sometimes possible to find out what these existing measures are from other EIAs where they have been listed. For example, Australia has in some of its EIAs, similarly to the USA, included all existing NCMs at the regional level of government in its Annex I, thus exempting all existing NCMs of the Australian states and territories from the key services disciplines.[34] In

---

[32] Ibid., 270.

[33] Marchetti, J. A. & Roy, M. (2008) *Opening Markets for Trade in Services: Countries and Sectors in Bilateral and WTO Negotiations.* Cambridge; New York: Cambridge University Press, 109–10.

[34] See e.g. Australia–United States FTA (2005), Schedule of Australia, Annex I, p. 1. In its Annex II, Australia reserves the right to adopt or maintain any measure at the regional

its later agreements with Korea (2014) and China (2015), Australia has, however, listed NCMs applied at the regional level as well.

From a practical and methodological point of view, it may, however, be difficult, or practically impossible, to map all existing non-conforming measures by regional entities in different countries and thus understand to what extent they do away with the amount of non-discriminatory treatment granted on the central level. That is the case especially when sub-central restrictions are not listed in a specific EIA (as in the US EIAs). Sometimes it may be possible. This is the situation in CETA.[35] The binding of provincial and local measures by Canada makes it possible to analyze whether Canada's commitments reach the thresholds of Art. V as a whole.

The following two chapters analyze selected services commitments of the USA, Canada and the EU. The emphasis of the book is on the EU but the USA and Canada have been chosen for comparison as examples of powerful federal states. The USA is an especially prominent example of a federal state with widely divided powers across different regulatory areas. The fifty American states are separate sovereigns, with their own state constitutions, state governments, and state courts. There are also significant differences between their legal systems. In terms of important service-related regulation, the states are responsible for health, education and welfare. They also have some authority over areas of justice, energy, environment and immigration.[36]

level of government that is not inconsistent with Australia's obligations under Article XVI of the GATS. This is similar to the USA and the earlier Canadian practice, even though the Canadian reservation applies to the regional level only. With regard to Mode 4 commitments, the reservation applies also to the central government (Australia's Annex II, p. 2).

[35] Canada has included in its schedule separate federal, and provincial and territorial annexes, which together form the entirety of its commitments. Canada's two schedules (under Annex I and Annex II) with federal measures take approximately seventy pages of the agreement, whereas the two schedules with provincial and territorial restrictions occupy almost 300 pages. Both the EU's and Canada's commitments follow the so-called negative scheduling practice. This is unusual for the EU, which until the CETA was using GATS-type scheduling practice in its EIAs. According to the EU, 'the clear and comprehensive listing of the reservations provides unprecedented transparency on existing measures, in particular at provincial level'. See 'CETA – Summary of the Final Negotiating Results' by the European Commission. Available at http://trade.ec.europa .eu/doclib/docs/2014/december/tradoc_152982.pdf (last accessed on 1 December 2018).

[36] For a useful overview of key federations and their division of powers, as well as participation to international trade negotiations, see Walker J., Negotiation of Trade Agreements in Federal Countries, SPICe Briefing, the Scottish Parliament, 17 November 2007, available at https://sp-bpr-en-prod-cdnep.azureedge.net/published/2017/11/17/Negotiation-of-Trade-Agreements-in-Federal-Countries/SB17-79.pdf (last accessed 15 December 2018). For

Canada, under the Constitution Act of 1867, was established as a federation and has formally distributed powers between the Parliament of Canada and the provincial legislatures. In the ten provinces of Canada, the provincial governments and parliaments are responsible for several policy areas including education, health care and agriculture.[37]

The EU, on the other hand, is made of twenty-eight sovereign states, each of which has its own constitutional structure, ranging from federations to unitary states. The EU itself has an internally differentiated constitutional structure. It strives for consistency in its external relations on two fronts: horizontally between its different institutions, structures and policies, as well as vertically between the Union and the Member States. The vertical division of competencies varies across different policy areas and the Union has different techniques to manage them, such as the technique of 'mixed agreements' as well as the duty of sincere cooperation.[38]

The challenges that the EU as a multi-state actor faces in concluding services trade agreements are often similar to countries that have a federal structure.[39] Trade liberalization by the EU reflects the combination of supranational and national jurisdiction over trade negotiation areas. Within the field of services, as in goods, the competence to conclude agreements with third parties is within the powers of the Union. However, due to the lack of internal harmonization of services regulations within the EU, the EU Member States keep scheduling their own nationally based restrictions to the common EU services schedule. In this sense, there are clear similarities to countries with de-centralized regulation of service activities.

III   The Case of the European Union

i   Development of the EU's Competences in the Field of Trade

This section gives a short overview of the EU's trade policy and the Union's competences in the field of external trade. The overview works

---

a comparison of the impact of federalism on the international relations in the EU and USA, see De Baere & Gutman (2012).

[37] See Government of Canada (29 March 1867). Constitution Acts, 1867 to 1982. Available at: http://laws.justice.gc.ca/eng/Const/page-4.html#h-17 (last accessed 15 January 2019).

[38] Barnard, C. and Peers, S. (2017) *European Union Law*, 2nd ed. Oxford: Oxford University Press, at 746. On different techniques to manage external relations, see Rosas, A. (2015) EU External Relations: Exclusive Competence Revisited. *Fordham International Law Journal*, 38(4), 1073.

[39] For a comparison between sub-national perspectives in Canada and the EU in the context of the CETA negotiations, see Omiunu (2017).

to show how the EU Member States function in trade and investment matters similarly to sub-national units in a federal state. They are independent states but have given their competence in trade and most investment matters to the EU. That does not mean that the Member States would not be participating in the EU's decision-making over external trade. The Member States are the ultimate decision-makers in the Council that finally decides on the conclusion of trade and investment agreements on behalf of the Union. During negotiations, the Member States are regularly consulted and informed by the Commission through the Trade Policy Committee of the Council. The European Parliament, on the other hand, is kept updated through the European Parliament Committee on International Trade (INTA).

As we have chosen some of the EU's EIAs as our data, the methodology of the book is adapted to the EU's practice of scheduling services commitments. An essential characteristic of this practice is that the EU's commitments are a compilation of separate commitments of a large number of different states. To understand and interpret the EU's EIAs, one needs to understand the Union's policy and competences in the field of trade. In the field of services, the extent to which the EU can act as a uniform actor externally is also closely related to the state of development of its own internal market in services. The following brief overview of the development of the EU's competencies in the area of external services trade helps in the interpretation of the EU's services commitments and the results of our study.

Trade in services is today, in its entirety, part of the EU's Common Commercial Policy (CCP). Due to the special, more politically sensitive nature of services, as compared to goods, the current state of affairs required a constitutional struggle regarding the scope of the CCP. Most modes of supply were first considered to be outside the CCP and even when included, the EU's exclusive competence did not apply in a number of services sectors. The Lisbon Treaty brought about a significant change in this respect: the main subject matters of the WTO, goods and services, were matched by the new formulation of the CCP.[40] Whereas the Nice Treaty had left agreements relating to certain sensitive service sectors subject to the common accord of the Union and the Member States, Art. 3 and Art. 207 TFEU clearly provide that trade in services, as well as

---

[40] Müller-Graff, P.-C. (2008) The Common Commercial Policy Enhanced by the Reform Treaty of Lisbon, in Dashwood, A. & Maresceau, M. (eds.), *Law and Practice of EU External Relations: Salient Features of a Changing Landscape*. Cambridge; New York: Cambridge University Press, 188–201, at 190.

commercial aspects of intellectual property and foreign direct investment, belong to the area of the CCP and thus to the category of the EU's
exclusive competence.[41] Under TFEU, trade agreements limited to issues
covered by the CCP could therefore, in principle, be concluded solely by
the Union without the need for participation by the Member States.
However, as will be explained below, the EU continues to sign its trade
agreements not alone but together with its Member States for several
reasons.

The formulation of the law on the EU's competences as it stands today
started with the advent of the WTO in the mid-1990s when the Uruguay
Round was closing and the Court was asked to give its opinion on the
question of who had the competence to conclude the new GATS and
TRIPS agreements embodying the results of the Round. Already much
earlier the Court had declared that the Community enjoyed exclusive
external competence in two fields in particular: the CCP (Opinion 1/75)[42]
and the common fisheries policy.[43] The rationale with regard to the CCP
(including only trade in goods at the time) was that there was no longer
room for the Member States' unilateral action. Instead, in a common
market where third country goods imported into any Member State were
treated as goods originating in the Community, unified rules and policies
were required to ensure an adequate direction for the Community's
external trade. A common position was also needed to avoid the
Community being weakened in its relations with third countries.[44]

However, at the advent of the WTO, the Court in Opinion 1/94[45]
established that the logic applied in Opinion 1/75 to trade in goods was
not suitable for all aspects of services trade. With respect to establishment
(Mode 3) and the movement of natural persons as recipients or suppliers
of services (Modes 2 and 4), the existence in the Treaty of specific
chapters on the free movement of natural and legal persons led the
Court to conclude that those matters did not fall within the CCP.

---

[41] Rosas, A. & Armati, L. (2010) *EU Constitutional Law: An Introduction*. Oxford: Hart,
at 205.

[42] Opinion 1/75, *Opinion of the Court of 11 November 1975 given pursuant to Article 228 of
the EEC Treaty* [1975], ECR 01355.

[43] Case 804/79, *Commission v. United Kingdom* [1981], ECR 1045.

[44] Leal-Arcas, R. (2003) Exclusive or Shared Competence in the Common Commercial
Policy: From Amsterdam to Nice. *Legal Issues of Economic Integration*, 30(1), 3–14, at 4.

[45] Opinion 1/94, *Opinion of the Court of 15 November 1994 – Competence of the Community
to conclude international agreements concerning services and the protection of intellectual
property* [1994] ECR I-05267. Regarding foreign investment, see Opinion 2/92, *Third
Revised Decision of the OECD on national treatment* [1995] ECR I-521.

Furthermore, the chapters were not inextricably linked to the treatment to be afforded in the Community to nationals of non-member countries. Therefore, in the absence of specific provisions to that effect, the treatment of TCNs crossing the external frontiers of the Member States was outside the ambit of the Community's exclusive competence. The Court concluded that only cross-border trade (Mode 1) fell within the CCP since it was 'not unlike trade in goods' and involved no movement of persons.

The Amsterdam Treaty (1999) empowered the Council to extend the scope of the CCP to services and intellectual property insofar as they were not already covered by it. The Council did not act upon the authorization but the reform was finally implemented by the Treaty of Nice (2003), in which the ambit of the CCP was expanded to all modes of services.[46] Agreements relating to trade in cultural and audio-visual services, educational services, and social and human health services were, however, still left within the shared competence of the Community and its Member States.[47] Consequently, in addition to the applicable Community decision-making procedure, the conclusion of agreements including such services required the separate approval of the Member States – as well as separate national ratifications in each of them.

The Lisbon Treaty attempted to rectify this impractical state of affairs by changing the law in two important ways. First, all service sectors, except for transport services, were brought within the exclusive competence of the Union. The idea was that as a consequence, national ratifications of agreements covering services and trade-related intellectual property rights could in principle be avoided, at least as long as no extensive liberalization of transport services is included.[48] Second, the

[46] In Opinion 1/08 the Court confirmed that the Community was, as a result of the Nice Treaty, competent to conclude international agreements relating to trade in services supplied also under modes 2, 3 and 4. Opinion 1/08, *Opinion of the Court (Grand Chamber) of 30 November 2009 – Opinion pursuant to Article 300(6) EC* [2009] ECR I-11129, paragraph 119. Opinion 1/08 concerned the modification and withdrawal of the EU's specific commitments under the GATS following the EU's enlargement in 2005. The Court confirmed that the adoption of the EU's common schedule for EU25 fell within the sphere of shared competence because of the agreements reached with affected WTO Members touched upon transport services.

[47] Art. 133(6)(2) EC. In Opinion 1/08 (paragraphs 135–140) the Court stated that also such agreements that concern neither exclusively nor predominantly sensitive sectors (cultural, audiovisual, educational, social and health services) fell within the shared competence.

[48] In the area of transport the competence between the Union and the Member States is shared (Art. 4(2)(g) TFEU). The number of transport services that still possibly remain

Lisbon Treaty made almost all trade and international agreements subject to the Consent Procedure and gave veto power to the European
Parliament (Art. 207 (6) TFEU).[49] Furthermore, in order to implement
the CCP, regulations could from now own be adopted by the European
Parliament and the Council in accordance with the ordinary legislative
procedure (Art. 207 (2) TFEU).

In 2013, the Court handed down two more important rulings on the
scope of the CCP. In *Daiichi Sankyo*,[50] the Court confirmed that the
Treaty amendments of the Lisbon Treaty brought the TRIPs Agreement
in its entirety within the scope of the CCP. In that case, as well as in
the second case, *Conditional Access Services*,[51] the Court also clarified
the relationship between Articles 114 and 207 TFEU. Art. 114 constitutes the main Treaty article used to enact harmonization measures in
the internal market. In both cases, one of the central issues was the
potential 'abuse' of Art. 207 TFEU as a means of externally harmonizing
the internal market and therefore infringing upon the EU competences
under Art. 114 TFEU. The Court did not find reason for such concern.

outside the Union's exclusive competence is significantly reduced by the development of
the Union's secondary law, which in combination with the ERTA principle and the
principle of loyal cooperation means that the Member States' action is significantly
limited and the Union's competence accordingly extended. Pursuant to the AETR/
ERTA judgment of 1971 (and the doctrine of implied powers), the Member States do
not have the right to undertake obligations with third countries which affect common
rules laid down by the Community (now the EU), only the EU itself can do so. As
a general rule, the doctrine means that the EU enjoys implied external competence in
areas where it enjoys internal competence. With the Lisbon Treaty, the principle is now
also codified in Articles 3(2) and 216(1) TFEU. See Rosas & Armati (2010), at 209 and
Case 22/70, *Commission v. Council* [1971] ECR 263. See also Eeckhout (2011), at 59. The
inclusion of several transport services under the EU's exclusive competence was later
dealt with and confirmed in Opinion 2/15 of the Court (see below). As noted by Rosas,
what is noticeable in the Court's case law on the AETR/ERTA principle is the Court's
focus in determining whether a specific legal regime is covered 'to a large extent' by
common EU rules, rather than each and every detail of this regime. See Rosas (2015), at
1095.

[49] In its decision-making, the Council acts by a qualified majority (Art. 207(4) TFEU). In
certain cases, and especially when unanimity is required for the adoption of the EU's
internal rules, the negotiation and conclusion of external agreements requires unanimity.
Moreover, Art. 207(6) provides that the exercise of the competences conferred by the
article 'shall not affect the delimitation of competences between the Union and the
Member States, and shall not lead to harmonisation of legislative or regulatory provisions
of the Member States in so far as the Treaties exclude such harmonisation'.

[50] Case C-414/11, *Daiichi Sankyo Co. Ltd, Sanofi-Aventis Deutschland GmbH v. DEMO
Anonimos Viomikhaniki kai Emporiki Etairia Farmakon* [2013] EU:C:2013:520.

[51] Case C-137/12, *Commission v. Council (Conditional Access Services)* [2013] EU:
C:2013:675.

The latter case concerned an international agreement on Conditional Access Services, an area for which a similar level of protection had already been established through the EU's internal legislation. The Court found that Art. 207, and not Art. 114 TFEU, was the correct legal basis for the conclusion of an international agreement which led to external harmonization of conditional access services with third countries, even if the agreement had certain internal effects. By applying the so-called 'centre of gravity' test in determining the correct legal basis for measures falling within separate competences, the Court concluded that the Convention's aim was not to promote conditional access services within the EU, but rather to protect EU service providers beyond the borders of the EU. Its primary objective had a specific connection with international trade in those services, and thus it could be legitimately linked to the CCP.[52]

In a similar vein, the Court in *Daiichi Sankyo* rejected the argument that allowing TRIPs to fall within the scope of the CCP would unduly affect the EU's competence in internal market matters by leading to indirect harmonization of the internal market or even deactivation of a shared competence.[53] The Court pointed out that the main objective of the TRIPS Agreement was to strengthen and harmonize the protection of intellectual property on a worldwide scale.[54] It remained open to the EU to legislate on intellectual property rights within the internal market. The Court admitted, however, that such competence must be exercised in conformity with TRIPs, 'as those rules are still, as previously, intended to standardize certain rules on the subject at world level and thereby to facilitate international trade'.[55]

Notwithstanding the Court's expansive interpretation of the scope of the CCP, the EU has, up until recently, continued to conclude its trade agreements as so-called mixed agreements, which means that both the

---

[52] In accordance with the center of gravity test, it is sufficient that the 'main purpose' of an agreement is the external harmonization for it to fall within the scope of the CCP. 'Incidental' internal harmonization does not require reference to another legal base (para. 53 of C-137/12, *Conditional Access Services*). See also Ankersmit, L. (2014) The Scope of the Common Commercial Policy after Lisbon: The Daiichi Sankyo and Conditional Access Services Grand Chamber Judgments. *Legal Issues of Economic Integration*, 41(2), 193–210. On the center of gravity test, see e.g. Van Vooren & Wessel (2014), 158–185.

[53] Ankersmit (2014), at 205.

[54] Para. 58 of C-414/11, *Daiichi Sankyo*.

[55] Para. 59, ibid.

EU and the Member States are signatories to the agreements.[56] That is partly because many of the EU's trade agreements include issues that are clearly outside the CCP (e.g. chapters relating to cultural cooperation), but also because it has still not been entirely clear whether certain issues are within the scope of the CCP or not. Especially the EU's powers in respect of foreign direct investment (FDI) has been a controversial issue since the Lisbon Treaty came into force. The Commission has interpreted the treaty broadly as allowing the EU the exclusive competence to negotiate and conclude agreements regarding all aspects of investment.[57] Many Member States, however, have taken an alternative interpretation, arguing that the EU has powers only in relation to the narrow category of FDI, admission of investment, and that the type of portfolio investments and post-establishment investment protection covered by BITs (including the so-called investor-state dispute settlement) do not fall within the concept of FDI. Such issues would thus remain within the scope of shared competence, needing approval from both the EU and individual Member States. The issue is significant, considering that all EU's most recent trade agreements include also chapters on investment.

In the process of concluding the EU–Singapore FTA in 2015, the Commission decided to address the question legally.[58] The Commission

---

[56] 'Mixed agreements' are international agreements concluded jointly by the EU (before, the Community) and the Member States because they include issues in shared competence. Cremona notes that this is a particular kind of shared competence, which requires joint action instead of permitting the Community and the Member States to act either alone or together. See Cremona, M. (2010) Balancing Union and Member State Interests: Opinion 1/2008, Choice of Legal Base and the Common Commercial Policy under the Treaty of Lisbon. *European Law Review*, 35(5), 678–94, at 679. Not all the EU's trade agreements are mixed. Especially older trade and cooperation agreements have often been signed by the Union alone. One recent example is the Stabilisation and Association Agreement concluded with Kosovo in February 2016 (Council Decision (EU) 2016/342 of 12 February 2016 on the conclusion, on behalf of the Union, of the Stabilisation and Association Agreement between the European Union and the European Atomic Energy Community, of the one part, and Kosovo, of the other part, OJ 2016 L 71/1). The European Atomic Energy Community (Euratom) is also a party to the agreement because of the competencies falling under its mandate. Euratom is a separate community but it has the same members as the European Union and is governed by the Commission and Council, operating under the jurisdiction of the European Court of Justice. Moreover, as will be noted below, the EU's most recent trade agreements with Singapore and Japan were concluded as 'EU-only' agreements (see footnotes 65–67).

[57] Reinisch, A. (2014) The EU on the Investment Path – Quo Vadis Europe? The Future of EU BITs and other Investment Agreements. *Santa Clara Journal of International Law*, 12 (1), 111–57, at 118.

[58] Request for an opinion submitted by the European Commission pursuant to Art. 218(11) TFEU (Opinion 2/15).

asked the Court to confirm whether the Union had the requisite competence to sign and conclude the FTA alone. Until then, most EU's trade
agreements had been concluded as mixed agreements, but in the EU–
Singapore FTA (EUSFTA) the Commission proposed to conclude the
agreement between the EU and the Republic of Singapore alone, without
the Member States appearing as parties to the agreement.[59] In its Opinion
the Court held that the EUSFTA covers shared competences with respect
to: (i) non-direct foreign investment, (ii) investor–state dispute settlement
(ISDS), and (iii) state-to-state dispute settlement relating to provisions
regarding portfolio investment and ISDS. In the form proposed by the
Commission, the agreement would therefore need to be concluded as
a 'mixed agreement'.[60] However, all subject matters outside investment
and ISDS were considered to be within the realms of the CCP and the
Union's exclusive competence, including all matters of services trade. This
applied also to all transport services as the Court, after a detailed examination of the EU's internal rules, came to the conclusion that all transport and
transport related services contained in the envisaged agreement fell within
areas which were already covered to a large extent by common EU rules.
Since the scope of those rules may be affected or altered by the commitments taken in the agreement, the Court decided that the competence of
the EU to approve the commitments is exclusive pursuant to Art. 3(2)
TFEU.[61]

In its latest judgments, the Court has therefore continued to consoli-
date the wide interpretation of the scope of the CCP – even if it did not go
as far as extending the exclusive competence to all areas of investment.

[59] However, later the Commission proposed 'mixity' for the agreement with Canada
(CETA). According to the Commission, the conclusion of CETA as a mixed agreement
was to allow for a swift signature and provisional application of the agreement (the parts
being clearly in the area of exclusive competence being provisionally applicable before the
rest of the agreement). At the same time the Commission noted that this was without
prejudice to its legal view, as expressed in the concerning the trade deal reached between
the EU and Singapore. See 'European Commission proposes signature and conclusion of
EU–Canada trade deal', 5 July 2016, available at http://europa.eu/rapid/press-release_IP-
16-2371_en.htm (last accessed on 23 August 2018). On the question of provisional
application of EU's trade agreements in the aftermath of Opinion 2/15 see Kleimann,
D. and Kübek, G. (2016), *The Signing, Provisional Application, and Conclusion of Trade
and Investment Agreements in the EU: The Case of CETA and Opinion 2/15*, EUI Working
Paper RSCAS 2016/58.
[60] Opinion 2/15, Opinion of the Court (Full Court) of 16 May 2017. See Puccio, Laura.
'CJEU Opinion on the EU-Singapore Agreement', European Parliament, Members'
Research Service, May 2017: www.europarl.europa.eu/RegData/etudes/ATAG/2017/
603955/EPRS_ATA(2017)603955_EN.pdf (last accessed on 20 September 2018).
[61] Opinion 2/15, paras. 168–218.

The possible effect of external harmonization on the EU's internal rules may bring up new questions as a result. For example, one can ask to what extent the EU's unified external trade commitments on third-country service suppliers' entry, stay and professional qualifications will affect their rights within the internal market. So far there is only limited EU legislation in that regard.[62] Therefore, it would seem that the Commission-led unification of conditions in trade agreements, so far seen at least in the EU's horizontal commitments on third-country service suppliers, is creating common rules that are the main source of EU rules on third-country service suppliers. However, the reach of such rules is limited considering that trade commitments do not extend to such third-country nationals who are legal residents in the EU and outside the limited scope of Mode 4.

As the recent Opinion on the EU–Singapore FTAs shows, the CCP is still not entirely in the domain of the Union as non-direct foreign investment and ISDS are not covered by it. For any agreements including those issues, there is a need for Member State ratifications also in the future. Also, were a trade deal to cover policies outside the EU's exclusive competence and involving issues that have not been harmonized in the EU, it would need to be concluded by the EU and Member States together.[63] However, in order to speed up the ratification process and to avoid trade and investment protection agreements becoming trapped in national and regional politics, the two types of agreements can be concluded separately, along the lines of competences.[64] Such a split has already been done with the EU's recent agreement with Singapore. In October 2018, the Council adopted decisions for the separate signing of the two agreements.[65] The Commission has proposed the same 'splitting'

[62] Mainly the EU rules on intra-company transfers. See Directive 2014/66/EU of the European Parliament and of the Council of 15 May 2014 on the conditions of entry and residence of third-country nationals in the framework of an intra-corporate transfer.

[63] Bungenberg, M. (2010) Going Global? The EU Common Commercial Policy after Lisbon, in Herrmann, C. & Terhechte, J. P. (eds.), *European Yearbook of International Economic Law* 2010. Heidelberg: Springer, 123–51, at 133. For example, in the fields such as social policy, health and culture intra-EU harmonization is largely absent or impossible.

[64] The trade and investment parts of the agreement can be procedurally divided and concluded separately with the EU Member States being parties only to the investment agreement. See Puccio (2017). This possibility is available if the trade part of the agreement does not grow to cover issues that are not within the CCP.

[65] On 18 April 2018, the European Commission proposed to the Council of the EU to sign and conclude two agreements with Singapore. These agreements were created by dividing the FTA reached between the EU and Singapore (EUSFTA) in 2014 into separate trade and investment protection agreements. The first is to be concluded by the EU alone,

procedure for the trade and investment agreement negotiated with Vietnam.[66] With Japan, on the other hand, no investment agreement has been reached so far. Instead, an Economic Partnership Agreement was concluded between Japan and the EU as an 'EU-only' agreement, without participation of the Member States. This trade agreement entered into force on 1 February 2019.[67]

ii The (Lack of) the EU's Internal Market of Services: Implications for External Trade

Even though goods and services are now equally located within the CCP and the EU's exclusive competence, the offers which the EU makes to its trading partners in respect of services look very different from its offers in respect of goods. Whereas goods are treated similarly in each Member State once they enter the territory of the Union, in services the diversity of national rules prevails. This is because the EU still, to a large extent, lacks harmonized legislation with regard to how services and services-related areas of law are regulated inside the Member States.[68] For example, in the

whereas the second is concluded by the EU and its Member States. The investment protection agreement is thus subject to ratification in each Member State. See EU Council Press Release, EU–Singapore: 'Council Adopts Decisions to Sign Trade and Investment Agreements', www.consilium.europa.eu/en/press/press-releases/2018/10/15/eu-singapore-council-adopts-decisions-to-sign-trade-and-investment-agreements/, 15 October 2018 (last accessed on 1 February 2019).

[66] The Free Trade Agreement and the Investment Protection Agreement between the EU and Vietnam were signed on 30 June 2019. Following the signatures, the agreements will, on the EU side, be presented to the European Parliament for its consent, as well as to the respective national parliaments of the EU Member States in the case of the Investment Protection Agreement. See Joint press statement by EU Trade Commissioner Cecilia Malmström and Minister of Industry and Trade Tran Tuan Anh on the occasion of the signing of the Free Trade Agreement and the Investment Protection Agreement between Viet Nam and the EU, 30 June 2019, http://trade.ec.europa.eu/doclib/press/index.cfm?id=2041 (last accessed on 3 July 2019).

[67] 'EU-Japan Agreement Enters into Force', European Commission Press Release, 31 January 2019, http://europa.eu/rapid/press-release_IP-19-785_en.htm (last accessed 1 February 2019). Regarding this new treaty making *modus operandi* in the EU's external economic governance, see Kleimann, D. (2018) Beyond the Shadow of the Veto: Economic Treaty Making in the European Union after Opinion 2/15, 165-183, in *Institutionalisation beyond the Nation State, Transatlantic Relations: Data, Privacy and Trade Law*, Fahey, E. (ed.), Cham: Springer International Publishing.

[68] See Langhammer who notes that given the significant amount of national sovereignties that remain in the services trade amongst EU Member States, the EU is not yet even a free trade area. Langhammer, R. J. (2005) The EU Offer of Service Trade Liberalization in the DOHA Round: Evidence of a Not-Yet-Perfect Customs Union. *Journal of Common Market Studies*, 43(2), 311–25, at 311.

absence of a genuine EU-wide immigration policy, service suppliers from third countries face a different immigration scheme in each Member State. Even if the Member States aim at formulating unified conditions relating to issues such as period of stay and prior employment, there is still a separate work and residence permit procedure in each Member State.[69] Another example is the absence of uniform rules regulating service professions (most relevant for sector-specific commitments under the GATS). Each Member State can apply its own qualification, licence and residence requirements across the sectors. The complex and Member State-specific sectoral commitments that the EU has offered under the GATS and its services PTAs illustrate how the incompleteness of the EU's internal services market appears in its external trade relations.

Even though the Commission is the exclusive trade negotiator of the Union and undoubtedly aims at as consistent a schedule as possible, each Member State ultimately puts forward its own limitations to be included in the EU's common services schedule. Significant differences still exist among Member States both in horizontal and sector-specific commitments. After the entry into force of the Lisbon Treaty in December 2009, the continuing diversity within the EU's services schedule can be seen in all of the EU's most recent trade agreements, as is shown also by our results.

A look at the EU's services schedules demonstrates the situation. Both in horizontal and sector-specific commitments, the description of reservations is prescribed separately by each Member State. In some cases two or more Member States have adopted the same position, in which case the relevant states are grouped together. On some occasions, the commitment or restriction is marked as being taken by the EU if all Member States share the same commitment or restriction. The following example in Table 4.1 concerning auditing services is from the EU's services schedule in the EU–Korea FTA.[70]

---

[69] The directive on a single application procedure for third-country national (TCN) workers does not apply to self-employed persons nor ICTs. See Art. 3 of Directive 2011/98/EU of the European Parliament and of the Council of 13 December 2011 on a single application procedure for a single permit for third-country nationals to reside and work in the territory of a Member State and on a common set of rights for third-country workers legally residing in a Member State. ICTs and the self-employed are outside the scope of application. Contractual service suppliers are sometimes required to obtain a work permit in the host country but the Directive applies only to workers whose employer is based in the EU.

[70] Free Trade Agreement between the European Union and its Member States, of the one part, and the Republic of Korea, of the other part, Official Journal of the European Union, L 127, 14 May 2011, ANNEX 7-A-1, EU Party, List of commitments in conformity with Article 7.7 (Cross-border supply of services).

Table 4.1 *EU and its Member States' reservations for auditing services under Establishment (Mode 3) in the EU–Korea EIA*

| 6. BUSINESS SERVICES
A. Professional Services
. . .
b) 2. Auditing services
(CPC 86211 and 86212
other than accounting
services) | AT: Korean auditors' (who must be authorised according to the law of Korea) equity participation and shares in the operating results of any Austrian legal entity may not exceed 25 per cent, if they are not members of the Austrian Professional Body.
CY: Access is subject to an economic needs test. Main criteria: the employment situation in the sub-sector.
CZ and SK: At least 60 per cent of capital share or voting rights are reserved to nationals.
DK: In order to enter into partnerships with Danish authorised accountants, foreign accountants have to obtain permission from the Danish Commerce and Companies Agency.
FI: Residency requirement for at least one of the auditors of a Finnish liability company.
LV: In a commercial company of sworn auditors more than 50 per cent of the voting capital shares shall be owned by sworn auditors or commercial companies of sworn auditors of the European Union.
LT: Not less than 75 per cent of shares should belong to auditors or auditing companies of the European Union.
SE: Only auditors approved in Sweden may perform legal auditing services in certain legal entities, *inter alia*, in all limited companies. Only such persons may be shareholders or form partnerships in companies which practice qualified auditing (for official purposes). Residency is required for approval.
SI: The share of foreign persons in auditing companies may not exceed 49 per cent of the equity. |

As the commitment shows, ten of the EU Member States have state-specific restrictions on the supply of auditing services in or to their territory. Between them, only two Member States provide for the same restriction (CZ and SK). For the seventeen Member States that have not prescribed restrictions, the sector is 'bound', meaning that they do not restrict the supply of auditing services by Korean nationals.

In practice, the Commission coordinates the Member States' positions that vary according to their national legislation. The Commission acts as the sole negotiator but in the formulation of the EU's offer on services, the content of the offer is largely dependent on how far each Member State is willing and able to go. International services negotiations are generally hampered by the challenge of coordinating various positions of national authorities in the fields such as taxation, social security, immigration. In the EU context, and similarly to many other federal entities, the Commission has to be particularly attentive to the prerequisites of the Member States. Running over the Member States and their various regulatory authorities would risk the Council not accepting the final agreement. Moreover, in case the agreement is concluded as a 'mixed' agreement between the EU and its Member States, it is additionally subject to national ratifications. Even in the case of EU-only agreements, national opposition can be channelled through the Council or the Parliament. The risk of political difficulties in the national sphere is emphasized by the civil society's interest in safeguarding public services, which makes various domestic stakeholders especially alert to trade agreements in the field of services.[71]

At this level of EU integration, a uniform, common services schedule is not likely to be achieved. Only a completed, largely harmonized internal market in services would make uniform conditions possible and allow a type of customs union in services to be formed. And even if the EU managed to harmonize its regulations across all services sectors, the

---

[71] The concern for the viability of public services has raised the interest of civil society representatives as well as regions and municipalities in international services negotiations. See 'Municipalities Concerned about CETA, TTIP and TISA', European Public Service Union EPSU, 28 October 2014: www.epsu.org/article/municipalities-concerned-about-ceta-ttip-and-tisa (last accessed on 30 September 2018). Intra-EU services trade has also been an object of passionate politics. A good example is the EU's Services Directive in which several service sectors were excluded for political reasons (Directive 2006/123/EC of the European Parliament and of the Council of 12 December 2006 on services in the internal market). In particular, the directive does not apply at all to healthcare services and audio-visual services. Social services are also largely excluded. For an extensive account of the Services Directive and its somewhat complicated relationship to the Court's case law, see Snell, J. (2008) Free Movement of Services and the Services Directive: The Legitimacy of the Case Law, in van de Gronden, J. (ed.), *EU and WTO Law on Services: Limits to the Realization of General Interest Policies within the Services Markets*. The Hague: Kluwer Law International, 31–54.

conditions towards third-country service suppliers would be uniform only if the Member States were able to agree also on issues such as the entry conditions for third-country service suppliers and acceptance of their professional qualifications. Entire Mode 4 is problematic as it is formally in the EU's exclusive competence as part of services trade but the EU's internal immigration and professional recognition rules are not.[72] Actually, EU Member States keep concluding bilateral migration agreements with third countries, which may, to a limited extent, include some overlap with temporary movement to supply services, which can be referred to as service mobility (Mode 4).[73] From an external point of view, the formal existence of the Union's exclusive competence in services may not seem to matter much as long as internal policies are not aligned.

In addition to immigration and intra-EU movement rules, there are significant legal and administrative barriers that apply horizontally across different services sectors. They include requirements for licences, economic needs tests, quotas, types of legal entities, and are sometimes directly discriminatory (residency and nationality requirements). These MA barriers and NT limitations vary across Member States, even if the EU's latest EIA schedules have less diversity than the original GATS commitments. The EU's Services Directive[74] has not changed the

---

[72] Certain service suppliers accessing the EU under Mode 4 may benefit from EU-wide rules, particularly the EU's ICT Directive (Directive 2014/66/EU of the European Parliament and of the Council of 15 May 2014 on the conditions of entry and residence of third-country nationals in the framework of an intra-corporate transfer) and the Seasonal Workers Directive (Directive 2014/36/EU of the European Parliament and of the Council of 26 February 2014 on the conditions of entry and stay of third-country nationals for the purpose of employment as seasonal workers). However, the self-employed, such as independent professionals, as well as contractual service suppliers must often apply for work permits in accordance with national rules and procedures. Each EU country alone decides on the volumes of work permits. Business visitors, another Mode 4 category, can often conclude their stay with a short-term visa where the Schengen rules provide for uniform entry conditions across twenty-six countries (twenty-two of which are EU Member States).

[73] Arguably, the GATS MFN clause acts as a tool to discipline bilateral immigration agreements. See Panizzon, M. (2010) International Law of Economic Migration: A Menage à Trois? GATS Mode 4, EPAs, and Bilateral Migration Agreements. *Journal of World Trade*, 44(6), 1207–52. However, there is no MFN obligation with regard to such rules that provide for an access to the host state's labour market as labor migration is outside the scope of Mode 4. Therefore, there is likely to be only a limited overlap between EU Member States' bilateral migration agreements and Mode 4. See Jacobsson, J. (2015) GATS Mode 4 and Labour Mobility: The Significance of Employment Market Access, in Panizzon, M., Zürcher, G. & Fornalé, E. (eds.), *The Palgrave Handbook of International Labour Migration: Law and Policy Perspectives*. Hampshire: Palgrave Macmillan, 61–94.

[74] Directive 2006/123/EC of the European Parliament and of the Council of 12 December 2006 on services in the internal market, OJ L 376, 27.12.2006, p. 36–68.

situation in this regard as it is not aimed at the harmonization of service regulations inside the EU but facilitating the exercise of the freedom of establishment for service providers and the free movement of services. Service activities are directly impacted by several fields of law, including environmental, urban planning, consumer protection, labour and social security law, with some of the applicable legislation introduced at EU level. But usually the applicable rules are a compilation of national and EU rules. The EU has highly harmonized rules for the practice of various professions in the EU's internal market, but such EU's internal professional recognition rules do not apply to third-country service suppliers.[75] The EU's services market remains greatly differentiated for them. The EU's internal diversity in this regard is not always visible in its EIA services schedules in case Member States' professional regulations do not include violations of NT.[76] However, the diversity of rules in itself (even when such rules are non-discriminatory towards third-country service suppliers) makes the access to the EU market additionally complicated and burdensome for non-EU service suppliers who are interested in selling their services across the Member States.[77]

Arguably for the purpose to show more coherence, the Commission is aiming at a more uniform services schedule for the EU. The quest for a more harmonized services offer was visible already in the EU's services offer made in the first years of the Doha Round (which now, over ten

---

[75] Under Art. 2 of the EU's professional qualifications directive, only EU nationals are covered by the general rules (Directive 2005/36/EC of the European Parliament and of the Council of 7 September 2005 on the recognition of professional qualifications). See also Guild, E. (2007) European Union and Third Party Service Trades: Four Essays on EU Services, Quaker United Nations Office, *Global Economic Issues Publications*, Working Paper, April 2007, at 2–3. The exclusion of third-country nationals from the coverage of the recognition rules is also specified in EU's EIAs.

[76] However, often they do include violations of NT as well. There are numerous Member State-specific examples of nationality and residency requirements in various service professions. The differences between the Member States' regulations (the diversity) is easily visible in such instances.

[77] This has been noted by the American transport company Uber when it has tried to access the Member State markets. Instead of being able to adopt an EU-wide strategy, it must adapt to the regulations applicable in each Member State. Moreover, taxi licensing powers in certain EU states, like in many other states, are in the hands of regional or local government, which calls for further adaptation in accordance with local rules. This encountered Uber in Spain where the Spanish government in late 2018 decided to transfer ride-sharing licensing regulations to its autonomous regions. See 'Spanish Government Will Let Cities Nullify Thousands of Uber, Cabify Licenses', *El País*, 28 September 2018, available at https://elpais.com/elpais/2018/09/28/inenglish/1538146835_960312.html (last accessed on 15 December 2018).

years later, is largely meaningless).[78] Following the EU's first GATS commitments at the end of the Uruguay Round, the EU made two offers as part of the Doha Round: one in 2003 and another, revised offer, in 2005.[79] The horizontal commitments of the EU's Doha Round offers reveal a reasonable unification especially of the general conditions for the entry and stay of non-EU service suppliers. Notwithstanding certain examples where a limited number of Member States have either gone further or remained below the EU's common standard, the offers on horizontal commitments significantly streamline the Member States' commitments as compared to their consolidated GATS commitments. The change is noteworthy considering that in the Community's original horizontal commitments concluded at the end of the Uruguay Round, the entry conditions and periods of stay largely vary between the Member States. Within the consolidated schedule of EU25 the diversity is manifold compared to the Doha Round offers.[80] However, the sectoral commitments offered in the Doha Round still reveal a considerable amount of Member State-specific limitations.

The EU's GATS offers of 2003 and 2005 also show that there are some occasions where the Member States' offers have deteriorated with the

[78] Klamert, M. (2015) *Services Liberalization in the EU and the WTO: Concepts, Standards and Regulatory Approaches*. Cambridge: Cambridge University Press, at 68–9 and Langhammer (2005), at 323. Since the EU's latest offer, the Doha Round has become embroiled in deep controversies and the offers are no longer relevant as such. Nonetheless, they can be reviewed to analyze to what extent the EU has managed to formulate a unified stand on services before the halt of the Doha Round.

[79] Communication from the European Communities and its Member States – Conditional Initial Offer, 10 June 2003, TN/S/O/EEC and Communication from the European Communities and its Member States – Conditional Revised Offer, 29 June 2005, TN/S/O/EEC/Rev.1.

[80] See a study on the EU's Doha Round offers on Mode 4 in Jacobsson, J. (2013) Liberalisation of Service Mobility in the EU's International Trade Agreements: As External as It Gets. *European Journal of Migration and Law*, 15(3), 245–61. The EU's draft consolidated schedule (EU25) is included in the WTO document S/C/W/279 of 9 October 2006. It has been a 'draft' for over a decade because of the slow pace of ratifications by EU Member States. The schedule was about to be finally adopted when the book went into publication. In November 2018 the Commission put forward a proposal for a Council decision on the matter, asking the Council to approve the agreements without finishing national ratifications (Commission Proposal for a Council Decision, COM(2018) 733 final, 8 November 2018). Opinion 2/15 had made clear that the Council may adopt its decision under the exclusive competence of the EU. National ratifications are therefore no longer needed. Once the EU25 consolidated schedule is formally adopted, the EU can start negotiations for the incorporation of the newest Member States' (Bulgaria, Romania and Croatia) national commitments into the EU schedule.

adoption of a more unified offer since the consolidated Uruguay Round commitments. However, their overall importance is not significant and there are also several examples of situations where individual Member States' commitments have ameliorated with the more streamlined EU offer.[81]

As noted by Hoekman and Sauvé, integration agreements, even when not formally seeking to establish a common external policy, often involve some degree of harmonization of regulatory policies at least in certain sectors. This may imply that some participating countries become more liberal, while others need to be more restrictive. As the authors note, harmonization up is nevertheless the more likely result than harmonization down and thus the balancing requirement of Art. V:4 towards outsiders is usually not risked.[82]

It is, however, important to keep in mind that the EU's more unified stand in the 2003 and 2005 offers has mostly not been attained by harmonizing EU legislation but by coordinating the positions of the Member States. The common position is thus dependent on the flexibility provided by the Member States' national legislation.

Eschenbach and Hoekman have carried out an interesting analysis of the EU's GATS commitments and Doha Round offers.[83] They use the index score (from zero to 100) of Hoekman to characterize the EU's GATS commitments.[84] As the authors note, the index used is a somewhat arbitrary measure of the depth of commitments in that its value is unlikely to be very informative of the actual policies that prevail. However, it provides a way of weighting commitments and allowing cross-country comparisons, thus permitting to assess the degree to which there is certain uniformity in GATS commitments across EU members. They find that the pre-Doha level of commitment for the

---

[81] Jacobsson, ibid., at 255–6.

[82] Hoekman, B. & Sauvé, P. (1994) Liberalizing Trade in Services. *World Bank Discussion Papers*, WDP243, at 58–9. The balancing requirement towards outsiders means that the overall level of barriers has not risen on a sectoral basis.

[83] Eschenbach, F. & Hoekman, B. (2006) Services Policies in Transition Economies: On the EU and WTO as Commitment Mechanisms. *World Trade Review*, 5(3), 415–43.

[84] As explained in Chapter 7 on methodology, the Hoekman method (1996) assigns a value of 1 to full commitment to liberalization; 0.5 (partial) to specific limitations; and 0 ('unbound') to instances where no commitments at all are made for a subsector. Average scores are provided for MA and NT (also combined) across all four modes and 155 sub-sectors. See Hoekman, B. (1996) Assessing the General Agreement on Trade in Services, in Martin, W. & Winters, A. L. (eds.), *The Uruguay Round and the Developing Countries*. Cambridge: Cambridge University Press, 88–124

EU-15 as a whole was 47 per cent. Most EU members do not deviate much from this average 'benchmark' in terms of national commitments across modes. At 46 per cent, the EU weighted average is only one percentage point below the benchmark value.

Among the most interesting findings is that the greatest variance in specific commitments is found for Mode 3. The standard deviation of the commitments is twice as high for Mode 3 commitments as for other modes on market access. Although Modes 1 and 4 are more 'sensitive' for all countries, the sensitivities on Mode 3 vary more between the Member States. They also find that the GATS Doha Round offers made by the EU substantially increase the EU's average commitment index. At the aggregate level, the standard deviation falls from 2 to 1.6, indicating an increase in uniformity at the EU Member State level. With the Doha offers, the variance across EU members would fall for Mode 3 market access commitments, but the structure of commitments remains similar to the pre-Doha status quo. They find that the 'lagging' countries are mostly the same – only Greece would converge to the EU average as a result of the offers that were on the table as of 2004.[85]

Langhammer[86] uses the same methodological approach as the Hoekman commitment index, except that he modifies the index by also taking account of differences in in-between commitments (ranging between 'unbound' and 'none) and assigning them values 0.25 and 0.75. Similarly to Hoekman and Eschenbach, he finds relatively low coefficients of variation. The average levels of commitments thus do not differ much between the Member States. Overall, there is most diversity under Mode 4.

Both studies give useful insight into the uniformity, or lack of uniformity, in the EU's services commitments. However, they only note the existence of restrictions and distinguish between severe and minor trade restrictions to a limited extent. The fact that with the Doha Round offers more EU Member States have a similar number of bounds, unbounds and partial commitments than in the original GATS commitments does not mean that the commitments provide for identical conditions towards third-country service suppliers. The actual content of the conditions would be very hard to index. As noted by Langhammer, because of the non-quantitative nature of trade restrictions in services, it is very difficult to assess how far the EU is from a customs union (common external

---

[85] Eschenbach & Hoekman (2006), at 421.
[86] Langhammer (2005).

policy) in services. The heterogeneity of both service sub-sectors and policy measures makes the quantification of services barriers virtually impossible.[87] Also the methodology introduced in this book only notes the existence or lack of NT, not the reason for it. To learn more of the types of differences existing between different Member States in their services commitments, a more qualitative study would be needed.

[87] Ibid., 313.

5

Application of GATS Art. V to Federal Entities

The previous chapter dealt with the importance of federalism in the efforts to liberalize trade externally. This chapter turns to a more scholarly question. It looks at federal entities' EIAs from the point of view of WTO law and asks how to assess them in light of Art. V GATS. The central proposal is that from a legal point of view sub-central measures can, in excessive amounts, be against GATS Art. V. That conclusion is considered necessary because the neglect of sub-central measures would seriously undermine the criterion of substantiality in the case of countries that have constitutionally divided powers in their internal regulation of service activities.

The chapter starts by examining those provisions of the GATS that specifically mention sub-central levels of government. Interestingly, such specific mentions are limited to Art. I and Art. XVI. However, considering that the agreement defines 'measures by Members' as 'measures taken by central, regional or local governments and authorities', it is hard to see how the regional and local levels of federal entities could escape the reach of the various GATS disciplines. The same proposition should apply to GATS Art. V that sets the rules for closer economic integration between individual Members. As Art. V aims to limit EIAs only to such agreements that provide for a substantial sectoral coverage and elimination of discrimination, it would make little sense to exclude measures taken by sub-central government of the participating countries.

I   The GATS and Sub-Central Levels of Government

The GATS applies to all measures taken by the WTO Members, including those of lower levels of government.[1] Under Art. I:3(a), 'measures by Members' means measures taken by:

(i) central, regional or local governments and authorities; and
(ii) non-governmental bodies in the exercise of powers delegated by central, regional or local governments or authorities.

The case law on services is limited but the central case of *Gambling* dealt with both federal and state measures that discriminated against foreign services suppliers. In *Gambling*, the AB emphasized that there must exist a 'nexus' between the responding Member and the 'measure', such that the 'measure' – whether an act or omission – must be 'attributable' to that Member.[2] The Panel in the *Gambling* case had concluded that certain state-level laws in the USA were against the US schedule of commitments under the GATS. The AB, on the contrary, reversed the Panel's finding that those state laws, namely, those of Louisiana, Massachusetts, South Dakota and Utah, were inconsistent with the USA's obligations under Art. XVI:1 and sub-paragraphs (a) and (c) of Art. XVI:2. However, the AB did not depart from the conclusion that the USA was responsible for measures applied by its states.

This is the standard position under customary international law. Under the principles of state responsibility, states are responsible for internationally wrongful acts that can be attributed to them.[3] A state's responsibility is engaged by conduct that is incompatible with its

---

[1] The term 'measure' itself is defined in Art. XXVIII(a) and means 'any measure by a Member, whether in the form of a law, regulation, rule, procedure, decision, administrative action, or any other form'. This includes a long, open list of regulatory instruments. As noted by Krajewski, any governmental action can be a 'measure' according to GATS, because the list extends to 'any other form'. Krajewski, M. (2003) *National Regulation and Trade Liberalization in Services: The Legal Impact of the General Agreement on Trade in Services (GATS) on National Regulatory Autonomy.* The Hague: Kluwer Law International, at 64.

[2] *United States – Measures Affecting the Cross-Border Supply of Gambling and Betting Services*, Report of the Appellate Body, WT/DS285/AB/R, circulated 7 April 2005, para. 121. See also the Panel report in *China-Publications*, para. 7.166, where the Panel concluded that 'measures' also included measures taken by the executive branch of the state as they could be attributed to the state. *China – Measures Affecting Trading Rights and Distribution Services for Certain Publications and Audiovisual Products*, WT/DS363/R, Report of the Panel, circulated 12 August 2009.

[3] See e.g. Brownlie, I. (1983) *System of the Law of Nations: State Responsibility*, Part I. Oxford, Clarendon Press.

international obligations, irrespective of the level of administration or government at which the conduct occurs. This is clearly stated in Art. 4 of the Draft Articles on State Responsibility.[4] Moreover, the Draft Articles provide that whether a state has committed an internationally wrongful act 'is not affected by the characterization of the same act as lawful by internal law' (Art. 3). The commentary to the Draft Articles notes that the principle of state responsibility stretching over the acts of organs of regional and local units has long been recognized. According to the commentary, the principle was strongly supported during the preparatory work for the 1930 Hague Conference. On that occasion, the participating Governments were expressly asked whether the state became responsible as a result of '[a]cts or omissions of bodies exercising public functions of a legislative or executive character (communes, provinces, etc.)'. All governments answered in the affirmative.[5]

Case law has confirmed that it does not matter for this purpose whether the territorial unit in question is a component unit of a federal state or a specific autonomous area. It appears equally irrelevant whether the internal law of the state in question gives the federal parliament power to compel the component unit to abide by the state's international obligations.[6] An especially enlightening example is the *LaGrand* case in which the International Court of Justice asserted the international responsibility of the USA for an act which was within the competence of the Governor of Arizona.[7]

---

[4] Draft Articles on Responsibility of States for Internationally Wrongful Acts, in Report of the International Law Commission on the Work of Its Fifty-Third Session, UN GAOR, 56th Sess., Supp. No. 10, at 43, UN Doc. A/56/10 (2001). Art. 4, para. 1, of the draft articles reads: 'The conduct of any State organ shall be considered an act of that State under international law, whether the organ exercises legislative, executive, judicial or any other functions, whatever position it holds in the organization of the State, and whatever its character as an organ of the central Government or of a territorial unit of the State'.

[5] Ibid., Commentary on Art. 4, p. 41.

[6] *Montijo* case (*US* v. *Colombia*) (1874), Moore, History and Digest, vol. II, p. 1440 and *Pellat* case, UNRIAA, vol. V (Sales No. 1952.V.3), p. 534, at p. 536 (1929). See Materials on the Responsibility of States for Internationally Wrongful Acts, United Nations Legislative Series, ST/LEG/SER B/25, New York 2012, pp. 34–5. As noted by Meyer, the state responsibility rules are bedrock principles of international law, confirmed by dozens of cases. For references to recent case law, see Meyer, T. (2017) Local Liability in International Economic Law. *North Carolina Law Review*, Vol. 95, 261–338, at 276–8.

[7] *LaGrand* (*Germany* v. *United States of America*), Order, Provisional Measures, 1999 I.C.J., para. 28. See also *LaGrand*, Judgment, I.C.J. Reports 2001, p. 466, at p. 495, para. 81. Similarly in *Avena and Other Mexican Nationals* (*Mex.* v. *US*), Judgment, 2004 I.C.J. Rep. 12 (Mar. 31).

States, especially federal states, vary widely in their structure and distribution or powers. In most cases, the constituent parts of a state have no separate international legal personality nor any treaty-making power. In certain cases, such as in the case of the Swiss Confederation, a constituent part of a state may be able to enter into international agreements on its own account.[8] The treaty party may agree to limit its recourse to the constituent part in the event of a breach. It is also possible that a treaty includes a federal clause and limits the state's responsibility for acts taken on lower levels of government.[9] These situations are, however, exceptions to the general principle and limited to the relations between the parties to the relevant treaties.[10]

Meyer differentiates between three different types of rules for the liability of lower levels of government in international economic agreements: (1) immunity, under which neither the sub-national nor national governments are answerable under international law for the actions of a sub-national government; (2) vicarious liability, under which nations are liable for the actions of their sub-national units even if they do not control them as a matter of domestic law; and (3) direct liability, under which a claimant's case is brought directly against the offending sub-national government.[11] Vicarious liability is still the default rule under the international law of state responsibility. However, as noted by Meyer, immunity is on the rise. It has been adopted under an increasing number of economic treaties, such as the TPP's investment and services chapters.[12] As the following chapter shows, immunity is common in the treaty practice of both Canada and USA. Direct liability, on the other hand, is rare but exists in certain investment agreements.[13] The economic agreements of the EU and its Member States provide another, although a more

---

[8] See articles 56, paragraph 3, and 172, paragraph 3, of the Constitution of the Swiss Confederation of 18 April 1999.

[9] See e.g. Art. 34 of the Convention for the Protection of the World Cultural and Natural Heritage.

[10] Materials on the Responsibility of States for Internationally Wrongful Acts, United Nations Legislative Series, ST/LEG/SER B/25, New York 2012, pp. 34–5.

[11] Meyer (2017), at 272–87. Meyer advocates direct liability as he considers that it best achieves the twin goals of fostering local governance and international cooperation.

[12] Ibid., 262.

[13] Under The International Convention on the Settlement of Investment Disputes ('ICSID Convention') nations have the possibility to render their local governments liable to direct suit, but, as noted by Meyer, few nations have used this opportunity. See Convention on the Settlement of Investment Disputes between States and Nationals of Other States, Art. 25(1) and Art. 25(3), opened for signature 18 March 1965, 17 U.S.T. 1270, 575 U.NT.S. 159 and Meyer (2017), at 269.

complicated version, of direct liability. In the context of the WTO Dispute Settlement System, the EU has been held responsible in all disputes brought against an EU Member State. The EU has also been willing to assume this responsibility.[14] However, there are other international economic agreements in which the institutional design does not necessarily foster the EU participation's and/or responsibility. This is the case specifically with international investment agreements where a significant number of treaties remain bilateral between a specific EU Member State and a third country.[15]

In accordance with the general state responsibility rule, the vicarious liability rule, WTO Members are responsible for breaches of the WTO agreements applied by actors whose acts or omissions can be attributed to the state. According to GATS Art. I:3, this covers lower levels of government, as well as non-governmental bodies in the exercise of powers delegated by public authorities. Interestingly, however, GATS gives certain additional guidance on this question. Art. I:3 lit. a, sentence 2 includes the following provision:

> In fulfilling its obligations and commitments under the Agreement, each Member shall take such reasonable measures as may be available to it to ensure their observance by regional and local governments and authorities and non-governmental bodies within its territory.

There would appear to be at least two possible ways to interpret the provision. The first interpretation is strict and the other more lenient. The strict interpretation is adopted by Zacharias and Krajewski, according

---

[14] Larik and Delgado Casteleiro note that the interrelation of the Union and its Member States in the WTO dispute settlement system highlights not only the special features of the EU, but also of its Member States as 'strange subjects' of international law. Rather than defending themselves, the Member States of the EU remain passive and let themselves be defended by the Union. This in turn is accepted by the other WTO Members. See Delgado Casteleiro, A. & Larik, J. (2013) The 'Odd Couple': The Responsibility of the EU at the WTO, in Evans, M. & Koutrakos, P. (eds.), *The International Responsibility of the European Union*. Oxford: Hart Publishing, 233–255.

[15] See Delgado Casteleiro, A. (2016), *The International Responsibility of the European Union, From Competence to Normative Control*. Cambridge: Cambridge University Press, at 195–223. In the new EU investment treaties, novel techniques are being implemented to share the responsibility. CETA, which includes an investment protection agreement between Canada and the EU and its Member States, includes a clause according to which the investor must 'deliver to the European Union a notice requesting a determination of the respondent'. In the event that the EU does not make a determination within fifty days, the EU is the default respondent unless the measures identified in the notice are exclusively measures of a specific Member State. See Article 8.21 of CETA.

to whom Art. I:3 reflects general international practice and makes it clear that the GATS applies to all measures taken by any entity of a WTO Member. They draw the parallel to state responsibility under customary international law and argue that similarly under the GATS states have the obligation to ensure the compliance of sub-central and non-governmental entities.[16]

However, another possible interpretation is more lenient. According to that interpretation one could argue that the GATS actually only demands a certain effort from the Members to ensure the observance of the obligations and commitments taken by them by their regional and local governments and authorities. The extent of the effort would be limited to 'reasonable measures as may be available' to the Member. It could then be argued that if no such reasonable measures were available, the breach of any obligations and commitments by local authorities would go unpunished. Munin takes this position by concluding that Members are not expected to take every possible step to prevent lower government levels from infringing GATS disciplines. In her opinion, it means that they are not expected to take measures which would involve an exaggerated extra-administrative effort or exceptional costs.[17]

It is hard to say what exactly are the reasonable measures that the Members can be expected to take and when would it be too much to ask them to stop infringements of WTO law by their regional authorities. The vagueness of the more lenient interpretation makes one ask whether such a departure from the general international law was the purpose of the GATS drafters. Moreover, there is another way to read the sentence about 'reasonable measures'. That is to read it as a positive obligation. According to this interpretation, the purpose is rather to underline the Members' obligation to take any reasonable measures that they possibly can in order to make sure that their regional and local governments and authorities observe the GATS law. The provision would thus aim at preventing a departure from the obligations in the first place. However, failing to take measures to ensure the observance of the rules would not release the Member of its responsibility. In the case of a dispute, the active

---

[16] Zacharias, D. (2008), at 57, 'Article I GATS', in Wolfrum, R., Stoll, P.-T. & Feinäugle, C. (eds.), *WTO – Trade in Services*. Leiden; Boston: Martinus Nijhoff Publishers and Krajewski (2003), at 64.

[17] Munin, N. (2010) *Legal Guide to GATS*. Alphen aan den Rijn: Kluwer Law International, at 67.

attempt of the central government to solve the issue could, nevertheless, be possibly considered a mitigating factor.

This position would appear reinforced by Art. 22:9 of the WTO Dispute Settlement Understanding ('DSU'). The provision reads:

> The dispute settlement provisions of the covered agreements may be invoked in respect of measures affecting their observance taken by regional or local governments or authorities within the territory of a Member. When the DSB has ruled that a provision of a covered agreement has not been observed, the responsible Member shall take such reasonable measures as may be available to it to ensure its observance. The provisions of the covered agreements and this Understanding relating to compensation and suspension of concessions or other obligations apply in cases where it has not been possible to secure such observance.[18]

Members must therefore ensure the observance of the covered agreements by sub-central government by taking such 'reasonable measures' that may be available to them. The language is very similar to Art. I GATS. But the DSU also specifies that where it has not been possible to secure such observance by regional and local governments, other Members have the right to apply the WTO rules regarding the compensation and suspension of concessions. Munin notes the same provision and considers that it balances the standard of 'reasonable measures' required from the Members under GATS Art. I:3.[19]

Another parallel can be drawn to the WTO's Technical Barriers to Trade Agreement ('TBT Agreement'). The TBT Agreement confirms not only that Members are responsible for the actions of their local governments; it also provides that '[m]embers shall formulate and implement positive measures and mechanisms in support of the observance of the provisions of Article 2 by other than central government bodies'.[20] The TBT Agreement thus not only establishes the Members' responsibility for the actions of their local governments, but also sets an obligation for the Members to control and support them in their observance of the TBT

---

[18] The paragraph includes a footnote (17) stating that 'Where the provisions of any covered agreement concerning measures taken by regional or local governments or authorities within the territory of a Member contain provisions different from the provisions of this paragraph, the provisions of such covered agreement shall prevail'.

[19] Munin (2010), at 67.

[20] Agreement on Technical Barriers to Trade art. 3.5, Apr. 15, 1994, Marrakesh Agreement Establishing the World Trade Organization, Annex 1A (providing with respect to local governments that '[m]embers are fully responsible under this Agreement for the observance of all provisions of Article 2[,]' which provides the main substantive rules of the TBT Agreement). See Meyer (2017), at 268.

disciplines. The language is different to GATS Art. I:3 lit. a, but the purpose is the same: to ensure that local governments observe the relevant WTO disciplines.[21] It may be that in the subject matters covered by the TBT Agreement many of the local measures are technical, rather than regulatory, in nature and can be more easily influenced by the central government. In the area of services regulation, on the other hand, the central government may simply lack the legal means to intervene. In any case, also in the area of services, the central government must take such *reasonable measures* as may be available to it to ensure the observance of the GATS by lower levels of the government.

The original parallel to the obligation to take 'reasonable measures' can be found in Art. XXIV:12 GATT. The Understanding on the Interpretation of Article XXIV states (para. 13) that 'Each Member is fully responsible for the observance of all provisions of the GATT 1994, and shall take such reasonable measures as may be available to it to ensure such observance by regional and local governments and authorities within its territory'. Moreover, where the DSB has ruled that a provision of the GATT has not been observed, 'the responsible Member shall take such reasonable measures as may be available to it to ensure its observance' (para. 14). Finally, paragraph 14 of the Understanding ends by stating that 'the provisions relating to compensation and suspension of concessions or other obligations apply in cases where it has not been possible to secure such observance'.

There is some case law relating to Art. XXIV:12 GATT. In *Canada–Gold Coins*[22], Canada suggested that each Member would be able to decide for itself what 'reasonable measures' meant. The Panel, however, rejected this proposal and noted that the only indication of the possible substantive content of the standard could be derived from the Interpretative Note to Art. III, which states that the application of Art. III:1 to internal taxes imposed by local governments and authorities within the territory of a contracting party is subject to the provisions of Art. XXIV:12 GATT. The interpretative note uses the example of taxation measures applied by local government and notes that the term 'reasonable measures' would permit a contracting party to eliminate inconsistent

---

[21] A similar provision can be found in Art. 105 of NAFTA. It provides that '[t]he Parties shall ensure that all necessary measures are taken in order to give effect to the provisions of this Agreement, including their observance, except as otherwise provided in this Agreement, by state and provincial governments'. See Meyer (2017), at 274.

[22] *Canada – Measures Affecting the Sale of Gold Coins*, Report of the Panel, L/5863, 17 September 1985, GATT Panel Report, unadopted.

taxation applied by a local government gradually over a transition period, if abrupt action would create serious administrative and financial difficulties.[23] In this case, the report of which was unadopted, the Panel gave some leeway to federal states and determined that Art. XXIV:12 limits the obligation of federal governments to secure the observance of their obligations by local governments. The provision would thus give a certain special right to federal states without giving an offsetting right to unitary states in order to meet the constitutional difficulties faced by federal states in the application of their GATT obligations on all levels of government.[24]

It is also possible to argue that the purpose of the GATT, as well as later the GATS, negotiators was to include a type of a 'federal clause' in the agreements.[25] It would give a certain leeway to federal states to default when the reason for the default is in the federal structure of the country. The loose wording of the 'reasonable measures' both in GATT Art. XXIV:12 and GATS Art. V:1 can be read as in support of such an interpretation. Also, when compared to the NAFTA Art. 105, the GATT and GATS clauses can be seen to be more lenient.

Jackson and Hayes have identified that the language of Art. XXIV:12 descended directly from the language included in the draft ITO Charter of 1948. The potential risks relating to the application of sub-central measures were foreseen very early on. Hayes has reported that originally the federal compliance clause was connected to the discipline on national treatment but was later inserted in the miscellaneous article XXIV presumably in view of the fact that the issue of federal compliance with the proposed multilateral trade agreement affected not only the national treatment provision but also other substantive provisions of the then proposed GATT.[26] From very early on, there were conflicting

---

[23] See a useful account of the GATT practice in Munin (2010), at 68–9.

[24] *Canada – Measures Affecting the Sale of Gold Coins*, paras. 59–63.

[25] Some states include so-called federal clauses when signing international treaties to inform other parties of possible difficulties that they may encounter in implementation because of the need to secure the cooperation of their sub-federal levels of government. For example, Canada has introduced such a clause in some of the treaties that it has signed to limit its liability under the treaty. See Dupras, D., NAFTA: Implementation and Participation of the Provinces, January 1993, Law and Government Division, Government of Canada. Available at: http://publications.gc.ca/Collection-R/LoPBdP/BP/bp324-e.htm (last accessed on 15 January 2019).

[26] See Jackson, J. H. (1967) The General Agreement on Tariffs and Trade in United States Domestic Law. *Mich L Rev*, 66(2), 249, at 304–6 and Hayes, E. (2004) Changing Notions of Sovereignty and Federalism in the International Economic System: A Reassessment of

interpretations as to what extent the 'reasonable measures' under Art. XXIV:12 were intended to be compelling or mandatory to the contracting parties.[27]

In any case, in accordance with both the DSU and the Understanding on the Interpretation of Article XXIV, other Members remain entitled to ask for compensation and suspend concessions or other obligations where it has not been possible to secure observance of the rules by local government. Moreover, the GATT case law makes clear that lower levels of government are formally bound by the same obligations as the central government, and to the same degree. This was the case, for example, in *United States–Malt Beverages*, where the Panel held the US federal government responsible for certain measures that were taken by certain US states. The Panel applied to the states the same standard as the one that it applied to the central government.[28]

No matter which interpretation of the GATS Art.I:3 lit. a one chooses, giving a wide scope of freedom to local governments would appear unsustainable. It would mean that Members with constitutionally divided powers over services regulation would have lesser obligations than Members with more centralized regulatory powers. Typically, this would mean that federations could commit to a significantly lesser degree than unitary states as federal states could simply argue that they cannot force any regional or local governments to comply, at least if those regions or communities had autonomy over the issues at stake. It is unlikely that unitary states would have agreed to such a wide carve-out. Moreover, as also pointed out by Zacharias and Krajewski, it would go against the traditional position adopted under international law.[29]

Finally, it is worth noting that the language of 'reasonable measures' in GATS Art. I:3 applies also to non-governmental bodies within the Member's territory. According to Art. I:3(a)(ii) 'measures by Members' means also measures taken by non-governmental bodies

---

WTO Regulation of Federal States and the Regional and Local Governments within Their Territories. *Nw J Intl L & Bus*, 25(1), 1, at 20.

[27] For more references and a more detailed account of the historical background of the federal compliance clause, see Omiunu, O. (2017) The Evolving Role of Sub-National Actors in the Mechanisms for International Trade Interactions: A Comparative Analysis of Belgium and Canada. *Global Journal of Comparative Law*, 6(2), 105–37.

[28] *United States – Malt Beverages*, DS23/R, 16 March 1992, GATT Panel Report. Similarly in the GATT 1947 case *Canada – Alcoholic Drinks*, DS17/R – 39S/27, 18 February 1992, GATT Panel Report. See also Munin (2010), at 68–9.

[29] Zacharias (2008), at 57 and Krajewski. (2003), at 64.

in the exercise of powers delegated by central, regional or local governments or authorities. If the lenient interpretation was adopted, it would mean that a breach of GATS commitments or obligations could go unpunished also when undertaken by a non-governmental body, as long as the Member concerned had taken 'reasonable measures' to avoid that. That would be a very strange interpretation considering that measures taken by non-governmental bodies must in accordance with Art. I:3(a)(ii) be delegated to them. Central governments can always take back any delegated powers, and should do so if their delegation leads to illegalities. A failure in this regard must lead to state responsibility. Such responsibility can hardly be subject to any 'reasonable measures' as may be available to the central government. Therefore, the requirement for the Member to take 'such reasonable measures as may be available to it' with regard to any powers delegated to non-governmental bodies is likely to mean that the central government has an active obligation to try to stop any breach undertaken by such entities. But it should not be interpreted as releasing the central government from its responsibility as to the breach. The same can be considered to apply to any regional or local governments and authorities, even if in that case the powers cannot typically be withdrawn. However, an active obligation to ensure compliance should apply. WTO Members must do their best in making sure that all levels of government uphold the obligations and commitments under WTO law, and specifically under the GATS. This is of important practical relevance as powers in the area of services regulation are typically divided across central and local authorities. Other Members thus have an interest in asking for active observance from all national authorities, and the central government should actively participate in this regard. Any failures should, however, be attributed to the state.

Another mention of internal divisions of WTO Members is included in GATS Art. XVI. The second paragraph defines the measures which a Member 'shall not maintain or adopt either on the basis of a regional subdivision or on the basis of its entire territory, unless otherwise specified in its Schedule'. As noted by Delimatsis and Molinuevo, this reference to the coverage of Art. XVI may seem superfluous since Art. I:3 lit. a already makes it clear that the GATS covers measures taken by all levels of government. However, in the context of Art. XVI the purpose seems to be to highlight that a Member has the right to specify market access limitations in its schedule and thus apply different conditions in different parts of its territory. For instance, the number of banks may be limited in a specific sub-federal region, whereas other regions may apply different conditions.[30]

As has been noted by Krajewski, the ordinary meaning of the term 'regional subdivision' would suggest that it is a unit which is smaller than the entire territory of a country but which is also larger than any particular local entity. According to Krajewski, regional subdivisions could be the states or provinces in a federal system or other larger administrative units in a centralized state. Since the term 'subdivision' implies that the entire territory of a country can be divided into regional subdivisions, a measure applying only to a particular, limited area or distinct units of the country (such as national parks or river basis) should not be covered.[31] This position is a sensible one. It draws a reasonable balance between making sure that all constituent parts of the state are covered, while not asking the WTO Members to include all possible limitations applied in very limited or distinct units of the country. However, where exactly to draw the limit of a unit that would be outside the application of Art. XVI:2 remains unclear.

II   What Is Required from Federal Entities under Art. V GATS?

As has been established in Part I of the book, the essence of Art. V is the requirement of elimination of discrimination. What does this entail when the EIA is entered into by a federal entity? The key question in this regard is whether Art. V covers measures taken on sub-central levels or on the central level only. We consider the first option to be correct. The required level of non-discrimination should be provided across all levels of government considering that the GATS covers measures taken by regional and local governments and authorities in addition to the measures taken by central government and authorities.

In the previous section it was noted that under GATS Art. I:3 each Member is expected to take reasonable measures to ensure that its obligations are observed by regional and local governments. This could mean that in certain situations a Member could escape from enforcing its obligations towards regional or local authorities if there were no reasonable measures available to ensure their respect on the regional or local

---

[30] Delimatsis, P. & Molinuevo, M. (2008) Article XVI GATS – Market Access, in Wolfrum, R., Stoll, P.-T. & Feinäugle, C. (eds.), WTO – Trade in Services. Leiden; Boston: Martinus Nijhoff Publishers, 267–395, at 375.

[31] Krajewski (2003), at 85.

level (even though the state would still be subject to countermeasures as authorized by Art. 22:9 DSU). How does this condition translate to the requirements set out by Art. V?

Art. V does not say anything about the level of government on which the preferential liberalization of services needs to take place. It mentions only 'between or among the parties', meaning two or several contracting parties. Nor does it include any reference to a 'regional subdivision'. It is therefore unclear to what extent sub-central measures are covered by the said provision. When putting forward their schedules under the GATS, Members choose the level of government on which they desire to liberalize and how much they desire to liberalize. They are free to exclude regional and local measures, as long as the exclusions are mentioned in their schedules. Art. V GATS, however, requires the elimination of *substantially all discrimination* between the parties with no exceptions made depending on the constitutional structure of the country concerned. Considering that in many countries, services activities are to a large extent regulated on sub-central levels, the application of the Art. V requirements only to the central government could potentially leave a significant amount of non-discrimination uncounted for. Some states and regions in federal countries are big economies on their own. For example, California's economy has surpassed that of the United Kingdom to become the world's fifth largest economy.[32] Therefore, to argue that sub-central measures would not be covered by Art. V would seem contradictory. There is also no reason to consider that Art. V would depart from the general definition of a 'measure' under Art. I (the agreement covering measures on any level of the government). Therefore, similarly to the scheduling of commitments under the GATS, parties to EIAs need to carve out any regional or local measures that they do not want to bind. However, when they do that, they should respect the requirement of Art. V, which is to eliminate substantially all discrimination. This, together with the requirement of substantial sectoral coverage, sets limits to the amount of sub-central measures that can be excluded. Furthermore, even if sub-central measures were not excluded per se, all applicable reservations on all levels of government should be listed as it is otherwise impossible to verify to what extent the elimination of discrimination applies.

---

[32] 'California now has the world's fifth largest economy', 4 May 2018, *CBS News*, www.cbsnews.com/news/california-now-has-the-worlds-5th-largest-economy/ (last accessed on 15 December 2018).

As was already noted above, federal states may have constitutional difficulties in enforcing international legal obligations against their own sub-federal authorities. Another difficulty may arise earlier on when the relevant treaty is being negotiated. If the powers for regulating certain service sectors are divided between different levels of government, ideally all the relevant actors commit to the liberalization undertaken with third countries. The modalities for the inclusion of sub-central actors in international treaty negotiations depends on each state. In some states such modalities, such as consultations or active participation, may be formal and necessitated by law, whereas in others they may be more ad hoc.

In a 2014 inquiry of the UK's House of Lords on the Transatlantic Trade and Investment Partnership (TTIP), a question was posed to a representative of the European Commission concerning the already concluded trade negotiations with Canada.[33] Lord Lamont of Lerwick wanted to know how the EU Member States and the Canadian provinces participated in the negotiations. To answer, Mauro Petriccione, Director of the European Commission, explained the EU system that is enshrined in the EU Treaties. The EU has decades of experience in running its external trade negotiations through the Trade Policy Committee and the Council at a political level. Therefore, for the EU, the CETA negotiations were run, as far as the EU Member States were concerned, like every other trade negotiation.[34] On the Canadian side,

[33] Unrevised transcript of evidence taken before The Select Committee on the European Union, External Affairs (Sub-Committee C), Inquiry on Transatlantic Trade and Investment Partnership, Evidence Session No. 17, Questions 186–197, 23 January 2014. Witness: Mauro Petriccione, Director, Asia and Latin America, DG Trade, European Commission. The transcript is available at www.parliament.uk/documents/lords-committees/eu-sub-com-c/TTIP/ucEUC230114ev17.pdf (last accessed on 15 December 2018).

[34] It should be pointed out that at a later stage the multi-level governance of the EU posed significant difficulties for the signing of the agreement by the EU. First, to accommodate certain Member States' grievances, the European Commission changed is course and decided that the agreement should be concluded not by the EU alone, but by the twenty-eight Member States as well (as a 'mixed agreement'). Later, in October 2016, the Council wished to adopt a decision authorizing the signing and provisional application of the EU–Canada agreement. However, the Belgian region of Wallonia – a region with a population of three million – refused to authorize the Belgian federal authorities to authorize the signing and provisional application of the agreement. After last-minute negotiations between the Walloon and Belgian federal authorities, as well as the European Commission and Canada's international trade minister, an agreement was reached. On 'EU only' and 'mixed agreements' especially in the context of the 'Wallonian saga', see Kleimann, D. & Kübek, G. (2016) *The Signing, Provisional Application, and Conclusion of Trade and Investment Agreements in the EU: The Case of CETA and Opinion 2/15*, EUI Working Paper RSCAS 2016/58.

however, the negotiations were carried out in a much more innovative manner. Mr Petriccione described the Canadian approach in the following manner:

> A basic political decision was taken by the Canadian federal Government that they would involve the provincial Governments directly this time. Traditionally, the Canadian federal Government negotiate the areas of federal competence directly and consult the provinces privately on the areas of their competence. They often refuse to negotiate international agreements in those areas. In this case, we made the point that some of the areas of provincial competence would be indispensable for a balanced agreement, and the EU would not be interested in an agreement that did not cover those areas. So the Canadians took the decision to consult the provinces and, this time, involve them directly in the negotiating process. In a way, they had to invent mechanisms for consultation similar to those that we have in the treaty for consulting member states. It has been a bit of a messy process but, in the end, it was very effective. We had a reasonably solid assurance that the provinces will implement the outcome in full for the areas of their competence.[35]

The inclusion of the Canadian provinces in the CETA negotiations appears to have been a type of ad hoc mechanism to allow for direct sub-federal involvement. A more established framework had developed over the decades to facilitate trade dialogue between the Canadian federal and provincial officials, but the CETA negotiations marked the first time when the representatives of the Canadian provinces were part of the Canadian official delegation. The direct participation made it possible to put forward pan-Canadian positions to the EU negotiators.[36]

The end result was successful, even though only time will tell how well the treaty will be put in practice by the Canadian provinces and territories. However, already the inclusion of sub-federal reservations can be considered a success as such, as it provides for an unprecedented

---

[35] Mauro Petriccione's answer to the question of Lord Lamont of Lerwick. Unrevised transcript of evidence taken before The Select Committee on the European Union, External Affairs (Sub-Committee C), Inquiry on Transatlantic Trade and Investment Partnership, Evidence Session No. 17, Questions 186–197, 23 January 2014.

[36] Walker J., Negotiation of Trade Agreements in Federal Countries, SPICe Briefing, The Scottish Parliament, 17 November 2017. Available at https://digitalpublications.parlia ment.scot/ResearchBriefings/Report/2017/11/17/Negotiation-of-Trade-Agreements-in-Federal-Countries# (last accessed on 15 December 2018). The paper provides a useful account of the provincial influence over the CETA negotiations and gives an overview of the negotiation of trade agreements in the federal countries of Canada, Belgium, Germany and the USA. See also the bibliography for a variety of references dealing with the role of sub-central authorities in international trade negotiations.

transparency in the Canadian EIAs. The innovative inclusion of Canadian provincial officials in Canada's negotiation team will hopefully not remain a one-time event.[37] The model is worth exporting too. A similar practice in other federal states could pave the way for deeper and more meaningful services liberalization. Both constitutional and practical limitations may of course exist. Kukucha has evaluated the impact of sub-federal governments in the Canadian and American foreign trade policy. He notes that the Canadian constitutional realities and institutional mechanisms allow for a greater sub-federal involvement than in the USA where state and regional interests are left to one committee of the United States Trade Representative (USTR) and to the ability of federal negotiators to correctly forecast sub-federal priorities.[38] However, there are unlikely to be too many barriers (legal ones at least) to the formation of negotiation teams across different levels of government. Moreover, the inclusion of sub-federal reservations in a state's services schedule should not be a problem as such reservations do not divert from the division of powers in that specific state but only describe what the applicable rules and regulations are. The inclusion of the sub-central levels of government in trade negotiations could also encourage liberalization, but a mere transparency increase over local regulations would already be valuable as such.

The language of GATS Art. I:3 does not refer only to federal states but it should be applied to any state with some type of division of powers between different levels of government. It should also be considered to apply to a supranational system, such as the EU. The reality is that the way in which powers between different levels of government are divided is different in almost any federal state or entity. This necessarily raises questions on how the WTO obligations should be applied and enforced

---

[37] Broschek and Goff note that the exceptional level of provincial participation in the CETA negotiations has not been replicated in subsequent negotiations. Teams from the larger Canadian provinces were on site at some talks for the TPP agreement, getting briefed by their federal colleagues. Similarly, the larger provinces sent teams to Washington, DC, to meet with their federal colleagues during the NAFTA renegotiations. However, unlike in CETA, there was no direct participation of the provinces. See Broschek, J. & Goff, P. (2018) Federalism and International Trade Policy: The Canadian Provinces in Comparative Perspective. IRPP Insight, No. 23 (Institute for Research on Public Policy, Montreal). See also Omiunu (2017)(who compares the role and participation of sub-national actors in international trade negotiations in Canada and Belgium).

[38] Kukucha, C. J. (2015) Federalism Matters: Evaluating the Impact of Sub-Federal Governments in Canadian and American Foreign Trade Policy. *Canadian Foreign Policy Journal*, 21(3), 224–37.

in each case. As argued by Meyer, these questions should no longer be ignored but international dispute resolution and the law of state responsibility need to evolve to take the increasing role of lower levels of government into account.[39]

The EU is probably the most interesting WTO Member in this regard. As the empirical studies of this book show, the EU's treaty practice in its EIAs shows that it acts similarly to a federation.[40] The EU's commitments are described on the level of the Union, while separate carve-outs are given for individual Member States. Furthermore, in the EU the issue of regional subdivision is relevant on two different levels. The first level is the individual Member States (the state/central level) and the second level is the regional and local governments in the Member States (the sub-national level). The second level consists of the potentially discriminatory regulations that are in force on the sub-national levels of individual Member States. But as the empirical study done for the purposes of the book discovered, there are only a few examples of such occasions in the reviewed schedules of the EU's EIAs. Such local measures have therefore not been taken into account in the study's scoring.[41] Similarly to the EU's EIAs, some appearances of local measures can also be found in the EU's

---

[39] Meyer (2017), 337.

[40] The division of liability for breaches of international law by EU Member States is, however, different to federal states. Whether a claim should be brought against the EU or a Member State directly depends on the allocation of competencies between the EU and its Member States. In WTO cases, panels and the AB have attributed Member States' action to the Union. See Hoffmeister, F. (2010) Litigating against the European Union and Its Member States – Who Responds under the ILC's Draft Articles on International Responsibility of International Organizations? *The European Journal of International Law*, 21, 723–47. See also, and partly differently, Marín Durán who notes that Member States enjoy a certain level of national discretion in some issues that come under the WTO law agreements, for example in trade defence measures, customs administration, internal taxation and consumer protection. She puts forward a specific competence/remedy model for the Member States' liability for breaches of EU law. She does not deal with services regulation but it could be proposed that also there liability could in certain cases fall upon individual Member States instead of the Union (where the issue at stake is not internally harmonized within the EU). See Marín Durán, G. (2017) Untangling the International Responsibility of the European Union and Its Member States in the World Trade Organization Post-Lisbon: A Competence/Remedy Model. *European Journal of International Law*, 28(3), 697–729. For a comprehensive treatment of the EU's international responsibility, in WTO dispute settlement, investment disputes and in certain other areas of international law, see Delgado Casteleiro, A. (2016).

[41] One of the few examples are the Åland Islands of Finland. The archipelago of Åland is a region of Finland, but compared to the other regions, it enjoys a high degree of home rule and some of Finland's commitments do not include Åland.

consolidated GATS schedule. For example, in the horizontal commit-ments on real estate purchases, Germany has specified that a 'purchase of real estate by foreigners in the Länder Berlin, Schleswig-Holstein and Saarland may be subject to authorization'. Another federal state, Austria, has specified that 'the acquisition, purchase as well as rent or lease of real estate by foreign natural persons and juridical persons requires an authorization by the competent regional authorities (Länder)'.[42] However, the amount of such regional or local measures is very limited also across the EU's GATS commitments. There appears to be two alternative ways to interpret this. The first possibility is that the lower levels of government in the EU Member States do not exercise policies that are more services trade-restrictive than the central govern-ment's policies and do not therefore significantly divert from the com-mitments given by the state as a whole. The second possibility is that the general liberalization level under both the GATS and the EU's EIAs is still so low that there has not been a need to specify all discriminatory local measures as they have not been more restrictive than the overall level of liberalization committed to across the Member State's territory.

The EU's schedule in CETA would appear to offer some support to the second interpretation. The CETA Annexes specify to which level of government each reservation applies to. The EU's annex includes first those reservations that are applied across the Union. After that, national lists of reservations follow. In the case of Germany, its national list of reservations includes a much higher number of sub-federal measures than what is visible in its GATS commitments. CETA has thus revealed the sub-federal measures that at the time of GATS were hiding under the surface. In addition to a higher liberalization level in CETA over the GATS, the negative scheduling technique used in CETA is likely to have a big role to play. In negative scheduling, all reservations must be specifi-cally mentioned. Instead of a tip of the iceberg, which was visible under the GATS, we are therefore seeing all sub-federal regulations that limit trade in services.[43] In the case of Austria and Belgium, the number of

---

[42] EU's Draft consolidated GATS Schedule, S/C/W/273, 9 October 2006.
[43] A certain comparison can be made to behind-the-border issues in trade in goods where nominal tariffs are only a small part of the barriers that face goods when they cross borders. Often a more significant barrier is formed by the various technical (regulatory) barriers to trade. They are the iceberg that is hiding under the surface. In the area of services, all trade barriers are regulatory in nature. However, if a federal country's service schedule reveals federal measures only, all sub-federal measures remain hidden below the surface. On the nature of trade protection in services, see Mavroidis, P. M & Hoekman, B. (2016) A Technical Barriers to Trade Agreement for Services?, in Roy, M. & Sauvé, P. (eds.),

national sub-federal reservations in CETA remains low. This may indicate that the sub-federal regions and Länder in those countries do not possess the necessary powers or have not practised their powers in a way that would pose problems to international service supply.[44]

The GATS schedules of USA and Canada, on the other hand, include a much higher degree of sub-federal measures than the federal states of the EU (Germany, Belgium and Austria). The following Tables 5.1 and 5.2 include two examples of the 1994 GATS commitments of Canada and the USA.[45] They describe the market access and national treatment limitations in two sub-sectors only but are good examples of the overall manner in which the two countries' commitments are described across their schedules. Limitations by states and provinces are abundant.

The high number of discrepancies between central and state/provincial measures in the Canadian and US GATS commitments shows that at least at the time of the two countries' certified GATS schedules (April 1994), there were significant differences in how services were regulated across their territories. Indeed, most of the service sectors in the US and Canadian schedules include exclusions and limitations applied by lower levels of government. The GATS commitments are, nevertheless, old and the situation may look different today.

The standard way to access information about WTO Members' current level of trade liberalization is to check their recent PTAs. Even if PTAs cover limited partners only, they give an idea of how far the Member has been willing, and able, to go in opening its market. However, in the case of the sub-federal measures applied by US states and Canadian provinces and territories such an analysis is impossible to carry out as the two countries have exempted all existing measures of

---

Research Handbook on Trade in Services. London: Edward Elgar. They do not deal with sub-central measures but identify elements of a possible TBT Agreement for the GATS.

[44] More research into the federal structure of those countries is needed to confirm the hypothesis. Also, it should be kept in mind that services regulation is often formulated in a manner that is not discriminatory (*de jure* at least). Therefore, even if services regulation may exist on various levels of government, it does not mean that such regulation is necessarily discriminatory and thus problematic from the point of view of international services agreements. On the other hand, the disciplines included in international services agreements (e.g. on domestic regulation) may limit the possibilities of both federal and sub-federal governments to exercise their powers.

[45] Canada, Schedule of Specific Commitments, GATS/SC/16, 15 April 1994, pp. 47–8 and The United States of America, Schedule of Specific Commitments, GATS/SC/90, 15 April 1994, pp. 60–1.

Table 5.1 *Canada's GATS commitments for wholesale trade services (Modes of supply: 1) Cross-border supply 2) Consumption abroad 3) Commercial presence 4) Presence of natural persons)*

Sector or sub-sector	Limitations on market access	Limitations on national treatment	Additional commitments

B*. Wholesale trade Services
Wholesale trade services (excepting agriculture and live animals in 6221; fisheries products in 62224; alcoholic beverages in 62226; musical scores, audio and video recordings in 62244; and books, magazines, newspapers, journals, periodicals and other printed matter in 62262; and 62251 of pharmaceutical and medical goods, and 62252, surgical and orthopaedic instruments and devices)
(CPC 622*)
	1) None, other than:
	   Sale of Amusement machines (Québec): Services must be supplied through a commercial presence
	   Marketing of Fish Products (Nova Scotia): Nova Scotia residents require ministerial approval to enter into agreements with non-residents
	   Sale of Motor Vehicles (Saskatchewan): Services must be supplied through a commercial presence Automobile Dealers and Salvage Dealers (Newfoundland): Services must be supplied through a commercial presence
	   Sale of Amusement Machines (Québec): Citizenship requirement in order to sell amusement machines
	2) None
	3) None, other than:
	   Fish Buyers (British Columbia): Mobile fish buyers licenses are not issued to foreigners
	4) Unbound except as indicated in the horizontal section
		1) None, other than:
		   Fish Buyers (Newfoundland): Non-residents must be registered and licensed in order to purchase unprocessed fish from primary producers and/or process fish
		2) None
		3) None
		4) Unbound except as indicated in the horizontal section	

Table 5.2 *The United States' GATS commitments for wholesale trade services (Modes of supply: 1) Cross-border supply 2) Consumption abroad 3) Commercial presence 4) Presence of natural persons)*

Sector or sub-sector	Limitations on market access	Limitations on national treatment	Additional commitments
7. FINANCIAL SERVICES			
A. INSURANCE			
Direct insurance [...]	1) None	1) None	
d) Services Auxiliary to Insurance:	2) None	2) Unbound	
i) Brokerage Services	3) Generally, brokerage firms can offer services in most states by obtaining licences as 'brokers' and in other states by obtaining licences to operate as 'agents'. Brokerage licences are not issued in: Florida, Iowa, Kentucky, Michigan, Minnesota, Mississippi, Oregon, Tennessee, Texas, Virginia, West Virginia, Wisconsin.	3) None	
		4) Brokerage licences are not issued to non-residents in: South Dakota, Wyoming. Brokerage licences are issued to non-residents for only certain lines of insurance in: Alabama (all except life, accident & health), Arkansas (property, casualty, surety & marine), Louisiana (property & casualty), New Mexico (property & casualty).	

Table 5.2 (*cont.*)

Sector or sub-sector	Limitations on market access	Limitations on national treatment	Additional commitments
	4) Unbound, except as indicated in the horizontal section. In addition, generally, brokerage firms can offer services in most states by obtaining licences as 'brokers' and in other states by obtaining licences to operate as 'agents'. Brokerage licences are not issued in: Florida, Iowa, Kentucky, Michigan, Minnesota, Mississippi, Oregon, Tennessee, Texas, Virginia, West Virginia, Wisconsin.	Higher licence fees for non-residents may be charged in: Alaska, Arizona, Arkansas, California, Georgia, Hawaii, Indiana, Kansas, Louisiana, Maine, Maryland, Massachusetts, Montana, Nebraska, Nevada, New Hampshire, New Jersey, New Mexico, North Carolina, North Dakota, Ohio, Oklahoma, Pennsylvania, Rhode Island, South Carolina, Utah, Vermont.	

sub-federal entities from the services schedules of their PTAs.[46] It is therefore not possible to review the level of discrimination applied across their territories. The only exception is the CETA. The agreement includes a significant number of reservations applied by Canadian provinces and territories. The sub-federal reservations are organized in a schedule that is separate from the schedule of federal reservations. The sub-federal schedule for Annex I – including the Canadian provincial and territorial reservations for existing measures – is over 200 pages long. The sub-federal schedule for Annex II – including the provincial and territorial reservations for future measures – is over eighty pages in length.[47] The respective schedules for the federal level are forty-nine and twenty-nine pages long.[48] Both schedules are clearly longer than Canada's schedule under the GATS. This does not mean that the CETA would be less liberalizing than the Canadian commitments at the time of the GATS; on the contrary, CETA goes further than what Canada committed to under the GATS. Because of the sub-federal coverage and new openings in certain service sectors across the country, it goes beyond Canada's previous EIAs as well.[49] The high number of reservations is due to the scheduling modality of CETA, which is based on a negative listing. The GATS commitments, on the other hand, are based on a positive listing. Under the GATS, the WTO Members liberalized only those service

[46] The existing levels of sub-central measures are 'grandfathered', meaning that sub-central levels of government can continue to apply all laws and regulations that were in force at the conclusion of the agreement, but they cannot adopt any new or more restrictive measures (unless such measures are allowed by the reservations made by the same state under Annex II).

[47] Comprehensive Economic and Trade Agreement (CETA) between Canada, of the one part, and the European Union and its Member States, of the other part, OJ L 11, 14.1.2017, p. 23–1079. The text and the annexes of CETA are available in a more readable format on a website by the European Commission: http://ec.europa.eu/trade/policy/in-focus/ceta/ceta-chapter-by-chapter/ (last accessed 1 December 2018).

[48] The federal reservations apply in all provinces and territories of Canada. It should be noted that the Canadian reservations (federal and regional level) include measures applying also to investment. Differently from the GATS, in CETA 'investment' covers also manufacturing activities and not just services activities.

[49] The EU claims that in services and investment CETA is the most far reaching agreement the EU has ever concluded. European Commission, 'CETA explained': http://ec.europa.eu/trade/policy/in-focus/ceta/ceta-explained/index_en.htm#service-markets, updated 21 September 2017 (last accessed on 1 December 2018). Moreover, the agreement provides 'unprecedented transparency' on existing measures, in particular at provincial level. Canada has also engaged in more far-going liberalization than in any of its previous services agreements. See European Commission, 'CETA – Summary of the final negotiation results': https://trade.ec.europa.eu/doclib/docs/2014/december/tradoc_152982.pdf, February 2016 (last accessed on 1 December 2018).

sectors that they specifically included in their schedules, and only to the extent that was described in their schedules. In negative listing, a country must specify every single reservation that it wants to keep (Annex I) or wants to have an option for introducing in the future (Annex II). This tends to lead to much more detailed schedules. At the same time, negatively listed agreements tend to be more liberalizing. Anything that is not mentioned, must be liberalized.[50]

In the case of Canada, the iceberg theory seems to hold ground. This is proved by Canada's lengthy CETA Annexes which include a higher number of reservations than what is visible in Canada's positively described GATS commitments (which already include a significant number of provincial measures). The deeper services commitments in CETA reveal all sub-central measures that are applied across the Canadian provinces and territories. In the case of the USA, on the other hand, the iceberg theory cannot be tested, for the moment at least. That would require a CETA-type mapping of measures applicable in all fifty US states. However, as explained, there is some indication of an increasing pressure towards the USA to engage in services liberalization also on lower levels of government. It is therefore possible that some type of a sub-federal iceberg will emerge and become visible in later US EIAs.

In the EU's EIAs, the progress made by individual Member States since the GATS can be analyzed since the reservations put forward by individual Member States are included in all EIAs concluded by the EU. As the results of our empirical analysis show, the EU's services commitments, to a large extent, continue to be determined individually by its Member States. Significant variations still exist among different Member States both in horizontal and sector-specific commitments. This is interesting considering that the EU has an exclusive competence in the area of trade and is otherwise functioning as a single operator in trade. However, as was explained in the previous chapter, the situation reflects the lack of a single services market within the EU. The level of harmonization of services rules inside the EU is still weak. From the point of view of GATS Art. V, what matters, however, is the attainment of the criteria of substantiality across the EU. Considering that the EU is a contracting party of the WTO and has exclusive external competence to conclude trade agreements also in the field of services, the level of liberalization of services should match the requirements of Art. V throughout all of its constituent territories. The methodology of the empirical analysis in this

---

[50] See more on differences between positive and negative listing in Chapter 9 of Part III.

the book has been designed to take account of the national differences. The liberalizations scores of the EU therefore reflect the number of Member States that have eliminated discrimination under each sector and sub-sector. This gives a more accurate picture of the EU's liberalization levels than a study that would focus on the EU level commitments only.

The EU's internal situation can be connected to the wider issue of how deep EIAs should be in order to escape claims of non-compliance. This book puts forward the question of how the exact coverage and level of non-discrimination should be assessed in a situation where commitments vary across different states or regions of the same contracting party and try to answer it with regard to a multi-level entity such as the EU (which does not have a fully harmonized commercial policy in the field of services). We suggest that in order to be in line with its international obligations, the EU (or any WTO Member with internally divided regulatory powers in services) should ensure that when signing EIAs, the commitments of all Member States (or, in the case of other WTO Members, all states/regions/other entities with regulatory powers in services) reach the GATS threshold of 'substantiality' in terms of sectoral coverage and elimination of discrimination.

The same applies to regional levels of government in federal states such as the USA and Canada. In order to be in line with their international obligations, all WTO Members with internally divided regulatory powers in services should ensure that when signing EIAs, the commitments of all sub-central entities with regulatory powers in services reach the GATS threshold of 'substantiality' in terms of sectoral coverage and elimination of discrimination. As the following chapter points out, this result has not been achieved in a number of EIAs signed by Canada and the USA. That is because both countries, up to the conclusion of CETA by Canada, have exempted all existing measures applied on sub-federal levels of government. The practice of providing immunity for sub-federal measures from liberalization means that large swaths of regulatory activity remain outside international economic law's disciplines. This way powerful regions in federal states are free to maintain discriminatory practices, whereas unitary states have to liberalize across their territory.[51] In federal states with significant powers delegated to lower levels of government this

---

[51] Meyer (2017), at 266–7. Meyer uses the example of the TPP (the originally negotiated draft agreement), under which California was free to continue its existing discriminatory practices while smaller economies such as Vietnam or New Zealand had to cease.

poses problems also in light of the GATS Art. V discipline. In the case of the EU, the same problem is present with regard to the measures applied on the level of the Member States. Even if no Member State's measures are entirely excluded or exempted from the EU's EIAs, such national measures affect the coverage of the EU's agreements. In some sectors such an affect is quite significant. Part IV of the book gives a detailed analysis on some of the EU's EIAs in this regard. The percentage value assigned to each service sector shows the number of Member States that have committed to national treatment but it also tells us about the internal diversion between the EU Member States. If one or two Member States have inserted limitations but most Member States have an identical commitment, the diversion is not significant. But if half of the Member States has a commitment and the other half does not, the diversion is at its peak.[52]

Before going to the study on the EU's EIAs, the last chapter of this part of the book gives an overview of the services schedules of CETA, NAFTA and the EIAs that the USA and Canada have concluded with South Korea. The purpose is to compare the scheduling practice of these federal entities and to understand what changes they have recently implemented with regard to the inclusion of sub-central entities. The commitments concerning lower levels of government are also contrasted with those that the same states undertook as part of the GATS.

---

[52] In that case, the score for the EU's commitment would be 0.5, that is 50 per cent (fourteen states having committed to NT and fourteen states not). The methodology is explained in detail in Part III of the book.

6

A Review of Federal Entities' Services Commitments under the GATS and Selected EIAs

The purpose of the present chapter is to analyze and compare the scheduling practice of the USA and Canada with regard to sub-central levels of government. It starts by looking into the said WTO Members' GATS commitments but then moves to selected EIAs. The chosen sample of agreements are the EIAs that both Members have concluded with South Korea.[1] The agreements with Korea are all recent and easily comparable as they have all been concluded with the same country. In addition, the services commitments of CETA (EU–Canada) and NAFTA (US–Canada–Mexico) are reviewed. At the end of the chapter, the results are presented in table format, in Tables 6.1 and 6.2. The purpose is not to draw conclusions on the agreements' compatibility with Art. V GATS but to shed more light on the scheduling practice of these three federal entities. A more comprehensive methodology to assess EIAs is presented in the following part of the book.

The chapter shows that there are crucial differences in the way that the USA and Canada engage in international services liberalization, as compared to the EU. First of all, almost all of their EIAs follow negative listing[2] and second, they do not list any limitations applied on the sub-

---

[1] Canada–Korea Free Trade Agreement, entry into force 1 January 2015, available at https://international.gc.ca/trade-commerce/trade-agreements-accords-commerciaux/agr-acc/korea-coree and The United State – Korea Free Trade Agreements, entry into force 15 March 2012, available at https://ustr.gov/trade-agreements/free-trade-agreements/korus-fta (both last accessed on 20 January 2019).

[2] The US–Jordan FTA (signed in 2000) follows a positive listing in its services schedules. However, the commitments appear to be copied from both states' GATS commitments of 1994. In the case of Jordan, its schedule includes some improvements to its GATS commitments. The sub-sectors, in which improvements occur, are marked in bold in its schedule. The FTA includes both parties' side letters on 'GATS Article 5'. The side letters confirm both parties' understanding that 'consistency with Article V of the GATS is the foundation of the commitments with regard to trade in services that both the United States

federal levels of government (CETA notwithstanding). All existing sub-federal measures are simply exempted, in trade language – 'grandfathered'.[3] Interestingly, the GATS schedules of both the USA and Canada include sub-federal measures. This may have to do with the fact that all WTO Members had to engage in a similar scheduling practice under the GATS, whereas in EIAs the partner countries agree among themselves if and how to include any sub-national limitations to the liberalization commitments. The GATS deliberately mentions measures taken by sub-central entities.[4] The exclusion of a Member's regional or local limitations from its schedule would thus go against the GATS. In their EIAs, however, the USA and Canada have had the practice to exempt any regional and local limitations to market access and national treatment commitments. This would have been harder or impossible to do under the GATS where the number of participating states was much higher and where especially unitary states (non-federations) were unlikely to accept the exclusion of regional governments in federal states.[5]

In contrast to their commitments under the GATS, limitations applied at the level of regional and local government are not specified in any EIAs of the USA and Canada (in the case of Canada, up until CETA).[6] Both the USA and Canada have in their EIAs decided not to list any existing non-

and Jordan have undertaken'. It is not clear what the statement is based on, especially considering that the limited improvements to the original GATS commitments appear one-sided. The agreement is available at https://ustr.gov/trade-agreements/free-trade-agreements/jordan-fta/final-text (last accessed on 20 January 2019).

[3] In general sense, a 'grandfather clause' is an exemption that allows an entity to continue with activities or operations that were approved before the implementation of new rules, regulations or laws. See Investopedia: www.investopedia.com/terms/g/grandfatherclause.asp (last accessed on 10 January 2019). On the use of the grandfathering clause, see e.g. Adlung, R. & Carzaniga, A. (2009) MFN Exemptions under the General Agreements on Trade in Services: Grandfathers Striving for Immortality. *Journal of International Economic Law*, 12(2), 357–92.

[4] See the previous Chapter on this question.

[5] There is extensive literature on the possibility of strong states to exert pressure on weaker or smaller states in bilateral trade negotiations and thus reach outcomes that are more favourable than what would be possible multilaterally. Reference can be made e.g. to Heydon, K. & Woolcock, S. (2009) *The Rise of Bilateralism: Comparing American, European and Asian Approaches to Preferential Trade Agreements*. Tokyo; New York; Paris: United Nations University Press. Notwithstanding possible negative effects of bilateralism/regionalism, meaningful service liberalization appears more likely to be achieved in smaller groups of countries than multilaterally. These questions are taken up in more detail in Part I of the book.

[6] In the case of the USA, the only exception is the US–Jordan EIA. However, the US commitments are copied from its GATS commitments and include the same sub-federal measures as its GATS schedule.

conforming measures (the so-called Annex I limitations) of their sub-federal entities (again, CETA notwithstanding).[7] Instead, they have included a blanket reservation which exempts all sub-federal measures. These two powerful federal states have thus managed to negotiate preferential agreements that allow them to forego any limitations to trade in services that appeared on the regional and local levels of government at the time of conclusion of the agreements.

This is noteworthy considering that EIAs should eliminate substantially all discrimination, as required by GATS Art. V. Moreover, the services chapters of the reviewed PTAs include a similar wording as GATS Art. I regarding the definition of covered measures. They include those taken by regional and local governments and authorities alike. Based on Art. V GATS and the coverage of the reviewed EIAs, one could thus expect the inclusion of sub-central measures, and maybe even expect them to go deeper than the respective GATS commitments. However, this is not the reality. Out of the reviewed agreements by the USA and Canada, only CETA by Canada engages in significant liberalization on the sub-central level. The USA has not included the sub-central level in any of its EIAs, not in the EIAs reviewed here nor in any other of its EIAs either. In its EIA with Korea, the USA has, for the first time, included an illustrative list of sub-central measures. However, the list is not legally binding.[8]

I Sub-Central Measures of the USA and Canada under the GATS

In the previous chapter it was concluded that based on a combined consideration of both Art. I and Art. XVI, it is clear that sub-central

---

[7] We checked this by going through all EIAs signed by the USA and Canada. The US EIAs are available on the website of the USTR: https://ustr.gov/trade-agreements/free-trade-agreements (last accessed on 15 January 2019). The USA has PTAs in force with fourteen countries. Thirteen of them include a services agreement. Sub-federal non-conforming measures are exempted through a blanket reservation included in Annex I of the agreements. The Canadian EIAs are available on the website of the Government of Canada: www.international.gc.ca/trade-commerce/trade-agreements-accords-commerciaux/agr-acc (last accessed on 15 January 2019). Canada has fourteen PTAs in force. Nine of them include an EIA. In some of the Canadian EIAs, existing non-conforming measures applied by Canadian sub-national governments are exempted already in the text of the agreement (see e.g. Art. 10.07 'Reservations' of the Canada–Panama FTA). In others, they are exempted through a separate clause in Annex I (e.g. Canada–Chile FTA, Canada's Annex I).

[8] The chapter reviews only a couple of PTAs but the author has reviewed also earlier PTAs of USA and Canada and found that they have very limited references to sub-central entities.

measures are covered by the GATS and need to be inscribed in the WTO Members' schedules of specific commitments when in breach of either Art. XVI or Art. XVII. The exclusion of a Member's regional or local limitations from its schedule would thus go against the GATS.

A look into the GATS commitments of the USA and Canada would appear to confirm this understanding. Both countries have included sub-central measures extensively. In its GATS schedule, the USA has specified measures across all levels of government – on federal, state and local levels. For legal services alone, the US schedule is twenty pages long because of differences in state-level regulation. Canada's GATS schedule also includes numerous mentions of the Canadian provinces and territories. They are usually named individually but on a couple of occasions they are referred to together as 'Federal and sub-central governments'.[9]

In comparison, the EU's GATS schedules also include commitments both for the entire EU as well as individual Member States. The second sub-central level of the EU consists of the regulations applied on the sub-national level of individual Member States. There are, however, only a few examples of limitations described on sub-national levels of the Member States in the reviewed schedules of the EU's GATS, as well as EIA, commitments.[10]

WTO Members' GATS commitments remain generally shallow. As there are many limitations and sectors that remain 'unbound', differences in the levels of openness inside a federal country may easily remain unnoticed when looking at the country's GATS schedule alone. If the country's general (central level) liberalization is low, that may hide internal differences between more and less liberal sub-central levels of government. Some WTO Members may also have chosen to liberalize according to the lowest common denominator in cases where there are

---

[9] See e.g. the horizontal commitments in Canada's GATS schedule. For 'commercial presence', Canada has inserted the following limitation on national treatment: 'Federal and sub-central tax measures (generally pertaining to small business) may result in a difference in treatment in respect of all or some "Canadian controlled private corporations" as defined by the Income Tax Act'. Canada, Schedule of Specific Commitments, GATS/SC/16, 15 April 1994.

[10] One example are the Åland Islands that form an autonomous region in Finland. In contrast to other Finnish regions, Åland enjoys a high degree of home rule. Limitations to the possibility to supply services in Åland are included in the horizontal commitments of Finland. See EU's Draft consolidated GATS Schedule, S/C/W/273, 9 October 2006. The commitments of Finland were upon its accession to the EU in 1995 included in the consolidated EU schedule but are based on the national GATS Schedule of Finland, GATS/SC/33, 15 April 1994.

differences in the openness levels between different regions or local levels of government. A look into different federal countries' GATS commitments shows that in some of their schedules sub-central entities appear widely across both the horizontal and sector-specific schedules (among such WTO Members are the EU, USA, Canada, Australia). In some other federal countries' GATS schedules sub-central entities make only occasional appearances (examples include Switzerland and Mexico with some mentions of regional/local measures) or zero appearances (an example is Russia with no mention of regional/local measures). The difference must be based on the way that services are regulated in the WTO Member in question (services regulated either centrally or across different levels of government) or, alternatively, it must be based on the degree of liberalization taken by the country in general (poor central level of liberalization can 'hide' differences between different lower levels of government). Finding out what exactly is at stake in each case would require qualitative analysis of the competences of the sub-central authorities in each particular WTO Member.

Another way to shed more light on the issue is to look into federal countries' EIAs. As services commitments in such agreements are supposed to go deeper than the same countries' GATS commitments, the agreements can reveal internal divisions that are hidden in the same countries' original GATS schedules. We now turn to the EIAs that were reviewed for the purposes of this chapter.

II Sub-Central Measures in Selected EIAs

The GATS commitments date to the early 1990s and are generally considered greatly outdated (as is increasingly the GATS itself). The main avenue for services liberalization today are EIAs. Earlier research has shown that the market access commitments in EIAs go significantly beyond the level of liberalization in the same countries GATS commitments.[11] However, even in EIAs the level of liberalization is still far from free trade. This is shown also by our results on the EU's EIAs. Very few countries have so far engaged in extensive opening of their services markets. The EU has the deepest EIA in this regard: service suppliers established in one EU Member State cannot be discriminated

---

[11] Roy, M. (2014) Services Commitments in Preferential Trade Agreements: Surveying the Empirical Landscape, in Sauvé, P. & Shingal, A. (eds.), *The Preferential Liberalization of Trade in Services: Comparative Regionalism*. Cheltenham: Edward Elgar.

against in other EU Member States. The elimination of obstacles is based on the non-discriminatory application of host state rules, with only a limited sectoral harmonization.[12]

In this chapter, we explain to what extent the reviewed EIAs include commitments taken by sub-central levels of government. We go through each agreement, starting from CETA and NAFTA and moving then to the EIAs concluded by the USA and Canada with South Korea. An overview of the presence of sub-central entities in these EIAs is included in a separate table at the end of the chapter.

i   CETA

CETA follows the negative scheduling method in its description of reservations.[13] This was new for the EU, which had earlier been using GATS-type positive scheduling practice in its EIAs. It was reported that the EU agreed to negative scheduling at least partially due to its motivation to effectively bind the Canadian provinces.[14]

NCMs are, across different chapters, specified as being maintained either by (i) the European Union, as set out in its Schedule to Annex I; (ii) a national government, as set out by that Party in its Schedule to Annex I; (iii) a provincial, territorial or regional government, as set out by that Party in its Schedule to Annex I; or (iv) a local government. Cross-border trade in services is included in Chapter 9 of the agreement, whereas Investment (Chapter 8), partly overlapping with Mode 3, and Temporary Entry and Stay of Natural Persons for Business Purposes (Chapter 10), overlapping with Mode 4, are separate chapters.

With regard to both existing and future measures applicable in Canada, Canada has included two different annexes. The first applies on the national level (federal level as well as provincial and territorial levels) and the second one applies only on the provincial and territorial

---

[12] Towards non-EU service suppliers this shows in the fragmentation of the EU's internal services market. Different national rules apply across the Member States of the EU.

[13] However, the commitments for the temporary entry and stay of natural persons for business purposes (the Mode 4 category of CETA) are described in positive manner, sector by sector. See Annexes from 10-B to 10-E of CETA. The negatively schedules reservations apply to Cross-Border Trade in Services (Modes 1 and 2) and Investment (covering Mode 3 but also non-services sector investment).

[14] Walker James, Negotiation of Trade Agreements in Federal Countries, SPICe Briefing, the Scottish Parliament, 17 November 2007, available at https://sp-bpr-en-prod-cdnep .azureedge.net/published/2017/11/17/Negotiation-of-Trade-Agreements-in-Federal-Countries/SB17-79.pdf.

level. Canada's list of Provincial and Territorial measures under Annex I is 271 pages long and under Annex II eighty-eight pages long. This is a radical departure from Canada's earlier EIAs where sub-federal NCMs have been exempted through a blanket reservation. It shows that Canada has engaged in deeper services liberalization with the EU by binding the restrictions applied also in provinces and territories. Through Annex I, the Canadian provinces and territories are bound to regulatory status quo and have committed to providing to the EU the benefits of autonomous liberalization in a number of important sectors (architectural, engineering, foreign legal consultancy, urban planning, tourism, business services).[15] In addition, Canada has bound the sub-federal levels of government also with regard to future measures (Annex II).

Unlike GATS Art. I:3, in CETA there is no general definition for the authorities whose measures are covered by the agreement's service disciplines. Art. 9.1 ('Definitions') and Art. 9.2 ('Scope') of Chapter 9 on Cross-Border Trade in Services do not mention anything about the sub-central levels of government. Neither do the respective provisions for Investment (Chapter 8) and for the Temporary Entry and Stay of Natural Persons for Business Purposes (Chapter 10).[16] Instead, the issue is taken up in the substantial obligations. For example, Art. 9.3 on NT in cross-border trade in services (Chapter 9) specifies the following:

1. Each Party shall accord to service suppliers and services of the other Party treatment no less favourable than that it accords, in like situations, to its own service suppliers and services.
2. For greater certainty, the treatment accorded by a Party pursuant to paragraph 1 means, with respect to a government in Canada other

---

[15] See 'CETA – Summary of the Final Negotiating Results' by the European Commission. Available at http://trade.ec.europa.eu/doclib/docs/2014/december/tradoc_152982.pdf (last accessed on 10 January 2019). Another area of major commercial interest in CETA is government procurement. Enhanced access to the Canadian public procurement market, including in particular access to the sub-federal levels of procurement, was a major negotiating aim of the EU in CETA. The final agreement provides full coverage of Canadian procurement, covering federal, provincial and municipal procurement, with relatively few explicit exceptions. See 'EU–Canada Comprehensive Economic and Trade Agreement (CETA)', European Parliament, Directorate-General for External Policies, Policy Department, EP/EXPO/B/INTA/FWC/2013–08/Lot7/02–03, December 2015, available at www.europarl.europa.eu/RegData/etudes/IDAN/2015/535016/EXPO_IDA (2015)535016_EN.pdf (last accessed on 10 January 2019).

[16] Chapter 9 of CETA corresponds to Modes 1 and 2, Chapter 8 corresponds to Mode 3 (even though 'Investment' in CETA covers also certain manufacturing activities) and Chapter 10 corresponds to Mode 4.

than at the federal level, or, with respect to a government of or in a Member State of the European Union, treatment no less favourable than the most favourable treatment accorded, in like situations, by that government to its own service suppliers and services.

The formulation thus clarifies that the obligation of NT applies beyond the central level of government and that the point of comparison should be the like service suppliers and services of that particular sub-central entity whose treatment is under scrutiny. In the case of the EU, reference is made both to the central governments of the Member States as well as to the lower levels of government within the Member States ('government of or in a Member State'), thus covering the two levels of sub-central authorities in the EU (national and sub-national).

Another reference to different levels of government is included in Art. 9.5 regarding MFN. Art. 9.6 includes the MA principle and specifies that the prohibited limitations shall not be adopted or maintained by a Party 'on the basis of its entire territory or on the basis of the territory of a national, provincial, territorial, regional or local level of government'.

Art. 9.7 ('Reservations') specifies in paragraph 1 that NT, MFN and MA disciplines do not apply to any existing non-conforming measure (NCM) that is maintained by a Party at the level of the EU, a national government or a provincial, territorial or regional government, as set out in the Parties' schedules to Annex I. The said obligations do not apply to existing NCMs of local governments either. Differently to provincial, territorial, or regional measures, such local measures do not need to be listed. There is no need to set them out in the Party's Schedule to Annex I. This means that local measures, such as municipal measures, remain unlisted in CETA. This can, however, be considered a minor shortcoming considering that Canada has in CETA for the first time listed the NCMs of its provinces and territories.

Reservations to future measures (the Annex II measures) are specified in the second paragraph. According to Art. 9.7 para. 2, NT, MFN and MA disciplines do not apply to a measure that 'a Party' adopts or maintains with respect to a sector, sub-sector or activity as set out in its Schedule to Annex II. The level of government is not specified. According to Art. 1.1 ('General definitions'), 'Parties' means, on the one hand, 'the European Union or its Member States' or 'the European Union and its Member States' within their respective areas of competence as derived from the EU Treaties, and on the other hand, 'Canada'. It is therefore not entirely clear what levels of sub-central government are covered by the reservations to future measures under Art. 9.7. para. 2. However, as Canada has included provincial and territorial NCMs in its schedule to Annex II, it appears that any future NCMs by sub-central entities are meant to be covered as well.

In addition, Art. 1.10 ('Persons exercising delegated governmental authority') states that unless otherwise specified in the agreement, each Party must ensure that persons with delegated regulatory, administrative or other governmental authority must act in accordance with the Party's obligations. It further specifies that the obligation applies 'at any level of government'. Furthermore, Art. 1.8 specifies that 'Each Party shall ensure that all necessary measures are taken in order to give effect to the provisions of this Agreement, including their observance at all levels of government'.[17]

Central government is defined in the Party-specific definitions of Art. 1.2. For Canada, it means the Government of Canada, and for the EU Party, it means 'the European Union or the national governments of its Member States'. The definition is interesting as it labels the EU as 'central government'. CETA thus appears to have the same approach as the present book in contrasting the relations of the EU and its Member States to federal states.

ii   NAFTA

NAFTA, an agreement predating the GATS, lacks a general definition of the authorities whose measures are covered by the agreement. Similarly to CETA, the extent to which state and provincial measures are covered is specified in the substantial obligations of the agreement.

Article 1202 of Chapter Twelve (Cross-Border Trade in Services) includes the discipline on NT:

1. Each Party shall accord to service providers of another Party treatment no less favorable than that it accords, in like circumstances, to its own service providers.
2. The treatment accorded by a Party under paragraph 1 means, with respect to a state or province, treatment no less favorable than the

---

[17] The provision can be contrasted with the obligation for WTO Members to take 'such reasonable measures as may be available to it' to ensure the observance of the GATS disciplines by regional and local governments and authorities and non-governmental bodies within their territory (Art. I:3(ii)). The language in CETA appears stronger as it requires each Party to 'ensure' compliance by taking any 'necessary measures' without any mention of them being 'reasonable' or 'available' to the Party. See more on the question of 'reasonable measures' as required under the GATS in the previous Chapter.

most favorable treatment accorded, in like circumstances, by that state or province to service providers of the Party of which it forms a part.

Article 1206 on 'Reservations' states that the NT, MFN and prohibition of local presence disciplines do not apply to existing NCMs listed in Annex I and maintained either at the federal level, by a state or province, or a local government. The explanatory note to Annex I mentions that each reservation sets out the level of government maintaining the measure for which a reservation is taken. In accordance with Art. 1206:1(a), only measures taken by local governments do not need to be listed. This appears to mean measures that are adopted on lower levels than state or province. The exclusion of local measures is again similar to CETA.

Unlike CETA, NAFTA, however, stops short from listing any NCMs that are applied by sub-federal levels of government (state and provincial level). This is because under the second paragraph of Art. 1206, 'Each Party may set out in its Schedule to Annex I, within two years of the date of entry into force of this Agreement, any existing non-conforming measure maintained by a state or province, not including a local government'. The Parties thus gave each other a period of two years to come up with a list of NCMs that were applied on the level of states and provinces with regard to the NT, MFN and local presence requirements.

The same timeline of two years is given for the listing of any NCMs at the state and provincial level for measures in breach of the rules on Investment (Art. 1108, 'Reservations and Exceptions' of Chapter Eleven).

NAFTA does not have an MA discipline similar to the GATS and later EIAs, but Article 1207 on Quantitative Restrictions specifies that any quantitative restrictions are set out in Annex V. Again, a specific timeline is given to set out restrictions maintained by a state or province (and not including a local government). However, under Art. 1207 the timeline for the listing of such sub-federal measures is only one year (Art. 1207:1).

The categories of measures covered by the NAFTA Articles 1206, 1207 and 1108 roughly correspond to Modes 1, 2 and 3.[18] The wording of the said articles confirms that NAFTA was meant to cover sub-central measures. However, such measures were not included in the Annexes. Instead, the inclusion of NCMs by lower levels of government was to take

---

[18] NAFTA does not include a list of NCMs for the Temporary Entry of Business Persons but the commitments for them are included in annexes and appendixes directly under the relevant Chapter Sixteen. The commitments appear to apply across all levels of government of all three Parties. There do not seem to be differences in the relevant immigration categories across the different levels of government of the three states.

place only at later dates, within the time periods specified in the chapters on Investment and Services.

The Parties returned to the issue two years later. They did that through an exchange of separate side letters in March 1996 (NAFTA entered into force on 1 January 1994). In those side letters all state and provincial measures of all three states were exempted in their entirety.[19] The detailed and legally binding listing of the sub-federal measures had apparently proved impossible, or overly burdensome.[20] Therefore, each Party ended up exempting all NCMs existing on sub-federal levels of government. The USA has exempted the NCMs applied by its states in all of its EIAs since NAFTA. It has put the blanket reservation forward at the signing of the agreement, without any attempt to come up with any such lists at a later stage. A similar practice (exemption of all sub-federal measures) was followed by Canada, all the way up until the conclusion of CETA with the EU in 2016.

[19] The side letters of the USA, Canada and Mexico are available on the webpage of the NAFTA Secretariat: www.nafta-sec-alena.org/Home/Texts-of-the-Agreement/North-American-Free-Trade-Agreement. See all three letters in Annex I, under 'Non-Conforming Measures' placed at the top of the page below 'Schedule of Canada'. Each state's side letter says that, 'for transparency', attached are documents that list NCMs maintained at the provincial and territorial level. However, such documents were not attached to the publicly available copies of the original side letters (which are scanned fax documents) and are not publicly available. The Canadian Government's North American Trade Policy Team confirmed to the author that the documents were exchanged amongst NAFTA Parties for transparency purposes. However, as the documents were not adopted as part of the final agreement, they are therefore not included on the NAFTA website (email correspondence, 11 March 2019). The lists are unlikely to have been very detailed considering that later lists included by the USA and Canada for 'transparency' purposes in their FTAs with Korea are very vague and non-binding illustrations of the types of measures applied. See below at footnote 22.

[20] The situation has not got any easier over the years. In the context of the TTIP negotiations between the USA and the EU it was reported that the Obama administration had claimed that an inventory of state-level measures would be a 'Herculean' task to complete. See Jutta Hennig, 'Under Pressure to Show TTIP Progress, US, EU Focus on Market Access', Inside US Trade – 04/18/2014, Vol. 32, No. 16 (posted 17 April 2014). Since NAFTA, the USA has only provided illustrative and non-exhaustive and non-binding lists of state-level measures as part of the FTA with Korea and the original draft TPP agreement. The recently negotiated USMCA (meant to replace NAFTA) exempts all existing sub-federal NCMs. No lists of such measures are available in the version that is currently available on the webpage of the USTR. Some types of non-binding lists of sub-federal NCMs were included in the NAFTA side letters (the lists are not publicly available). But legally binding and exhaustive lists of sub-federal measures have thus so far proved impossible. This is probably due to a variety of reasons – economic and political, but probably also technical. Going through all such measures may be a Herculean endeavour indeed.

iii   US–Korea

The US–Korea Free Trade Agreement (KORUS) entered into force on 15 March 2012. Similarly to NAFTA and most US EIAs, its service commitments follow a negative scheduling method. Art. 12.1, paragraph 2, of Chapter Twelve on Cross-Border Trade in Services includes the same definition for 'measures' as GATS Art. 1:3. KORUS thus covers measures adopted or maintained by central, regional, or local governments and authorities. Art. 12.3 of KORUS also includes a reference to 'a regional subdivision', similarly to GATS Art. XVI.

Even if the definition of 'measures' follows the GATS, with regard to the actual commitments of the sub-federal levels of government KORUS follows the established practice of the USA since NAFTA. It exempts all existing NCMs of 'all states of the United States, the District of Columbia, and Puerto Rico'.[21] The reservation applies to NT (Articles 11.3 and 12.2 KORUS), MNF (Articles 11.4 and 12.3 KORUS), Local Presence (Article 12.5 KORUS), Performance Requirements (Article 11.8 KORUS) and Senior Management and Boards of Directors (Article 11.9 KORUS). The formulation is similar to all earlier US EIAs since NAFTA and was followed by the USA also in the draft TPP agreement (from which the USA later withdrew).

What is new is the illustrative list of state-level NCMs that is provided on the following page of Annex I, as Appendix I-A.[22] However, the NCMs illustrated at the state and local level are provided for transparency purposes only and are not bound by the services provisions of these PTAs.[23] Annex I states 'For purposes of transparency, Appendix I-A sets out an illustrative, non-binding list of non-conforming measures maintained at the regional level of government'. Footnote 1 specifies that the 'document is provided for transparency purposes only, and is neither exhaustive nor binding. The information contained in this document is drawn from US commitments under the General Agreement on Trade in

---

[21] See p. 12 of KORUS, Annex I, the schedule of the United States and Appendix I-A to the same schedule

[22] The same list was put forward along the US services commitments in the TPP. The original text and schedules of commitments is provided on the website of the USTR 'for reference purposes': https://ustr.gov/trade-agreements/free-trade-agreements/trans-pacific-partnership/tpp-full-text (last accessed on 20 January 2019).

[23] Ibid. In the original TPP agreement, the information can be similarly found in Annex I, the schedule of the United States and Appendix I-A to the same schedule, at p. 16. The USA has withdrawn from the TPP but the originally negotiated commitments are available at https://ustr.gov/trade-agreements/free-trade-agreements/trans-pacific-partnership/tpp-full-text (last accessed on 20 June 2018).

Services, the May 2005 Revised US Services Offer under the Doha Development Agenda negotiations, and related documents'. This would seem to indicate that the USA is informing its treaty partner of potential sub-central measures (to the extent that they were committed to under the GATS and the Doha Round Offer and revealed by those and related documents) but has not undertaken an updated review to find out what the currently applied measures are. The list is 'not exhaustive', which would seem to indicate that also other sub-central measures may be applied, especially if introduced after the GATS. Furthermore, KORUS does not provide for any liberalization of sub-central measures – the list is provided for mapping purposes only. The list of existing sub-central measures is neither binding and thus cannot be relied upon based on the FTA. However, it should be considered a slight improvement to US scheduling practice as it gives some information on restrictive measures that are applied on the level of the states.

Korea managed to negotiate also another concession related to the sub-federal levels of government. Annex 12-C of KORUS integrates a possibility for a party to request 'consultations regarding non-conforming measures maintained by a regional level of government'. The annex includes only one paragraph which reads:

> If a Party considers that an Annex I non-conforming measure applied by a regional level of government of the other Party creates a material impediment to a service supplier of the Party, an investor of the Party, or a covered investment, it may request consultations with regard to that measure. The Parties shall enter into consultations with a view to exchanging information on the operation of the measure and to considering whether further steps are necessary and appropriate.

The concession may be modest and does not guarantee that any changes to problematic sub-central measures would be agreed upon, but it shows that there is an increasing pressure to open up services markets also on the level of sub-central levels of government.[24] In KORUS, the pressure

---

[24] In the context of the TiSA negotiations the same pressure is visible in the bilateral market access request by the EU to the USA. The EU would like the USA to update its TiSA offer by providing full transparency for sub-federal measures. As an alternative option, the EU requests the USA to provide transparency related to local content in all sectors where the USA has MA commitments and to take a commitment to provide the remaining information on transparency with respect to other sectors after TiSA enters into force. See 'TiSA – Bilateral Market Access Request by the European Union' (June 2016), Copy for the Council and the European Parliament. Available at: www.bilaterals.org/?tisa-bilateral-market-access&lang=en (source: Wikileaks, last accessed on 21 December 2018).

may have been exerted both ways. Korea has a system of local autonomies where the number of high-level local governments was in 2012 increased to seventeen. The local levels of government, and especially the high-level local governments, may exercise regulatory powers that affect Korea's services commitments.[25]

Interestingly, the USA has not exempted sub-central measures with regard to MA commitments under Art. 12:4. As was mentioned above, the exemption of sub-federal measures in Annex I applies to the articles on NT, MFN, local presence and a few other disciplines. This omission seems to relate to another Appendix that the USA has included as part of its Annex II. That Appendix II-A specifies that 'The United States reserves the right to adopt or maintain any measure that is not inconsistent with the United States' obligations under Article XVI of the General Agreement on Trade in Services as set out in the US Schedule of Specific Commitments under the GATS'.[26] Considering the blanket reservation included therein, this appears to confirm that the USA has not given any new market access commitments under KORUS but limits itself to those given under the GATS. For this purpose, sub-federal measures do not need to be specifically exempted as they in any case are tied to the level provided already under the GATS. However, it is also specified that 'For purposes of this entry only, the US Schedule of Specific Commitments is modified as indicated in Appendix II-A'. Appendix II-A includes limited improvements to the US GATS schedule on market access. The improvements are mostly given at the federal level (at least no regional specification is mentioned), but a few are improvements to state-level measures.[27] However, the list of improvements is short and limited to a few sectors only.[28] It indicates a poor improvement to the US market access commitments as compared to its GATS commitments, both on the federal as well as the sub-federal level.

---

[25] These high-level local governments are Seoul Special City, six metropolises, eight provinces, and Jeju Special Self-Governing Province. See the webpage of the Korean Culture and Information Service: www.korea.net/Government/Constitution-and-Government/Local-Governments (last accessed on 21 December 2018). Korea's Annex I in KORUS reveals some sub-central measures applied on local levels of Korean government.

[26] See p. 8 of Appendix II-A of Annex II-US.

[27] Appendix II-A starts by the following statement: 'For the following Sectors, US obligations under Article XVI of the General Agreement on Trade in Services as set out in the US Schedule of Specific Commitments under the GATS (GATS/SC/90, GATS/SC/90/Suppl.1, GATS/SC/90/Suppl.2, and GATS/SC/90/Suppl.3) are improved as described'.

[28] See p. 11 of Appendix II-A of Annex II-US.

It is worth noting that the USA has included a similar reservation to MA in all of its EIAs since the conclusion of the GATS. The reservations are included at the end or towards the end of the US Annex II. The formulations differ to some extent, but all set the US GATS commitments as the baseline of its MA commitments under the EIA.[29] The formulation below is from the US–Peru FTA of 2009:

> Sector: All
> Obligations Concerned: Market Access (Article 11.4)
> Description: Cross-Border Services
> The United States reserves the right to adopt or maintain any measure that is not inconsistent with the United States' obligations under Article XVI of the General Agreement on Trade in Services.[30]

The blanket reservation and the fixing of the US commitments to the level of the GATS is surprising and has been paid little attention to.[31] In light of our approach to Art. V, the lack of new openings on MA is not problematic as Art. V calls for the elimination of discrimination, not MA limitations. Limitations to MA are, however, an issue in case they include discriminatory elements or in case MA is left unbound. Examples of both situations can be found in the US GATS commitments, both on the federal and sub-federal level. Moreover, since the GATS is based on positive listing – meaning that the Members picked the services that they wanted to take commitment on – the US commitments under the GATS do not reveal possible MA limitations applied in the excluded sectors.

In this sense, the KORUS agreement is a step forward as it provides for improvements to the USA's MA commitments as compared to the GATS.[32] As already mentioned, a few of the improvements are made to

---

[29] The US–Morocco EIA includes the following addition to the reservation: 'If Morocco believes that such a non-conforming measure would materially affect its interests under this Agreement, it may request consultations under this entry. The United States agrees to engage in such consultations and to give due consideration to the views expressed by Morocco in this respect'. United States – Morocco Free Trade Agreement (2004), Schedule of the United States, Annex II, p. 8. In the US–Singapore FTA, the reservation is included in Annex I, which in that particular EIA is exceptionally 'Annex 8A' (United States – Singapore Free Trade Agreement of 2003).

[30] The United States – Peru Trade Promotion Agreement, Annex II, Schedule of the United States, p. 7.

[31] Actually, we have not come across any mention of this reservation in literature. This, of course, does not mean that it would not have been noticed.

[32] The USA included an identical list of improvements to its Annex II under the draft TPP. See p. 13 of Appendix II-A of Annex II, Schedule of the United States to Trans-Pacific Partnership, available at: https://ustr.gov/trade-agreements/free-trade-agreements/trans-pacific-partnership/tpp-full-text (last accessed on 20 January 2019).

measures applied by US states (Appendix II-A of Annex II). The significance of such new commitments is, however, limited as they relate to a small number of states only and apply in the sole sub-sector of Foreign Legal Consulting Services. Overall, the number and level of improvements is modest.

iv   Canada–Korea

The Canada–Korea Free Trade Agreement (CKFTA) has been in force since 1 January 2015. 'Measures' are defined similarly to the GATS (Art. 9.1:2, 'Scope and Coverage', Chapter Nine: Cross-Border Trade in Services). In addition, the second paragraph of Art. 9.2 on NT specifies that 'the treatment accorded by a Party under paragraph 1 means, with respect to a sub-national government, treatment no less favourable than the most favourable treatment accorded, in like circumstances, by that sub-national government to service suppliers of the Party of which it forms a part'. Art. 9.4 on MA applies to measures imposed 'either on the basis of its [Party's] entire territory or on the basis of a sub-national government'. It can thus be interpreted that Canada has agreed to NT and MA disciplines on all levels of the government.

The agreement includes a list of national reservations for existing (Annex I) and future (Annex II) NCMs. The NCMs are set on the federal level but a couple horizontal limitations include a mention of the Canadian provinces. An example is the following measure restricting foreign ownership of land in the Western province of Alberta.[33]

Sector: All Sectors
Sub-sector:
Industry Classification:
Type of Reservation: National Treatment (Article 8.3)
Measures:
Citizenship Act, R.S.C. 1985, c. C-29
Foreign Ownership of Land Regulations, SOR/79-416

Description: Investment

1. The *Foreign Ownership of Land Regulations* are made pursuant to the *Citizenship Act* and the *Agricultural and Recreational Land*

---

[33]   Annex I, Schedule of Canada.

(Continued)

Ownership Act, RSA 1980, c. A-9. In Alberta, an ineligible person or foreign-owned or -controlled corporation may only hold an interest in controlled land consisting of a maximum of 2 parcels containing, in the aggregate, a maximum of 20 acres.

2. For the purposes of this reservation:ineligible person means:

- (a) a natural person who is not a Canadian citizen or permanent resident;
- (b) a foreign government or foreign government agency; or
- (c) a corporation incorporated in a country other than Canada;

controlled land means land in Alberta but does not include:

- (a land of the Crown in right of Alberta;
- (b) land within a city, town, new town, village or summer village; and
- (c) mines or minerals.

However, the appearance of sub-federal measures in Canada's national schedule is only occasional. Otherwise, Canada has included a similar carve-out for sub-federal measures as is included in NAFTA. Canada's schedule to Annex I of the agreement is identical to NAFTA in this regard: it includes a reservation for all existing non-conforming measures of all provinces and territories. The measures are not listed. In addition, and very interestingly, Canada's Appendix I-A sets out 'an illustrative, non-binding list of non-conforming measures maintained at the sub-national level of government'. The list is provided '[f]or purposes of transparency only'.[34]

The logic of the listing is the same as in the non-binding and illustrative list of state measures included by the USA in KORUS (also called Appendix I-A). The wording regarding the nature of the list as 'illustrative' and 'non-binding' is almost identical between the two agreements. The list of sub-federal measures in the Canada–Korea agreement is also very general and does not explain in detail what the sub-federal measures consist of. Instead, it simply lists which states have existing measures

---

[34] Footnote 2 to the Appendix notes that the document is provided for 'transparency purposes only', and is 'neither exhaustive nor binding'. Furthermore, it states that the information contained in the document is drawn from Canada's May 2005 Revised Conditional Offer on Services (TN/S/O/CAN/Rev.1, 23 May 2005).

affecting citizenship, residency, local presence, economic needs tests, taxation, corporate form or training requirements. Both Canada and the USA have included the illustrative list of sub-federal NCMs only in their FTAs with Korea. It may thus be that the lists exist thanks to Korean negotiators' efforts to shed some light on the various service-related measures applied by the American and Canadian states and provinces. Interestingly, Canada and the USA have provided the same lists as part of their Annex I schedules to the original TPP agreement. The Canadian list is still part of the re-negotiated Comprehensive and Progressive Agreement for Trans-Pacific Partnership (CPTPP), which was concluded by the remaining eleven TPP states after the withdrawal of the USA.[35]

Canada's approach to MA commitments is also the same as in the post-GATS EIAs concluded by the USA. Canada has in its EIAs tied its commitments to its MA commitments under the GATS. The binding of the Canadian MA commitments to the level of the GATS is included in all Canadian EIAs, except for CETA. In addition, and again similarly to the KORUS, Appendix II-A to Canada's schedule of NCMs in the Canada–Korea EIA includes a list of commitments that somewhat improve Canada's obligations under Art. XVI of the GATS. The list also includes some improvements to Canada's GATS commitments on the level of provinces, across various service sectors.[36]

Art. 9.6 ('Non-conforming measures') of the Canada–Korea EIA notes that Annex 9-A sets out specific commitments with regard to consultation regarding a non-conforming measures adopted or maintained by a sub-national government. Annex 9-A states the following:

> If a Party considers that an Annex I non-conforming measure applied by a sub national government of the other Party creates a material impediment to a service supplier of the Party, an investor of the Party, or a covered investment, it may request consultations with regard to that measure. If a Party considers that an Annex I non conforming measure

---

[35] See Annex I of Canada to the CPTPP, available at https://international.gc.ca/trade-commerce/trade-agreements-accords-commerciaux/agr-acc/cptpp-ptpgp/ (last accessed on 22 January 2019). At the time of the book's going into publication, the agreement had entered into force for seven of the eleven states that signed it (including Canada). The original US commitments under the draft TPP are available on the webpage of the USTR.

[36] Many of the new commitments consist of the removal of discriminatory MA requirements, such as commercial presence requirements or foreign ownership restrictions. Several removed restrictions seem to apply to NT, rather than MA, e.g. those that remove citizenship or residence requirements. Therefore, even if the list is provided as an improvement to Canada's MA commitments as compared to the GATS, it does also provide for a limited number of new NT commitments for Canadian provinces.

applied by a sub-national government of the other Party prevents the development of a mutual recognition agreement or arrangement or prevents a service supplier of a Party from receiving the benefits of such an agreement or arrangement, it may also request consultations with regard to that measure. The Parties shall enter into consultations with a view to exchanging information on the operation of the measure and to considering whether further steps are necessary and appropriate.

The EIAs concluded by Canada and the USA are surprisingly similar, all the way up until the conclusion of CETA. The USA and Canada[37] have in NAFTA exempted all existing NCMs (Annex I limitations) of all sub-federal entities. However, with regard to future measures (Annex II)[38] the agreements have a liberalizing effect also on state and provincial levels. The reviewed EIAs of USA and Canada do not include Annex II measures for sub-national levels of government and it would thus seem that they do not allow for the introduction of new sub-federal limitations, beyond the existing ones. However, as the existing NCMs are not explained in detail, it may be hard to keep track of the commitments on the sub-federal level in the first place. If a service supplier from a partner country wants to challenge a restrictive measure applied by a US state or a Canadian province, it needs to check the measure's legislative background and try to understand if the measure existed already at the time of conclusion of the EIA. Annex I measures are subject to a 'ratchet' clause.[39] Therefore, any unilateral liberalization should not be subsequently withdrawn. But again, it may be hard for foreign service suppliers to keep track of such developments. Transparency is of vital importance when any non-conforming measures are put forward. Therefore, the detailed inclusion of the measures applied by the

[37] Also Mexico has done the same.
[38] The difference between Annex I and Annex II measures is that existing measures that do not comply with the disciplines of the services agreement must be listed in Annex I and cannot be made more restrictive. Annex II includes a list of measures for which the state wants to maintain the freedom to introduce them at a later stage. Either way, a measure must be listed under one of the annexes to be upheld. Typically, an Annex I measure needs to be amended, continued or renewed in order to be validly upheld. If it is discontinued, the trading partner gets to benefit from autonomous liberalization and the measure cannot be re-introduced at a later stage, unless it has been included also in Annex II.
[39] Art. 12:6 of KORUS excludes 'the continuation or prompt renewal of any non-conforming measure' and 'an amendment to any non-conforming measure referred to in subparagraph (a) to the extent that the amendment does not decrease the conformity of the measure, as it existed immediately before the amendment'. Unless an outdated measure is promptly renewed, it is therefore liberalized. A similar ratchet clause is included in Art. 9.7 of CETA. It is not entirely clear what a 'prompt renewal' consists of.

Canadian provinces and territories in the CETA agreement is an important step forward. It makes the sub-federal level accountable in a way that is radically different to the earlier treaty practice of Canada and the USA.

v Summarizing Tables

Table 6.1 *Sub-central entities in the GATS commitments of the USA, Canada and the EU*

Country/entity	Sub-central measures covered in the treaty text	Inclusion of sub-central commitments in the sector-specific commitments	Comments
United States	Yes	Yes	Sub-central measures appear widely
Canada	Yes	Yes	Sub-central measures appear widely
European Union	Yes	Yes (on the level of EU Member States)	A very limited appearance of EU MSs' internal (national) sub-central measures

Table 6.2 *Sub-central entities in the EIA commitments of KORUS, Canada–Korea, EU–Korea, CETA and NAFTA*

Agreement	Sub-central measures covered in the treaty text	Inclusion of sub-central commitments in sector-specific commitments by USA, Canada and EU	Comments
KORUS	Yes	No	Reservation for all existing sub-central non-conforming measures (a non-binding list is provided)
Canada–Korea	Yes	No	The same as in KORUS
EU–Korea	Yes	Yes (on the level of EU Member States)	A very limited appearance of EU MSs' internal (national) sub-central measures
CETA	Yes	Yes	Sub-central non-conforming measures described in detail
NAFTA	Yes	No	Reservation for all existing sub-central non-conforming measures

PART III

Methodology for a Legal-Empirical Analysis of EIAs

7

Empirical Research on Services Preferentialism

I Introduction to the Chapter on Methodology

This chapter explains the technical details of the empirical methodology that is put forward in this book for the study of EIAs. The methodology is based on the findings of the first part of the book. It is designed for the evaluation of services agreements in light of the GATS-discipline on EIAs. The method consists of a textual analysis of the EIAs, including both the text of the agreement and the schedules of services commitments. However, the focus is on the commitments, especially on sector-specific commitments.

In Part IV of the book, the methodology is applied to four EIAs of the EU. Only the EU side's commitments are analyzed: the purpose is to find out the approximate level of liberalization reached by the EU, as well as to assess how the EU's method of liberalization corresponds to the Art. V criteria. Thus, no conclusions can be drawn on the agreements in their entirety. Since the EU has concluded EIAs with very different types of countries from several different regions, the agreements are useful material for an analysis under the various elements of Art. V GATS. Yet considering that all EU Member States are highly developed countries and advanced economies, the flexibility that Art. V provides for developing countries does not apply to the EU side. Whereas the overall purpose of the agreement can be considered in the analysis under Art. V, especially with regard to the possibility of 'wider integration', it is argued that the EU side's level of liberalization should always correspond to the strict requirement of 'substantiality' in terms of sectoral coverage and elimination of discrimination.

In the interpretation of the results in light of the WTO rules, particularly Art. V GATS, specific attention is paid to the EU's commitments under Mode 4. That is because Mode 4 commitments are scheduled differently to the rest of the modes and must therefore be approached differently from Modes 1, 2 and 3. In this context, we also aim to assess how the EU understands the scope of Mode 4. As with the other modes, we also try to evaluate how the liberalization level in the EU's Mode 4 commitments corresponds to the criteria of Art. V.

The methodological approach is adapted to take into account the special circumstances of services trade liberalization by the EU towards third countries, especially the fact that regulation of services, unlike goods, is not uniform throughout the Union. However, it is proposed that such special circumstances are relevant not only in the study of the EU, but in the study of all WTO Members with constitutionally divided powers in the regulation of service activities.[1] Therefore, the proposed methodology can be used to study the EIA commitments of any federal entities, including federal states such as the USA and Canada.[2] Similar circumstances are likely to rise also with regard to any other existing or future free trade area that would start concluding services agreements independently in its own name, similarly to the EU.[3]

---

[1] 'Regulation' in this book is understood as a broad, general political and legal concept that includes all governmental policies and measures that are aimed at influencing, controlling and guiding all private activities with impacts on others. See Krajewski, M. (2003) *National Regulation and Trade Liberalization in Services: The Legal Impact of the General Agreement on Trade in Services (GATS) on National Regulatory Autonomy*, The Hague: Kluwer Law International, at 4. Similarly to Krajewski, reference can be made to Reagan who defines regulation as 'a process or activity in which government requires or proscribes certain activities or behaviour on the part of individuals and institutions, mostly private, but sometimes public'. See Reagan, M. (1987) *Regulation – The Politics of Policy*. Boston and Toronto: Little, Brown and Company, at 15. Regulation can take place on all levels of a state, as well as on supranational and international level.

[2] In case the federal state has engaged in liberalization on the sub-central levels of government. In case sub-federal commitments are not included and the sub-federal levels of government have significant regulatory powers in the area of services, the EIA cannot be adequately studied in light of Art. V.

[3] So far, to our knowledge, the EU is the only free trade/common market area that is clearly concluding trade agreements in its own name in addition to its Member States (and thus binding itself legally too). It is also the only organization that is a Member of the WTO in its own right, in addition to its Member States. This might, however, change, as more regions are engaging in deeper integration. The EU, for its own part, is interested in agreements with other free-trade areas or common markets. Negotiations for an Association Agreement are on-going with Mercosur. Mercosur appears as the contracting party or negotiating party to several trade agreements but it is the individual Member

The challenges that the EU as a multi-state actor faces in concluding services trade agreements are indeed often similar to countries that have a federal structure. Trade liberalization by the EU reflects the combination of supranational and national jurisdiction over trade negotiation areas. Within the field of services, as in goods, the competence to conclude agreements with third parties is within the powers of the Union.[4] However, due to the lack of comprehensive internal harmonization of services regulations within the EU, the EU Member States keep scheduling their own nationally based restrictions to the common EU services schedule in PTAs. In this sense, there are similarities to countries with decentralized regulation of services. However, as was explained in Part II of the book, in the case of some federal states such non-central measures are not explained in detail in the country's services schedule.

This book asks how such sub-central limitations to cross-border services trade should be taken into account when analyzing the Art. V criteria for substantiality. In the empirical study presented in Part IV of the book, the focus is on the EU. The study analyzes to what extent the EU's and its Member States' EIA commitments reach the Art.

States rather than Mercosur that are the formal contracting parties to those agreements. The EU has expressed wishing one day to integrate its separate deals/negotiations with certain Southeast Asian countries and conclude a region-to-region trade agreement with the Association of Southeast Asian Nations (ASEAN). See European Commission's memo 'The EU's Bilateral Trade and Investment Agreements – Where Are We' of December 3, 2013, available at http://trade.ec.europa.eu/doclib/docs/2012/november/tradoc_150129 .pdf (last accessed on 17 September 2018). Whether any future agreement would bind the ASEAN as an organization naturally depends on the level of integration and legal structure that ASEAN countries are willing to adopt for the organization. According to its Charter, ASEAN has been accorded legal personality as well as an explicit international treaty-making power. In most cases, however, all Member States of the ASEAN are listed as parties to the agreement. See Cremona, M., Kleimann, D., Larik, J., Lee, R. & Vennesson, P. (2015) *ASEAN's External Agreements: Law, Practice and the Quest for Collective Action.* Cambridge: Cambridge University Press, at 84–7.

[4] Originally, in Opinion 1/94, the Court of Justice of the European Union had concluded that only cross-border trade (Mode 1) fell within the Union's Common Commercial Policy (CCP) since it was 'not unlike trade in goods' and involved no movement of persons. See Opinion 1/94, *Opinion of the Court of 15 November 1994 – Competence of the Community to conclude international agreements concerning services and the protection of intellectual property* [1994] ECR I-05267. The Amsterdam Treaty and the Treaty of Nice extended the Union's competences in the field of external trade. However, prior to the Lisbon Treaty, the EU's exclusive competence did not apply in a number of services sectors. Since the entry into force of the Lisbon Treaty on 1 December 2009, Art. 3 and Art. 207 of the Treaty on the Functioning of the European Union (TFEU) provide that trade in services, as well as commercial aspects of intellectual property and foreign direct investment, belong to the area of the CCP and thus to the category of the EU's exclusive competence.

V threshold of substantiality as regards the sectoral coverage and the level of non-discrimination in the reviewed agreements. The same research question and methodology can, however, be applied to any countries that have a federal structure or that otherwise regulate services on sub-central levels. To demonstrate how the methodology would work in the case of a federal state outside the EU, Part IV of the book applies the method also to the CETA agreement. The analysis is limited to one service sector only and no EIA-wide conclusions are thus made with regard to that agreement. The comparison to the CETA is done also to show how the method works with EIAs that use negative scheduling.

In the WTO, the EU has been one of the most active proponents of service trade liberalization. This is logical considering that the EU is the world's biggest exporter of commercial services.[5] During the past decade the EU has become active in liberalizing services trade also in PTAs with third countries. Especially in the recent, so-called deep and comprehensive free trade agreements (DCFTAs), new market opening in services has been one of the main goals of the negotiations. New openings in services was among the EU's top priorities also in the negotiations with Canada, Japan and Singapore.[6] In addition to these new generation PTAs, detailed commitments on the liberalization of services can also be found in certain other types of agreements concluded by the EU with third countries in the past. These agreements include two association

---

[5] World Trade Statistical Review 2018, p. 69, available at www.wto.org/english/res_e/sta tis_e/wts2018_e/wts2018_e.pdf (last accessed on 28 January 2019). If looking at individual countries, the biggest exporter of commercial services is the United States. In the EU, the single biggest exporters are United Kingdom, Germany and France.

[6] The first such 'deep and comprehensive' FTA, as labelled by the EU, was the EU–South Korea Free Trade Agreement of 2011. A similarly labelled FTA with Singapore was reached in 2013 but was subsequently amended in 2017 to bring the agreement in line with the EU's new approach to investment protection and dispute resolution as a result of the Court of Justice of the EU Opinion 2/15. In 2013, the EU reached 'deep' trade agreements also as part of Association Agreements with Moldova and Georgia. A deep and comprehensive trade agreement was signed with Ukraine in 2014 and it has been in provisional application since January 2016. Trade and investment negotiations with Vietnam were launched in 2012 and completed in December 2015. Following the Court of Justice Opinion 2/15, and in a similar way to what had been done with the EU–Singapore agreement, the result of negotiations with Vietnam was adjusted to create a separate FTA and an Investment Protection Agreement (IPA). CETA, a deep and comprehensive trade agreement with Canada, entered into force provisionally on 21 September 2017. National parliaments in EU countries have still to approve it before it can take full effect. See 'Overview of FTA and Other Trade Negotiations', updated December 2018, available on the webpage of the European Commission: http://trade.ec.europa.eu/doclib/docs/2006/december/tradoc_118238.pdf (last accessed on 28 January 2019).

agreements, one economic partnership agreement and one agreement simply referred to as 'trade agreement'.[7] The empirical analysis conducted for the purposes of the book covers four EU EIAs belonging to three different groups of agreements (AA, FTA and EPA). The results partly reflect differences in these three types of agreements. However, overall, and maybe surprisingly, the differences are revealed to be relatively modest.

II   Earlier Empirical Research on EIAs

While there is decades' worth of research on the nature and magnitude of goods trade, we know much less about services trade and impediments to it. Data on cross-border transactions in services became available only in the last decade and data on service trade impediments have been collected and made available even more recently.[8] Knowledge about the main driving factors and consequences of barriers in services trade is now being constantly developed. A growing amount of literature is also focusing on preferentialism in the services context. That research still pales in comparison with studies on preferentialism in goods trade but since services have become an important feature of PTAs their study is attracting a growing interest. There is also an increasing amount of research being carried out on services commitments, both under the GATS and EIAs. Several of such studies employ empiric methods.

As is noted by Shingal and Egger, most research on services preferentialism has so far been devoted to studying the trade effect of services accords on aggregate and disaggregated services trade flows. The impact of different levels of regulation and various barriers to trade in services and to trade costs are the object of an increasing number of research projects.[9] Empirically oriented legal and/or economic literature has evolved to

---

[7] Association Agreements (AAs) are international agreements that the EU has concluded with third countries with the aim of setting up an all-embracing framework to conduct bilateral relations. These agreements normally provide for the progressive liberalization of trade and, in certain cases, they prepare for future membership of the European Union. Economic Partnership Agreements (EPAs) are trade and development agreements negotiated between the EU and African, Caribbean and Pacific countries. Their aim is to contribute, through trade and investment, to sustainable development and poverty reduction. All PTAs notified by the EU to the WTO are listed in Appendix 1. For the list of agreements included in the empirical study see Appendix 2.

[8] Shingal, A. & Egger, P. (2014) Determinants of Services Trade Agreements: Regulatory Incidence and Convergence. *NCCR Trade Working Papers*, No. 2014/06, at 3.

[9] See references to recent literature in ibid., at 4.

explain services commitments in the GATS and EIAs,[10] reciprocal services commitments[11] as well as GATS+ commitments in PTAs.[12]

So far, there is only limited empirical research that would consider specific EIAs in light of the criteria of Art. V GATS. Most studies focus only on certain modes of delivery, most often on Modes 1 and 3. Their point of departure is not Art. V but rather the level of liberalization set by the chosen Members GATS commitments. Most studies also do not differentiate between market access (MA) and national treatment (NT) limitations but group them together. In such an analysis, every improvement or deterioration to a commitment under either field leads to a higher or lower value in the index. This contrasts with the present study that indexes limitations regarding NT separately. Since Art. V requires the elimination of existing discriminatory measures and/or prohibition of new or more discriminatory measures, any commitment falling short of full NT (whether no commitment at all or a partial commitment) brings in this study the value for that specific commitment to zero. Naturally, it can be argued that partial commitments are better than nothing but since the book applies the Art. V criteria, arguably only commitments providing for full non-discrimination should pass the test of compliance with the GATS discipline on EIAs. Moreover, a simple methodology based on existence of discrimination makes it easier to compare EIAs with each other. It also facilitates the analysis of federal entities where individual discriminatory measures are often not applied on the level of the federation but by sub-federal levels of government. In that case, our method shows the percentage share of sub-federal entities that have discriminatory exemptions in place.

The authors of empiric studies on services commitments readily acknowledge the inherent difficulties in approaching services agreements

---

[10] Hoekman, B. (1996) Assessing the General Agreement on Trade in Services, in Martin, W. & Winters, A. L. (eds.), *The Uruguay Round and the Developing Countries.* Cambridge: Cambridge University Press, 88–124; Marchetti, J. A. & Roy, M. (2008) *Opening Markets for Trade in Services: Countries and Sectors in Bilateral and WTO Negotiations.* Cambridge; New York: Cambridge University Press; Roy, M. (2011) Services Commitments in Preferential Trade Agreements: An Expanded Dataset, *WTO Staff Working Paper*, ERSD-2011-18.

[11] Marchetti, J., Roy, M. & Zoratto, L. (2012) Is There Reciprocity in Preferential Trade Agreements on Services? *WTO Staff Working Paper*, ERSD-2012-16.

[12] Roy, M., Marchetti, J. & Lim, H. (2007) Services Liberalization in the New Generation of Preferential Trade Agreements (PTAs): How Much Further than the GATS? *World Trade Review*, 6(2), 155–92; Van der Marel, E. & Miroudot, S. (2014) The Economics and Political Economy of Going Beyond the GATS. *The Review of International Organizations*, 9(2), 205–39.

empirically. Contrary to the GATT, the measures addressed in the GATS are not primarily about pricing but are qualitative in nature. To convert qualitative information into a numerical assessment of the degree of trade restrictiveness can be approached through a variety of methods ranging from the so-called frequency indices to price equivalents.[13] Hoekman explains the challenges relating to such efforts to 'quantify' the coverage of service commitments.[14] Hoekman himself focuses on GATS commitments but similar difficulties arise in quantifying commitments in EIAs. A simple method used by most quantifying studies is to count all sectors and modes where commitments are made or employ a weighting scheme that is a function of the type of commitment made.

As Hoekman notes, even if a country submits an 'unbound' in its schedule, its actual policy may be much more liberal in practice.[15] However, when characterizing commitments in an empiric legal study this is not relevant: 'unbound' means that there is no commitment. Weighing a full commitment or no commitment is straightforward but much more challenging is to weigh the various restrictions and specifications that countries list across various service sectors and modes of supply. As Hoekman points out, this is analogous to the problem affecting efforts to characterize the restrictiveness of national policy stances through indices. A simple and transparent way adopted by Hoekman himself is to give a weight of zero to 'unbound' type commitments; a weight of one to full commitments (i.e. the party has subscribed 'none', meaning there are no limitations), and a weight of 0.5 to commitments where restrictions are specified. This methodology was first adopted by Hoekman[16] and it has subsequently been used and extended by numerous authors.[17]

---

[13] Langhammer, R. J. (2005) The EU Offer of Service Trade Liberalization in the DOHA Round: Evidence of a Not-Yet-Perfect Customs Union. *Journal of Common Market Studies*, 43(2), 311–25, at 314.

[14] Hoekman, B. (2006) Liberalizing Trade in Services: A Survey. *World Bank Policy Research Working Paper*, No. 4030, at 34.

[15] 'Unbound' is part of GATS language and used by WTO Members in accordance with the WTO Secretariat's Scheduling Guidelines. 'Unbound' means that the Member has not submitted any commitments but remains free to impose any limitations under the relevant sector and mode. On the contrary, 'none' means that the relevant mode and sector is fully committed and no derogations from MA and/or NT are allowed.

[16] Hoekman, B. (1995) Tentative First Steps: An Assessment of the Uruguay Round Agreement on Services, Volume 1. *World Bank Policy Research Working Paper*, No. 1455, at 60, and Hoekman, B. (1996) Assessing the General Agreement on Trade in Services, in Martin, W. & Winters, A. L. (eds.), *The Uruguay Round and the Developing Countries*. Cambridge: Cambridge University Press, 88–124.

[17] Hoekman (2006), at 34.

One of the most interesting studies is by Marchetti and Roy[18] who have built an impressive dataset of EIA commitments. The dataset demonstrates the preferentiality of various countries' EIA commitments as compared to the same countries' MFN commitments under the GATS. The approach taken by the authors builds upon Hoekman.[19] The main difference to Hoekman is that rather than giving a score of 0.5 to all partial commitments, the index gives a higher score for each improvement in a Member's partial commitments. For each step, half the difference between the score for a full commitment (one) and the score of the partial commitment being improved is added. For example, a partial commitment that is improved by way of a foreign equity limit moving from 49 to 51 per cent would obtain a score of 0.75. A further improvement by the Member in the same sub-sector and mode would get a score of 0.875 (e.g. the foreign equity limit moving up to 60 per cent).[20]

Thus, Roy and Marchetti's index takes into account the level of commitments undertaken. The information also permits to compare a Member's commitments across its different EIAs. Overall, their results highlight that, on average, commitments undertaken in EIAs far outweigh those contained in Members' GATS schedules, but also those offered in the current Doha Round of negotiations. This stands for both Modes 1 and 3, and for countries of different levels of development. Naturally, as the authors note, the level of GATS+ commitments varies significantly across Members.[21]

Importantly, their index analyzes commitments only under Modes 1 and 3. Another shortcoming is that the evaluation of the extent to which EIAs provide for new and improved bindings necessarily involves a degree of value judgement. As the authors point out, this is the case especially when comparing commitments framed under a positive-list approach and others under a negative-list one. Therefore, the authors highlight that their overview does not in any way amount to a legal evaluation of commitments.[22]

---

[18] Marchetti, J. A. & Roy, M. (2008) *Opening Markets for Trade in Services: Countries and Sectors in Bilateral and WTO Negotiations*. Cambridge; New York: Cambridge University Press. Their study is developed further in Roy, M. (2011) Services Commitments in Preferential Trade Agreements: An Expanded Dataset, *WTO Staff Working Paper*, ERSD-2011-18. Their dataset is available at www.wto.org/english/tratop_e/serv_e/data set_e/dataset_e.htm. The publication of 2011 also updates the information collected on the basis of an index of GATS+ commitments in EIAs (Roy, Marchetti & Lim (2007)).

[19] Hoekman (1995); Hoekman (1996).

[20] Roy (2011), at 8.

[21] Ibid., 14.

[22] Marchetti & Roy (2008), at 109–10.

This contrasts with this book's methodology that aims at a legal evaluation of EIAs. The goal of legal accuracy, especially with respect to
finding the level of discrimination in the EIA commitments, requires
a somewhat simpler methodology than the methods employed in the
studies mentioned above. Since in this study EIA commitments are
mapped only with regard to sectoral coverage and full national treatment,
there is less space for such value judgement that is present in studies that
quantify different types of limitations in the commitments. Naturally,
also in the present study, there is always the possibility of errors. Our
analysis also requires interpreting provisions, in particular for comparison purposes (e.g. when the EU does not entirely follow the WTO's
Services Sectoral Classification List (MTN.GNS/W/120)) and especially
in cases where it is not completely certain whether a specific limitation in
a commitment is discriminatory or not. Therefore, the results of all
empirical studies on services commitments, ours included, should be
regarded more as an 'approximation' of the reviewed commitments
rather than a completely accurate representation of the content of
a specific EIA.

Fink and Molinuevo offer an assessment of EIAs in East Asia, focusing
on their liberalization content and their compliance with WTO rules on
regional integration. Their analysis is divided into two parts. The first part
evaluates to what extent the chosen twenty-five EIAs have offered liberalization undertakings that go beyond those to which countries are committed under the GATS. Also their dataset presents the value added by EIA
undertakings relative to pre-existing GATS commitments. They cover all
the four modes of supply. Moreover, they use the database to empirically
assess the effect of the scheduling approach on the depth and breadth of
liberalization.[23] The second part is similar to our approach in the sense that
it seeks to shed light on whether the twenty-five East Asian services EIAs
are compatible with Art. V GATS. As the authors note, while a number of
authors have commented on the disciplines of Art. V, only few studies have
confronted specific agreements with these disciplines.[24] By using the first
parameter of Art. V (sectoral coverage), the authors conclude that current
commitments under the investigated EIAs do not manifestly provide for
substantial sectoral coverage. As an obvious shortcoming, the authors'

---

[23] Their outcome suggests that negative lists appear to induce wider but not deeper PTA
commitments than positive lists. See Fink, C. & Molinuevo, M. (2008) East Asian
Preferential Trade Agreements in Services: Liberalization Content and WTO Rules.
World Trade Review, 7(4), 641–73, at 666.

[24] Ibid., at 644.

database does not separately record MA and NT commitments. However, they do observe that none of the East Asian EIAs provides for full NT across all sectors and modes. In cases where sub-sectors have been scheduled, Modes 1 and 2 are subject to the least number of explicit discriminatory measures. In many of the agreements, however, parties require the establishment of a commercial presence or the registration with local professional bodies as a prerequisite for supplying services. The authors consider that even if such restrictions are *de jure* non-discriminatory and are inscribed as MA limitations, they may be considered *de facto* discriminatory and thus be taken into account in an assessment of whether substantially all discrimination is eliminated. With regard to Mode 3, most agreements feature horizontal limitations that are relatively far-reaching and allow for the maintenance of significant discriminatory measures. Under Mode 4, the value added of the EIAs' commitments relative to the GATS is minor. Fink and Molinuevo conclude that the reviewed EIAs currently do not comply with the requirements of substantial sectoral coverage and elimination of substantially all discrimination. They contemplate that if the agreements were legally tested by the WTO, much would depend on what is considered a 'reasonable' time-frame for achieving those requirements.[25]

A study by Miroudot et al. also follows the methodology used by Hoekman,[26] Roy et al.,[27] Marchetti and Roy[28] and Fink and Molinuevo.[29] They assess the preferential content of the studied EIAs through an analysis of MA and NT commitments at the level of the 155 sub-sectors of the GATS Sectoral Classification List. Additionally, the authors have broken down partial commitments into nine categories accounting for different types of trade restrictive measures (four for MA and five for NT). These categories of limitations correspond to 'partial' commitments, where countries decide to take MA and/or NT commitments but maintain non-conforming measures. As the point of departure is to measure how preferential EIAs are, the commitments are compared to the parties' GATS commitments. The report confirms that

---

[25] Ibid, at 666.
[26] Hoekman (1995); Hoekman (1996).
[27] Roy et al. (2007).
[28] Marchetti & Roy (2008).
[29] Fink & Molinuevo (2008); Miroudot, S., Sauvage, J. & Sudreau, M. (2010) Multilateralising Regionalism: How Preferential Are Services Commitments in Regional Trade Agreements?, *OECD Trade Policy Working Papers*, No. 106. They examine services schedules of commitments in fifty-six EIAs where an OECD country is a party.

on average RTAs in services go beyond GATS with commitments in about 72 per cent of sub-sectors, among which 42 per cent correspond to preferential bindings (GATS-plus commitments). The authors have collected plenty of information on the reviewed EIAs in their database. Based on their results, we can also draw some conclusions on the level of NT reached in the agreements as they map all NT restrictions separately from MA commitments. However, their empirical analysis is not built to measure compliance against the criteria of Art. V but to show the percentage of sub-sectors covered by full or partial commitments in the EIAs as compared to the countries' GATS commitments.

Interestingly, Miroudot et al. touch upon the issue of measures taken at the sub-national or sub-central level.[30] However, because of difficulties relating to the question of how non-conforming measures in a given region should affect MA for the whole country, they decided not to take into account any sub-national or sub-federal level restrictions in the categorisation of commitments. As they note, the choice has important consequences in the analysis of the schedules of commitments of EIAs signed by the EU. According to the authors, they should ideally have done the analysis at the level of the EU Member States as restrictions are clearly different among EU members and fully listed both in the EU's consolidated GATS schedule and in EIAs. But understandably, the authors found it to be too much to analyze twenty-seven schedules of commitments for each agreement where the EU was a party at once. This affects all their results in cases where there are reservations listed for specific EU Member States. When a sector is unbound or when all EU Members have no restriction, the results are not affected. The design of the otherwise excellent study by Miroudot et al. shows the need to develop more methodologies capable of counting in restrictions taken on sub-central levels of EIA partners.

We are aware of two studies that take the internal divergence within the EU into account: Langhammer[31] and Eschenbach and Hoekman[32]. Both studies use a methodology that enables to assess the degree of uniformity across the EU Member States' commitments. Eschenbach and Hoekman look into the EU's and its post-GATS accession countries' (and certain other transition economies') commitments under the GATS and in the context of the Doha Round offers. Langhammer, on the other

[30] Ibid., at 34.
[31] Langhammer (2005).
[32] Eschenbach, F. & Hoekman, B. (2006) Services Policies in Transition Economies: On the EU and WTO as Commitment Mechanisms. *World Trade Review*, 5(3), 415–43.

hand, analyzes the EU Member States' commitments solely under the EU's services offer during the WTO's Doha Round (the EU including fifteen Member States at the time).

Eschenbach and Hoekman's study assesses the following four main issues: (a) the formal degree of service sector openness reflected in the commitments made by EU Member States in the GATS; (b) the extent to which the Member States deviate from the EU 'baseline' by imposing country-specific restrictions; (c) the degree of uniformity across Member States' commitments; and (d) the extent to which greater convergence is implied by the offers made by the EU and its members as in the context of the Doha Round. The deviation from the EU's baseline is found by setting a benchmark score for the EU as a whole, based on which it is assessed to what extent each EU Member State imposes country-specific restrictions. The authors find that the pre-Doha level of commitment for the EU-15 as a whole was 47 per cent and that most Member States do not deviate significantly from this average 'benchmark' in terms of national commitments across modes. Using Langhammer's data[33] on the EU's Doha Round offer, the authors calculate that the offer substantially increases the average commitment index from 46 per cent to slightly above 58 per cent. At the aggregate level, the standard deviation among the Member States would with such an offer fall from two under the GATS to 1.6 under the offer, indicating an increase in uniformity at the Member State level.

Langhammer's central argument is that in the field of services, the EU's level of integration is not yet comparable to the attainment of a full customs union in goods. Given the remaining national sovereignties in regulating service trade also against other EU Member States, the EU is arguably not yet even a free trade area. The author measures the EU's distance from a customs union by calculating frequency indices of trade measures by refining the 1995 Hoekman index. His database is the EU's first offer in service trade in the Doha Round in February 2003.

In order to identify differences between sector-specific concessions of individual EU Member States Langhammer modifies and expands Hoekman's method with respect to the in-between category 0.5 (ranging between 'unbound' and 'none'). Because of the importance of service trade enabled by factor flows, he gives a higher weight to Modes 3 and 4 in the assessment of openness to service trade. The author then calculates the so-called overlap or similarity index and asks which proportion of

[33] Langhammer (2005).

Member State A's concession is 'matched' by concessions of Member State B in the same service sector. The index ranges between zero (no overlap) and 100 (total overlap). A total overlap would point to identical concessions towards third countries and thus would indicate a complete customs union. In contrast to his central argument of a far-from-complete customs union, Langhammer, however, concludes that the similarity is high, at between 90 per cent and 100 per cent. Some elements of national 'specialities' of trade policy sovereignty remain, especially in three Member States who were the last ones to join the Union at the time (Austria, Finland and Sweden).[34]

These two studies concentrate on the EU's commitments under the GATS (including the EU's more recent Doha Round offer) and they give valuable information of the relative openness of the EU Member States under the GATS and the Doha Round offer (at EU-15). Unlike Eschenbach and Hoekman, we do not compare the EU Member States' commitments to each other. This information is of relevance also to us as one of the central arguments of the book is that the internal diversity in a WTO Members' commitments affects the conformity analysis of an EIA under the Art. V criteria. Our methodology, however, is focused on showing the attainment of non-discrimination per each sector as a percentage of EU Member States. Since in the EU's EIAs there is a significant degree of variation between the Member States in the number of non-discriminatory commitments offered, a percentage value quickly shows under which sectors the biggest number of Member States have provided for such a treatment. Under our analysis, this is most relevant as we argue that a contracting party with an internally divided structure in the regulation of services must reach the threshold of eliminating substantially all discrimination across its entire territory. The percentage of states thus shows to what degree such coverage is reached.

---

[34] The results of both studies appear to imply that the EU Member States' commitments towards third-country suppliers are relatively uniform. As explained in more detail in Part II where we discuss the EU's trade policy in services, we question this end result to some extent as similarities, or even identical concessions, on the part of the EU Member States do not necessarily mean that the conditions for third-country service suppliers are the same or even similar. For example, a similar measure, such as an economic-needs test (ENT), in one Member State is not necessarily applied according to the same criteria as an ENT applied by another Member State. Unless the conditions to access a specific service sector and to supply one's services post-access have been harmonized within the EU, a uniformity analysis would need to go much further in order to confirm that the conditions of service supply for third-country operators are indeed the same (as they should be in a real free trade are in services).

In Langhammer's study the EU's average score of openness is calculated by weighing the EU Member States' regulations with the share of the states in the EU's gross national income.[35] Such an approach could arguably be apt also for our method as there are significant differences in the sizes and economic weight of different EU Member States. We have, however, chosen to give the same weight to each Member State. The choice reflects the EU's structure as a union of sovereign states where each state retains powers also as an independent WTO Member. Also from the point of view of service suppliers, national boundaries still mean more in services than in the field of goods. Suppliers may choose a specific EU Member State as point of access due to proximity, cultural and language factors – not necessarily because of its economic significance. The methodology can, however, be easily adapted to take economic significance of a state into account. This could be a useful approach especially in case of a federal state with some regional powers in the regulation of services (e.g. Canada and the USA).

To summarize, our methodology differs from previous empirical studies on EIAs in two important respects. First, whereas most studies are primarily econometric in their design, our method is adapted for a purely legal analysis. It shows how EIAs correspond to the exact requirements set for EIAs by Art. V:1 GATS under all four modes of supply. It therefore allows for a legal analysis of the level of substantial coverage and non-discrimination in EIAs. Second, our methodology enables to take into account sub-central differences in the liberalization of services. In this study, such differences are accounted for among the EU Member States but the method can be used for any federal entity. In that case, the method shows the level on which the federal entity has committed to non-discriminatory liberalization as a whole.

III   New Directions in the Empirical Legal Research of PTAs

There is an increasing amount of innovative and data-driven empirical analysis carried out on trade agreements. Even if most of such studies have so far not focused specifically on EIAs,[36] they are worth mentioning for

---

[35] Langhammer (2005), at 316.
[36] A recent exception is the database of East Asian EIAs built by Fink and Molinuevo (2008). They use their database of twenty-five EIAs to empirically assess the effect of the scheduling approach (negative/positive) on the depth and breadth of liberalization undertakings. Their study is explained in more detail above in this same chapter under 'Earlier Empirical Research on EIAs'.

their overall value to the study of PTAs and for the potential that they carry also for the study of services commitments. The most interesting projects of the moment are those that employ computational analysis of legal data. A number of such studies were published in a special issue of the *Journal of International Economic Law (JIEL)* in June 2017.[37] For example, Allee, Elsig and Lugg[38] compare post-Uruguay Round PTAs to WTO agreements and reveal a strong presence of the WTO in PTAs. They note that nearly all recent PTAs reference WTO agreements explicitly, often dozens of times across multiple chapters. Likewise, they find that in many of those same PTAs substantial portions of treaty language are copied verbatim from a WTO agreement. Moreover, they carry out multiple regression analyses which reveal that larger countries and those that are most active in going preferential are also most likely to include a strong WTO presence in their PTAs. They also note that the presence of the WTO in PTAs has increased over time. In light of their research, the ties between the WTO and PTAs appear to be more solid than has been realized.[39]

A project by Alschner, Skougarevskiy and Seiermann is making a digitized and annotated set of 450 PTA full texts in English, French and Spanish publicly available. The team is carrying out research on this new corpus and showcasing how text-as-data techniques can be used to automatically map the PTA landscape. Their work is innovative in its use of automated analysis made possible by recent computational advances making it possible to treat text as data. So far, the team has digitized PTA texts and used textual similarity tools to assess PTA design patters on global, national and chapter level.[40] As noted in their preliminary results,

---

[37] Special JIEL Issue: New Frontiers in Empirical Legal Research: Text-as-Data and Network Analysis of International Economic Law, *Journal of International Economic Law*, 20(2), 1 June 2017. For references to data-driven empirical literature, see the special issue's 'Suggested, Non-Exhaustive Bibliography, Databases and Software to Carry Out Data-Driven Empirical Research of International Economic Law', pp. 419–26.

[38] Allee, T., Elsig, M. & Lugg, A. The Ties between the World Trade Organization and Preferential Trade Agreements: A Textual Analysis. *Journal of International Economic Law*, 20(2), 333–63.

[39] The paper by Allee, Elsig and Lugg (2017) is part of the efforts of the DESTA team based at the World Trade Institute (Bern). The Design of Trade Agreements (DESTA) project aims to systematically collect data on various types of PTAs. They inform to have manually coded design features for more than 620 agreements (as of February 2017). The team's website is available at www.designoftradeagreements.org (last accessed on 29 January 2019).

[40] Alschner, W., Seiermann, J. & Skougarevskiy, D., *Text-as-Data Analysis of Preferential Trade Agreements: Mapping the PTA Landscape*, UNCTAD Research Paper No. 5, UNCTAD/SER.RP/2017/5, July 2017.

their research method is especially useful for the analysis of treaty design choices. Various similarity indexes also offer new insights into the processes of normative convergence between different legal regimes, such as trade and investment law.

A growing number of databases are being built to count for the various developments taking place in preferential trading arrangements. Even if manually coded, they allow for comparisons among impressive numbers of PTAs. In one of the earlier studies in this vein, Horn, Mavroidis and Sapir examine to what extent PTAs involving the EU and the USA include obligations in areas that are not currently covered by the WTO Agreements.[41] Their first step consists of listing all the policy areas contained in the twenty-eight agreements and dividing them into fourteen 'WTO' and thirty-eight 'WTO-X' areas, where WTO provisions come under the current mandate of the WTO, and WTO-X provisions deal with issues lying outside the current WTO mandate. After that they evaluate each provision in each agreement for the extent to which it specifies at least some obligation that is clearly defined, and that is likely to be legally enforceable. They find that the EU's agreements contain almost four times as many instances of WTO-X provisions as the US agreements, but the US agreements contain more enforceable WTO-X provisions than the EU agreements.

Building on the methodology developed by Horn, Mavroidis and Sapir, a bigger database has been put together at the World Bank by Hofmann, Osnago and Ruta.[42] Their work offers a detailed assessment of the content of 279 PTAs, examining the coverage and legal enforceability of their provisions. Based on the analysis of the data, they conclude that PTAs have become deeper over time. A growing number of agreements cover an extended set of policy areas and frequently with legally enforceable provisions, including in four leading areas outside the current WTO mandate: competition policy, investment, movements of capital, and intellectual property rights protection.

[41] Horn, H., Mavroidis, P. C. & Sapir, A. (2010) Beyond the WTO? An Anatomy of EU and US Preferential Trade Agreements, *The World Economy*, 33(11), 1565–88. The authors refer to the EU as 'EC' because it was until 30 November 2009 known officially in the WTO as the European Communities.

[42] Hofmann, C., Osnago, A. & Ruta, M. (2017) *Horizontal Depth: A New Database on the Content of Preferential Trade Agreements*, Policy Research Working Paper No. WPS 7981, Washington, DC, World Bank Group. Their database covers 279 agreements signed by 189 countries between 1958 and 2015, and reflecting the entire set of PTAs in force and notified to the WTO as of 2015.

Manual coding of PTA content has been developed also by other authors.[43] Such work is needed to understand the fast development of preferential trading rules and their relationship to the WTO disciplines. The obvious shortcoming in the coding of international treaties is the subjectivity that the analysis of treaty language necessarily entails. Moreover, reading through agreements is slow and allows for a limited number of observations to be made at a time. This is the case also with our methodology.

With new applications for computational analysis and the use of big data, empirical legal research is set to become more accurate and capable of analyzing much wider samples of information than what has been possible so far. As declared by Alschner, Pauwelyn, and Puig, the time seems ripe for data-driven empirical analysis of international law.[44] They note that manual coding and analysis forces empirical legal scholars to limit themselves to convenience or random samples or to taking of other shortcuts. For example, instead of studying the entire pool of investment agreements, researchers standardly limit themselves to the analysis of model treaties to describe trends and treaty making practices. Yet, as correctly pointed out by the three authors, a host of problems can arise once researchers draw inferences from such samples or substitutes. They note the issue of selection bias in sampling, missing observations or unwarranted generalizations, which may produce a skewed or misleading picture of the larger universe in question.

Text-as-data analysis and other computational methods indeed open many new avenues to the study of trade and investment agreements. At the moment, this is especially fruitful when used to compare and draw connections between different texts and actors. However, computational analysis is not yet readily suitable for deeply qualitative analysis of legal text. For example, the research carried out for the purposes of this book required the reading and legal interpretation of the services commitments of the EU and all of its Member States – all formulated in varying legal terms and language. Without the presence of clear key words (such as 'discriminatory' or 'nationality' indicating that a specific commitment is against national treatment), the drawing of legal conclusions on the content of the commitments appears so far unattainable

---

[43] For more such research, see the references in ibid., at 3–4.
[44] Alschner, W., Pauwelyn, J. & Puig, S. (2017) Introduction to Special Issue on New Frontiers in Empirical Legal Research: The Data-Driven Future of International Economic Law, *Journal of International Economic Law*, 20(2), 217–31.

for a computer.[45] However, improvements in computer programs and especially advancements in the employment of artificial intelligence can probably already quite soon enable the use of computational analysis also in more qualitative legal research requiring normative interpretation. In order to facilitate progress towards AI enabled legal research, treaty negotiators should modify treaty templates and make them more understandable by computers. More coherence should be the goal especially in the description of services and investment commitments as they include much more qualitative information than tariff schedules. Also, standard terms should be used to describe similar events.[46] The EU's EIAs reveal that we are still far from that. Each EU Member State describes its commitments in its own way, making it sometimes challenging even for a human lawyer to understand the legal implications of the language used. The next chapter presents the methodology employed in this book and describes some of the challenges relating to the qualitative analysis of services commitments.

---

[45] Some preliminary conclusions can, however, be made based on computational analysis. For example, by searching for words that indicate discrimination, such as nationality and residence requirements. Moreover, treaty parties tend to use similar language across different PTAs. Textual comparison tools can therefore make the manual coding work much easier. Even if the final conclusion on the legal meaning of the commitment is left to the researcher, much of the process is becoming more easily automatized.

[46] For example, states often employ economic needs tests (ENTs) in their services schedules. They are among some of the most common types of barriers to services trade. However, only the specific way in which the ENT is described reveals whether it is discriminatory towards foreign service suppliers or not. Sometimes that is not entirely clear – the commitment may simply state that 'an ENT is in use'. The same issue applies to many other regulatory instruments, such as licences. A services commitment of a party to an EIA may specify that a licence is required without further specifying what are the elements to take into account in the granting of the licence. Sometimes a reference to national laws is included. The possibly discriminatory nature of the commitment is then revealed only by reading the relevant national provisions.

8

A New Methodology for the Study of EIAs

I An Overview of the Empirical Part

This chapter explains the technical details of the empirical methodology that is put forward for the study of EIAs. The methodology is based on the findings of the first part of the book and it is designed for the evaluation of services agreements in light of Art. V of the GATS. The method consists of a textual analysis of EIAs, including both the text of the agreement and the schedules of services commitments. However, the focus is on the commitments, especially on sector-specific commitments. The coding of national treatment (non-discriminatory treatment) in the sector-specific commitments allows the commitments to be directly compared to the discipline of Art. V:1 GATS, which requires the elimination of substantially all discrimination, combined with the requirement of a substantial sectoral coverage.

In Part IV of the book, the methodology is applied to four EIAs of the EU. The reviewed agreements differ from a commercially oriented FTA to a more development-oriented Economic Partnership Agreement (EPA). Only the EU side's commitments are analyzed: the purpose is to find out the approximate level of liberalization reached by the EU in those EIAs, as well as to assess how the EU's method of liberalization corresponds to the Art. V criteria. Thus, no conclusions can be drawn on the agreements in their entirety. Since the EU has concluded EIAs with very different types of countries from several different regions, the agreements are useful material for an analysis under the various elements of Art. V GATS. Yet considering that all EU Member States are highly developed countries and advanced economies, the flexibility that Art. V provides for developing countries does not apply to the EU side. Whereas the overall purpose of the agreement can be considered in the analysis under Art. V, it is argued that the EU side's level of liberalization should always correspond to the strict requirement of 'substantiality' in terms of sectoral coverage and elimination of discrimination.

In the interpretation of the results in light of the WTO rules, particularly Art. V GATS, specific attention is paid to the EU's commitments under Mode 4. In the EU's EIAs, as tends to be the case in EIAs in general, the movement of natural persons is liberalized differently to the other modes. The commitments for the entry of natural persons supplying services are usually laid out in the horizontal commitments of the party's schedule, or sometimes already in the text of the agreement itself. Their coding is thus necessarily somewhat different to the other modes where the bindings and reservations are laid out specifically for each service sector. With some modifications of the method, we try to evaluate also the EU's Mode 4 commitments and see how their liberalization level corresponds to the criteria of Art. V:1 (which in its footnote 1 asks for the substantial coverage to apply across all modes).

The EU has included a large number of external agreements with provisions on services. Many of them provide for a long-term service liberalization but do not contain GATS-type specific commitments providing clear indications as to the extent of liberalization sector by sector. Some of the agreements are oriented towards preparation for possible future accession to the EU and their primary aim is a deep integration with the EU with a type of across-the-border liberalization model. The methodology presented in this chapter is in Part IV of the book applied to agreements which all include a GATS-type, positively listed services schedule. However, the methodology can be applied also to negatively listed services schedules. In the case of negative lists each reservation has to be individually 'picked up' and reflected against the list of service sectors.[1] Therefore, the application of the method to negatively listed EIAs is more cumbersome and time-consuming. Part IV of the book shows how this can be done by using the CETA as example. The method is there applied to Canada's services commitments under one service sector. The modification of the method for negatively listed agreements is

---

[1] For this list, we use the services sectoral classification list traditionally used in the WTO and also in most EIAs, Note by the Secretariat, WTO document MTN.GNS/W/120, 10 July 1991. More on the choice below.

taken up at the end of this chapter. The choice of the EU agreements that have been reviewed in detail is explained in the beginning of the results of the empirical analysis in Part IV of the book.

II   The Methods of the Empirical Study

The purpose of the empirical review is to analyze, first, how the EU has liberalized services trade in different EIAs, and, second, to what extent the selected EIAs correspond to the requirements of Art. V GATS. Under these requirements, a specific agreement should reach the threshold of 'substantiality' both in terms of sectoral coverage and elimination of discrimination. A central element of the analysis is to show, first, how the level of liberalization varies among the EU Member States and second, how the type of the agreement affects the level of liberalization reached in the agreement on the EU side. The goal is not to reach any definite conclusion on the reviewed agreements' compliance with the GATS discipline. For that purpose, also the other party's commitments should be reviewed as well as other aspects of the agreements. Our method is particularly relevant for analyzing the level of national treatment offered, both by unitary (non-federal states) and federal entities (whether multi-level actors such as the EU or federal states). The result is an approximation of the NT as applied across the different services sectors covered by the agreement. As we do not know what exactly is meant by the elimination of 'substantially' all discrimination, we cannot say if the EU's commitments comply with GATS Art. V. However, some ideas on this are presented in Part IV.

The methodology used in the study corresponds to the core requirements of Art. V GATS regarding sectoral coverage and non-discrimination. A numerical score representing the number (percentage) of committed EU Member States is counted separately for both requirements. This way, each mode of service supply gets two scores: one for sectoral coverage and another for the level of non-discrimination.[2] This is considered useful as Art. V distinguishes the two requirements. Even if in light of Art. V only those sectors where non-discrimination is

---

[2] The scores represent the percentage of EU Member States that have included a binding commitment for a specific sector (MA) and the percentage of Member States who have granted NT. A score of 0,5 means that fourteen Member States out of twenty-eight have done that (=50 per cent). The empirical analysis is carried out on EIAs in which the EU Party had twenty-seven Member States (Croatia had not yet joined the EU). The maximum number of Member States in them is thus twenty-seven.

guaranteed are counted towards the threshold of substantial coverage, separating sectoral coverage from NT gives more information on a specific agreement. This approach is also useful for taking note of such instances where discrimination is eliminated only within a specific time-frame (something that is allowed under Art. V:1(b)).

All service sectors are given the same weight in the analysis. An alternative approach would be to give more weight to the most important sectors. They could be chosen by economic relevance in terms of value or volume. Footnote 1 to Art. V states that the condition of 'substantial sectoral coverage' is to be understood in terms of 'number of sectors, volume of trade affected and modes of supply'. Volume of trade is thus relevant. However, since Art. V does not give any clear guidance on how these different factors should be weighed, it was considered more adequate for the purposes of this study to treat all modes and sectors equally. Volume of trade is a changing factor and we do not know what is the relevant point in time.[3] Moreover, there are problems relating to the availability of reliable data on volumes of services trade.

For informative purposes, we provide aggregated results for a few service sectors regarding each reviewed EIA (Part IV, Chapter 10: Detailed Results on the EIAs). Those sectors are professional services, other business services, communication services, financial services and transport services. The aggregated results, however, express averages across several sub-sectors and for more correct results the sub-sector specific results should be consulted. The detailed results showing the numerical score for each mode and sub-sector are included in Appendix 3 at the end of the book. That Appendix comprises a review sheet on each analyzed agreement in table format. Each sheet starts with basic facts of the agreement in question (the name and parties to the agreement, the dates of signature, coming into force, notification to the WTO and full implementation of the agreement in case such a date has been agreed upon). The development level of the agreement refers to the other party's status as a developing or developed country. It is also marked whether the

---

[3] The liberalization of a specific sector can grow the volume significantly. Also, should a normally very important service sector (e.g. financial services) be given less weight only because the volume of trade in that specific sector happens to be low between the partners to a specific EIA? How to weigh the importance of supply through a specific mode is also problematic. As noted by Hoekman, establishing 'mode-of-supply' weights on a sector-by-sector basis would be a monumental task. See Hoekman, B. (1995) Tentative First Steps: An Assessment of the Uruguay Round Agreement on Services, Volume 1. *World Bank Policy Research Working Paper*, No. 1455, at 14.

EIA has been concluded bilaterally with one state ('bilateral') or with a region/group of states ('regional').

The following part of the review sheet takes note of the elements in the agreement that relate to non-discrimination. These are clauses relating to MFN (necessary in order to conclude that the agreement provides for non-discrimination) and standstill obligations (prohibition of new or more discriminatory measures in the future).

After that, the elements relating to a wider process of economic integration are taken note of. We have chosen twenty elements that we consider representing not just economic but closer political, social or cultural approximation of countries. We consider them to be the types of elements that can be considered under Art. V:2 GATS ('a wider process of economic integration or trade liberalization').

After these elements, the review sheet contains the scoring of the most important element of each EIA: the sector-specific commitments. The sectoral coverage of the EU's commitments is marked by 'SC' and national treatment by 'NT'. The scores are usually given on the level of sub-sectors. In some cases, however, the EU has not separated a sector into sub-sectors, in which case the score is given on the level of the entire sector. In case the EU has excluded a specific sector or sub-sector from its commitments, such excluded sectors are coloured in grey. Thus, a review sheet with big parts in grey reflects a large number of excluded sectors or sub-sectors.

In the review sheet, we have decided to follow the WTO Secretariat's services sectoral classification list that is to a large extent based on the United Nations' product classification list (marked as corresponding CPC).[4] In the following, the WTO Secretariat's sectoral classification list is generally referred to as 'W/120'. There are some problems relating to the use of W/120. First, it is only one means to categorize services into sectors. W/120 is not part of the GATS but has been suggested for use by the WTO Members in the Scheduling Guidelines that have been approved by the WTO's Council for Trade in Services.[5] Second, W/120

---

[4] Services sectoral classification list, Note by the Secretariat, WTO document MTN.GNS/W/120, 10 July 1991. The list was prepared by the WTO Secretariat based on comments from participating Members. The GATS does not require WTO Members to use this or any other specific classification list but most Members are using the W/120. CPC is the Central Products Classification as set out in Statistical Office of the United Nations, Statistical Papers, Series M, No. 77, CPC Prov, 1991.

[5] Guidelines for the scheduling of specific commitments under the General Agreement of Trade in Services (GATS), WTO's document S/L/92 of 28 March 2001. Adopted by the Council for Trade in Services on 23 March 2001. On page 8 it is specified that 'in general

is based on an aggregated system that sometimes combines certain services sectors that appear separated in some other classification systems, notably the UN's CPC classification system. There is some discretion in the way that sectors have been aggregated. For example, financial services and telecommunications are divided into a number of detailed sub-sectors while health related and social services receive only four overall categories with no further sub-sectors whatsoever.[6]

However, as many WTO Members use the W/120 classification and it is an agreed reference point for the categorization of services,[7] we consider it to be the most appropriate template for the comparison of services commitments in EIAs in light of Art. V. At the same time, it should be acknowledged that it does not give a perfect representation of the universe of services. Naturally, the choice also leads to certain approximation in the results, as practically no schedule is identical to another schedule in its classification of services sectors. In some instances, the EU has moved certain sectors to another location in its schedule. This, however, does not affect the results of our study and the value for such sub-sectors is marked in the relevant place in the W/120 classification. On some other occasions, however, the EU has divided a specific sub-sector of the W/120 classification list into smaller sub-sectors. In this case the EU's commitments in these smaller sub-sectors are aggregated so that the lowest score among the EU's own sub-sectors becomes the overall score for the sub-sector in the review sheet.[8] In some instances, the EU has prescribed an 'unbound' for a sub-sector which is in

---

the classification of sectors and sub-sectors should be based on the Secretariat's Services Sectoral Classification List'. In addition, it is stated that 'Where it is necessary to refine further a sectoral classification, this should be done on the basis of the CPC or other internationally recognized classification (e.g. Financial Services Annex)'.

[6] Krajewski, M. (2003) *National Regulation and Trade Liberalization in Services: The Legal Impact of the General Agreement on Trade in Services (GATS) on National Regulatory Autonomy.* The Hague: Kluwer Law International, at 101.

[7] Ibid.

[8] For example, in the EU–Korea FTA the EU has divided placement and supply services of personnel (grouped together in the WTO Secretariat's list as CPC 872) into executive search (CPC 87201), placement services (CPC 87202), supply services of office supply personnel (CPC 87203) and supply services of domestic help personnel, other commercial or industrial workers, nursing and other personnel (CPCs 87204/05/06 and 87209). Overall, the EU's commitments across all of these sub-sectors are low but the lowest score (unbound for twenty-six out of twenty-seven Member States) in placement services (Mode 1) and supply services of domestic help personnel etc. (Mode 1 and Mode 2) gives the aggregate score 0,04 (bound only for one out of twenty-seven Member States) for the entire sector of placement services.

a more aggregate form in W/120.[9] In this case, the lack of commitment in the sub-sector used by the EU nullifies the commitment for the entire sub-sector in the W/120 classification. The EU has also scheduled certain sub-sectors that are not included in the W/120 classification. These EU's own sub-sectors are not taken into account in the review sheets but are taken note of and included in the annexed sheets containing the detailed explanations on each reviewed agreement.

These last three methodological choices somewhat reduce the real value of the EU's commitments, but these cases are overall rare. The exclusion of the additional sectors liberalized by the EU is necessary so that the scheduling modalities of the classification list prepared by the WTO Secretariat can be followed. The chosen method makes the EU's commitments comparable to other WTO Members' commitments scheduled according to the same classification model (or according to slight variations of it).

As the idea behind the methodology is not to find out how restrictive the commitments are, their level is not rated. This would be difficult, as such rating would require a careful qualitative analysis of each commitment.[10] Instead, the purpose is, to provide a relatively simple and straightforward tool to analyze EIAs in light of Art. V GATS, and more specifically in light of the first paragraph of Art. V. Thus, the method is primarily designed to find out the number of sectors providing for full non-discrimination.

i The Scoring of Sector-Specific Commitments

The coverage of the agreement is revealed by the numerical scores given to all sector-specific commitments of a party. Under this method, in the case of a contracting party that has made its commitments only on the level of the central government (no sub-central commitments included), the value given to each commitment is either one or zero. Under the

---

[9] An example are related scientific and technical consulting services (CPC 8675) under which the EU has otherwise committed a full binding but has specified 'unbound' for exploration services under Mode 1. Even though exploration services are only part of the larger service sector CPC 8675, the lack of commitment in part of the sector nullifies the commitment for the rest of the sector.

[10] Something that is recognized by Roy, Marchetti and Lim in their empirical study on the preferentiality of WTO Members PTA commitments as compared to their GATS commitments. See Roy, M., Marchetti, J. & Lim, H. (2007) Services Liberalization in the New Generation of Preferential Trade Agreements (PTAs): How Much Further than the GATS? *World Trade Review*, 6(2), 155–92.

column of sectoral coverage (SC), value one means that there is some type (any type) of a commitment under the relevant sector or sub-sector. Value zero means that the relevant sector or sub-sector has been completely excluded from the party's commitments. Under the NT column, value one means full commitment (i.e. full NT) and value zero means that the specific sector or sub-sector is unbound or that the commitment is qualified (limited) in a way that does not provide for full NT.

In the case of the EU, the numerical scores reveal the internal dispersion among the commitments between different Member States. In addition to the EU, the same application of the method can be used for any federal entity that has internal dispersion in its services commitments (such as many federal states). The overall number of EU Member States depends on how many Member States the EU had at the time of conclusion of the agreement. For the reviewed EIAs, the number of Member States is either twenty-seven (the EIAs with CARIFORUM, South Korea and Central America), or twenty-eight (the EIA with Georgia). The maximum possible score for the EU party is one, corresponding to 100 per cent of the Member States (all Member States committed), and the minimum score is zero (no Member State has given a commitment). If the score for SC is one, it means that all the Member States have some type of a commitment for the sector or sub-sector in question. As the commitment is for sectoral coverage only, the commitment does not need to provide for full NT, a qualified commitment suffices. If, for example, all twenty-seven Member States signatory to the EIA have a full or a qualified commitment on a specific sector, the score for that sector's coverage is 100 per cent. If twenty of them have a commitment, the score is 20/27, that is 0,74, which represents 74 per cent of the Member States. If, for example, only five Member States have some type of a commitment for a specific sector, the score is 5/27, which makes 19 per cent (0,19).

With regard to the column on NT, score one indicates that all EU Member States provide for non-discriminatory treatment in respect of the other party's service suppliers. If the score is zero, no Member State has prescribed a non-discriminatory commitment. In most cases, however, the score is something between zero and one. For example, if ten out of twenty-seven Member States have committed to NT, the NT commitment for that specific sector or sub-sector gets the score 10/27 which equals 0,37. This is the same as 37 per cent of the Member States. For example, in the EU–Korea EIA, under taxation services (CPC 863) and concerning Mode 1, four out of twenty-seven Member States have prescribed 'unbound' which

Table 8.1 *EU and its Member States' Mode 1 reservations for taxation services in EU–Korea EIA*

1. BUSINESS SERVICES	For Mode 1
A. Professional Services	AT: Nationality condition for representation before competent authorities.
c) Taxation services (CPC 863)	CY: Tax agents must be duly authorised by the Minister of Finance. Authorisation is subject to an economic needs test. The criteria used are analogous to those for granting permission for foreign investment (listed in horizontal section). As these criteria apply to this sub-sector, the employment situation in the sub-sector is always taken into consideration. BG, MT, RO, SI: Unbound.

means that twenty-three Member States have some kind of a binding (see Table 8.1). Twenty-three Member States out of twenty-seven represent 85 per cent, which gives the relevant sub-sector of professional services the score 0.85 for sectoral coverage (SC). Under NT, however, two of the committed Member States have included a discriminatory specification. Therefore, for NT the score is slightly lower, representing twenty-one out of twenty-seven Member States (0,78, i.e. 78 per cent).[11]

Under the NT column, only such bindings that provide for full NT are taken into account in the score. The bindings can be somehow qualified, but they cannot be overtly discriminatory. For example, a Member State may have prescribed a quota but if the quota is directed towards the other party's service suppliers only, the Member State's score for NT in that sub-sector is zero. If, on the other hand, the quota appears to be applied in a non-discriminatory way to all service suppliers willing to offer their services in the market (domestic and foreign alike), it does not affect the Member State's NT score. Even though even non-discriminatory quotas are MA limitations under the GATS, they are not relevant in our study as our methodology is based on an interpretation of Art. V GATS that requires the elimination of discrimination without the need to eliminate

---

[11] Cyprus has inscribed a requirement of authorization that is subject to an economic needs test applied only to foreigners (as explained in its horizontal commitments). Austrian commitment includes a nationality condition for representation before competent authorities.

non-discriminatory MA limitations such as those listed in Art. XVI GATS.

Problems in interpretation arise in the very often-occurring case of qualified commitments, i.e. commitments that provide for some type of limitations. The separation of discriminatory limitations from non-discriminatory ones is the most challenging aspect of the chosen approach. The EU follows a scheduling practice that generally does not separate discriminatory MA restrictions from non-discriminatory ones. Instead, the EU's EIA schedules include only two columns, of which the first one contains the relevant sector and the second one the 'description of reservations'. This practice is likely to result from the EU's interpretation of the GATS[12] and especially Art. XVI on MA.[13] The list of prohibited MA limitations of Art. XVI does not differentiate between discriminatory and non-discriminatory limitations. Many WTO Members, including the EU, have decided not to differentiate between the two types of limitations in their EIA schedules. This scheduling practice, however, differs from the GATS. In the EU's GATS schedule, as in the case of all other Members' GATS schedules, there are altogether four columns. The first column includes the sectors and sub-sectors, after which there are two separate columns: one for 'Limitations on Market Access' and another one for 'Limitations on National Treatment'. The fourth column is reserved for 'Additional Commitments'.[14]

---

[12] The issue is not completely clear under the GATS. There is a scholarly debate concerning the applicability of Art. XVI GATS to non-discriminatory MA limitations. The general opinion appears to favour the view that also non-discriminatory limitations are covered as long as they come under the list of measures included in Art. XVI:2 GATS. See especially Pauwelyn, J. (2005) Rien ne Va Plus? Distinguishing Domestic Regulation from Market Access in GATT and GATS. *World Trade Review*, 4(2), 131–70, and Mavroidis, P. C. (2007) Highway XVI ReVisited: The Road from Non-Discrimination to Market Access in GATS. *World Trade Review*, 6(1), 1–23.

[13] The EU's EIAs follow closely the wording of the GATS in its provisions on MA and NT. See e.g. in the EU–Korea EIA, Art. 7.5 (MA) and Art. 7.6 (NT) with regard to Cross-Border Supply and Art. 7.11 (MA) and Art. 7.12 (NT) with regard to Establishment. The section on 'Temporary presence of Natural Persons for Business' does not have provisions on MA and NT.

[14] Entries in this column are not obligatory and rarely used. If a Member so wishes, it may in a given sector make additional commitments relating to measures other than those subject to scheduling under Articles XVI and XVII. These commitments can deal, for example, with qualifications, standards and licensing matters. The column should be used to indicate positive undertakings, not to list additional limitations or restrictions. See the WTO Secretariat's Guidelines for the Scheduling of Specific Commitments under the General Agreement on Trade in Services (GATS), adopted by the Council for Trade in Services on 23 March 2001, S/L/92, 28 March 2001 ('Scheduling Guidelines').

The combination of MA and NT limitations means that if a specific sector or sub-sector is prescribed as 'unbound' (no commitment at all), the score is automatically zero for SC and NT alike. If a Member State, or the EU as a whole, has prescribed 'none', it means that the sector or sub-sector is bound and there is full NT. This practice has its positive sides. When all restrictions are in one column, one does not need to contemplate how a commitment in the MA column affects the commitment in the NT column. This problem was at issue in *China–Electronic Payment Services* where it was considered in what case an 'unbound' in the MA column takes over the notation 'none' in the national treatment column.[15] In the EU's schedule, an 'unbound' is clearly effective for both MA and NT.

However, the combination of MA and NT limitations under one column in the EU's EIAs makes it difficult, and sometimes impossible, to understand whether a specific restriction is applied on a discriminatory basis or not. This is the case, for example, with conditions relating to quotas or economic needs tests that do not always specify whether the conditions are applied only to foreigners or to domestic and foreign service suppliers alike. In most cases, however, it is possible to understand which type of measure is in question. Therefore, if it is obvious that restricting measures such as standards and licensing requirements are applied to domestic and foreign suppliers alike, they are considered non-discriminatory.

The EU has paid attention to the issue of scheduling of measures that apply to domestic and foreign service suppliers alike. The EU prescribes MA limitations listed in Art. XVI GATS but does not prescribe measures that somehow restrict the supply of services but do not constitute MA or NT limitations. The EU has included the following statement in the beginning of its services schedules on all modes:

> The list below does not include measures relating to qualification requirements and procedures, technical standards and licensing requirements and procedures when they do not constitute a market access or a national treatment limitation within the meaning of Articles 7.5 and 7.6. Those

---

[15] Panel Report, *China – Measures Affecting Electronic Payment Services*, WT/DS413/R, adopted 31 August 2012, paras. 7.661–7.669. The Panel found that the special scheduling rule in Art. XX:2 GATS applied to China's inscription of 'Unbound' under the MA column for the cross-border supply of electronic payment services under Mode 1 even though with regard to NT China had inscribed 'none'. China was therefore allowed to maintain the full range of limitations expressed in Art. XVI:2, whether discriminatory or not. According to Art. XX:2 GATS, 'measures inconsistent with both Articles XVI and XVII shall be inscribed in the column relating to Article XVI. In this case the inscription will be considered to provide a condition or qualification to Article XVII as well'.

measures (e.g. need to obtain a licence, universal service obligations, need to obtain recognition of qualifications in regulated sectors and need to pass specific examinations, including language examinations), even if not listed, apply in any case to services and service suppliers of [Korea].[16]

The types of measures described typically relate to NT (they are not part of the quantitative limitations included in Art. XVI GATS on MA). The EU's statement makes the empirical analysis thus easier in the sense that if a Member State or the EU as a whole has included a measure listed above, it can be assumed to be a limitation to NT. Therefore, if a specific licensing requirement has been set out in a schedule, it can be assumed that it is applied to foreign services or service suppliers only.

Some of the most challenging limitations to interpret are quotas and economic needs tests (ENTs). The EU's practice appears to be to list both discriminatory and non-discriminatory MA limitations such as these two types of measures. It is not often clear whether they apply only to foreigners or to all service suppliers, domestic and foreigners alike.[17] In the review, there is a certain margin of error in this regard. Sometimes it is possible to interpret that a certain ENT applies to all service suppliers (domestic and foreigners alike), in which case it is considered a non-discriminatory MA limitation and it thus does not affect the relevant commitment's NT score. In certain other cases, however, the field of application of the ENT remains a mystery, as it is often not specified whether ENTs are applied on a discriminatory or non-discriminatory basis. There are, however, differences between the Member States in this regard. An example of a clearly formulated condition of a non-discriminatory ENT is Italy's commitment under services auxiliary to transport (heading 17 A) in the EU–Korea EIA. It includes a footnote 75 specifying that an ENT is applied on a non-discriminatory basis. An example of an unclear scheduling is France's commitment under legal services (CPC 861) which specifies that lawyers' access to the profession of 'avocat auprès de la Cour de Cassation' and 'avocat auprès du Conseil d'État' is subject to quotas and to a nationality condition. It is not specified whether the quota applies also to France's own nationals. The

---

[16] Annex 7-A-1 of the EU–Korea FTA, p. 1165. The EU's other EIAs include similar statements.

[17] The same problem relates also to other WTO Members' schedules. Many schedules do not provide a precise description as to whether the origin of the service or service supplier is a criterion of the test. Sometimes the discriminatory criterion may be inferred from the commitment. See the WTO Secretariat's Note 'Economic Needs Tests', WTO document S/CSS/W/118, 30 November 2001, Council for Trade in Services, Special Session.

nationality condition, however, ensures that the service supply by Korean nationals is prohibited and there is thus no NT.

The analysis of ENTs therefore requires a careful case-by-case analysis based on the wording of each commitment. If there is no sign of discrimination, there is no effect on the score for NT. In case the field of application of the measure is unspecified, the score for NT goes to zero as the Member State in question can, in principle, claim that it is free to apply the quota or ENT as it wishes. There is thus at least a possibility of discrimination. One specific case of ENTs are those that are applied to the groups of persons admitted to the Member States under Mode 4. The EU has in its annexes on the reservations applying to Mode 4 specified that in those sectors where ENTs are applied, 'their main criteria will be the assessment of the relevant market situation in the Members State of the European Union or the region where the service is to be provided, including with respect to the number of, and the impact on, existing service suppliers'.[18] Considering that the assessment is extremely open-ended ('relevant market situation') and conducted with respect to the number of *existing* service suppliers, it is likely to affect foreign service suppliers differently from domestic suppliers. Foreigners' access to the market is often subject to visas or some other type of entry permission. ENTs are usually applied at the point of entry to the country. ENTs can be applied to domestic service suppliers as well but typically only in certain regulated professions. Open-ended ENTs under Mode 4 are therefore considered discriminatory by definition as Member States remain free to deny entry to the country altogether.

The biggest challenge in our method of interpretation and legal analysis relates to reservations that appear especially burdensome for foreign suppliers. As has already been discussed in Part I of the book, Art. XVII GATS prohibits both *de jure* and *de facto* discrimination.[19] In accordance with paragraph 2, 'treatment no less favourable' is attained by according to services and service suppliers of any other Member, either formally identical treatment or formally different treatment than the treatment accorded to the Member's own like services and service suppliers. Under paragraph 3, the treatment is to be considered less favourable if it

---

[18] See e.g. Annex IV D to the EU–CARIFORUM EIA.

[19] The EU's EIAs have almost identical NT provisions to the GATS Art. XVII:3. For example, Art. 7(6) of the EU–Korea EIA reads as follows: 'Formally identical or formally different treatment shall be considered to be less favourable if it modifies the conditions of competition in favour of services or service suppliers of a Party compared to like services or service suppliers of the other Party'.

modifies the conditions of competition in favour of services or service suppliers of the Member compared to like services or service suppliers of any other Member.

A modification in the conditions of competition in favour of a Member's own services or service suppliers can be hard to establish in a real-life situation and it is possibly even harder to establish based on a simply-worded commitment in a service schedule. Under the GATS, the requirement to provide 'treatment no less favourable' than to one's own like services and service suppliers depends, to a large extent, on the definition of 'likeness'. Likeness can be hard to prove in any given context, let alone in an abstract situation of a scheduled commitment. In addition, even though Art. XVII clearly covers also *de facto* discrimination, its exact meaning and scope remains unclear. As explained by Krajewski, a measure can be considered to constitute *de facto* discrimination if it (a) does not formally discriminate against foreign services and service suppliers but (b) has the same or similar effects as a formally discriminating measure. The absence of formal discrimination is usually easy to determine on the basis of the plain language of the measure but the existence of a situation under condition (b) is harder to ascertain, as it requires the determination of a discriminatory effect.[20] Therefore, to know whether a Member should in any particular case apply formally identical or formally different treatment to a foreign service or service suppliers often depends on the particularities of the specific case and on the effects that the measure has in that specific case.[21]

So far, the case law on 'likeness' in the context of the GATS remains elusive. With regard to NT under Art. XVII, the Panel in *China – Publications and Audiovisual Products* held that likeness is established when origin is the only factor on which a measure bases a difference of treatment between domestic and foreign service suppliers.[22] Such a 'presumption of likeness' was confirmed in the recent case *Argentina – Financial Services*, where the AB considered that a complainant may establish 'likeness' by demonstrating that the measure at issue makes

---

[20] Krajewski (2003), at 108. In addition, the GATS-case law on non-discrimination is very limited and we do not have much guidance on the issue of what types of discrimination *de facto* are covered by the agreement.

[21] On the concept of national treatment and likeness under the GATS, see especially Diebold, N. F. (2010) *Non-Discrimination in International Trade in Services: 'Likeness' in WTO/GATS*. Cambridge; New York: Cambridge University Press, at 50–62.

[22] *China – Measures Affecting Trading Rights and Distribution Services for Certain Publications and Audiovisual Products*, WT/DS363/R, Report of the Panel, circulated 12 August 2009, para. 7.975.

a distinction between services and service suppliers based exclusively on origin.[23] The AB also noted that 'measures allowing the application of a presumption of "likeness" will typically be measures involving a *de jure* distinction between products of different origin'.[24] If there are issues other than origin, a more detailed analysis becomes necessary. The panel engaged in a somewhat deeper analysis in *China – Electronic Payment Services*, where it concluded that like services are to be in a competitive relationship with each other. In any case, a case-by-case analysis is required.[25]

This is the challenge with an *ex ante* review. A case-by-case review cannot be engaged in with regard to each commitment with potential implications of indirect discrimination. Moreover, the analysis of 'likeness' requires the establishment of a *competitive relationship* between services considered like. With no real-life services and service suppliers this is impossible. Any analysis is bound to stay on the level of speculation. In addition, as noted by the AB in *Argentina – Financial Services*, the scope for a 'presumption of likeness' under the GATS should be more limited than in the context of trade in goods. According to the AB, establishing 'likeness' based on the presumption may often involve greater complexity in trade in services, due to the fact that the determination of 'likeness' under Articles II:1 and XVII:1 GATS involves consideration of both the service and the service supplier. This may render it more complex to analyze whether or not a distinction is based exclusively on origin, in particular, due to the role that domestic regulation plays in shaping the characteristics of services and service suppliers and consumers' preferences. In addition, in the field of services there are notable complexities of determining origin and whether a distinction is based exclusively on origin. Furthermore, an additional layer of complexity stems from the existence of different modes of supply and their implications for the determination of the origin of services and service suppliers.[26]

Due to these inherent challenges in determining likeness in the context of services, as a general rule, our analysis can only take account of *de jure* discrimination and the most blatant forms of *de facto* discrimination.

---

[23] *Argentina – Measures Relating to Trade in Goods and Services*, WT/DS453/AB/R, Report of the Appellate Body, circulated 14 April 2016, para. 6.38.

[24] Ibid., para. 6.36.

[25] *China – Electronic Payment Services*, WT/DS413/R, Report of the Panel, circulated 16 July 2012, paras. 7.700–7.702.

[26] *Argentina – Measures Relating to Trade in Goods and Services*, paras. 6.38–6.40.

The most obvious cases of discrimination are nationality requirements. All limitations requiring residency in the host state are also considered discriminatory as they effectively preclude the supply of services through Modes 1, 2 and 4.[27] Under Mode 3 residency requirements, on the other hand, are considered discriminatory only when they go further than requiring establishment (e.g. by requiring permanent establishment for a specific period of time prior to granting full non-discriminatory treatment). Measures that require specific types of legal entity or joint venture through which a service must be supplied are also considered discriminatory in case they apply only to foreign service suppliers.[28]

On the contrary, potentially indirectly discriminatory requirements can escape our analysis. Such requirements can relate to various aspects of host-state legislation relating, for example, to specific quality requirements or professional requirements that are not openly discriminatory but can be more easily fulfilled by host state nationals, for example, due to their education, language skills or acquired experience in the host state. In principle, Art. XVII could possibly be considered to prohibit excessive requirements relating to host-state permissions, qualifications and procedures that modify the conditions of competition in favour of local service suppliers compared to like services or service suppliers of the other party.[29] However, since service schedule commitments are typically

---

[27] Also conditions that *in practice* necessitate extensive prior residence are considered discriminatory. For example, in the EU–Korea EIA, Denmark requires that marketing of legal advice services under Mode 1 is reserved to lawyers with a Danish licence to practice and to law firms registered in Denmark. In addition, there is a requirement of a Danish legal examination to obtain a Danish licence. In the case of an individual lawyer, this would usually necessitate university studies in Denmark and thus prior residence there. For law firms, it is not clear what registration in Denmark means but it is likely to require some type of establishment, which contravenes the essence of Mode 1 that is to supply services across borders without local presence.

[28] Such measures appear under subsection (e) of Art. XVI:2 on MA. However, measures requiring a special type of legal entity from foreigner service suppliers are clearly discriminatory so such measures must be considered to be in breach of Art. XVII. The same conclusion applies to subsection (f) of Art. XVI:2 (limitations on the participation of foreign capital in terms of maximum percentage limit on foreign shareholding or the total value of individual or aggregate foreign investment).

[29] When considering the scope of *de facto* discrimination, the interpretative footnote to Art. XVII:1 must be considered. The footnote states 'Specific commitments assumed under this Article shall not be construed to require any Member to compensate for any inherent competitive disadvantages which result from the foreign character of the relevant services or service suppliers'. The footnote implies that inherent characteristics of a foreign service supplier working to the supplier's disadvantage need to be separated from a disadvantage

extremely vague and we do not have any specific, real-life service suppliers whose situation to analyze, such potential breaches of the NT obligation cannot be included in an empirical analysis such as the one in the present study. Uninformed estimations one way or another could skew the final outcome considerably if incorrectly analyzed. Therefore, in this study only clearly discriminatory limitations are noted. More covert indirect discrimination may thus escape the analysis and qualify as a full NT commitment.

However, we estimate that such cases are very limited. Considering that NT is not an all-encompassing concept under the GATS but available only in situations where Members have opted in for NT through their commitments, it would be far-fetched to assume that any measure causing adverse effects on service suppliers of other countries would amount to discrimination. Such measures would be extremely hard to schedule, as their effects are often not foreseeable. We agree with Krajewski who argues that only such measures should be considered discriminatory that can at least theoretically be scheduled. A broader interpretation of the NT obligation of Art. XVII could be detrimental to national regulatory autonomy.[30] Therefore, even though a certain margin of error exists, our analysis should be able to catch most forms of discrimination according to this approach. Another issue is that measures, which are not considered discriminatory by a Member, are typically not prescribed in its schedule. Their discriminatory effect may be revealed only in dispute settlement. Naturally, such measures escape any empirical analysis, as we can only consider measures that are scheduled. We of course cannot exclude that certain measures considered non-discriminatory by a Member are actually violations of the NT obligation, but as long as they are not included in the Member's schedule, they cannot in any case be taken into account. They would be revealed only *ex post*, when faced with a foreign service supplier in a real-life situation.

Last, state monopolies, even though not discriminatory per se (they are listed under Art. XVI GATS on MA), are considered of equal value to

created by *de facto* discrimination. Therefore, only 'true' discrimination should be considered as a violation of Art. XVII. In addition, the existence of a separate discipline on domestic regulation (Art. VI) suggests that Art. XVII should be clearly distinguished from non-discriminatory measures subject to Art. VI:4. See the discussion in Krajewski (2003), at 108–14 and Diebold (2010), at 58–9. On drawing the limits between the disciplines on domestic regulation, MA and NT see also Pauwelyn, J. (2005) Rien ne Va Plus? Distinguishing Domestic Regulation from Market Access in GATT and GATS. *World Trade Review*, 4(2), 131–70, and Mavroidis (2007).

[30] Krajewski (2003), at 113–14.

'unbound' in the review since state monopolies in practice make it impossible for a foreign service supplier to access the market. State monopolies therefore nullify the score for both sectoral coverage and NT for the Member State in question.[31] In addition, in light of the recent WTO dispute settlement case *China – Electronic payment services*, monopolies can be considered NT violations if not scheduled as limitations.[32]

ii   The Treatment of Horizontal Limitations

In addition to sector-specific commitments, most services schedules include a section referred to as 'horizontal commitments'. They include commitments, typically limitations, applying to all of the sectors included in the schedule. They often refer to a particular mode of supply, in most cases to Modes 3 and 4. Any evaluation of sector-specific commitments must therefore take any such horizontal entries into account.

Quantifying the restrictiveness of horizontal limitations is, however, especially problematic. While they apply to all modes of supply across all the sectors, the effects they have on particular sectors greatly differ from each other.[33] In the EU's EIAs, horizontal limitations for Modes 1 and 2 typically concern real estate. In the case of Mode 3, they concern real estate, public utilities, some aspects of investment and types of establishment. Under Mode 4, the horizontal limitations relate to ENTs and certain categories of persons, their residence and qualifications. Since the limitations are in most cases discriminatory, taking them into account under each separate sector would nullify most of the commitments altogether.

While horizontal commitments are often discriminatory, we consider that there must be some room for them and the rest of the analysis on sector-specific commitments should be separated from them. Naturally, the horizontal limitations must be taken into account in the overall assessment as their extent may largely affect the conditions of service

---

[31] Under wholesale trade services (Section B of the EU–Korea FTA) the state monopolies on tobacco are not taken into account in the score as their significance in the entire sector is minor.

[32] Hoekman, B. & Meagher, N. (2014) China – Electronic Payment Services: Discrimination, Economic Development and the GATS. *World Trade Review*, 13(2), 409–42, at 439. See the Panel Report in *China – Measures Affecting Electronic Payment Services*, WT/DS413/R, adopted on 31 August 2012.

[33] Hoekman, B. (1996) Assessing the General Agreement on Trade in Services, in Martin, W. & Winters, A. L. (eds.), *The Uruguay Round and the Developing Countries*. Cambridge: Cambridge University Press, 88–124, at 14.

supply. This is the case especially under Mode 4, where the horizontal commitments in principle determine the conditions of entry for foreign suppliers.

Authors of empirical studies have treated horizontal commitments in varying ways. Fink and Molinuevo treat them as if they were inscribed in each scheduled sub-sector. They consider the approach most appropriate from a legal perspective as it directly follows the scheduling guidelines under the GATS.[34] Since their method in analyzing sectoral commitments is less aggregated than ours, it accommodates such an approach. Hoekman takes horizontal limitations into account with regard to Mode 4.[35] Roy et al., on their part, also assess the horizontal limitations. However, so as not to overestimate their effect, they only factor into the scoring the more stringent types of horizontal limitations (and improvements to them). In their analysis, those are foreign equity restrictions, limitations on the number of suppliers, including through economic needs tests, joint-venture requirements and nationality requirements.[36]

In our analysis, we review all the horizontal limitations in the EU's EIA schedules. However, so as not to overestimate their impact on the sector-specific analysis, we only take note of them and do not factor them into the non-discrimination analysis. Naturally, in assessing the extent of non-discriminatory treatment granted to each EIA partner, the horizontal part of the commitments is relevant and it is thus separately analyzed in connection with each agreement.

iii   Issues Relating to a Wider Process of Economic Integration or Trade Liberalization

In addition, the review sheet takes into account the wide array of disciplines included in the EU's modern PTAs. They are considered to form part of the larger context that can be seen reflected in Art. V:2 GATS which gives consideration to a 'wider process of economic integration or trade liberalization'. The existence or non-existence of these elements does not affect the scoring and they are thus simply noted in the beginning of each review sheet (see Appendix 3). The disciplines taken note of

---

[34] Fink, C. & Molinuevo M. (2008) East Asian Preferential Trade Agreements in Services: Liberalization Content and WTO Rules. *World Trade Review*, 7(4), 641–73, at 671.

[35] Hoekman (1995), 15: 'In all cases where a reference is made under the temporary entry mode of supply to a horizontal commitment (restriction), a value of 0.5 was entered'.

[36] Roy, M. (2011) Services Commitments in Preferential Trade Agreements: An Expanded Dataset. *WTO Staff Working Paper*, ERSD-2011-18, at 18.

include areas such as harmonization and mutual recognition schemes, domestic regulation and regulatory cooperation schemes. We also note the presence of WTO-X areas such as competition policy, investment protection and labour mobility (immigration) schemes.[37]

iv   Review of Commitments on Mode 4

Mode 4 liberalization commitments are typically crafted along somewhat different parameters than the other modes and are also subject to specific disciplines. In the EU's EIAs, the types of categories of persons admitted under Mode 4 are specified in the text of the agreement. Limitations to Mode 4 are sometimes included also in the horizontal section of the commitments. The text of the agreement already specifies what type of service suppliers are allowed to enter the EU under Mode 4. The structure of commitments thus critically differs from the rest of the modes, as the possibility of supply through Mode 4 greatly depends on the categories of persons admitted. The analysis of Mode 4 thus necessarily requires a somewhat different assessment. This is done in connection with each agreement through a separate analysis of the EU's Mode 4 commitments. The sector-specific Mode 4 commitments applicable to these specified-categories of persons are, in addition, taken into account normally in the sector-specific analysis and marked into the review sheet. It should, however, be noted that the value of the sector-specific commitments under Mode 4 greatly depends on the types and number of categories of persons admitted in the first place. These categories are noted in the explanation of the results in Chapter 10, Part IV of the book.

Under Mode 4, the most often-occurring limitations are citizenship, nationality and residency requirements. They are considered discrimi-natory as they in essence prohibit the supply of a service by a foreign national through temporary presence. The biggest challenges in inter-pretation relate to ENTs. The cover page of the EU's schedules on Mode 4 contains a statement on ENTs that is not present in the cover page on Modes 1–3. The statement includes the criteria used for ENTs but does not specify whether they are applied in a discriminatory or non-discriminatory manner.[38] However, it is worth noting that under Mode 4 ENTs are likely to be applied in a discriminatory manner as they

---

[37] For a full list of the noted areas, see the review sheets in Appendix 3 and the list of issues under 'wider process of economic integration'.
[38] See e.g. Annex 7-A-3 in the EU–Korea EIA.

typically concern the right to work in fields where no economic criteria are applied to EU Member States' own nationals.[39] As is also noted in the WTO's Secretariat's Note on ENTs, in cases where movement of natural persons is subject to an ENT, the limitation is typically intended to discriminate between foreign and local workers. This is clearest when an ENT limits access to situations where there is a 'lack of availability in the local labour market', or a 'lack of domestic supply'.[40]

Before going to the results on the reviewed EIAs, the following chapter addresses some of the challenges that are present in the empirical analysis of services commitments. It explains some alternative approaches that could be used to adapt the methodology to different scheduling practices (especially to negative listing) and to take into account economic differences between different service sectors and sub-central actors.

---

[39] In the EU, occupations are usually subject to quotas only in some regulated professions. Moreover, non-discriminatory ENTs usually include detailed specifications on the criteria applied. For example, the EU Member States have prescribed ENTs with regard to certain social and health care services (e.g. hospital and ambulance services). The criteria typically applied are the number of and impact on existing establishments, transport infrastructure, population density, geographic spread, and creation of new employment. In these cases, the measure's application to all service suppliers can often be inferred (though a margin of error does exist). In the case of Mode 4, the EU Member States usually impose an ENT without any further criteria and in such sectors where access to employment would not typically be restricted with regard to one's own nationals.

[40] See the WTO Secretariat's Note 'Economic Needs Tests', WTO document S/CSS/W/118, 30 November 2001, Council for Trade in Services, Special Session, p. 6.

9

Adaption to Scheduling Differences
and Economic Realities

I On Modes and Sectors

Liberalization of services is a complex exercise and it can be conducted in a number of ways. Art. V GATS includes a significant degree of choice as to the method of liberalization. In contrast to the elimination of duties,[1] WTO Members are not under a legal obligation to use any specific template for scheduling their commitments across services sectors.[2] In the GATS, commitments were generally scheduled in accordance with the W/120 template recommended to be used by the WTO Secretariat.[3] However, there are some differences in the grouping of the sectors, and

---

[1] In their tariff schedules, WTO Members' must use an international nomenclature, the Harmonized System (HS), developed by the World Customs Organization, which is arranged in six-digit codes allowing all participating countries to classify traded goods on a common basis. Beyond the six-digit level, countries are free to introduce national distinctions for tariffs and many other purposes. See Dayong, Y. (2008) *The Harmonized System – Amendments and Their Impact on WTO Members' Schedules*, WTO Staff Working Paper ERSD-2008–02.

[2] Guidelines adopted by the WTO Council for Trade in Services (2001) note that '[i]n general, the classification of sectors and sub-sectors should be based on the Secretariat's Services Sectoral Classification List'. In that list, each sector is identified by the corresponding UN Central Product Classification (CPC) number. It is further noted that where it is necessary to refine a sectoral classification, this should be done on the basis of the CPC or other internationally recognized classification (e.g. Financial Services Annex). If a Member cannot provide concordance with the CPC (e.g. when using its own sub-sectoral classification or definitions), it should give a sufficiently detailed definition to avoid any ambiguity as to the scope of its commitment. See WTO, 'Guidelines for the Scheduling of Specific Commitments under the General Agreement on Trade in Services (GATS)', Adopted by the Council for Trade in Services on 23 March 200, S/L/92, 28 March 2001.

[3] MTN.GNS/W/120, dated 10 July 1991, Note by the Secretariat 'Services Sectoral Classification List'.

particularly smaller sub-sectors, across the Members' GATS commitments. This is even more evident in EIAs where approaches to services liberalization are more varied than in the WTO context. The comparison of services schedules can therefore be challenging, especially in the case of agreements that employ methodologies that significantly differ from the GATS method of scheduling.

The empirical methodology presented in the previous chapter is based on the scheduling logic of the GATS. It therefore builds on the modal and sectoral approach used in that agreement. The choice is appropriate considering that the same logic, or some alterations of it, are followed also in most EIAs adopted since the entry into force of the GATS. However, WTO Members are increasingly adopting new tactics in their approach to services liberalization. These changes affect both the modes and sectors, as well as the way in which the parties' commitments are scheduled.

One of the most visible changes is the increasing merging of Modes 1 and 2. The two modes have been grouped together as 'Cross-Border Trade in Services' in EIAs followed by some of the key services exporters, such as the EU, USA, Canada and Australia. A possible change to merge the two modes was discussed among the WTO Members already soon after the conclusion of the GATS.[4] In PTAs, several WTO Members have followed the GATS model. Others have followed the NAFTA-model which had only one chapter on Cross-Border Trade in Services and described reservations without formal separation between Modes 1 and 2. The EU's EIAs after the GATS have included a chapter on 'Cross-border supply of services' (covering both modes) but its commitments have been divided into four separate modes as in the GATS.[5]

In CETA, the EU has, however, embraced the NAFTA model and agreed to schedule its commitments according to a negative listing

---

[4] A new definition of the coverage of Modes 1 and 2, or the merging of the two modes, was discussed in the context of financial services but the general view among the delegations was that any definitive agreement or understanding on the distinction between the two modes would necessarily apply to other services as well as financial services. See Job No. 3706, dated 3 July 1997, Informal Note by the Secretariat for the Committee on Trade in Financial Services, Report of Informal Consultations held on 27 June 1997 on the Distinction between Modes 1 and 2 in Financial Services (also included in the WTO document S/FIN/W/14).

[5] E.g. in the EU–Korea FTA, 'Cross-border supply of services' is defined as the supply of a service (i) from the territory of a Party into the territory of the other Party and (ii) in the territory of a Party to the service consumer of the other Party. This responds to the definitions of the first two ways to supply services in GATS Art. I:2.

(except for Mode 4 where a modified version of positive listing is followed). The CETA also did away with the formal division to Mode 1 and 2. All the EU's and its Member State's reservations to Modes 1, 2 and 3 are set out as reservations either to 'Cross-Border Trade in Services'[6] or 'Investment'. The grouping of the Mode 1 and 2 reservations together under cross-border trade makes sense considering the low level of limitations that is applied to Mode 2 (consumption abroad). In cases where such limitations are applied, they can be specifically formulated in the reservation.

Interestingly, the empirical analysis carried out for the book showed that in those cases where the EU and its Member States had described a limitation to Mode 2, they had always described a limitation to Mode 1 as well. We did not come across any situation where the Member States would have given a binding commitment for Mode 1 but no binding commitment for Mode 2. Therefore, the NT score for Mode 2 is always at least the same and usually higher than for Mode 1.[7]

Another relatively recent tendency in PTAs is to include disciplines on investment. A growing number of PTAs include a chapter on investment, thus incorporating rules that used to be the substance of bilateral investment treaties (BITs).[8] The exact scope of such chapter differs. Some PTAs provide only for post-establishment treatment and investment

---

[6] Note, also the language has changed from 'supply of services' to 'trade in services', the same as in NAFTA-modeled EIAs (e.g. most agreements concluded by the USA, Canada and Australia). In CETA, the commitments for the movement of natural persons (Mode 4) are organized in separate annexes (Annexes 10-B, 10-C, 10-D and 10-E), which are connected to the relevant chapter (Chapter Ten – Temporary Entry and Stay of Natural Persons for Business Purposes). The reservations to the different categories of natural persons are marked in a hybrid manner (sectors positively, Member State specific restrictions negatively). This is in contrast to the rest of the modes where both the EU and the Canadian reservations are marked in a negative manner.

[7] See the review sheets for each analyzed EIA in Appendix 3.

[8] Meltzer notes that there has been a rapid growth in the number of PTAs containing investment provisions. By 2015, 282 PTAs included investment provisions, with approximately 90 per cent of these agreements having been concluded since the 1990s. See Meltzer, J. (2015) Investment, in Lester, S., Mercurio, B. & Bartels, L. *Bilateral and Regional Trade Agreements: Commentary and Analysis (Volume 1)*. Cambridge: Cambridge University Press, 245–99. Currently a key issue for countries looking to negotiate investment in their FTAs is to decide whether to include a clause on politically controversial investor-state dispute settlement (ISDS). In the EU, ISDS was one of the legal questions in Opinion 2/15 of the Court of Justice (see Chapter 4 in Part II of this book). The EU Court decided that ISDS falls within shared competence between the EU and the Member States, and any EU PTA including such a dispute settlement regime is therefore subject to the Member States' consent.

protection, whereas some cover market access as well. The USA has been the champion of agreements with the full coverage, but the EU has caught up. The EU–Chile FTA, which was signed in November 2002, became the EU's first PTA with a dedicated chapter on investment liberalization and post-establishment treatment commitments for services and non-services sectors. All following EU PTAs contain similar provisions.[9]

The new modus operandi by the EU is to have in its PTAs a separate chapter on Cross-Border Trade in Services (corresponding to Modes 1 and 2), another one on Investment (corresponding partly to Mode 3) and another on Temporary Entry for Business Purposes (corresponding partly to Mode 4). Investment covers both manufacturing and services activities.[10] And similarly to investment, temporary entry for business (and sometimes some other) purposes covers also such business people who are engaged in trade in goods or in the conduct of investment activities.[11] This is in contrast with GATS Mode 4, which covers the movement of natural persons for the supply of services only.

In addition to the reorganization of modes, there are differences in the listing and classification of the services sectors across different EIAs. To improve coherence and facilitate comparative analysis, it would be the best if all EIA partners were to use the Services Sectoral Classification List (W120) used in WTO/GATS as the basis of their commitments.[12] In

[9] Basedow, R. (2016) The European Union's New International Investment Policy: Product of Commission Entrepreneurship or Business Lobbying? *European Foreign Affairs Review*, 21(4), 469–91. According to Basedow, the wider coverage of investment in EU's PTAs has been due to competitive pressure coming from European business.

[10] In the case of the EU, CETA is the first agreement where the EU uses the term 'Investment' instead of the earlier term 'Establishment'. In CETA, Investment (Chapter 8) covers market access and investment protection in all economic activities (except for the activities excluded in Art. 8:2). In a few PTAs signed prior to CETA, the EU used the term 'Establishment' instead. On the prior agreements and especially the changes made in the EU–Korea FTA, see Mathis, J. H. & Laurenza, E. (2012) Services and Investment in the EU-South Korea Free-Trade, Area: Implications of a New Approach for GATS V Agreements and for Bilateral Investment Treaties, *The Journal of World Investment & Trade*, 13(2), 157–85.

[11] See e.g. the recently negotiated trade agreement between the USA, Mexico and Canada (USMCA, not yet in force). The agreement's Chapter 16 includes the rules for the temporary entry of business persons. A 'business person' is defined as 'a citizen of a Party who is engaged in trade in goods, the supply of services or the conduct of investment activities' (Art. 16.1 'Definitions'). The USMCA, which is meant to replace NAFTA, was signed on 30 November 2018 and is available on the website of the USTR: https://ustr.gov/trade-agreements/free-trade-agreements/united-states-mexico-canada-agreement (last accessed on 30 January 2019).

[12] See the Scheduling Guidelines of the WTO Council for Trade in Services, S/L/92, 28 March 2001. For financial services, specific classification is typically used. Already in

reality, however, countries use various modifications of that list, or, they base their schedules on the United Nations CPC classification (of which the W/120 list is a simplified version) and modified versions of that. This is understandable. The original W/120 list is far from complete. Also, we have today services that did not exist, or were only emerging, when the GATS was negotiated. Moreover, several services cut across many sectors and cannot easily fit in the traditional listing. Shadikhodjaev gives the interesting example of smart grid services which comprise some elements of telecommunications services, computer services and services incidental to energy distribution. Another example is carbon capture and storage, which involves business, transport and other services, and which can be argued not to be covered by the W/120 regime.[13] Some of the scheduling issues are solved by the 'technological neutrality' principle, which means that the GATS commitments cover all technologies for the mode of delivery in question.[14] However, even if that is the case, there are likely to be changes in the scheduling of services in future EIAs to better respond to new technologies and fast-developing business realities.

Changes in the organization and coverage of modes and sectors, however, makes empirical analyses more complicated to carry out. Each agreement is different, which means that the same method and scoring template cannot be used for all EIAs. This of course affects the comparability and objectivity of the analysis. The EIAs that are reviewed in the next chapter all follow the same logic in the organization of modes and sectors. They did not therefore pose too many problems for comparison. For other EIAs, alterations of the method may need to be made. However, it should be kept in mind that all empirical studies of services commitments are, out of necessity, rough approximations, and too strict conclusions should therefore be avoided.

---

the GATS the Members used the categorization provided in the Annex on Financial Services.

[13] Shadikhodjaev, S. (2018) Regulation of Renewable Energy Trade in the Megaregionals Era: Current Issues and Prospects for Rule-Making Reforms, in Peng, S., Liu H.-W. & Lin C.-F. (eds.), *Governing Science and Technology in the Era of Megaregionals*. London: Edward Elgar, at 180. See also Peng, S. (2014) Regulating New Services through Litigation? – Electronic Commerce as a Case Study on the Evaluation of 'Judicial Activism' in the WTO, *Journal of World Trade*, 48(6), 1189–222.

[14] This was confirmed in *US–Gambling* and *China–Publications*. It was established that Mode 1 encompasses all possible means of supplying services from the territory of one Member into the territory of another. On digital services, see Weber, R. H. & Burri, M. (2012) *Classification of Services in the Digital Economy*. Berlin: Springer.

II Negative vs. Positive Listing

Another key challenge in comparing services schedules are the different scheduling modalities. There are two principal methods to schedule services commitments: the so-called positive and negative scheduling, often referred to as 'top-down' (negative) and 'bottom-up' (positive) approach. In negative listing, a country covers all services except those listed, while in positive listing a country covers only those services that are listed. In negatively listed schedules a state must therefore carefully formulate a reservation for each instance where its internal measures fall short of the disciplines agreed upon in the EIA. The most famous example of a top-down agreement is the NAFTA, whereas the GATS is a positively listed agreement.

Whereas, in principle, both methods can lead to identical level of liberalization, there are, however, a variety of opinions as to the supposed superiority of one of the methods to the other one. It is often considered that, at least in practice, negative scheduling leads to higher levels of liberalization.[15] Negative scheduling starts from an empty board and only non-conforming measures are inscribed. This may, partly maybe even for psychological reasons, lead to fewer restrictions being inscribed. In positive scheduling, the listing of restrictions takes place through a specific set of service sectors (e.g. based on the W/120 list) and the state can decide with each sector whether it wants to include and liberalize it or not. However, also under this method, the restrictions applied under each sector must be inscribed 'negatively'.[16] From the national authorities' point of view, it may be easier to grasp the types of national measures requiring explicit limitations under positive scheduling. However, if the state has already liberalized trade through a positive schedule earlier, it is likely to be easier to adjust the desired restrictions to the negative model in another agreement.[17]

---

[15] On differences between the approaches and on possible implications for the resulting level of liberalization, see e.g. Houde, M., Kolse-Patil, A. & Miroudot, S. (2007) The Interaction between Investment and Services Chapters in Selected Regional Trade Agreements. OECD Trade Policy Papers No. 55. See also Adlung, R. & Mamdouh, H. (2014) How to Design Trade Agreements in Services: Top Down or Bottom-Up? *Journal of World Trade*, 48(2), 191–218.

[16] Therefore, in reality, also the GATS approach is 'hybrid' as only sectors are inscribed positively. Restrictions, on the other hand, are inscribed negatively.

[17] Most Members use positive scheduling on the basis of the CPC Product Classification (used in the WTO's Sectoral Classification List). The USA generally uses negative scheduling and also a specific NAFTA classification system. See NAFTA Appendix 1001.1b-2-B: Common Classification System. Anderson, R. D. & Müller, A. C. (2008) Market Access for the Government Procurement of Services: Comparing Recent PTAs with WTO Achievements, in Marchetti, J. A. & Roy, M. (eds.), *Opening Markets for Trade*

The potentially more liberalizing effect of negative listing has been noted also by civil society actors. Both the TiSA and CETA have been targeted by campaigners worrying about the effect that the agreements may have on states' regulatory autonomy. Their key concern appears to be the negative listing, as well as the standstill and ratchet provisions.[18] All three mechanisms are familiar from EIAs based on the NAFTA model.[19] A standstill clause requires that the current level of liberalization in each country is locked in and cannot be made worse. A ratchet means that a country cannot reintroduce a measure that it had previously and unilaterally removed in an area where a binding commitment was made.[20] Agreements that incorporate these mechanisms can lead to freer services trade than agreements that do not include such clauses. This is the case especially with the ratchet clause. For example, under the ratchet mechanism, if a state removes a limit for foreign equity in a specific service sector, it cannot reintroduce it later. In most positively listed agreements no such clause exists. Therefore, if the original commitment allows for a foreign equity cap, it can be removed and reintroduced freely.

Adlung and Mamdouh are of the opinion that the method of scheduling nevertheless has limited, if any, impact on the results achieved. They consider that what ultimately matters are not negotiating or scheduling

---

in Services: Countries and Sectors in Bilateral and WTO Negotiations. Cambridge: Cambridge University Press, at 450–1.

[18] See e.g. Sinclair, S. (2017) 'TISA Troubles: Services, Democracy and Corporate Rule in the Trump Era, Rosa Luxemburg Stiftung and Canadian Centre for Policy Alternatives', available at www.rosalux.eu/fileadmin/user_upload/Publications/2017/TISA-UK.pdf (last accessed on 25 January 2019).

[19] Standstill clauses are extensively used in positively listed agreements as well, including in some EU EIAs. See e.g. Art. 7.7(2) of the EU–Korea FTA. On the use of standstill and ratchet clauses in different types of EIAs, see Latrille, P. (2016) Services Rules in Regional Trade Agreements: How Diverse or Creative Are They Compared to the Multilateral Rules?, in Acharya, R. (ed.), *Regional Trade Agreements and the Multilateral Trading System*. Cambridge: Cambridge University Press, at 455.

[20] For a standstill clause related to NT, see 'TiSA Draft Core Text' of 14 July 2016, Art. II:2.2. 'The conditions and qualifications on national treatment set out in Section B of Part I or Part II of each Party's Schedule shall be limited to measures that a Party maintains on the date this Agreement takes effect, or the continuation or prompt renewal of any such measures'. For a ratchet clause, see Art. II:2.3 of the same draft: 'If a Party amends a measure referred to in paragraph 2 in a way that reduces or eliminates the inconsistency of that measure with the treatment provided for in Article I-4 (National Treatment), as it existed immediately before the amendment, a Party may not subsequently amend that measure in a way that increases the inconsistency with the treatment provided for in Article I-4 (National Treatment)'. The draft text is available at www.bilaterals.org/IMG/pdf/core_text.pdf (last accessed on 25 January 2019).

techniques, but the political impetus that the governments concerned are ready to generate.[21]

Such a political impetus may be visible in the EU's scheduling practice. Whereas the EU has traditionally engaged in GATS-type positive scheduling, in its current trade negotiations the EU is actively using both methods. In CETA with Canada, the parties opted for negative scheduling across all modes. They also adopted the standstill and the ratchet mechanism. Incidentally, CETA is also the EU's most far-going EIA so far. The EU used negative listing also in the recently concluded agreement with Japan. In the other two recently negotiated PTAs with Singapore and Vietnam, on the other hand, a positive listing was used.[22]

Services commitments in any type of agreement are challenging material for analysis. Our methodology works best with positively listed EIAs. The method can be used for negatively listed commitments too, but the starting point is different. Instead of going through the schedule sector by sector, one needs to go through each reservation and note to which sector (or often, sectors) the reservation applies to. The analysis is therefore much more burdensome in the case of negatively listed schedules.[23] We have not used our method to analyze any negatively listed EIA in its entirety. However, to show how that can be done, in Part IV of the book we use the method to analyze Canada's commitments under one sector of CETA.

For the analysis of TiSA offers, if more of them were to be made, our method would appear to work well. In the first TiSA draft, limitations to MA were planned to be set through a positive listing. Only NT limitations would be listed negatively.[24] At least in the EU's TiSA offer of 2016 this is done similarly to positively listed agreements where all MA and NT limitations are laid out sector by sector.[25] Even if for NT reservations the starting point is

[21] Adlung & Mamdouh (2014).

[22] See the Commission's brochure 'Services and investment in EU trade deals: Using "positive" and "negative" lists'. Available at http://trade.ec.europa.eu/doclib/docs/2016/april/tradoc_154427.pdf (last accessed on 25 January 2019).

[23] As was mentioned at the end of the previous chapter, computational analysis tools can possibly make this task easier. Also, machine learning can maybe be used to allow computers to read and analyze services commitments.

[24] European Commission, Trade in Services Agreement (TiSA) Factsheet, 26 September 2016, available at http://trade.ec.europa.eu/doclib/docs/2016/september/tradoc_154971.doc.pdf (last accessed on 20 January 2019).

[25] The EU's revised TiSA offer (26 May 2016) is publicly available on the TiSA-focused webpage of the European Commission: http://ec.europa.eu/trade/policy/in-focus/tisa/, last update 14 July 2017 (last accessed on 20 January 2019). According to the Commission, the TiSA negotiations are on hold and are expected to resume when the political context allows. There is no formally set deadline for ending the negotiations

Table 9.1 *EU and its Member States' reservations for freight transport agency services in the EU's TiSA offer of 2016*

Sector or sub-sector	Limitations on market access	Limitations on national treatment	Additional commitments
E. Services auxiliary to air transport services c) Freight transport agency services (part of CPC 748)	1) EU: None 2) EU: None 3) EU: None except: In CY, CZ, HU, MT, PL, RO, SK: Unbound. In BG: Foreign persons can supply services only through participation in Bulgarian companies with 49 per cent limitation on equity participation and through branches. 4) BVEP; ICT; SeSe: Unbound except as indicated in the horizontal section.	1, 3) In BG: Supply of services by foreign persons is allowed only through participation in Bulgarian companies, with 49 per cent limitation on equity participation and through branches.	

that no text means full liberalization, the reservations to NT are easy to spot as the schedule and the reservations are organized sector by sector. Moreover, TiSA follows the modal logic of the GATS; commitments are organized under the four modes. The following example in Table 9.1 is from the EU's TiSA offer of 2016:[26]

The EU's scheduling of limitations in its TiSA offer can be contrasted with its commitments in the services schedule of CETA. There the EU has followed a negative scheduling. Both in Annex I and II the EU first lists

(the same European Commission webpage). Some TiSA documents have been leaked through Wikileaks but to our knowledge only the EU offer has been made officially available.

[26] Ibid. Numbers 1, 2, 3 and 4 refer to the four modes. 'BVEP' (business visitors for establishment purposes), 'ICT' (intra-corporate transferees) and 'SeSe' (service sellers) are Mode 4 categories under the draft TiSA.

reservations that apply across the entire EU. After that, Member State specific reservations follow. Each Member State has set out its reservations separately, running alphabetically from Belgium to the United Kingdom. Canada has done the same with regard to its federal and sub-federal levels of government. Each Canadian province and territory has listed its reservations after the federal level. The reservations are challenging to group and connect to specific service sectors, but they give a good idea of the number of reservations applied in individual Member States or provinces/territories. For example, the additional EU+ reservations[27] applied by the UK in CETA are only four pages long, whereas the reservations of France stretch over eleven pages and the reservations of Germany over twenty-four pages. The German reservations in CETA are particularly interesting, as they reveal a large number of sub-federal measures applied by the German Länder.[28] In general, the lists of reservations of both Canada and the EU are very long as every single measure on each level of government had to be specifically mentioned.[29]

III   Adaption to Economic Realities: Adding Weights

Finally, the question of the economic significance of the different modes and sectors should be considered. It can be very reasonably argued that the GATS Art. V requirement of substantial sectoral coverage should take the economic significance of each sector and each mode into account. This is supported also by footnote 1 to Art. V GATS, according to which the condition of substantial sectoral coverage is understood in terms of number of sectors, volume of trade affected and modes of supply. As noted by Hoekman in his foundational 1995 study, a first step could consist of determining the total value of output represented by a Member's scheduled sectors as a proportion of its GDP. If country A schedules only 5 per cent of its service sector in GDP terms, while country B schedules 15 per cent, one can say that in an absolute sense B has offered three times as much as A.[30] However, countries do not

---

[27] EU+ meaning the national, Member State specific reservations added to the reservations taken by the EU as a whole in the beginning of the schedule.

[28] See the German reservations in Annex I of CETA, pp. 384–407 (EU/CA/R/Annex I/ en 384).

[29] EU's Annex I is 265 pages long. Canada's federal and sub-federal reservations take almost exactly as many pages.

[30] The example is provided by Hoekman. See Hoekman, B. (1995) Tentative First Steps: An Assessment of the Uruguay Round Agreement on Services, Volume 1. *World Bank Policy Research Working Paper*, No. 1455, at 12.

collect data on the basis of the services sectors listed in services agreements. Statistics are usually collected for the most significant service sectors only and they are typically not organized in accordance with the GATS and EIA categories. Moreover, a correct economic weight would also need to factor in the restrictiveness of each measure applied – thus taking into account how much each measure affects MA and NT. It is not clear how exactly this could be done. In the study by Hoekman, he uses economic weights in an aggregated manner to count for the relative importance (size) of individual service sectors.[31]

Another challenge relates to how to count accurate volumes of trade for each sector and mode. As was already noted in the previous chapter, volume of trade is a changing factor and we do not know what the relevant point in time is to count such volume. Moreover, there are serious problems in the availability of reliable statistics.

Another question relates to the economic significance of each sub-central entity. Carrying out the empirical analysis, we chose to give the same weight to each EU Member State. The choice reflects the particularities that relate to the EU where each Member State is also a sovereign state and a WTO Member in its own right. Moreover, from the point of view of service suppliers, it may be of relevance to see what percentage of EU states allows access under various modes and sectors, even if there are considerable differences in the sizes of the Member State economies.

The methodology can, however, be adapted to take the economic significance of each state into account. This can, in principle, be done by giving a weight to each Member State's commitments in light of its economic significance. One starting point could be the volume of services trade that each Member State is responsible for. The problem again is how exactly this should be calculated. Across modes or across sectors? The problem relating to the significance of each mode and sector remains. Moreover, even if we decide to base the weight in a simplified manner, for instance, on the sum of imports and exports of services in each Member State, we would be left with the problem of finding such accurate statistics. However, certain rough estimates could be used.[32]

---

[31] Ibid., see table 5 on page 19 and the 2-digit output weights in Annex 1.

[32] The new services statistics prepared by Eurostat could possibly be used for this purpose. They separate imports and exports on the level of the Member States. See Eurostat, 'Statistics Explained', Services trade statistics by mode of supply, available at https://ec .europa.eu/eurostat/statistics-explained/index.php/Services_trade_statistics_by_modes_ of_supply (last accessed on 15 January 2019).

In the case of federal states, the adding of weights is particularly complex as the economic significance of different sub-federal regions would need to be calculated. Some federations may have statistics on the supply of services in and out of different regions, but most federal states are not likely to have very detailed data as services statistics are usually collected on the level of countries.[33]

Notwithstanding these challenges, certain economic weights can certainly be used. However, advanced programming and computational analysis is likely to be needed. For the moment, and for the purposes of the analysis carried out in this book, we have to settle with equal weights across modes, sectors and states.

---

[33] See e.g. OECD statistics where all OECD countries compile their data according to the System of National Accounts (SNA): OECD Data, Trade in Services: https://data.oecd.org /trade/trade-in-services.htm. National accounts or national account systems are the implementation of complete and consistent accounting techniques for measuring the economic activity of a nation. See the System of National Accounts (SNA), United Nations Statistics Division, https://unstats.un.org/unsd/nationalaccount/sna.asp.

PART IV

Analysis of the Selected Services Agreements

10

The Results of the Empirical Study

I   An Overview of the Reviewed EIAs

The method presented in Part III of the book is in this Part applied to a chosen set of four EIAs concluded by the EU. The reviewed agreements include four different international agreements concluded between the EU and its Member States on the one hand and partner countries on the other hand. The agreements represent three different types of the EU's trade agreements: they comprise an economic and partnership agreement (EPA), a free trade agreement (FTA) and two association agreements (AAs). Two of the agreements are bilateral (EU–South Korea FTA and EU–Georgia AA) and two regional (EU–Central America AA and EU–CARIFORUM EPA). The first of the four agreements, with CARIFORUM countries, was concluded in 2008 and the last one, with Georgia, in 2014. The EU–Georgia AA entered into force in July 2016.

Of the analyzed agreements, the EU–South Korea Free Trade Agreement of 2011[1] is the first of the EU's new generation PTAs, DCFTAs,[2] and according to the EU, presented a stepping-stone for future liberalization. At the time of its conclusion, the agreement with Korea went further than any of the EU's previous agreements in lifting

---

[1] The agreement was signed in October 2010. The agreement was provisionally applied from 1 July 2011, and entered into force on 13 December 2015, after having been ratified by all signatories. See European Commission, 'Annual Report on the Implementation of the EU–Korea Free Trade Agreement', COM(2016) 268 final, 30 June 2016.

[2] Deep and Comprehensive Free Trade Areas (or 'Agreements' instead of 'Areas').

trade barriers in services.[3] Since then, the EU has negotiated DCFTAs also with Moldova, Ukraine, Singapore, Japan, Vietnam and Canada. The agreements with Singapore and Vietnam have not yet entered into force (as of February 2019), whereas the Economic Partnership Agreement with Japan entered into force on 1 February 2019.[4] The goods and services chapters of the agreement with Canada (CETA) have been in provisional application since September 2017.[5] CETA is a turning point in the EU's services agreements because of the scheduling modality of its services commitments. In CETA, the EU, for the first time, engaged in the so-called negative listing of reservations. Instead of giving specific, 'positive' commitments for chosen service sectors, both Canada's and the EU's (and its Member States') reservations are included in two annexes. The annexes have the same logic as the annexes included in the American and Canadian EIAs since NAFTA (1994). Reservations to existing measures and liberalization commitments are listed under Annex I and reservations to future measures are listed in Annex II.[6] Up until CETA, the EU was hesitant to engage in negative listing of its services commitments but has since then agreed to the same method also in the EPA with Japan. So

---

[3] See the European Commission's information page on the EU–South Korea Free Trade Agreement, available at http://ec.europa.eu/trade/policy/countries-and-regions/coun tries/south-korea/ (last accessed on 1 November 2018).

[4] The negotiations for the EPA with Japan were concluded in December 2017. The European Parliament gave its consent to the agreement in December 2018. The entry into force took place on 1 February 2019, at the same time when the book was sent for publication. See European Commission Press Release, 'EU–Japan Trade Agreement Enters into Force', http://trade.ec.europa.eu/doclib/press/index.cfm?id=1976 (last accessed on 1 February 2019). The negotiations for investment protection and related dispute settlement were still continued at that time.

[5] European Commission, 'EU–Canada Trade Agreement Enters into Force', Press release, 20 September 2017, http://europa.eu/rapid/press-release_IP-17-3121_en.htm (last accessed on 31 January 2019). National parliaments in EU Member States – and in some cases regional parliaments too – will need to approve CETA before it can take full effect. Altogether the approval of thirty-eight national and regional EU Member State Parliaments is required. See Gantz, D. A. (2017) The CETA Ratification Saga: The Demise of ISDS in EU Trade Agreements? *Loyola Univ. Chicago L. Rev.*, 49, 361. On the Canadian side, the necessary parliamentary approval processes were carried out already in 2017. See ICTSD Bridges, 'Canadian Senate Approves CETA Implementation Bill', 18 May 2017, www.ictsd.org/bridges-news/bridges/news/canadian-senate-approves-ceta-implementation-bill (last accessed on 31 January 2019).

[6] A more extensive analysis of CETA is included in Part II of the book. As noted there, Canada has included separate annexes for federal and sub-federal measures both under Annex I and II. On the EU side, both the Union's and the individual Member States' reservations are included in the same annex. The EU Party's Annex I is 265 pages long and Annex II is 190 pages long. Most of the content especially in Annex I comes from Member State specific reservations.

far, Canada and Japan are the only partners with which the EU has agreed to that method. The EU was pushed to adopt negative scheduling also in the TiSA negotiations, but in the end agreed only to a hybrid approach that mixes positive scheduling of MA commitments to a negative scheduling of NT commitments.[7] In services and investment, CETA has been labelled as the most far reaching trade agreement that the EU has ever concluded.[8] The negative scheduling is likely to have contributed to that result.[9]

The EU's new generation, commercially driven PTAs are based on primarily economic criteria and according to the EU, go beyond the market opening that can be achieved in the WTO context.[10] The EU–Korea FTA was the first agreement to have this outspoken goal. The agreement can be seen as the flagship of the EU's Global Europe strategy of 2006, which marked the debut for bilateral trade negotiations with

---

[7] The plurilateral initiative for a new international services agreement originated form the US and Australia, which are both used to the negative scheduling model. The EU negotiators were originally against the negative listing approach and keen to proceed similarly to the GATS, which follows the positive listing model. Broude and Moses provide a detailed account of how the EU got on board and approved a partial negative listing through the hybrid approach. See Broude, T. & Moses, S. (2016) The Behavioural Dynamics of Positive and Negative Listing in Services Trade Liberalization: A Look at the Trade in Services Agreement (TiSA) Negotiations, in Roy, M. & Sauvé, P. (eds.), *Research Handbook on Trade in Services*. London: Edgar Elgar, 401–11. At the time of writing, the negotiations on TiSA were not actively pursued.

[8] See European Commission, 'CETA Explained', last updated 21 September 2017, http://ec .europa.eu/trade/policy/in-focus/ceta/ceta-explained/index_en.htm#service-markets (last accessed on 15 January 2019). Since then, the EPA with Japan has entered into force. A qualitative comparison of the services commitments of CETA and the EPA with Japan (EUJEPA) is needed to verify which one goes deeper (e.g. by using our methodology). However, reading the EU's own statements, the CETA would appear to go further in services than EUJEPA. Similarly strong statements about the liberalization effect over services have not been included in the press releases regarding the EUJEPA. The economic effect of EUJEPA is bigger but it relates to the size of the Japanese economy. It should also be noted that the discussion about the most far-reaching services agreements does not include the agreements concluded with the countries aiming at accessing the EU (candidate countries and potential candidates). The logic of liberalization in those agreements is radically different and aimed at progressive alignment with the internal market rules of the EU. See e.g. the EU–Albania Stabilization and Association Agreement (entered into force in April 2009), Title V on 'Movement of Workers, Establishment, Supply of Services, Current Payments and Movement of Capital'.

[9] The question of negative scheduling, as compared to positive scheduling, is dealt with more detail in the previous chapter regarding challenges in the empirical study of EIAs (Chapter 9, Part III).

[10] See the Commission's Quick Reading Guide to the EU–South Korea FTA, October 2010, http://trade.ec.europa.eu/doclib/docs/2009/october/tradoc_145203.pdf (last accessed on 1 November 2018).

commercially meaningful partner countries with limited non-trade agendas.[11] Many other EU agreements also include a strong trade component but have additional goals as well. For example, the trade pact of the agreement with Georgia is part of an Association Agreement (AA), the purpose of which is wider than the objectives behind the more economically oriented EU–Korea FTA. The AA relates to the EU's framework of the European Neighbourhood Policy and its eastern regional dimension, the Eastern Partnership. The key goal is to extend the EU's influence in its close neighbourhood and to bring Georgia closer to the EU by requiring it to adopt a significant amount of the Union's internal market regulation. After implementing the agreement, Georgian business may access the EU's internal market in selected sectors and will function in those sectors in the same regulatory environment as businesses in the EU. An important part of the AA with Georgia is therefore the approximation of Georgian trade-related laws to the selected pieces of the EU's legal framework.[12]

This is visible in the commitments taken under the agreement's Chapter 6 that concerns 'Establishment, trade in services and electronic commerce'.[13] The chapter aims at integrating Georgia as much as possible into the EU market. It provides for both the freedom of establishment in services and non-services sectors, subject to limited reservations, and the expansion of the internal market for a set of key services sectors once

---

[11] The Global Europe agenda marked a strategic shift in the EU's trade policy. It ended the EU's PTA moratorium, which the Commission had put in place to focus on the WTO's Doha Round. Bilateral engagement between the richest economies of the world were seen to undermine the Doha Agenda but ever since 2006, the Commission, backed by a trade-oriented coalition of Member States in the Council, has been aiming at creating economic growth through 'deep and comprehensive' trade integration with some of the most commercially attractive regions of the world. See Kleimann, D. (ed.) (2013) *EU Preferential Trade Agreements: Commerce, Foreign Policy, and Development Aspects*. Global Governance Programme, European University Institute (ebook). Available at http://cadmus.eui.eu/handle/1814/27661 (last accessed on 18 January 2019), at 5.

[12] According to the EU, the adoption of EU approaches to policy-making will improve the quality of governance, strengthen the rule of law and provide more economic opportunities in Georgia, as well as in Moldova and Ukraine with whom similar agreements have been concluded. See the European Commission's country sheets on Georgia, Moldova and Ukraine, available at http://ec.europa.eu/trade/policy/countries-and-regions/coun tries/georgia/, http://ec.europa.eu/trade/policy/countries-and-regions/countries/mol dova/ and http://ec.europa.eu/trade/policy/countries-and-regions/countries/ukraine/ (last accessed on 1 November 2018).

[13] See the Commission's Reading guide on the similarly structured EU–Ukraine Deep and Comprehensive Free Trade Area, available at http://trade.ec.europa.eu/doclib/docs/2013/ april/tradoc_150981.pdf (last accessed on 15 January 2019).

Georgia effectively implements the relevant EU *acquis*. The agreement thus provides for a right of establishment (as opposed to commercial presence under Mode 3) in both services and non-services sectors. In contrast to the other reviewed EU EIAs, the reservations to this right are provided in a negative list and automatic coverage for new services and further liberalization not listed as exceptions is guaranteed. The rest of the services commitments are scheduled according to a traditional GATS-type schedule.[14]

In addition to the agreements with Korea and Georgia, the empirical method is applied to the EU's AA with Central America and EPA with the CARIFORUM states. AAs and EPAs are based on a wide array of motivations. The agreements have a combination of objectives relating to commercial purposes, development, and economic and political integration between the EU and the country or countries concerned.[15]

The AA with Central America is the EU's first ever region-to-region AA. It aims at closer political and economic cooperation between the EU and the participating countries by relying on three mutually reinforcing pillars, namely political dialogue, cooperation and a trade agreement.[16] The agreement, however, does not require the Central American countries to adopt EU legislation similarly to the Eastern Neighbourhood AAs. Instead, the Central America AA aims at supporting the region's own integration process. An important factor in the negotiations for the agreement was the need to replace the unilateral preferential access to the EU market, which was granted to Central America under the EU's General Scheme of Preferences (GSP). Being subject to expiration, GSP preferences are more unpredictable than preferences given under a PTA, and countries having achieved high or upper-middle income per capita no longer benefit from the scheme. One of the main benefits of the AA

---

[14] The agreements with Georgia, Ukraine and Moldova differ from the agreements concluded with the EU's candidate countries in the sense that the method of liberalization with Georgia, Ukraine and Moldova follows the EU's commercial FTAs, including in services (they have a GATS-type services schedule). The stabilization and association agreements with candidate countries do not have a GATS-type EIA but include mechanisms for progressive alignment with the EU's internal market rules.

[15] See Cremona, M. (2010) The European Union and Regional Trade Agreements, in Herrmann, C. & Terhechte, J. P. (eds.), *European Yearbook of International Economic Law 2010*. Heidelberg: Springer, 245–68, at 245–6.

[16] The trade pillar of the AA has been provisionally applied since 1 August 2013 with Honduras, Nicaragua and Panama, since 1 October 2013 with Costa Rica and El Salvador, and since 1 December 2013 with Guatemala.

with Central America was thus considered to be a unilateral system with a stable, predictable and reciprocal framework.[17]

Out of the four reviewed agreements, the EU–CARIFORUM EPA[18] has the strongest development agenda. Epas are EU's development-oriented PTAs that are being concluded with African, Caribbean and Pacific (ACP) countries that participate to the Cotonou Agreement.[19] The ACP–EU Partnership Agreement, signed in Cotonou on 23 June 2000, was concluded for a twenty-year period from 2000 to 2020. It is a comprehensive partnership agreement and has been the framework for EU's relations with the seventy-nine ACP countries. With the expiry of the WTO waiver that allowed their existence, the trade preferences of the agreement expired at the end of 2007. EPAs have been negotiated to replace the preferences. According to the EU, EPAs are WTO-compatible agreements but go beyond free trade by focusing on ACP countries' development, taking account of their socio-economic circumstances and including co-operation and assistance. They are reciprocal but allow ACP countries long transition periods to open up

---

[17] The Commission's webpage on the trade agreement with Central America, available at: http://ec.europa.eu/trade/policy/countries-and-regions/regions/central-america/ (last accessed on 15 November 2018). According to the Commission, the strengthening of the regional integration process in Central America in practical terms means the creation of a customs union and economic integration between the region's countries. The EU supports this process through the trade agreement and its trade-related technical cooperation programs. For a comparison of different trends of regional integration and on the links between the EU and other regional processes, see Warleigh-Lack, A., Robinson, N. & Rosamond, B. (eds.) (2011) *New Regionalism and the European Union*. New York: Routledge. On the effects of EU trade preferences on developing countries' exports, see Persson, M. & Wilhelmsson, F. (2007) Assessing the Effects of EU Trade Preferences for Developing Countries, in Bourdet, Y., Gullstrand, J. & Olofsdotter, K. (eds.), *The European Union and Developing Countries*. Cheltenham; Northampton: Edward Elgar.

[18] CARIFORUM's membership comprises Antigua and Barbuda, The Bahamas, Barbados, Belize, Dominica, Grenada, Guyana, Jamaica, Saint Lucia, Saint Vincent and the Grenadines, Saint Kitts and Nevis, Surinam, Trinidad, Tobago, and the Dominican Republic.

[19] The relations between the EU and the ACP countries date back to 1975 and the first Lomé convention. The latter was a successor to the first Convention of Yaoundé in 1963, binding the then European Economic Community and former colonies of some of its Member States. Since then, successive partnership agreements have been concluded until the present time. The currently applied Cotonou Agreement was revised in 2005 and 2010. It was concluded for a twenty-year period and will expire on 29 February 2020. On the Cotonou Agreement, the EPAs and the participating countries' capacity to implement them, see Gathii, J. T. (2013) The Cotonou Agreement and Economic Partnership Agreements, in *Realizing the Right to Development: Essays in Commemoration of 25 Years of the United Nations Declaration on the Right to Development*. The Office of the High Commissioner for Human Rights. New York; Geneva: United Nations.

partially to EU imports while providing protection for sensitive sectors. EU tariffs are liberalized immediately.[20] The story is, however, very different for services, as our results show. ACP' countries access to the EU's services market is restrained, as it is in all EU's EIAs.

The different motivations behind the EU's trade agreements can arguably be taken into account in accordance with Art. V:2 GATS. The provision allows flexibility in assessing compliance with the criteria of the first paragraph of the article depending on the relationship of the agreement to a wider process of economic integration or trade liberalization among the countries concerned. In our analysis, we map these wider elements of the reviewed agreement and in the discussion, we address the question of how these features should affect the analysis of the EU's EIAs under GATS Art. V – or if they should at all.

II   The Findings

The section on the results is structured as follows. First, we note some of the common features in all of the reviewed EIAs. These are the type of features that directly affect the level of liberalization granted by the agreement. As our analysis is focused on assessing the agreements' level of discrimination in terms of NT, the issues brought up in our review are directly related to that aspect. After presenting the common features affecting NT across the agreements, we provide separate results for each agreement. In this section we give the average scores for each mode across the entire EIA as well as for certain selected service sectors. Here the results are summarized but the detailed results for each single sub-sector can be viewed in Appendix 3, which includes the sector-specific analysis of each EIA. The detailed review sheets of Appendix 3 also note such ingredients of the EIAs that we consider to be relevant for the so-called 'wider process of

---

[20] See the Commission's webpage on EPAs: http://ec.europa.eu/trade/policy/countries-and-regions/development/economic-partnerships/ (last accessed on 19 November 2018). In practice, the negotiations of EPAs have proved difficult. According to critics, the EU has sent mixed signals: its partners have believed that the main idea was to make existing preferential relationships WTO compatible whereas the EU wanted to move forward on trade. The EU also seems to have underestimated how difficult it is for partners from regional organizations of developing countries to negotiate trade deals in view of their poor capacities and the need to find agreement among one another. See Ramdoo, I. & Bilal, S. (2013) European Trade Policy, Economic Partnership Agreements and Regional Integration in Africa, in Kleimann, D. (ed.), *EU Preferential Trade Agreements: Commerce, Foreign Policy, and Development Aspects.* Florence: European University Institute (e-book).

economic integration' under Art. V:2 GATS. These additional ingredients are analyzed in more detail in the following chapter where the results presented here are assessed in light of the GATS discipline on EIAs.

i Key Features of the EIAs

In all of the reviewed EIAs, the EU has grouped Modes 1 and 2 together as 'Cross-Border Supply of Services'. The two modes are defined similarly to the GATS. In the EU–CARIFORUM EIA, Mode 3 is referred to as 'Commercial presence' (using the GATS terminology), but in the three other EIAs the term 'Establishment' has been used. Mode 4 is referred to as 'Temporary presence of natural persons for business' in all of the agreements. All modes of supply are thus covered by the agreements, even though the level of commitments greatly differs depending on the mode and the sectors. There are commitments in most of the sectors by at least some EU Member States. However, each agreement has excluded certain sectors.[21] In addition, in certain sub-sectors the NT score is zero because the commitments (the EU's as well as the individual Member States' commitments) do not provide for non-discriminatory treatment. All such 'zero sectors' are marked with grey colour in the review sheets of Appendix 3.

According to Art. 65 of the EU–CARIFORUM EIA, commercial presence means 'any type of business or professional establishment' through constitution, acquisition or maintenance of a juridical person or the creation or maintenance of a branch or representative office within the territory of the EU for the purpose of performing an economic activity. The other EIAs define 'establishment' in a similar manner. For the EU, the two concepts thus appear to have the same meaning.[22] Both concepts

---

[21] The excluded service sectors are the same for each EIA (see the results below). They include e.g. audio-visual services and some air transport services. The EU has secured similar carve-outs in all of its trade agreements, including the latest EIAs with Canada and Japan.

[22] In EU–CARIFORUM EIA, another concept, 'Investment', is used in the heading of Title II ('Investment, trade in services and e-commerce'). 'Investment' seems to be equivalent to GATS Mode 3, combined with investment in key non-services sectors (agriculture, manufacturing, mining). The content of the chapter on 'Commercial presence' (Mode 3) is, however, similar to 'Establishment' in the other agreements (which also include non-service sectors). If not in the title, all the agreements seem to use the term 'investment' interchangeably with Establishment/Commercial Presence at least under certain provisions (e.g. in the Article 'Review of the Investment Legal Framework' at the end of each chapter on Establishment, except for EU–Georgia). Also in the EU's later agreements 'Investment' covers MA and NT commitments for both service and non-service sectors

cover also branches and representative offices, in accordance with the definition of commercial presence in Art. XXVIII GATS. Considering that the establishment of branches and representative offices is an essential and legally accepted part of commercial presence also under the EU's EIAs, limitations to their use have been considered discriminatory in the review. The denial of their use modifies conditions of competition in favour of services suppliers of national origin as foreign service suppliers are required to fully establish themselves even though they already have a legal establishment in their home country. As to domestic suppliers, limitations to the use of branches do not concern them at all.[23] The EU's scheduling practice also appears to support the conclusion that the requirement of a subsidiary or other type of incorporation in the EU Member States is to be considered discriminatory. All reviewed EIAs include a statement according to which non-discriminatory requirements as regards the types of legal form of an establishment are not included in the schedules of commitments.[24] However, reservations on the use of branches are inscribed as limitations in the EU's schedules. In addition to a few sector-specific limitations, certain Member States have set horizontal limitations to the use of branches in all of the EIAs. As we have not factored horizontal limitations in the scores, limitations to the use of branches or representative offices do not affect the sector-specific scores. However, they are taken note of in the explanation of the results as horizontal limitations to the type of establishment.

(the scope of non-service activities has been gradually extended). In CETA and EUJEPA (EU–Japan), reservations to Investment and Trade in services are scheduled in a negative manner. In the EU–Singapore FTA, the term 'Establishment' is still used. With Canada, Singapore and Vietnam the EU has also negotiated investment protection rules. With Singapore and Vietnam the investment protection rules are included in a separate agreement to facilitate the adoption of the trade agreement by the EU alone. The investment protection rules are subject to Member State ratifications in accordance with Opinion 2/15 of the EU Court of Justice. For a comparison of the EU's EIA with the GATS architecture, see South Centre (2009) Negotiating Services Free Trade Agreements (FTAs) with the European Union: Some Issues for Developing Countries to Consider. Analytical Note SC/AN/TDP/EPA/21, June 2009.

[23] Setting up of a subsidiary instead of a branch may bring with it many advantages, for example in terms of liabilities (because the subsidiary and the parent company are distinct legal entities, the parent company is not usually exposed to any liabilities of its subsidiary). What is central here is, however, the free choice among the types of establishment enabled by Mode 3. We recognize that it may sometimes be desirable for public policy reasons to demand incorporation, but the requirement goes against the nature of Mode 3. The same applies to residency requirements for natural persons under Mode 4.

[24] See e.g. para. 5 of Annex 7-A-2 of the EU–South Korea EIA ('List of commitments in conformity with Article 7.13 (Establishment)').

Under Mode 3, the Member States have undertaken commitments relating also to such economic activities that are not in the field of services. Such commitments relate to agriculture, hunting, forestry, logging, fishing and aquaculture, mining and quarrying and manufacturing (referred to by the EU typically as non-service activities). Mode 3 (Establishment/Investment) commitments are scheduled based on a negative listing.[25] They are listed before or after the section 'Business Services' which starts the commitments for Modes 1 and 2 in accordance with positive scheduling and following a services list that corresponds to a large extent to the WTO's Sectoral Classification List. The Member States have on some occasions included certain service activities that are not included in the WTO's Classification.[26] As they extend the scope of the agreement, such extra service activities are listed in the results for each EIA below.

Each reviewed EIA specifies in the beginning of each schedule that it does not apply to any subsidies or grants provided by any of the EU Member States, including government-supported loans, guarantees and insurance. It is also separately specified under some sectors (especially under Research and Development Services (1.C.) that publicly funded R&D services, exclusive rights and/or authorizations can only be granted to EU nationals and to EU juridical persons having their headquarters in the EU.[27] Thus, even though the EU's commitments on R&D services under Computer and Related Services are liberal, public funding covers EU establishments only.

In the commitments regarding health services and social services, as well as most education services, it is specified that the commitments cover only privately funded services. None of the EU Member States have thus allowed access to their publicly funded education and health services networks. In addition, in the EU–Korea, EU–Central America and EU–CARIFORUM EIAs it is specified that the participation of private operators in the education network is subject to concessions.

In financial services, the EU Member States have typically grouped several sub-sectors together under the two main sectors. Therefore, there

---

[25] They, however, look quite different to the negative lists in CETA and EUJEPA as the EU and Member State specific reservations are listed together under each sector for which reservations are set out. The EU's reservations in CETA and EUJEPA are organized in two annexes in accordance with the NAFTA model and cover all four modes.

[26] It is possible that the extra services are on some occasions part of 'Other services' that is an additional category in the Classification under some of the main service sectors.

[27] E.g. EU–CARIFORUM EIA, Annex IV A (Mode 3) and Annex IV B (Modes 1 and 2).

are only two overall scores: one for insurance-related services and one for banking and other financial services. The EU's scores are very low for both insurance and banking services. This is due to the high number of discriminatory limitations that the Member States have set out and which therefore bring the score close to zero. There is also a high number of 'unbounds' in many Member States and that often brings also the sectoral coverage (SC) score close to zero.

It is noteworthy that the EU's Mode 1 commitments are sometimes relatively low also for such services that are not easily supplied cross-border (such as maintenance and repair of vessels and pushing and towing services as well as beauty services). It is not always easy to understand what goals such reservations serve. On some occasions it may mean that the Member States want to limit cross-border consulting relating to such services.

Under Mode 4, there is a large number of sub-sectors with zero commitments across the EIAs. They are easily visible as the areas coloured in grey in the review sheets of Appendix 3. The most often-occurring NT limitations are nationality and residency requirements. It is crucial to notice that the EU's commitments apply only to the limited categories of persons covered by each EIA. The commitments on key personnel and graduate trainees apply only with regard to services liberalized under Mode 3. The entry of foreign nationals is also subject to many other criteria regarding their legal entry and stay. There are many variations in these rules across the Member States. In line with the GATS, the EU's commitments for natural persons do not allow for access to the Member States' employment markets.[28]

All the EIAs' cover pages for the Mode 4 schedules include a statement on economic needs tests (ENTs).[29] They state the criteria used for ENTs but do not specify whether ENTs are applied in a discriminatory or non-discriminatory manner. However, we consider that under Mode 4 ENTs are especially likely to be applied in a discriminatory manner. EU Member States do not usually restrict the employment of their own nationals and thus ENTs applied to natural persons are likely to concern

---

[28] The GATS Annex on Movement of Natural Persons Supplying Services specifies that the GATS does not apply to measures affecting natural persons seeking access to the employment market of a WTO Member.

[29] The main criteria are 'the assessment of the relevant market situation in the Member State of the European Union or the region where the service is to be provided, including with respect to the number of, and the impact on, existing services suppliers'. See e.g. para. 6 of Annex IV D of the EU–CARIFORUM EIA.

third-country nationals only. However, it is possible that in certain regulated professions, EU Member States may restrict the entry of new suppliers among their own nationals as well. As we have regarded all ENTs discriminatory under Mode 4, there is some scope for interpretation errors in the reading of the schedules in this sense.

All schedules on Mode 4 also note that the lists of commitments do not include measures relating to qualification requirements and procedures, technical standards and licensing requirements and procedures when they do not constitute a limitation within the meaning of NT. Those measures (e.g. need to obtain a licence or need to pass specific examinations) apply to the categories of admitted natural persons even if not listed in the EU's schedule. Among such measures the EU has included also the 'need to have a legal domicile in the territory where the economic activity is performed'. In our view, such a measure is discriminatory under Mode 4 if it requires residence. In our analysis, all explicit residency requirements in the scheduled commitments reduce NT to zero.

Finally, the definitions regarding sub-central levels of government largely match those of the GATS in all four EIAs. For example, in the EU–Korea EIA, a definition for 'measure' is included in Art. 7.2 ('Definitions') of Chapter Seven on Trade in Services, Establishment and Electronic Commerce. The wording is not completely identical to the GATS, but extremely similar and the provision clearly covers all levels of government (central, regional and local governments). The provision regarding MA (Art. 7.5.2) also includes a reference to 'a regional subdivision' similarly to GATS Art. XVI. It specifies that neither party may adopt or maintain either on the basis of a regional subdivision or on the basis of its entire territory market access limitations similar to those included in GATS Art. XVI.

ii   Detailed Results on the EIAs

Below, each of the four EIAs is presented separately. We first give the average scores for each mode across the entire services schedule of the agreement. All scores represent percentages and are shown as decimals between zero and one in order to follow the presentation model of the detailed review sheets of Annex 3. Thus, a score of 0,75 refers to 75 per cent of the EU Member States (twenty-seven or twenty-eight states, depending on the agreement).

There are two different scores: the first for sectoral coverage (SC) and the second for national treatment (NT). The SC score shows the percentage of EU Member States that have given a binding commitment under each mode. The commitments counted under SC do not need to provide for NT but any commitment suffices. This method of providing a separate score for SC allows to note the overall number of sectors covered by the EIA even without full NT. For example, in the EU–Korea EIA, the EU's SC score for Mode 1 is 0,40, which means that, on average, 40 per cent of the Member States have given some type of a commitment across all sectors of the WTO's Sectoral Classification under Mode 1. A score under SC therefore refers to any type of commitment that is not 'unbound' or which does not constitute complete exclusion of the sector or sub-sector from the EU's schedule (e.g. the exclusion of audio-visual services). An 'unbound' or outright exclusion always gives the score zero.

The second score, NT, on the other hand, gives the score that we are most interested in: the percentage of EU Member States that have granted full NT. This score gives the number of Member States providing non-discriminatory treatment under each sector and sub-sector. It is important to note that sectoral exclusions do not affect the overall average score for NT. This is because under Art. V:1(b), there is a requirement to eliminate discrimination only in the sectors covered by the agreement. Even though it is not entirely clear what this requirement means, we have opted to provide the overall NT score only for such sectors that the EU has not excluded from its specific commitments.[30] Therefore, as the NT score is provided only for sectors that are included, the average NT score across sectors is occasionally higher than the SC score.[31] However, in general both scores are very close to each other. Only under Mode 4 there is a significantly lower score for SC than for NT. This tells about the high number of sectoral exclusions that the EU has applied throughout Mode 4.

The following Table 10.1 gives an example of the coding of the EU's commitments for communication services in the EU–Georgia AA. The first scores (0,75 and 1,00) on the level of the main services sector (2. Communication services) are the average SC and NT scores across both

---

[30] See the explanation for choosing this more conservative method in Chapter 8, in Part III (methodology).

[31] Some of the sectoral (or sub-sectoral) exclusions apply to all four modes, some only to one or two of them. As sectoral coverage is understood in terms of number of sectors *and* modes of supply, the average NT score under a specific mode is not affected by a sectoral exclusion even if only that specific mode has been excluded in the sector in question. The NT score gives the level of non-discrimination in the sectors covered under each mode.

Table 10.1 *Scores for communication services in the EU–Georgia AA (M = mode; SC = sectoral coverage, NT = national treatment)*

	M1: SC	M1: NT	M2: SC	M2: NT	M3: SC	M3: NT	M4: SC	M4: NT
2. Communication services	**0,75**	**1,00**	**0,75**	**1,00**	**0,75**	**1,00**	**0,00**	
A. Postal services	1,00	1,00	1,00	1,00	1,00	1,00	0,00	
B. Courier services	1,00	1,00	1,00	1,00	1,00	1,00	0,00	
C. Telecommunication services	1,00	1,00	1,00	1,00	1,00	1,00	0,00	
D. Audio-visual services	0,00	1,00	0,00	1,00	0,00	0,00	0,00	

modes. The scores for each sub-sector follow. They show that all EU Member States (1,00 = 100 per cent) have given a full NT commitment for postal, courier and telecommunication services. However, audio-visual services are excluded in their entirety. Therefore, the score for sectoral coverage (SC) is 0,00 for audio-visual services and there is no score for NT for that particular sub-sector. A score for NT would be given only if at least some type of commitment existed.

The average scores for both SC and NT under each mode are counted on the highest sectoral level (e.g. 1. BUSINESS SERVICES). In case the main sector is divided further into two lower sub-groups (on the level of A, B, C . . . and further into a, b, c . . .), the average scores for both the numerical level (1, 2, 3 . . .) and the following sectoral level (A, B, C . . .) are marked with a bold font in the review sheet. If no sub-sectors (a, b, c . . .) are specified, the upper sector (A, B, C . . .) alone is marked by a bold font. In some instances the Member States have given identical commitments under all sub-sectors of a specific sector in which case the sub-sectors have been hidden to save space (the scores being the same and thus giving an identical average).[32] There are also certain occasions where the Member States have given their sub-sectoral commitments combined on a higher sectoral level (e.g. in the EU's EIAs all sub-sectors are combined under '1B. Computer and Related Services'). In that case, the smallest sub-sectors are also hidden. The overall average score for each mode ('AVERAGE FOR MODE') is the combined average of the highest level of sectors (the main service sectors from 1 to 11)[33]. The score for each main sector from 1 to 11, on the other hand, is the average of the scores for the sectors below it (A, B, C . . .), which themselves are the average of the scores for the lowest level of sub-sectors (a, b, c . . .). Each average is marked by a bold font in the review sheet.

When looking at specific sectors and sub-sectors one soon notices that there are significant differences in the scores between them. Therefore,

---

[32] The full list of sectors and sub-sectors is as described in the WTO's Services Sectoral Classification list, MTN.GNS/W/120, 10 July 1991.

[33] In the WTO's Sectoral Classification list there are altogether twelve main service sectors. Because the EU has not included any commitments under sector 12 ('Other services not included elsewhere'), that sector is not shown in the review sheets. The fact that there are no EU commitments under this 'left-over' sector, has not affected the results. It is not clear as to what exactly should be included under the sector from the point of view of sectoral coverage. It was thus left outside the analysis.

instead of focusing on the overall average scores across the modes, it is much more informative to look at the average scores across specific sectors and particularly at the exact scores for specific sub-sectors.

Below, we have chosen a few important service sectors for which we provide the average NT score across the entire sector. The score is the average NT score across the sub-sectors for that specific sector. For example, in the EU–Korea EIA the NT score for professional services under Mode 1 is 0,45 – meaning that, on average, 45 per cent of the EU Member States have given non-discriminatory commitments to Korean service suppliers in professional services under Mode 1. The more specific scores by sub-sector should be viewed in Annex 3. There one can see that, for example, in the sub-sector of engineering services (CPC 8672), the EU's score is 0,70. Thus, 70 per cent of the EU Member States give full NT for engineering services through Mode 1. That can be compared to the 'services provided by midwives, nurses, physiotherapists and para-medical personnel' where the EU's score is as low as 0,04 – meaning that only 4 per cent of the Member States have given full NT to Korean professionals in this specific sub-sector (representing actually just one Member State). That shows that the average scores are not informative in cases where there are big differences between different sub-sectors.

The EIAs with the CARIFORUM countries and Georgia include two different categories of Mode 4 service suppliers. In addition to key personnel and graduate trainees that appear in all reviewed EIAs and are marked as Category 1 (Cat. 1) in these two EIAs, these two agreements include specific commitments also on contractual service suppliers (CSSs) and independent professionals (IPs). CSSs and IPs are marked as Category 2 (Cat. 2). In the EU–Georgia EIA, the EU has scheduled specific commitments for business sellers (good and services) together with key personnel and graduate trainees, and they are thus all included in Cat. 1. In the EU–CARIFORUM EIA, there is an endeavour to facilitate visits for business services sellers and short-term visitors for business purposes, but there are no specific commitments on these two groups of natural persons.

The EU's EIA with South Korea has specific commitments with regard to key personnel, graduate trainees and business services sellers. They are scheduled together and thus noted as one group under Mode 4. The EIA with the Central American countries has specific commitments in respect of key personnel and graduate trainees only (they are scheduled together).

In our review, we have noted all the horizontal limitations applied by the EU Member States. As they are not factored in the scores, they deserve special attention. On some occasions, such horizontal limitations applied across the sectors can greatly diminish the value of the sector-specific commitments. The limitations are analyzed in more detail in the following chapter. Here below, in the results concerning horizontal limitations, the number in the parentheses indicates the number of EU Member States having inscribed some type of a horizontal limitation for the type of issue in question. For example, 'types of establishment (EU (branches) + 10)' means that all EU Member States have included a reservation on allowing the use of branches across all service sectors in addition to which ten Member States have inscribed some other types of cross-cutting discriminatory reservations concerning the types of establishment available to service suppliers of the partner country. These measures are discriminatory if the foreign service suppliers' choice of legal form for the establishment is restricted as compared to domestic suppliers or if the foreign suppliers are subjected to more burdensome establishment requirements than domestic suppliers.

The detailed scores on SC and NT can be viewed in the review sheets of Appendix 3. In the beginning of each review sheet of Appendix 3, we have noted issues that may be considered relevant under Art. V:2 (the wider process of economic integration or trade liberalization). The presentation of the service sectors depends on the EU's commitments. Where the commitments are identical across the entire main sector (as they generally are e.g. for all sub-sectors of 'Computer and Related Services'), only the main sector is shown. Where the EU has provided different commitments across the sub-sectors, the scores are provided separately for each sub-sector.

We present the summary of our results in the following order, from the oldest to the most recent agreement (the year refers to the timing of the signing of the agreement):

EU–CARIFORUM EPA 2008
EU–Korea FTA 2010
EU–Central America AA 2012
EU–Georgia AA 2014

To provide a full picture of the agreements, we also take note of such service activities for which the EU has included commitments, but which are not part of the WTO's Sectoral Classification List. The different modes are marked as M1, M2, M3 and M4. Under Mode 4, key personnel and graduate trainees are marked as Category 1 (Cat. 1). Contractual service suppliers and independent professionals are marked as Category 2 (Cat. 2).

EU–CARIFORUM EPA 2008

AVERAGE SCORES (Twenty-seven Member States)

SC = sectoral coverage
NT = national treatment (the level of non-discrimination)
All Mode 1 commitments (averages on the level of the main sectors)
SC: 0,40
NT: 0,43

All Mode 2 commitments

SC: 0,70
NT: 0,76

All Mode 3 commitments

SC: 0,78
NT: 0,72

All Mode 4 commitments

Category 1	Category 2 (CSSs and IPs)
(key personnel and graduate trainees)	
SC: 0,51	SC: 0,22
NT: 0,82	NT: 0,33

The average level of non-discrimination (NT) in certain sectors and sub-sectors:

Professional Services

Mode 1: 0,44
Mode 2: 0,95
Mode 3: 0,85
Mode 4 Cat 1: 0,66 / Cat. 2: 0,31

Other Business Services

Mode 1: 0,72
Mode 2: 0,88

Mode 3: 0,86
Mode 4: Commitments only in certain sub-sectors

Communication Services

Mode 1: 1,00
Mode 2: 1,00
Mode 3: 1,00
Mode 4: Excluded in its entirety

Financial Services

Mode 1: Insurance 0,04 / Banking and other 0,00
Mode 2: Insurance 0,07 / Banking and other 0,93
Mode 3: Insurance 0,63 / Banking and other 0,52
Mode 4: Insurance 0,81 / Banking and other 0,81 (Cat. 1 only, Cat. 2 excluded in its entirety)

Transport Services (Excludes Much of Air Transport Services and All Space Transport Services)

Mode 1: 0,40
Mode 2: 0,79
Mode 3: 0,62
Mode 4: 0,64 (Cat. 1 only, Cat. 2 mostly excluded)

HORIZONTAL LIMITATIONS OF THE EU MEMBER STATES

Modes 1 and 2:
Real estate (18)
Mode 3:
Real estate (19)
Public utilities (all EU)
Types of establishment (7)
Investment (1)
Geographical zones (1)
Mode 4:
Certain Member States have prescribed horizontal reservations relating to:
Economic needs test for graduate trainees (2)
Scope of intra-corporate transfers (2)
Residency and citizenship requirements for managing directors and/or auditors (5)

Mutual recognition directives apply to EU citizens only (EU)
Transitional periods (12)

The EU Has Excluded the Following Sectors:

Mining, manufacturing and processing of nuclear materials;
Production of or trade in arms, munitions and war material;
Audiovisual services;
National maritime cabotage; and

Most national and international air transport services (excl. aircraft repair and maintenance, selling and marketing of air transport services, computer reservation system services, and other ancillary services that facilitate the operation of air carriers as contained in the specific commitments).

In addition, the EU's schedule shows that there are no commitments on space transport services.

The EU Has Commitments in the Following Services Not Appearing in the WTO's Classification:

The EU has included certain sub-sectors of energy services that do not appear in the WTO's model list (see section 18. Energy Services). They include wholesale trade services of solid, liquid and gaseous fuels and related products (CPC 62271), wholesale trade services of electricity, steam and hot water (NB: the horizontal limitation on public utilities applies), and retailing services of motor fuel (CPC 613) as well as retail sales of fuel oil, bottled gas coal and wood (CPC 63297) and retailing services of electricity, (non bottled) gas, steam and hot water. However, the Member States' commitments under these sub-sectors are modest (except for Mode 2 where the EU has given full commitments almost under each of these sub-sectors).

Under business services (F. Other Business Services), the EU has included certain services that appear in the WTO's model list only in the aggregated form 'Other' (CPC 8790) under F. 'Other Business Services'. The EU's schedule specifies translation and interpretation services (M1 89 per cent / M2 100 per cent / M3 81 per cent / M4 Cat. 1 93 per cent),[34] interior design services (M1 100 per cent / M2 100 per cent / M3

---

[34] Cat. 1 = key personnel and graduate trainees / Cat. 2 = contractual service suppliers and independent professionals. All values represent NT. If there is no value for a specific mode, it means that the value is zero.

100 per cent), collection agency services (M1 7 per cent / M2 7 per cent / M3 93 per cent / M4 Cat. 1 89 per cent), credit reporting services (M1 7 per cent / M2 7 per cent / M3 88 per cent / M4 Cat. 1 89 per cent), duplicating services (M1 4 per cent / M2 100 per cent / M3 100 per cent), telecommunications consulting services (M1 / 100 per cent and M2 / 100 per cent) and telephone answering services (M1 100 per cent / M2 100 per cent / M3 100 per cent).

In addition, under section 12 (services auxiliary to transport), the EU has included certain sub-categories that are not part of the CPC system and thus are not present in the WTO's model list. The services in question are customs clearance services, container station and depot services, maritime agency services and maritime freight forwarding services. The EU has given a full commitment for these services both for M1 and M2. Under M3, the score is 96 per cent for customs clearance and 100 per cent for the rest of these sub-sectors. Under M4, there are no non-discriminatory commitments.

Under the heading 'Other services not included elsewhere' (Included under 12. 'Other services not included elsewhere' in the WTO's model list), the EU has prescribed the following: washing (M2 100 per cent / M3 100 per cent), hairdressing (M2 100 per cent / M3 96 per cent), cosmetic treatment (M2 100 per cent / M3 96 per cent), other beauty treatment services (M2 100 per cent / M3: 96 per cent) and spa services (M2 100 per cent / M3 100 per cent). Included here are also telecommunications connection services (M1, M2 and M3 100 per cent). For Mode 4 Cat. 1, there is no coverage for telecommunications connections services and all the commitments for the rest of these sub-sectors are discriminatory.

Under rental/leasing services without operators, the EU has included telecommunications equipment rental (CPC 7541) (100 per cent for M1, M2 and M3, no NT for M4). In addition, there are retail sales of pharmaceuticals and retail sales of medical and orthopaedical goods (CPC 63211) and other services supplied by pharmacists (M1 4 per cent / M2 100 per cent / M3 22 per cent / M4 Cat. 1 74 per cent).

Concerning Mode 4

The EIA with CARIFORUM includes six different types of natural persons – more than in any of the other reviewed EIAs. There are specific commitments on four of them: key personnel and graduate trainees (Category 1) and CSSs and IPs (Category 2). The key personnel includes business visitors setting up a commercial presence and intra-corporate transferees. In addition, there are short-term business visitors – a type of Mode 4 appearing only in this EIA out of the four agreements. However, there are no binding commitments: Art. 84 includes an endeavour to facilitate short-term business visits for specific purposes (such as for research and design, training seminars, trade fairs and exhibitions). The last category comprises business services sellers for which there are no specific commitments but under Art. 82 their entry and stay is allowed for a period of up to ninety days in any twelve-month period, subject to the EU's scheduled reservations across the liberalized service sectors.

   The commitments on key personnel and graduate trainees include a limited commitment for a manufacturing activity outside business services: publishing, printing and reproductions of recorded media (Section 4 H).

   According to Art. 81 of the EIA, the temporary entry and stay of key personnel and graduate trainees shall be permitted for a period of up to three years for intra-corporate transferees, one year for graduate trainees, and ninety days in any twelve-month period for business visitors and business services sellers. Art. 83 includes the requirements for CSSs and IPs. Their entry and stay is subject to a number of conditions. Most importantly, the natural persons must be engaged in the supply of a service on a temporary basis as employees of a juridical person, which has obtained a service contract for a period not exceeding twelve months. In addition, the temporary entry and stay of CSSs and IPs shall be for 'a cumulative period of not more than six months or, in the case of Luxembourg, 25 weeks, in any 12-month period or for the duration of the contract, whichever is less'. The EU's sector-specific commitments on CSSs and IPs are so heavily restricted that only a small part of the sectors are in reality covered.

EU–South Korea FTA 2010

AVERAGE SCORES (Twenty-seven Member States)

All Mode 1 commitments (averages on the level of the main sectors)

SC: 0,44
NT: 0,46

   All Mode 2 commitments

SC: 0,73

NT: 0,79

All Mode 3 commitments

SC: 0,80
NT: 0,79

All Mode 4 commitments

SC: 0,48
NT: 0,84

The average level of non-discrimination (NT) in certain sectors:

Professional Services

Mode 1: 0,45
Mode 2: 0,95
Mode 3: 0,81
Mode 4: 0,73

Other Business Services

Mode 1: 0,72
Mode 2: 0,88
Mode 3: 0,84
Mode 4: Mostly no commitments

Communication Services

Mode 1: 1,00
Mode 2: 1,00
Mode 3: 1,00
Mode 4: Excluded in its entirety

Financial Services

Mode 1: Insurance 0,07 / Banking and other 0,00
Mode 2: Insurance 0,11 / Banking and other 0,93
Mode 3: Insurance 0,59 / Banking and other 0,00
Mode 4: Insurance 0,81 / Banking and other 0,81

Transport Services (Excludes Much of Air Transport Services and All Space Transport Services)

Mode 1: 0,43

Mode 2: 0,75
Mode 3: 0,76
Mode 4: 0,83 (some sub-sectors completely excluded)

Horizontal Limitations of the EU Member States

Modes 1 and 2:
Real estate (16)
Mode 3:
Real estate (18)
Public utilities (EU)
Types of establishment (EU (branches) + 10)
Investment (6)
Geographical zones (1)
Mode 4:
Certain Member States have prescribed reservations relating to:
Economic needs test for graduate trainees (2)
Scope of intra-corporate transferees (2)
Training of graduate trainees (5)
Residency and citizenship requirements for managing directors and/or
    auditors (5)
Mutual recognition directives apply to EU citizens only (EU)

The EU Has Excluded the Following Sectors:

The same as in the EU–CARIFORUM EIA (see above).

The EU Has Commitments in the Following Services Not
Appearing in the WTO's Classification:

Energy services: certain sub-sectors (similar to the EU–CARIFORUM
EIA, see above).

Under business services (F. Other Business Services): translation and
interpretation services (M1 89 per cent / M2 100 per cent), interior
design services (M1 100 per cent / M2 100 per cent), collection agency
services (M1 7 per cent / M2 7 per cent), credit reporting services (M1
7 per cent / M2 7 per cent), duplicating services (M1 4 per cent /
M2 100 per cent) and telephone answering services (M1 100 per cent /
M2 100 per cent).

In addition, under section 12 (services auxiliary to transport), the EU
has included the following 'Other services not included elsewhere':

washing, hairdressing, cosmetic treatment and spa services. All are unbound for M1 (100 per cent) provide full NT for M2 (100 per cent) and M3 (100 per cent).

Under rental/leasing services without operators, the EU has included telecommunications equipment rental (CPC 7541) (100 per cent for M1, M2 and M3, 0 per cent for M4). There are also commitments on the retail sales of pharmaceuticals and retail sales of medical and orthopaedical goods (CPC 63211) and other services supplied by pharmacists (M3: 22 per cent, M4: 74 per cent).

Concerning Mode 4

The EU's schedule on Mode 4 includes a limited commitment for one manufacturing activity: publishing, printing and reproductions of recorded media (Section 4 H).

According to Art. 7.18 of the EIA, the temporary entry and stay of key personnel and graduate trainees shall be permitted for a period of up to three years for intra-corporate transferees, one year for graduate trainees, and ninety days in any twelve-month period for business visitors and business services sellers. The scheduled commitments concern only key personnel (including business visitors responsible for setting up an establishment), graduate trainees and business service sellers. There are no commitments on CSSs and IPs. Instead, Art. 7.20(1) provides that 'the Parties reaffirm their respective obligations arising from their commitments under the GATS'. According to the second paragraph, the Parties' commitments in respect of CSSs and IPs depend on the results of the Doha Round and thus remain to be negotiated.

EU–Central America AA 2012

AVERAGE SCORES (Twenty-seven Member States)

All Mode 1 commitments (averages on the level of the main sectors)

SC: 0,41
NT: 0,44

All Mode 2 commitments

SC: 0,77
NT: 0,83

All Mode 3 commitments

SC: 0,77
NT: 0,67

All Mode 4 commitments

SC: 0,51
NT: 0,84

The average level of non-discrimination (NT) in certain sectors:

Professional Services

Mode 1: 0,44
Mode 2: 0,94
Mode 3: 0,85
Mode 4: 0,67

Other Business Services

Mode 1: 0,72
Mode 2: 0,89
Mode 3: 0,87
Mode 4: Commitments only in certain sub-sectors

Communication Services

Mode 1: 1,00
Mode 2: 1,00
Mode 3: 1,00
Mode 4: Excluded in its entirety

Financial Services

Mode 1: Insurance 0,00 / Banking and other 0,00
Mode 2: Insurance 0,11 / Banking and other 0,96
Mode 3: Insurance 0,56 / Banking and other 0,00
Mode 4: Insurance 0,81 / Banking and other 0,81

Transport Services (Excludes Much of Air Transport
Services and All Space Transport Services)

Mode 1: 0,38
Mode 2: 0,74
Mode 3: 0,56
Mode 4: 0,80

Horizontal Limitations of the EU Member States

Modes 1 and 2:
Real estate (18)
Mode 3:
Real estate (19)
Public utilities (EU)
Types of establishment (EU (branches) + 9)
Investment (6)
Geographical zones (1)
Mode 4 (key personnel and graduate trainees):
Certain Member States have prescribed reservations relating to:
Economic needs test for graduate trainees (2)
Scope of intra-corporate transferees (2)
Training of graduate trainees (5)
Residency and citizenship requirements for managing directors and/or
   auditors (5)
Mutual recognition directives apply to EU citizens only (EU)

The EU Has Excluded the Following Sectors:

The same as in the EU–CARIFORUM EIA (see above).

The EU Has Commitments in the Following Services Not
Appearing in the WTO's Classification:

Energy services: certain sub-sectors (similar to the EU–CARIFORUM
EIA, see above).

Under business services (F. Other Business Services), translation and
interpretation services (M1 89 per cent / M2 100 per cent / M3
81 per cent / M4 93 per cent), interior design services (M1, M2 and
M3 100 per cent), collection agency services (M1 7 per cent / M2
7 per cent / M3 93 per cent / M4 89 per cent), credit reporting services
(M1 7 per cent / M2 7 per cent / M3 89 per cent / M4 89 per cent),
duplicating services (M1 4 per cent / M2 and M3 100 per cent) and
telephone answering services (M1, M2 and M3 100 per cent).

Under section 12.A. (services auxiliary to maritime transport), the EU
has included customs clearance services, container station and depot
services, maritime agency services and maritime freight forwarding services. The EU has given a full commitment for these services only under
M2. Under M1, there is a full binding only for maritime agency services

and maritime freight forwarding services (unbound for customs clearance services and container station and depot services). Under M3, the score is 96 per cent for customs clearance and 100 per cent for the rest.

'Other services not included elsewhere': washing, cleaning and dyeing services; hairdressing services; cosmetic treatment, manicuring and pedicuring services; other beauty treatment services and spa and non-therapeutical services (non-medical): unbound for M1 and M4 and bound for M2 (100 per cent) and M3 (100 per cent). Included here are also telecommunications connection services (M1, M2 and M3 100 per cent).

Under rental/leasing services without operators, the EU has included telecommunications equipment rental (CPC 7541) (100 per cent for M1, M2 and M3). Retails sales of pharmaceuticals and retail sales of medical and orthopaedical goods (CPC 63211) and other services supplied by pharmacists (M1 4 per cent / M2 100 per cent / M3 22 per cent / M4 74 per cent).

For Environmental Services, the EU has included some more subsectors than specified in the WTO's model list (sub-sectors C-G of 6. Environmental Services). However, under Mode 1 they are unbound except for consulting services. Under Mode 2, there are no reservations.

Concerning Modes 1 and 2

In this agreement, the EU has more tendency to schedule simple 'unbounds' under Modes 1 and 2 instead of qualifying discriminatory reservations. Therefore the score is often the same for SC and NT for both modes.

Concerning Mode 4

The AA with Central America covers the same categories of persons as the EU–Korea FTA. A slight difference is that there are no sector-specific commitments but the entry of Mode 4 service suppliers is subject to commitments under the other modes (entry and stay is similarly allowed for a period of up to ninety days in any twelve-month period). There are no commitments on CSSs and IPs but parties simply reaffirm their respective commitments under the GATS.

EU–Georgia AA 2014

AVERAGE SCORES (Twenty-eight Member States)

All Mode 1 commitments (averages on the level of the main sectors)

SC: 0,44
NT: 0,46

All Mode 2 commitments

SC: 0,77
NT: 0,83

All Mode 3 commitments

SC: 0,93
NT: 0,74

All Mode 4 commitments

Category 1	Category 2
SC: 0,50	SC: 0,19
NT: 0,84	NT: 0,40

The average level of non-discrimination (NT) in certain sectors:
Professional Services

Mode 1: 0,45
Mode 2: 0,95
Mode 3: 0,79
Mode 4: Cat 1: 0,66 / Cat. 2: 0,43

Other Business Services

Mode 1: 0,72
Mode 2: 0,91
Mode 3: 0,83
Mode 4: Commitments only in certain sub-sectors

Communication Services

Mode 1: 1,00
Mode 2: 1,00
Mode 3: 1,00
Mode 4: Excluded in its entirety

Financial Services

Mode 1: Insurance 0,00 / Banking and other 0,00
Mode 2: Insurance 0,11 / Banking and other 0,93
Mode 3: Insurance 0,54 / Banking and other 0,54
Mode 4: Insurance 0,79 / Banking and other 0,79

Transport Services (Excludes Much of Air Transport Services
and All Space Transport Services)

Mode 1: 0,29
Mode 2: 0,70
Mode 3: 0,86
Mode 4: Cat 1: 0,79 / Cat. 2: 0,54 (several sub-sectors excluded in both categories)

Horizontal Limitations of the EU Member States

Modes 1 and 2:
No horizontal limitations. Only subsidies are mentioned in the beginning of the annex (in accordance with Art. 76(3) of the agreement).
Mode 3:
Real estate (16)
Public utilities (EU)
Types of establishment (EU (branches) + 9)
Investment (6)
Mode 4:
Certain Member States have prescribed reservations relating to:
Economic needs test for graduate trainees (2)
Scope of intracorporate transferees (2)
Training of graduate trainees (6)
Residency and citizenship requirements for managing directors and/or auditors (5)
Mutual recognition directives apply to EU citizens only (EU)

The EU Has Excluded the Following Sectors:

The same as in the EU–CARIFORUM EIA (see above).

The EU Has Commitments in the Following Services Not
Appearing in the WTO's Classification:

Energy services: certain sub-sectors (similar to the EU–CARIFORUM EIA, see above).

Under business services (F. Other Business Services, translation and interpretation services (M1 86 per cent / M2 100 per cent / M3 per cent

86 per cent / M4 Cat. 1 96 per cent, for Cat. 2 only translation services: 39 per cent), interior design services (M1 96 per cent / M2 100 per cent), collection agency services (M1 7 per cent / M2 7 per cent / M3 93 per cent / M4 Cat 1. 89 per cent, not covered for Cat. 2), credit reporting services (M1 7 per cent / M2 7 per cent / M3 93 per cent / M4 Cat. 1 89 per cent, not covered for Cat. 2), duplicating services (M1 4 per cent / M2 100 per cent and M3 per cent / M4 Cat. 1 0 per cent, not covered for Cat. 2) and telephone answering services (M1, M2 100 per cent). Included here are also telecommunications connection services (M1, M2 100 per cent).

For Environmental Services, the EU has included some more sub-sectors than specified in the WTO's model list (sub-sectors C-G of 6. Environmental Services). However, under Mode 1 they are mostly unbound (only three to five Member States bound) except for consulting services. Under Mode 2, there are no reservations. Under professional services, there are retail sales of pharmaceuticals and retail sales of medical and orthopaedical goods (CPC 63211) and other services supplied by pharmacists (M1 7 per cent / M2 100 per cent / M4 Cat. 1 75 per cent, not covered for Cat. 2).

Under section 12.A. (services auxiliary to maritime transport), the EU has included customs clearance services, container station and depot services, maritime agency services and maritime freight forwarding services. The EU has given a full commitment for these services only under M2. Under M1, there is a 96 per cent binding only for maritime agency services and maritime freight forwarding services (unbound for customs clearance services and container station and depot services). These auxiliary services are not mentioned in the negatively listed Mode 3 commitments and are therefore presumably covered by Mode 3.

In addition, the EU has included a section 13. Other transport services, which includes 'Provision of combined transport services'. The score is 46 per cent for Modes 1 and 2 but it is specified that the commitment is without prejudice to the EU's schedules' limitations affecting any given mode of transport.

'Other services not included elsewhere': washing, cleaning and dyeing services; hairdressing services; cosmetic treatment, manicuring and pedicuring services; other beauty treatment services and spa and non-therapeutical services (non-medical): unbound for M1 and for a part of M4 (0 per cent for specialists and for graduate trainees, otherwise 100 per cent) and bound for M2 (100 per cent) and M3 (100 per cent).

Included here are also telecommunications connection services (M1, M2 and M3 100 per cent).

Mode 4 Cat. 2 includes site investigation work (CPC 5111) where NT score is 61 per cent (covers CSSs only).

Concerning Mode 3

A negative scheduling modality. MFN exceptions are included in the sector-specific commitments whereas in the other EIAs they are listed in a separate annex. Similar horizontal limitations and sectoral exclusions to the other EIAs (Art. 78: audiovisual services, national maritime cabotage and most of air transport services excluded completely) but a high coverage of sectors and sub-sectors in the sector-specific commitments (SC 93 per cent).

Relating to air transport services: the conditions of mutual market access in air transport are to be dealt with by the Common Aviation Area Agreement between the EU and Georgia.

Concerning Mode 4

There are five different Mode 4 categories covered by the agreement (the same as in the EU–CARIFORUM EIA, except for short-term visitors for business purposes who are not included).

The conditions for the entry of key personnel, graduate trainees, CSSs and IPs are very similar to the text of the agreement in the EU–CARIFORUM EIA. A slight difference is that in the agreement with Georgia, there are sector-specific commitments on business service sellers (scheduled together with key personnel and graduate trainees). In the agreement with CARIFORUM, the entry and stay of service sellers is subject to the reservations across the other modes. In addition, in the agreement with Georgia, the specific group of natural persons is referred to as 'business sellers' as the EU covers in this agreement the sellers of both goods and services (except for the UK that covers only the sellers of services).

11

Legal Analysis of the Results

I Introduction to the Discussion of the Results

In the present chapter we give a concise view on the reviewed EIAs from the point of view of Art. V GATS. In accordance with our methodology, our analysis is focused on the level of liberalization included in the EU's sector-specific commitments. Where necessary, we bring up issues in the actual texts of the agreements but instead of interpreting the articles of the agreements, we focus on discussing the EU's EIAs' relationship to the Art. V:1 requirements of sectoral coverage and elimination of discrimination.[1] First it can be noted that only one of the reviewed EIAs includes a statement on the agreement's compatibility with the GATS. In the EU–South Korea FTA the parties list among the objectives of the agreement 'to liberalize trade in services and investment between the Parties, in conformity with Article V of the General Agreement on Trade in Services'. It is hard to say what type of conclusions can be drawn in this regard. At the time of the conclusion of the agreement, the Commission stated that the FTA goes further than any previous EU agreement in lifting trade barriers.[2] The Commission also stated that 'both in terms of

---

[1] For a recent and comprehensive interpretation of the EU's treaty obligations both under the GATS and EIAs, see Natens, B. (2016) *Regulatory Autonomy and International Trade in Services: The EU under GATS and RTAs.* Cheltenham; Northampton: Edward Elgar. The author analyzes the EU's obligations especially from the point of view of regulatory autonomy.

[2] The Commission's web page on the EU-South Korea FTA, available at http://ec.europa.eu/trade/policy/countries-and-regions/countries/south-korea/ (last accessed on 1 September 2018).

sectoral coverage and depth of market access commitments, the EU–Korea FTA is by far the most ambitious services FTA ever concluded by the EU and goes beyond any services agreement Korea has concluded so far'.[3]

The fact that the EU has not included a similar compatibility statement in its other EIAs does not necessarily mean that the EU has doubts about those EIAs' compliance with Art. V GATS. But the conclusion of the statement in the EIA with South Korea may mean that the EU wants to explicitly underline its view of WTO-compliance in respect of this specific agreement. Strictly legally, all the EU's EIAs should comply with Art. V. However, the EU may be especially willing to emphasize such compatibility with its most commercially driven PTA as that agreement lacks such other factors that could be considered to contribute to extensive trade liberalization in the longer term.[4] Moreover, for this particular PTA's economic significance and strategic importance (concluded with a central Asian economy), the emphasis on GATS-compatibility may also be planned to play down legal threats by other Members.

In this chapter we give some appraisal of the level of liberalization reached in the four reviewed EIAs. However, we refrain from a judgement on their GATS-compatibility. Reaching any exact conclusions in that regard would be challenging for two reasons. First, our methodology is only one possible way to analyze EIAs and it does not give any ultimate correct answer in this regard. Our results show how many Member States have provided NT under each sub-sector of the WTO's Sectoral Classification List. Our methodology does not take into account differences in the gravity of the limitations to NT. However, we consider such an approach to be in line with Art. V:1(b) since it defines non-discrimination in terms of NT. One either grants NT or does not. The empirical exercise of the four EIAs revealed that a large number of the inscribed reservations were serious NT limitations, for example nationality and residency requirements. However, it should be kept in mind that also small discriminatory elements in the commitments bring the value of the commitment to zero. Under the SC column, however, we have included all types of commitments, also discriminatory ones. One can thus see the difference between a binding (any kind of binding) and

---

[3] The EU Commission's brochure 'The EU-Korea Free Trade Agreement in Practice', available at http://trade.ec.europa.eu/doclib/docs/2011/october/tradoc_148303.pdf (last accessed on 1 September 2018).

[4] Such long-term trade liberalization and/or economic integration being a possible factor in the consideration under Art. V:2 GATS.

a non-discriminatory binding by comparing the SC and NT scores on the lowest sub-sectoral level. The score for SC is often higher, but only slightly. That shows that in a large number of the Member States' commitments only non-discriminatory bindings are given. The other alternative is a simple 'unbound' (giving a zero also under SC). In the average scores, which are counted across several sub-sectors, the SC score is sometimes lower than the corresponding NT score. That is because sectoral exclusions affect the SC score but do not affect the NT score. The choice is based on Art. V:1(b) which requires the elimination of discrimination only in the sectors covered by the agreement.

All in all, the results are most informative on the lowest sub-sectoral level. That relates to the second challenge in our chosen methodology. The EU's own structure as an FTA itself makes it hard to come up with any exact scores as to the sectoral coverage and level of non-discrimination provided in the EU's EIAs. The EU's commitments in the reviewed EIAs comprise the commitments of twenty-seven or twenty-eight different countries, depending on the agreement. Even though in some instances there is an identical commitment from all Member States, the much more often occurring situation is that there are at least a few different types of commitments with varying degrees of restrictiveness. On some occasions, often in the most sensitive sectors (e.g. in financial services and health services), there are over twenty different commitments. We have tried to solve this challenge by giving percentage values to the EU's commitments under each sub-sector. Thus, our results do not give the percentage of sectoral coverage and level of non-discrimination granted by the EU as a whole.[5] What they do give is the percentage of EU Member States providing for sectoral coverage (by granting some type of a commitment) and non-discrimination (by granting NT) under each sub-sector of the WTO's Sectoral Classification List. This can be considered to give some guidance as to the overall coverage of each EIA by the EU as a whole. However, one should not focus on the average percentages counted across all the sectors. They do not give very relevant information because there is a great variety in the sector-specific percentage scores.

---

[5] If the methodology was applied to a singular state giving one commitment for its entire territory in each sub-sector, the score under each sub-sector would be either one or zero. In that case, the average score across all the sectors would directly show the level of sectoral coverage and non-discrimination granted by that state in the entire agreement and thus corresponding directly to the Art. V GATS criterion of the elimination of 'substantially all discrimination' across a substantial number of sectors.

In a specific sub-sector the score may be 100 per cent (NT by twenty-eight Member States) and in another it may be 0 per cent (a discriminatory commitment by twenty-eight Member States). An average of 50 per cent of these two sub-sectors does not tell much. The averages should therefore be approached cautiously, and mainly to compare different EIAs to each other. Our analysis is best suited for looking at the scores on the sub-sectoral level. They show what percentage of the EU in terms of Member States provides for NT in each sub-sector. They also show the degree of dispersion among the Member States. Very high and very low scores tell of similarity in policies, whereas the scores closest to the middle tell about large diversity in the Member States' policies in that specific sub-sector.

We discuss the EU's commitments under Mode 4 in more depth than the other modes as there are particularities relating to how they are scheduled. An essential caveat to keep in mind is that the assessment of Mode 4 commitments is especially difficult since it is hard to say what exactly are the categories of persons that should be covered from the point of view of Art. V. With respect to Mode 4 the question is not only 'to what extent' but also 'in respect of who'.

II Results in Light of the Key Provisions of Art. V GATS

i Issues of Interpretation

In the reviewed EIAs, the EU has used the so-called positive method for the scheduling of its sector-specific commitments. The only exception is the chapter on 'Establishment' with Georgia where negative scheduling is used. In the case of the EU–Georgia EIA, the negatively listed restrictions are nevertheless organized under the same eleven main sectors as in the WTO's Sectoral Classification List, which facilitated our work. Altogether, it was, however, hard to understand which sub-sectors were meant to be covered by the negative schedule. We assumed that the liberalized sectors were meant to be the same as under the other modes of the same agreement. However, if all modes were negatively scheduled, one would not know with certainty which sectoral classification list to use as a point of comparison, unless that was specifically specified in the agreement.

In the EU–Georgia EIA, the EU has included in its commitments under Modes 1, 2 and 3 certain sub-sectors which do not appear under the WTO's Sectoral Classification List (the relevant sub-sectors are all written out in the chapter on results).[6] Most of these sub-sectors are not mentioned under the negatively scheduled chapter on Establishment. Considering that the sub-sectors are liberalized to a certain extent under the other modes, one could maybe assume that they are meant to be covered also under Establishment. However, we cannot be certain, as it is not clear towards which list of service sectors the commitments under the negatively listed Establishment should be compared to.

By far the most challenging part of our empirical analysis is, nevertheless, the interpretation of the EU's sector-specific restrictions. In this context it is maybe more correct to say 'the Member States' restrictions' as the difficulty is most often related to the specific way that each Member State has formulated its commitments. Some Member States are clearer than others. The repetition of the same restrictions under several sectors and across the agreements, however, helps the exercise.

Pursuant to Art. XX:3 GATS, the Members' schedules form an integral part of the agreement. In principle, services schedules are thus interpreted as any other kind of treaty language.[7] That means that the interpretational rules of Articles 31 and 32 of the Vienna Convention on the Law of Treaties apply also to services schedules. Their interpretation must thus take into account the common intention of the Members.[8]

However, as noted by the Appellate Body, each schedule has its own intrinsic logic.[9] Other Members' schedules are of 'limited utility in elucidating the meaning of the entry to be interpreted'.[10] This finding is clearly evident in our analysis. In practice, service schedules follow their own intrinsic logic. That is because they are formulated only by one side to the agreement and because they form a certain collective entity where the

---

[6] Such 'additional' sub-sectors could possibly be referred to as GATS-x services similarly to WTO-x areas in PTAs. 'WTO-x' has been used to signify commitments dealing with issues going beyond the current WTO mandate. See Horn, H., Mavroidis, P. C. & Sapir, A. (2010) Beyond the WTO? An Anatomy of EU and US Preferential Trade Agreements. *The World Economy*, 33(11), 1565–88. The EU's EIA commitments in non-service activities could also be labeled as GATS-x.

[7] For an extensive account of the interpretation of WTO Members schedules both under the GATT and the GATS, see Van Damme, I. (2009) *Treaty Interpretation by the WTO Appellate Body*. Oxford; New York: Oxford University Press, at 305–53.

[8] *United States - Measures Affecting the Cross-Border Supply of Gambling and Betting Services*, Report of the Appellate Body, WT/DS285/AB/R, circulated 7 April 2005, para. 160 and *China - Measures Affecting Trading Rights and Distribution Services for Certain Publication and Audiovisual Entertainment Products*, WT/DS363/AB/R, Report of the Appellate Body, circulated 21 December 2009, para. 405.

[9] *US-Gambling*, para. 182.

[10] *China–Publications and Audiovisual Products*, para. 383.

meaning of each commitment is often revealed only in connection with the other commitments of the same party. Naturally, the general rules of treaty interpretation must be applied but in an empirical exercise that goes through hundreds, or even thousands of commitments, certain short cuts must be created. Therefore, in unclear situations, we opted to give to particularly blurry commitments the value zero (mainly under NT). That is because of the lack of clarity as regards the value of the commitment: the state may, in practice, choose to apply it in a discriminatory way. A good example of such a situation are economic needs tests (ENTs) for which certain EU Member States do not always specify whether they apply them only to foreigners or to the state's own nationals as well. As there is a wide margin of discretion left to the state in this regard, we have chosen to give such unclear ENTs the score zero under NT.

There are two different ways of interpreting the results. First, the higher the score for NT, the higher is the level of non-discriminatory access to the EU market for the partner countries' service suppliers. The lower the score, the lower the access. However, as the scores represent percentages of Member States providing for SC and NT under each sector, the scores do not directly show the level of sectoral coverage and non-discrimination for the entire EU party. The second way to interpret the results is to consider the internal dispersion across the EU Member States. The very high and the very low scores show that either the majority or the minority of the Member States is willing to provide SC and NT. The commitments are often not identical and the reasons for the denial of NT may differ, but the result is that the foreign service supplier either has or does not have non-discriminatory access to the EU market. But there is also a large number of scores that are somewhere in the middle, on either side of 50 per cent. In these cases there is more dispersion among the Member States as a large number of them provide for NT and an equally, or close to equally, large number do not.

ii   Sectoral Coverage

In the following, we make some observations on the results of the empirical analysis concerning the sectoral coverage, the modal coverage and the level of non-discrimination of the four reviewed EIAs. We focus on certain general remarks only. The detailed results on each agreement can be viewed in Annex 3, in addition to which a summary of the results on each EIA has been presented above in the previous chapter.

As has been noted by Krajewski, the development of the scope of the CCP with regard to trade in services can be described as 'movement from sensitive modes to sensitive sectors'.[11] This development relates to the extension of the EU's external trade competencies from a partial coverage of services trade to complete competence in the field. Whereas there are no longer any specific decision-making procedures applying to any particular modes, the sensitivity of certain modes can still be visible in the EU Member States' sector-specific commitments.

All four modes are covered in all of the reviewed agreements but there are significant differences in coverage as well as in the level of non-discrimination. The results show that, on average, the EU Member States have given the highest number of sectoral commitments under Mode 3. The average score for the percentage of Member States having given commitments across all the sectors under Mode 3 is 77 per cent in the EIA with Central America, 78 per cent with CARIFORUM, 80 per cent with Korea and as high as 93 per cent with Georgia. As the Mode 3 Chapter with Georgia has been negatively scheduled, it is possible that the negative scheduling modality has increased the overall level of coverage by the EU Member States in that specific agreement. However, the high number of sectoral commitments under Mode 3 with Georgia may also relate to one of the main objectives of the agreement, which is the gradual approximation of the Georgian trade-relevant legislation to that of the EU's. This integration aspect of the agreement may have prompted a more liberal attitude from the Member States as they can already anticipate future approximation in regulation. The especially high score for SC in the EU–Georgia EIA for Mode 3 is, however, not reflected in the NT score (74 per cent), which is on the level of the other agreements.

The overall average score for Mode 3 is higher for SC than for NT in all of the reviewed agreements. This is different to the other modes and is because of the lower level of sectoral exclusions under Mode 3 than under other modes.[12]

---

[11] Krajewski, M. (2008) Of Modes and Sectors: External Relations, Internal Debates, and the Special Case of (Trade in) Services, in Cremona, M. (ed.), *Developments in EU External Relations Law*. Oxford: Oxford University Press, 172–215, at 195.

[12] Of the four EIAs reviewed in this study, three of them refer to Mode 3 as 'establishment'. As an exception, the oldest of the agreements, EU–CARIFORUM EIA of 2008, employs the traditional GATS term, 'Commercial Presence'. The EU's most recently negotiated trade and investment agreements with Vietnam and Canada employ the term 'investment'. In the negotiated, and also not yet concluded, agreement with Singapore the term 'Establishment' is used. The CETA and Vietnam agreements are the first examples of deals where the EU's 'Investment' chapter combines Mode 3 with one overall framework for the market access and

The overall lowest sectoral coverage scores are found to apply to CSSs and IPs under Mode 4. The movement of CSSs and IPs has, however, been liberalized only in two of the agreements. In the agreement with CARIFORUM, there are, on average, commitments from 22 per cent of the Member States across the sectors. For the EU–Georgia EIA, the score is 19 per cent. The low scores reflect the high number of sectoral exclusions for the CSSs and IPs. A quick look into the score sheets of Annex 3 shows that about half of the sectors are excluded. In addition to outright exclusions of certain sectors on the level of the text of the agreement, several and sometimes all Member States have excluded more sub-sectors in their sector-specific commitments. The average scores for the first category of Mode 4 (key personnel and graduate trainees, i.e. ICTs) are also relatively low: around 50 per cent in each agreement. However, direct comparison of scores under Mode 4 to the scores under other modes is problematic as treatment under Mode 4 is provided to a few limited categories of persons only. We give more insight into the Member States' commitments on Mode 4 below.

Notwithstanding the very limited category of CSSs and IPs, the lowest average number of Member States having given sectoral commitments is found under Mode 1. The result is the same in each agreement. The lowest numbers of Member States have given commitments in services relating to transport, energy distribution ('services incidental to energy distribution') and certain professional services (e.g. nurses, midwives and physiotherapists; accountants and auditors and veterinarians). Only one or two Member States have provided any commitments on the placement and supply services of personnel as well as on

protection of investments, including investor–state dispute settlement. The consolidated text of the CETA has been made available by the Commission at http://trade.ec.europa.eu/doclib/docs/2014/september/tradoc_152806.pdf (last accessed on 15 February 2019). In CETA, there are separate chapters for 'Investment', 'Cross-Border Trade in Services' (Modes 1 and 2) and 'Temporary Entry and Stay of Natural Persons for Business Purposes' (Mode 4). The EU's proposal in the TTIP agreement follows the same logic: there is no separate chapter or section on Mode 3 but one common chapter for investment which covers both service and non-service activities. The EU's proposal for 'Trade in Services, Investment and E-Commerce' in the TTIP negotiations is available at http://trade.ec.europa.eu/doclib/docs/2015/july/tradoc_153669.pdf (published in July 2016, last accessed on 1 December 2018). In the EU's previous trade agreements, the chapters on Establishment/Commercial Presence have concentrated on Mode 3 type of investment and covered non-service activities only in a very limited extent. On the overlap of GATS Mode 3 with the provisions of BITs, see Adlung, R. (2016) International Rules Governing Foreign Direct Investment in Services: Investment Treaties versus the GATS. *The Journal of World Investment and Trade*, 17(1), 47–85.

investigation and security services. A low number of bindings applies also to wholesale trade services.

In the important sector of financial services, there are almost no binding commitments under Mode 1. However, this does not mean that no insurance or banking services were liberalized at all. The grouping of financial services is quite special in the sense that they are grouped together under the large headings of 'All insurance and insurance-related services' and 'Banking and other financial services'. Typically, each Member State has provided an 'unbound' with regard to at least certain sub-sectors that belong to these two big categories. However, the exclusion of even a small fraction of insurance and/or banking services takes the score to zero for the entire sector. This is why the scores for the financial services sector are low. Under Mode 1, there are no completely non-discriminatory commitments in any of the reviewed EIAs. Each Member State has set out at least one discriminatory restriction, which takes the score to zero for the entire sector. Under Mode 3, the situation is more diverse as in the agreements with Georgia and the CARIFORUM states about a half of the Member States have provided non-discriminatory access to their banking sector whereas in the agreements with Korea and Central America no Member States have given completely discrimination-free commitments.

Overall, we should be especially wary about making far-reaching conclusions on the average scores across entire modes or even across specific service sectors. Because the scores are averages, they are not very informative as to the level of liberalization reached in each individual sub-sector. A better way to read the results is to look at individual sub-sectors and draw conclusions on the overall impression that the scores give. The average scores on sectoral and modal level give only some guidance on the openness of the EU Member States as a whole. What is especially noteworthy in the average scores, however, is how similar they are across the agreements. The sectoral exclusions are almost identical across the reviewed EIAs (meaning no commitments from any of the Member States). Between the EIAs, certain differences in excluded sectors are to be found mainly under Mode 4 only.

iii   The Level of Non-Discrimination

The scores for NT are occasionally higher than for SC. This is because we have counted the NT score only for such sectors that have been bound.

According to Art. V:1(b) GATS, elimination of substantially all discrimination is required only in the sectors covered by the agreement. If the NT score was provided for all sectors, also to such sub-sectors that have been excluded by the EU, the final scores for NT would be slightly lower.

Our results show that the number of Member States providing for full NT under the agreements varies on the level of entire modes between 40 per cent and 80 per cent. However, there are big differences between different modes and sectors. The lowest level of liberalization is granted under Mode 1. This applies to all of the reviewed EIAs. The average NT scores for Mode 1 in all of the agreements are between 43 per cent and 46 per cent. The low numbers are not due only to one or two sectors but there is a large number of sectors that are more poorly liberalized under Mode 1 than under the rest of the modes. Especially poor levels of liberalization appear under professional services. The same applies to real estate services, certain tourism and travel-related services, health services, recreational and cultural services, as well as transport services. Only in computer and related services, R&D services, educational services[13] as well as construction and related services the number of Member States providing for NT is on the level of the other modes. The low commitment levels under Mode 1 may reflect the difficulty in regulating services supplied especially through the internet. Whereas countries may more easily retain control over movement taking place under the other modes, provision of services under Mode 1 may be especially disruptive. A significant part of discrimination under Mode 1 is due to residency requirements, which, in practice, make empty any commitments for the supply of services through the internet. Such requirements are thus scored at zero for NT.

Under Mode 3, there is in most cases some type of commitment from all of the Member States (bringing the sectoral coverage to 100 per cent) but the commitment is then qualified by a discriminatory element. The most often appearing discriminatory elements are limitations to the participation of foreign capital in terms of maximum percentage limit on foreign shareholding or measures which restrict or require specific types of legal entity or joint venture through which the service can be supplied. The latter is considered discriminatory if the specific form of legal entity clearly applies to foreigners only.

The average levels of Member States providing for NT are quite similar under Modes 2 and 3. The NT scores for Modes 2 and 3 are the highest

---

[13] Only privately funded educational services are covered by the EU's EIAs.

across the four modes. Mode 2 is typically the most liberalized mode in
EIAs. However, the Member States' commitments show that they remain
wary also under this particular mode. There is a lack of NT typically in
the same sectors as under the other modes. The denial of NT in the case of
movement of one's own consumers may reflect caution in accepting
regulatory difference especially in sensitive sectors, even if the consumption of the service would take place outside the national territory.
Limitations to Mode 2 typically also relate to sectors that may affect
domestic employment. For example, placement and supply services of
personnel are heavily limited under all modes, also under Mode 2. The
same concerns, for instance, technical testing and analysis services (CPC
8676). Some types of testing services may be supplied relatively easily
over the internet. The limitations under Mode 2 may reflect the purpose
of making sure that both supply side (Mode 1) and demand side (Mode 2)
are covered by the limitations.[14]

The average level of NT under Mode 3 is 79 per cent in the EU–Korea
EIA, 74 per cent with Georgia, 72 per cent with the CARIFORUM states
and 67 per cent with the Central-American states. Whereas the negatively
scheduled Mode 3 chapter with Georgia scored the highest average for SC
(93 per cent), a similar level of liberalization does not apply to NT. The
EU's NT score with Georgia is in line with the provision of NT under
Mode 3 to Korea and the CARIFORUM states. The NT score with
Central America is somewhat lower at 67 per cent. The results show
that, on average, EU Member States are slightly more discriminatory
towards Georgian undertakings willing to establish in the EU than
towards undertakings originating in Korea, and slightly less discriminatory than towards undertakings originating in the CARIFORUM states.

Overall, there is a somewhat higher number of Member States providing NT under the agreements with Korea and Georgia than in the EIAs
with the CARIFORUM and Central American states. However, differences are small and depend on the mode and sectors. It is not possible to
point towards a generally much higher liberalization level in any of the
agreements. What is common to the agreements, is the generally low

---

[14] A low number of NT bindings from the Member States for Mode 2 are found also under
investigation and security services, commission agents' and wholesale trade services,
insurance and insurance-related services, certain transport services as well as – quite
surprisingly – library, archives, museums and other cultural services. The rational for
reserving the right to place restrictions on the use of foreign insurances by one's own
nationals is maybe more comprehensible than reserving the right to limit the use of
foreign libraries.

levels of NT especially under Modes 1 and 4 (a low number of Member States providing for NT under several sectors) and the higher NT scores under Modes 2 and 3. Under these two modes, in most sectors more than half of the Member States have provided for NT. In general, the results are best interpreted on a sub-sectoral basis.

The second paragraph of Art. V:1 allows for the elimination of existing discriminatory measures and/or prohibition of new or more discriminatory measures to take place on the basis of a reasonable time-frame. We have identified only one instance where the EU has provided for liberalizing measures to take place on a later date. In the EIA with the CARIFORUM certain EU Member States have applied transitional periods to their commitments with regard to CSSs and IPs. Ten Member States have stated that their commitments enter into force on 1 January 2011, and two Member States have provided for an entry into force on 1 January 2014.[15] The dates have already passed, and we have not taken them into account in our analysis. The results thus reflect the level of liberalization in the EU's EIAs as they stand in their final form.

The AA with Georgia is a special case as it provides for a gradual approximation of a significant part of Georgia's trade-relevant legislation with the EU's legislation. Therefore, a full implementation of the agreement is to be attained only through such a gradual process. This special characteristic of the agreement with Georgia, however, does not affect the way the EU has given its commitments. They can thus be analyzed similarly to the other agreements. It is possible that the gradual integration process leads to a more level playing field for Georgian service suppliers in the long-term but any higher level of elimination of discrimination is not visible in the sector-specific commitments as they stand today as compared to the other types of EIAs (the most visible difference being the wider than usual sectoral coverage under Mode 3). The overall process of integrating Georgia further into the EU's legislative framework can possibly be taken into account under Art. V:2 to which we now turn.

iv   Wider Process of Economic Integration

Art. V:2 includes a possible remedy for EIAs remaining below the required level of non-discrimination. Its provisions give the possibility to take the wider process of economic integration or trade liberalization into account in the estimation of the attainment of the conditions under

[15] Annex IV D of the EU–CARIFORUM EIA (p. 1699 of the agreement).

Art. V:1(b). However, the provision does not give any leeway as to the requirement of substantial sectoral coverage of Art. V:1(a).

As has been noted in Part I of the book, there is no consensus as to the exact issues that can be taken into account under Art. V:2. The most common understanding is that the 'wider process of economic integration' refers especially to the liberalization of trade in goods in the terms of Art. XXIV:5 GATT.[16] However, it is not specified how the relationship should be considered.[17]

In our review of the EU's EIAs, we have noted a wide range of issues that may tell about a wider economic integration or trade liberalization taking place between the contracting parties. We do not argue that all these issues should definitely be taken into account and we cannot say how they should affect the assessment of the liberalization levels of any specific agreement. The purpose is to shed some light into the overall framework in which services liberalization is taking place. Such liberalization does not happen in a vacuum but often requires different types and levels of cooperation between national authorities. For example, cooperation in the fields of mutual recognition or transparency may be required for countries to open their markets to foreign suppliers.

Within the issues listed under 'Wider process of economic integration' in the review sheets of Appendix 3, we have included different topics ranging from harmonization and regulatory cooperation to policies on competition and environment. The list is not based on any specific formula but is exemplary of the types of issues included in modern trade agreements. We have not given much detail but simply marked whether such disciplines are included in the EIAs, without paying attention to their legal enforceability. The noted issues do not affect the sector-specific scores in any way but bring some additional light into the contents of each agreement.

One way to approach elements of a 'wider process' is to analyze the relationship of the liberalization levels of each agreement to the extent that such elements are included in an EIA. When comparing the lists of

---

[16] Members' views on the issue are found e.g. in the document WT/REG/W/34, 'Systemic Issues Arising from Article V of the GATS', Communication from Hong Kong, China, Committee of Regional Trade Agreements, 19 February 1999, para. 11. See also WTO (2000) *Synopsis of 'Systemic' Issues Related to Regional Trade Agreements*, Note by the Secretariat, Committee on Regional Trade Agreements, WTO Doc. WT/REG/W/37 of 2 March 2000, para. 85.

[17] Cottier, T. & Molinuevo, M. (2008) Article V GATS, in Wolfrum, R., Stoll, P.-T. & Feinäugle, C. (eds.), *WTO – Trade in Services*. Leiden; Boston: Martinus Nijhoff Publishers, 125–64, at 139.

issues in the analyzed agreements, one notices, once again, that they are quite similar to each other. Even though the reviewed agreements range from a development-oriented agreement (the EPA with the CARIFORUM) to a commercially driven 'deep' FTA with a highly developed industrial nation (the FTA with Korea), they all follow similar patterns. The similarity in the negotiation templates that the EU is using is visible both in the types of issues covered (both in general and especially in relation to services) as well as in the liberalization levels in the field of services, both in terms of SC and NT. The most significant difference between the types of issues covered in the four EIAs is the inclusion of regulatory cooperation in the agreements with Korea and Georgia. Whereas the EIAs with the CARIFORUM and the Central American states provide for regulatory dialogues only, the agreements with Korea and Georgia include a more specialized institutional setting for regulatory cooperation.[18] Such a setting is taken the furthest in the EU–Georgia EIA, which is the only EIA among the four agreements that provides also for harmonization (to take place through Georgia's approximation to the EU legislation). These two agreements are also the ones providing for the highest levels of SC and NT across the four EIAs.

All in all, it would seem that the specific characteristics of a specific type of an agreement (AA, EPA, FTA etc.) can be considered to explain only to a modest degree the level of liberalization achieved in the reviewed EIAs.

v   The Scope and Depth of Mode 4 Commitments

In order to be GATS-consistent, EIAs should not, a priori, exclude any mode of supply.[19] The question of coverage is especially complicated with Mode 4, which is liberalized through different categories of persons. Such categories do not have their basis in the GATS but have been formed in the Members' practice. Each country determines its own

---

[18] The EU–Korea FTA establishes a Trade Committee, as well as more specialized committees and working groups that are responsible for ensuring the operation of the agreement. According to the Commission, the different bodies provide an opportunity both to seek resolution of market access concerns and to engage in closer regulatory cooperation. See the Commission's brochure 'The EU-Korea FTA in Practice', available at http://trade.ec.europa .eu/doclib/docs/2011/october/tradoc_148303.pdf (last accessed on 5 September 2018). Even if most regulatory cooperation relates to trade in goods, institutionalized contacts between each party's authorities may improve transparency and reduce regulatory conflicts also in other areas.

[19] The footnote to Art. V:1(a) GATS.

categories and there is thus great variety in the types of persons admitted as well as in the conditions for their entry and stay.

In the GATS, Mode 4 is defined as the supply of a service 'by a service supplier of one Member, through presence of natural persons of a Member in the territory of any other Member'.[20] Further indications as to the types of situations covered by Mode 4 are given under Art. XXVIII ('Definitions'). We are not aware of any WTO Member having liberalized the supply of services by all natural persons of other Members without any further specifications.[21] Typically, the main types of specifications relate to the type of persons admitted and to the period of their stay. In light of Art. XXVIII GATS and taking into account the Members' practice, it is therefore possible to conclude that Mode 4 does not need to cover all possible service supply by natural persons. Instead, Mode 4 can be liberalized through specific categories of persons. However, we are left in the dark as to how many and what types of categories exactly should there be and what type of entry and stay conditions should be applied.

What appears to be clear is that some movement of natural persons should be allowed at least. In this respect, it would seem that the USA is in an outright breach of Art. V as no PTA negotiated by the USA for over a decade has contained commitments aimed to facilitate the movement of natural persons.[22] The exclusion of an entire mode of supply cannot fulfil the requirement of substantial sectoral coverage under Art. V GATS, especially as the condition is understood not only in terms of number of sectors and volume of trade affected but also in terms of modes of supply.[23]

---

[20] Art. 1:2(d) GATS.

[21] See Jacobsson, J. (2015) GATS Mode 4 and Labour Mobility: The Significance of Employment Market Access, in Panizzon, M., Zürcher, G. & Fornalé, E. (eds.), *The Palgrave Handbook of International Labour Migration: Law and Policy Perspectives.* Hampshire: Palgrave Macmillan, 61–94.

[22] See e.g. Art. 12:1(7) of the FTA between the USA and South Korea, which states that 'Nothing in this Chapter or any other provision of this Agreement shall be construed to impose any obligation on a Party regarding its immigration measures, including admission or conditions of admission for temporary entry'. According to a report prepared for the Members and Committees of the US Congress by the Congressional Research Service, 'No U.S. FTA negotiated after the agreements with Chile and Singapore agreements includes provisions on the temporary movement of personnel'. See 'The Trans-Pacific Partnership (TPP): Negotiations and Issues for Congress', March 20, 2015, available at www.fas.org/sgp/crs/row/R42694.pdf (last accessed on 15 August 2018). See also Stephenson, S. M. & Hufbauer, G. (2011) Labor Mobility, in Chauffour, J.-P. & Maur, J.-C. (eds.), *Preferential Trade Agreement Policies for Development: A Handbook.* Washington, DC: World Bank, 275–306, at 282.

[23] Footnote to Art. V:1(a) GATS.

The EU is in a much safer zone in this regard. All of the reviewed EIAs include commitments on Mode 4. They thus seem to comply with the requirement that EIAs should not provide for the *a priori* exclusion of any mode of supply. Altogether another question is to what extent Mode 4 is covered in the EU's agreements. The GATS does not appear to extend to labour immigration per se, and the exclusion of immigration (with labour market access) in EIAs does thus not amount to a violation of Art. V. Parties should, nevertheless, cover the scope of Mode 4 as provided by the GATS.[24]

Therefore, whereas under Modes 1–3 there are two essential issues to check (the level of SC and NT), under Mode 4 there are three separate issues that arise. The first issue is the categories of persons covered, and only then come the sectoral coverage and the level of non-discrimination provided to such persons. Whereas one could argue that also under Mode 3 there are several ways to access the host state and that countries impose requirements as to the use of specific legal entities, the GATS clearly provides that 'commercial presence' (Mode 3) for the purpose of supplying a service means 'any type of business or professional establishment', including through 'the constitution, acquisition or maintenance of a juridical person' or 'the creation or maintenance of a branch or a representative office'.[25] Thus, the parameters for Mode 3 are largely set by the GATS, whereas the types of natural persons to be admitted under Mode 4 is, in practice at least, determined by the Members themselves. The GATS gives some guidance as to types of persons covered, but there are no legal definitions for the exact categories of persons covered and the conditions for their entry and stay.

The four basic categories of persons that are usually considered to result from the GATS and the Members' commitments on Mode 4 are 1) independent professionals (IPs), 2) intra-company transferees (ICTs), 3) contractual service suppliers (CSSs), and 4) business visitors (BVs) and services salespersons.[26] Only two of the EU's EIAs cover all these categories: the EIAs with the CARIFORUM and Georgia. The two other EIAs do not contain any commitments on CSSs and IPs but simply refer to possible advancement to be made in the GATS negotiations.

---

[24] Similarly in Cottier & Molinuevo (2008), at 134–5.

[25] Art. XXVIII GATS ('Definitions'). Moreover, under the MA discipline of the GATS (Art. XVI), measures which restrict or require specific types of legal entity or joint ventures are prohibited unless otherwise specified in the schedule. As we have explained earlier, such requirements go against Art. V in case they are discriminatory.

[26] See Jacobsson (2015).

The covered categories of persons are thus not identical across the EU's agreements. Among the reviewed EIAs, the most extensive Mode 4 coverage is found in the EU–CARIFORUM agreement. The agreement covers six different types of natural persons: CSSs, IPs, key personnel, graduate trainees, short-term business visitors and business services sellers. 'Key personnel' covers business visitors (responsible for setting up a commercial presence) and ICTs (which is further divided into managers and specialists). 'Graduate trainees' are, in essence, a sub-group of ICTs as they cover persons who have been employed by the transferring undertaking in the home country for at least one year and are temporarily transferred to a commercial presence or to the parent company of the same undertaking in the host state. They must possess a university degree and the transfer must take place for career development purposes or to obtain training in business techniques or methods. Business services sellers, on the other hand, are representatives of a service supplier seeking temporary entry for the purpose of negotiating the sale of services or to enter into agreements to sell services in the host state. It is specifically specified that they cannot engage in making direct sales to the general public or receive remuneration from a source located within the host state. However, the EU's sector-specific commitments under Category 2 of Mode 4 (CSSs and IPs) cover IPs only in about 50 per cent of the commitments.[27]

In the beginning of its schedule for CSS and IPs, the EU has chosen to specify the sectors in which the movement of CSSs and IPs is liberalized. That is probably to make clear in which (limited) sectors commitments for such service supply are taken. Both lists represent less than 50 per cent of all service sectors but the list for IPs is even shorter than for CSSs. Both lists include a mix of main service sectors and sub-sectors. It is also specifically highlighted that 'the Union does not undertake any commitment for contractual service suppliers and independent professions for any sector of economic activity other than those which are explicitly listed below'.[28]

As there are commitments on CSSs and IPs only in two of the EIAs, the overall coverage for Mode 4 in terms of categories of persons cannot be considered comprehensive. Most of the EU's commitments apply to

---

[27] The exclusion of IPs under about a half of the EU's Category 2 commitments in the EIAs with CARIFORUM and Georgia has not been noted in the review sheets of Appendix 3 as it would have excessively complicated their reading.

[28] E.g. the front page of Annex XIV-D of the EU–Georgia EIA.

ICTs and business visitors and service sellers only. There are numerous sectoral exclusions and discriminatory limitations that apply to CSSs and IPs in the two EIAs that cover them. There is also another factor that is questionable from the point of view of Art. V requirements. The EU's Mode 4 commitments are not subjected to the MFN and NT disciplines as the rest of the modes are.[29] The chapters on the temporary presence of natural persons for business purposes simply provide for the definitions of the persons covered but do not grant any non-discrimination obligations for them. Therefore, it would seem that the EU is not promising any non-discrimination in terms of MFN and NT to service suppliers under Mode 4. The level of treatment that is granted is revealed solely by reading the sector-specific commitments. There, as shown by our results, the level of NT is revealed. But it is noteworthy that there is no GATS-like NT treatment discipline on the level of the text of the agreement. Moreover, MFN does not seem to apply to Mode 4 at all. This is probably due to the EU's, or all contracting parties', desire to protect their policy space with admitting persons on more favourable conditions from other countries. However, such exclusion of MFN and NT does not find support in the GATS discipline on EIAs as the provisions of Art. V do not differentiate between the modes of supply in this regard.

In addition to this obvious shortcoming, once one turns into the actual commitments, one notices that also the sector-specific commitments under Mode 4 are quite modest. In general, there is also a large number of sectoral exclusions. There are more exclusions under Mode 4 than under any other mode in the EU's EIAs. That is easy to spot by viewing Annex 3 where the sectoral exclusions are marked by grey colour. As to the level of non-discrimination, the level of NT provided to ICTs is, in the average, higher than under Mode 1 but lower than under Modes 2 and 3. However, this applies only to the first category of Mode 4. For the second category (CSSs and IPs), the NT scores are much lower and an even higher number of sectoral exclusions are applied. The most common applied restriction are nationality and residence requirements. They immediately take the NT score to zero, which greatly decreases the value of the EU's commitments under Mode 4.

---

[29] In the EU–Georgia EIA, MFN applies only to Establishment (Art. 79(1) and 79(2), subject to reservations in Annex XIV-A and XIV-E). All of the other EIAs are subject to MFN reservations as well but a general MFN discipline is granted under the Modes 1–3.

It should also be noted that similarly to Mode 3, not all of the economic activities listed by the EU relate to services activities. Mode 4 has thus been partly extended to manufacturing businesses.[30]

Finally, it is worth analyzing the EU's approach to the scope of Mode 4. Among the three modes, Mode 4 is arguably the most ambiguous. It is unclear what categories of persons should be covered by the mode and to what extent their stay in the host state should be facilitated. Moreover, it is not entirely clear what are the limits of service supply and labor migration. It has generally been considered that the GATS does not cover labor migration but is limited to a specific service mobility taking place outside the host state's employment market.[31] Regarding this issue, it is interesting to note the approach that the EU has taken in its EIAs towards the issue of employment market access. All of the reviewed EIAs include the following statements in the beginning of the chapter on services:

> This Chapter shall not apply to measures affecting natural persons seeking access to the employment market of a Party, nor shall it apply to measures regarding citizenship, residence or employment on a permanent basis.
>
> Nothing in this Title shall prevent the [Parties or the Signatory CARIFORUM States] from applying measures to regulate the entry of natural persons into, or their temporary stay in, their territory, including those measures necessary to protect the integrity of, and to ensure the orderly movement of natural persons across their borders, provided that such measures are not applied in such a manner as to nullify or impair the benefits accruing to any Party under the terms of a specific commitment.[32]

In addition to these straightforward carve-outs designed to protect the integrity of the EU Member States' labour markets and national borders, a careful reading of the definitions of the categories of persons covered in the texts of the agreement reveals that the purpose is to avoid employment market access from taking place.

In that light, it is somewhat contradictory that the Member States have included so many limitations in their sector-specific commitments. There is a large number of nationality and residency conditions for

---

[30] See Descheemaeker, S. (2016) Ubiquitous Uncertainty: The Overlap between Trade in Services and Foreign Investment in the GATS and EU RTAs. *Legal Issues of Economic Integration*, 43(3), 265–94. She deals with the EU's practice of extending Mode 3 and Mode 4 to non-services sectors.

[31] On this question, see Jacobsson (2015).

[32] See e.g. Art. 60 of the Chapter on 'Investment, Trade in Services and E-Commerce' in the EU–CARIFORUM EIA.

ICTs, as well as occasional ENTs. Such requirements show that the Member States choose to retain the opportunity to give preference to local workers. This is understandable in the case of CSSs (for whom such requirements are applied even more often) but creates blurriness around the issue of employment market access in the case of ICTs. According to the EU's own definition of ICTs, their movement is designed to facilitate the business motivations of the foreign service supplier. ICTs must either get training in the host state or help in the development of the host state undertaking. A critical factor is that they have company-specific knowledge, which is typically confirmed by prior-employment requirements in the same undertaking. It is thus hard to imagine that they would be replaced by local workers who lack such a connection to the undertaking and the country of origin. Nevertheless, the EU Member States' commitments do not always reflect this reality.

In the EU's EIAs, Mode 4 is clearly temporary in nature. 'Temporary' is included already in the title of the chapters on Mode 4 ('Temporary entry and stay of natural persons for business purposes'). Clear time limits are provided for the stay in each category of persons covered.[33] With regard to the periods of stay (as well as to the definitions of the categories of persons), the EU Member States are perfectly aligned. However, there is once again no clarity as to what is required by Art. V. Beyond the exclusion of permanent migration, the GATS does not draw lines concerning periods of stay. For example, Japan's GATS commitments allow foreign business travellers to stay for a maximum of 90 days, but certain categories of ICTs can stay up to five years.[34]

When using foreign labour, the situation of TCN service suppliers established outside the EU is different to service suppliers who are established within the Union. In the EU, according to the Court's established case law, service suppliers posting workers to another EU Member State do not need to obtain work permits for their TCN employees (unless they are temporary work agencies). In contrast, third-country service suppliers established outside the EU typically must do so, although in some instances the service supply may take place with no permit if the service supplier is established in a country whose nationals

---

[33] For example, the temporary entry and stay of key personnel and graduate trainees 'shall be for a period of up to three years for intra-corporate transfers, 90 days in any 12-month period for business visitors, and one year for graduate trainees'. See Art. 81 in the EU–CARIFORUM EIA. The periods are the same across the reviewed EIAs.

[34] Mattoo, A. & Carzaniga, A. (eds.) (2003) *Moving People to Deliver Services*. Washington, DC: World Bank and Oxford University Press, at 3.

do not need any visa to enter the Union. In this regard, there is internal EU diversity depending on whether the EU Member State is in the Schengen area or not.

The EU case law in question relates to the use of non-EU national workers in the intra-EU provision of services.[35] In that line of case law, the Court of Justice has built its legal analysis of cross-border service supply around the question of employment market access.[36] In 2011, the Court ruled that hired workers (temp-agency workers) are a group of service suppliers that specifically seek access to the host state's employment market and thus belong to the category of workers.[37] In cases where such workers are not EU nationals and are sent from one EU Member State to work in another, work permits may still be required (a requirement otherwise prohibited in intra-EU provision of services).[38]

---

[35] When analyzing the EU's own case law, it is important to keep in mind that services are understood in somewhat different terms in the EU and in the WTO. The GATS drafters did not use the EU example. Instead, they followed a four-mode typology developed by economists Gary Sampson and Richard Snape. See Sampson, G. & Snape, R. (1985) Identifying Issues in Trade in Services. *The World Economy*, 8(2), 171–82. Only Modes 1, 2 and 4 coincide with the concept of services as it stands in EU law. Mode 3, by contrast, is the closest equivalent to the EU's freedom of establishment. In respect of Mode 4, the basic concept in EU law is the free movement of services, which, similarly to the GATS, encompasses legal entities and self-employed persons alike. EU law makes an important differentiation between workers and service suppliers. The dividing line is the relationship between the service supplier and the service recipient. If the relationship can be characterized as one of employment, the rules governing free movement of workers apply. Under the GATS, the exact division depends on each Member's national regime. See for EU case law Hatzopoulos, V. & Do, T. U. (2006) The Case Law of the ECJ Concerning the Free Provision of Services: 2000–2005. *Common Market Law Review*, 43 (4), 923–91, at 951.

[36] See especially cases C-113/89, *Rush Portuguesa Ldª* v. *Office national d'immigration* [1990] ECR I-1417, paras. 13–15, C-43/93, *Raymond Vander Elst* v. *Office des migrations Internationales* [1994] ECR I-3803, para. 21, joined cases C-49/98, C-50/98, C-52/98 to C-54/98 and C-68/98 to C-71/98 *Finalarte and Others* [2001] ECR I-7831, para. 22 and case C-445/03 *Commission* v. *Luxembourg* [2004] ECR I-10191, para. 38.

[37] Joined Cases C-307/09 to C-309/09, *Vicoplus* [2011] ECR I-00453.

[38] In one case the Court did not only reject the work permit/specific authorization requirement, but it also rejected the automatic expulsion of such third-country workers who had entered the host state's territory unlawfully. The Court concluded that by making it impossible to regularize the situation of a TCN worker that was lawfully posted by an undertaking established in another Member State but who had entered the host state without a required visa, the host state was imposing a restriction on that undertaking's freedom to provide services. Such an act exposes the worker in question to the risk of being excluded from the national territory, which is liable to jeopardize the planned posting. See Case C-168/04, *Commission* v. *Austria* [2006] ECR I-9041, para. 61. The posted TCN workers did not enjoy any free movement rights on their own but rather a derived right stemming from their employer's freedom to provide services in the EU's

The situation is different in the case of posted workers who are not hired out to the host-country company but are engaged in the direct provision of services by their home-state company under a service con-tract (corresponding to CSSs). According to the Court, such workers, employed by an undertaking established in one Member State and temporarily sent to another Member State to provide services, 'do not in any way seek access to the labour market in that second State, if they return to their country of origin or residence after completion of their work'.[39] Requiring work permits from such TCN service suppliers in the internal market has been illegal already for over twenty years, as it hinders the service provision by their employer. However, it is not difficult to imagine that sometimes separating such contractual service suppliers from hired temp-agency workers may be challenging.[40] The EU's Posted Workers Directive covers both situations, but the applic-ability of local labour laws is, to a certain extent at least, dependent on the national legislation.[41]

---

internal market. The concept of 'derived rights' is typically used in connection with TCN family members who sometimes enjoy a derived right to move within the EU together with their EU national family member. As with posted workers, in reality it is rather the EU national who has the right to move with his or her TCN family member. See Craig, P. P. & De Búrca, G. (2015) *EU Law: Text, Cases, and Materials*, Sixth edition. Oxford: Oxford University Press, at 857.

[39] Para. 21 of C-43/93, *Raymond Vander Elst* v. *Office des migrations Internationales* [1994] ECR I-3803.

[40] To help in drawing the difference, the Court of Justice has put forward a method that is often employed in domestic and European employment law. The Court emphasized that one should look into under whose control and direction the workers perform their duties. In the *Vicoplus* case, the Court said that 'as has been noted by all of the Governments which have submitted observations to the Court and also by the Commission, a worker who is hired out, within the meaning of Article 1(3)(c) of Directive 96/71 [The Directive on Posted Workers], works under the control and direction of the user undertaking. That is the corollary of the fact that such a worker does not carry out his work in the context of a provision of services undertaken by his employer in the host Member State'. See Joined Cases C-307/09 to C-309/09, *Vicoplus* [2011] ECR I-00453, para. 47. In practice, however, it is not always straightforward to say under whose control and direction CSSs work. For example, one can imagine a construction site where workers posted by a sub-contractor in another Member State perform their part of the project in close cooperation with the main contractor. Their superiors might be in another country and the workers, in effect, under the direction of the main contractor.

[41] The Posted Workers Directive ('PWD') covers three categories of workers, two of which correspond roughly to the GATS-type CSSs and ICTs. The third category is temp-agency workers. The PWD sets the mandatory, host-state rules of employment that must be applied to all intra-EU posted workers (including the host state's minimum rates of pay). See Art. 3 of Directive 96/71/EC of the European Parliament and of the Council of 16 December 1996 concerning the posting of workers in the framework of the provision

The EU's internal development with regard to temporary supply of personnel is reflected also in the EU's EIA commitments. All Member States have excluded the temporary supply of personnel in their Mode 4 commitments. Also under other modes, the commitments are of very limited nature.[42] There are, however, differences between the agreements. There are only one or two Member States that have given a commitment under Mode 1 in all of the four EIAs, but under Mode 3 there is an NT commitment from 37 per cent of the Member States in the EIAs with Central America and the CARIFORUM states (ten Member States out of twenty-seven providing for non-discrimination under Mode 3). In the EU-Korea EIA, the score is 4 per cent (one Member State out of twenty-seven) and with Georgia it is 7 per cent (two Member States out of twenty-eight). The higher levels with the Central American and the CARIFORUM states may relate to less concern over those countries' service suppliers' potential activity in the placement services of personnel, or to a growing concern in the EU Member States over the liberalization of temp-agency services since the conclusion of those agreements and up to the conclusion of the more recent agreements with Korea and Georgia.

Considering the complexity involved in the liberalization of Mode 4, it is impossible to give any clear answer to the level of non-discrimination provided by the EU's EIAs. As has been noted before, the conditions to access a country through Mode 4 are typically by their nature discriminatory. The movement of natural persons is never entirely liberalized – passports and visas are required to access any country. Even within the EU, the EU citizens do not enjoy unlimited right to remain in each other's territory. Keeping the overall restrictiveness of Mode 4 in mind, the EU's EIAs show that the EU is relatively liberal as to the categories of persons covered. However, the especially

---

of services. The applicability to intra-EU CSSs of certain local labour laws and/or collective agreements outside the mandatory rules for minimum protection of the PWD has been restricted in the Court's case law. See especially Case C-341/05, *Laval un Partneri Ltd* [2007] ECR I-11767 (paras. 80–1). Because of the political controversy concerning the PWD, especially after the judgment in *Laval*, the Commission has, under pressure from several Member States, recently proposed modifications to the Directive. See Proposal for a Directive of the European Parliament and of the Council amending Directive 96/71/EC of the European Parliament and of the Council of 16 December 1996 concerning the posting of workers in the framework of the provision of services, see COM (2016), 128 final.

[42] 'Placement and supply services of personnel' are listed under (k.) in F. Other Business Services which is located in the main sector of 1. Business Services.

meaningful categories of IPs and CSSs are covered only by two of the four agreements (EU–CARIFORUM EPA and EU–GEORGIA AA), and even in them the sectoral coverage especially for IPs is low. The average sector-specific scores for sectoral coverage are relatively low but for NT they are at around 80 per cent. Here one must, however, pay attention to the definitions of the Mode 4 categories already in the text of the agreement. The value of the NT score is limited. In the case of CSSs and IPs, the average non-discrimination score is as low as 33 per cent in the CARIFORUM EIA. In this sense, the coverage of Mode 4 is most extensive in the Georgia EIA, where the average NT score for ICTs (key personnel and graduate trainees) is 84 per cent and 40 per cent for CSS and IPs. However, all in all, and considering especially the overall poor level of commitments for CSSs and IPs, the EU can be considered to stay quite far from attaining the threshold of eliminating substantially all discrimination towards its preferential partners' service suppliers supplying services through the presence of natural persons.

III   Conclusion

Overall, there is much similarity in the scores for individual sub-sectors in all of the reviewed EIAs. The similarity in the commitments across the agreements is confirmed by reading the schedules. They are not identical and in some instances there are significant differences (the most radical being the higher than average sectoral coverage under Mode 3 in the EU–Georgia EIA), but the overall impression based on reading hundreds of pages of commitments is that many of the same restrictions keep repeating from one agreement to the other. The finding applies both to horizontal as well as sector-specific commitments. The reviewed agreements have been concluded within a relatively short period of time (2008–2014). It may be that the commitments reflect a status quo – a level of accession conditions that has taken place mostly through unilateral opening. They would thus not provide for new opening but simply lock-in the access conditions that are already applied. Another option is that the EU Member States have chosen to provide a relatively similar level of market opening across the agreements. However, considering that liberalization of service regulations is typically put into effect in a non-discriminatory manner (except maybe for Mode 4), any new openings granted in earlier agreements may possibly feed into later agreements as they have already become applied on an MFN basis in any case.[43]

This may be reflected also in the EU's EIAs. Instead of providing for new liberalization, they may rather reflect the status quo.[44] Our results show a significant degree of similarity in the commitments between the agreements even if more detailed analysis would be needed to find out the exact extent to which the Member States' commitments have changed from the EPA with the CARIFORUM (2008) to the AA with Georgia (2014).[45] However, our results give reason to conclude that the number of Member States having granted non-discriminatory access conditions to service suppliers of the partner countries in each agreement has not changed in any significant amount.

---

[43] Roy, Marchetti and Lim note that it is very difficult to identify with exactitude the extent to which EIAs lead to real liberalization (i.e. to the removal of applied restrictions). Some countries may bind the status quo (the applied regime) while others may decide to withdraw certain restrictions and accordingly not list them as reservations or limitations in the agreement. One can ascertain the level of actual liberalization only by going through the laws and regulations of each country and compare the applied regime before and after the conclusion of the agreement. See Roy, M., Marchetti, J. & Lim, H. (2007) Services Liberalization in the New Generation of Preferential Trade Agreements (PTAs): How Much Further than the GATS?, *World Trade Review*, 6(2), 155–92, at 178.

[44] Considering the generally low levels of liberalization in EIAs, binding the currently applied regulations may already be considered some sort of an achievement. Mattoo and Sauvé note that a negative list approach can be more effective in locking in the regulatory status quo, whereas positive scheduling can more easily lead to levels below it. See Mattoo, A. & Sauvé, P. (2010) The Preferential Liberalization of Services Trade. *NCCR Trade Regulation Working Paper*, No. 2010/13.

[45] Tracking changes can be done, for example, by measuring consistency in the language of the commitments. One method for measuring consistency in treaty language is used by Alschner and Skougarevskiy who measure the textual similarity of investment treaties through a specific 'heat map' which shows the overlap of the various textual components of each investigated agreement. See Alschner, W. & Skougarevskiy, D. (2016) Mapping the Universe of International Investment Agreements. *Journal of International Economic Law*, 19(3), 561–88.

12

Application of Art. V GATS to the EU's EIAs

The results draw an interesting picture of the EU's practice of scheduling its external services commitments. All reviewed services schedules show a significant degree of discrepancy between the Member States' commitments. The Member State specific limitations are visible also in the EU's latest EIAs with Canada (CETA) and Japan (JEEPA). The services schedules of CETA and JEEPA are negatively listed but reveal the internal diversity of the EU's internal services regulation as almost all reservations set out by the EU are based on individually formulated reservations by the Member States.

Interestingly, our analysis has shown that the differences between the four reviewed agreements are quite small. The EU and its Member States have not engaged in significantly deeper or lower services liberalization in any of them. Art. V:2 GATS allows for a wider process of economic integration or trade liberalization to be taken into account in the evaluation of the fulfilment of the criteria in Art. V:1. The reviewed agreements were chosen with the intention of including agreements that provide for very different types of economic integration, varying from the development-oriented EPA with the CARIFORUM states to the commercially driven FTA with Korea. The Association Agreement with Georgia, on the other hand, had as its outspoken aim the close economic and political integration of Georgia with the EU. These different aims of the agreements are, however, not reflected in the levels of non-discrimination provided by the EU to the partner states. It could be argued that at least in the case of the agreement with Georgia the wider process of economic integration could affect the evaluation of the fulfilment of the GATS

Table 12.1 *Average number of EU Member States providing for national treatment in the reviewed agreements*

	Average number of Member States providing for NT			
	EU–CARIFORUM	EU–KOREA	EU–CENTRAL AMERICA	EU–GEORGIA
Mode 1	43 %	46 %	44 %	46 %
Mode 2	76 %	79 %	83 %	83 %
Mode 3	72 %	79 %	67 %	74 %
Mode 4 (category 1 / category 2 if the agreement provides for two categories); note that many sectoral exclusions apply	82 % / 33 %	84 %	84 %	84 % / 40 %

criteria. But our results show that the EU–Georgia EIA has a non-discrimination level that is very similar to the other three EIAs, as seen in Table 12.1. That does not mean that the commitments are identical as in counting averages one commitment under one sector can compensate for the lack of commitment under other. However, when going through the detailed results sub-sector by sub-sector (Annex 3) one quickly sees that the numbers are quite similar across the agreements.

The differences in the level of non-discrimination provided by the EU Member States are altogether small. Under most modes and between all agreements, they are within a few decimals of percentage points as counted across the average levels of the EU Member States' NT commitments. Under Mode 3, the EIA with Central America stands out as there the average level of non-discrimination provided by the EU Member States for Mode 3 is 67 per cent, meaning that on average 67 per cent of the Member States provide for non-discrimination under Mode 3 to Central America (average across the sectors). In the other EIAs over 70 per cent of the Member States have, in average across the sectors, committed to full NT. In the EIA with CARIFORUM the score is

72 per cent, with Georgia it is 74 per cent and with Korea it is as high as 79 per cent. This may relate to the commercial interest of Mode 3 to Korea and to the higher willingness of the EU to engage in liberalization with Korea over this Mode.

In general, the results show very varying degrees of liberalization across different service sectors and different modes. The average level of non-discrimination across Modes 2, 3 and 4 is above 70 per cent in all of the reviewed EIAs, except for Mode 3 in the EIA with Central America. For Mode 1, the results show more moderate levels of non-discrimination across the Member States, staying below 50 per cent on average. For Mode 4, it is important to note that all four EIAs provide for several sectoral exclusions[1] and that the average scores of non-discrimination represent a few select service sectors only. Based on the sector-specific commitments, one can see that Mode 4 is poorly liberalized due to the many exclusions.

As Art. V GATS requires elimination of substantially all discrimination and across all modes, it would appear that the EU Member States struggle with this requirement particularly under Mode 1. In many service sectors, especially on the sub-sectoral level, less than half of the Member States provide for non-discrimination. If one looks at the level of NT across the main service sectors under Mode 1, there are only three sectors out of eleven (Business Services, Communication Services and Construction and Related Engineering Services) in which over 70 per cent of the Member States have, in average, provided for non-discrimination in all of the four EIAs. Also, in many important services sectors, such as banking and insurance services and certain transport services, the number of Member States providing for non-discrimination is relatively low and stays around 50 per cent or below under Mode 3. For Mode 4, several sectoral exclusions mean that the entire Mode is poorly liberalized across the EU. However, it should be kept in mind that the numerical results are averages and reflect the internal diversity that exists in the EU Member States' commitments. In case of unitary states without internal differences due to various sub-national levels of government the score would give the exact level of non-discrimination (one meaning non-discrimination and zero meaning denial of NT). In the case of federal states, the method applied here to the EU can be used. However, it should be remembered that the scores show the average number of sub-central levels of government providing for non-discrimination under each mode. Counting the exact percentage of sectors

---

[1] Marked in grey colour in the result sheets of Appendix 3.

that are liberalized is hard to do with federal states as the treatment varies depending on the region. To take fully into account the Art. V criterion of 'elimination of substantially all discrimination' with a substantial sectoral coverage, one needs to further see in how many service sectors has a sufficient degree of the Member States provided for non-discrimination (NT).

All in all, a large number of sub-sectors have low scores on national treatment across the four EU's EIAs, meaning that there is only a small part of the EU providing for a non-discriminatory access in those sectors. The practical relevance of that 'part of the EU' depends on the signifi-cance of those individual Member States' markets to the foreign service supplier, either for selling services there or as an access point to other EU Member States. As there is no legal clarity on the exact meaning of the Art. V requirements, nor on their application to an entity such as the EU, we cannot say what percentage exactly of the EU is required to reach compliance with Art. V. Moreover, as our results show the percentage of Member States committed under each sub-sector, the adding of eco-nomic weights may be needed to reflect the economic significance of each Member State as well as each service sector. However, it could be proposed that in order to reach the Art. V thresholds there would need to be enough Member States providing for non-discriminatory treat-ment. A particular percentage of the Member States (e.g. 80–90 per cent) could be considered to show committal by the EU 'as a whole'. Moreover, such numbers should cover a substantial part of the service sectors. Depending on how one understands 'substantial sectoral coverage', this is where the EU may fall short because, as the results show, there are many sub-sectors where only a low number of Member States has provided for NT.

One way to approach the issue would be to compare the EU's EIAs to other Members' agreements. Similar (low) levels of liberalization in other agreements could demonstrate a Members' practice in this regard, or at least a general negligent attitude towards Art. V. It is not just the EU's EIAs, but EIAs in general, that have so far provided for only modest levels of liberalization. Nevertheless, we would consider that no matter how low the overall level of liberalization is in the Members' EIAs in general, it would be questionable to let it affect the interpretation of Art. V in any significant manner. It may be possible to debate, in light of or regardless of the Members' practice, whether 'substantially all' means the provision of non-discrimination (NT) in 60 per cent or 90 per cent of all the service sectors. However, it would be far-fetched to claim that 'substantial' or 'substantially all' could correspond to a number that is lower than half (50 per cent) of the goal that is sought after (non-discrimination). That would appear to go against the ordinary meaning of the term. However, counting what exactly is 50 per cent or 90 per cent is close to an impossible task as it is not clear on what level the analysis of non-discrimination should be carried out (on the level of the main sectors or on the basis of each individual sub-sector). Also, it is not clear how the economic weight of each sector should be counted.

At the same time, it is not realistic to ask for very high levels of non-discrimination as that would in practice equal to free trade in services. Such a requirement, if enforced, would likely dissuade Members from engaging in services liberalization altogether. A more realistic understanding of the level to be reached could encourage Members to negotiate towards reaching such a level. More research should therefore be done to understand what are the current levels of non-discrimination provided across the Members' EIAs.

In case of federal states it is practically impossible to count the percentage share of service sectors that are liberalized across the country because of the internal diversity across regions. Instead, it could be proposed that a significant part of sub-central actors should provide for the elimination of substantially all discrimination. For example, if a significant part was considered to be equal to 80 per cent, in the case of the EU it would mean that at least 80 per cent of the Member States should be behind liberalizing a given service sector. In addition, the agreement should provide for the elimination of substantially all discrimination across the various modes and sectors (arguably to the extent that covers at least 50 per cent of the different service sectors, even if the meaning of 'substantially all' may be higher than that as well). Our results show the EU's average results across modes as a share of EU Member States providing for non-liberalization. In addition, the results show how many Member States have provided for non-liberalization under each service sector. Those sector-specific scores should be looked at to analyze the EU's results fully under Art. V:1. They show that at least some EU Member States have provided for NT (non-discrimination) under each main service sector, but they also show that there are big differences in the number of Member States behind liberalization across the different sectors. For example, for communication services (service sector number 2) all twenty-seven or twenty-eight Member States, depending on the agreement, have agreed to non-discrimination in Modes 1, 2 and 3 across the four agreements. Under Mode 4 there are no commitments. On the other hand, in transport services (service sector number 11) there is a varying degree of commitments across the four EIAs and big discrepancies between the Member States in each individual sub-sector. The same applies to banking services where the number of Member States committed to NT is either about a half or zero depending on the agreement.

By virtue of its exclusive competence in trade, including services trade based on Art. 207 TFEU, the EU is competent to negotiate and conclude services agreements on behalf of the Union and the Member States. However, as our study has shown, the level of commitments greatly varies across the Member States. Considering the exclusive competence of the EU in the area, we would nevertheless argue that the internal diversion across the Member States should be treated similarly to federal states such as the USA and Canada. In those states, sub-federal levels of government have powers in the area of services regulation but in accordance with the traditional theory of state responsibility it is the federal state that is ultimately responsible for any breaches of WTO law. Federal states sometimes try to overcome that responsibility and may have some support for invoking difficulties of enforcement through the requirement to take 'reasonable measures' to bring sub-central actors into compliance.[2] However, in relations between WTO Members it is the central state that ultimately carries the responsibility for compliance across its entire territory.

Marín Durán has noted how the EU has been eager to come forward as a single litigant and to assume sole responsibility in WTO disputes, even for alleged breaches by its Member States.[3] However, she argues that as long as the EU Member States remain members of the WTO in their own right, it is the allocation and exercise of internal regulatory powers between the EU and its Member States that is key in deciding who is responsible for breaches of WTO law. Thus she argues, in contrast to the traditional competence model[4], that it is not the division of *external* (i.e. treaty-making) competences between the EU and its Member States that

---

[2] As has been explained in Chapter 5 of Part II of the book, both the GATT and the GATS ask the Members to take 'reasonable measures' to ensure the observance of the agreements' disciplines by sub-central actors. Many other trade agreements include a similar requirement.

[3] Marín Durán, G. (2017) Untangling the International Responsibility of the European Union and Its Member States in the World Trade Organization Post-Lisbon: A Competence/Remedy Model. *European Journal of International Law*, 28(3), 697–729.

[4] Presented e.g. in Kuijper, P. J. and Paasivirta, E. (2013) EU International Responsibility and Its Attribution: From the Inside Looking Out, in Evans, E. & Koutrakos. P. (eds.), *The*

is of primordial importance for the purpose of assigning international responsibility in the WTO. Rather, it is the division and exercise of *internal* (i.e. treaty-infringing/treaty-performing) competences that matters. She points out that 'from the perspective of providing juridical restitution (i.e. the WTO-preferred remedy), what matters is who (i.e. the EU, its Member States or both) has the actual power to remove (or modify) the measure that is found to be WTO inconsistent', whereas the allocation of external competences under EU law is largely irrelevant to answer this question.

The general rules of international responsibility do not specifically address the question of how to determine the division of obligations between an international organization and its Member States where both are parties to an international treaty. In the EU Commission's view, it is the internal rules of the organization that matter. Therefore it has argued that as the sole bearer of WTO obligations in a post-Lisbon setting, only the EU is capable of incurring international responsibility in the WTO.[5] From the point of view of international law this is, however, problematic as long as both the Union and the Member States remain parties to the WTO Agreement. There is no textual basis for any division of responsibility between the EU and the Member States in the WTO agreement. The EU's GATS commitments may actually be the only exception in this regard as the EU's original services schedule only covers twelve Member States that were members of the European Communities in 1994, while the consolidated schedule negotiated following the EU enlargements had not yet, at the time of writing, entered into force. However, that may change soon as the Commission has recently made a new proposal to the Council on the matter. Opinion 2/15 of the Court of Justice appears to have finally cleared any doubts that may still have existed concerning the adoption of the EU's modified, common GATS schedule based on the EU's exclusive competence.[6] Up until that moment, the individual

---

International Responsibility of the European Union: European and International Perspectives. Oxford: Hart Publishing.

[5] ILC, Responsibility of International Organisations: Comments and Observations Received from International Organisations (ARIO Comments), Doc. A/CN.4/545, 25 July 2004, at 26, para. 2. For full references and discussion in light of the work of the International Law Commission (ILC) on the Articles on the Responsibility of International Organizations, see Marín Durán (2017), at 697–700.

[6] The EU Member States that have acceded to the EU after 1994 have continued to maintain their individual GATS schedules, which were adopted prior to their accession to the EU. In May 2004, the EU notified to the WTO the modification and withdrawal of certain commitments included in the EU's original GATS schedule in order to include the

schedules of all Member States that have acceded the EU since 1995 still remain in force.

Even with a certified common GATS schedule, internal differences in services regulations across the Member States have not disappeared. In line with the arguments of Marín Durán, internally EU Member States retain a regulatory autonomy for many trade-related rules that are not fully harmonized at the EU level. She gives the examples of taxation, patent law and some aspects of consumer and environmental protection (when going above the minimum levels of harmonization agreed upon on the level of the Union).[7] In the area of services trade, rules regulating certain services sectors such as financial, transport and audio-visual services, as well as overarching rules such as those regulating the entry of non-EU nationals and the rules regarding various professional activities, are some examples of regulatory areas which have not been exhaustively harmonized on the EU level. Even if the Member States should, in line with the ERTA principle, no longer enter into agreements on most of those matters with third countries the fact of divergent internal regulation remains.

From the point of view of international law, it may therefore be problematic to propose that the EU should be the sole carrier of

commitments of thirteen new Member States in the EU's common GATS schedule. This had to be done in order to ensure that those thirteen Member States did not maintain commitments which would be in breach of the *acquis communautaire* and that they were covered by the horizontal limitations included in the EU's GATS schedule. The EU then engaged in negotiations with eighteen WTO Members who claimed to be affected by these modifications and withdrawals, under Art. XXI of GATS. The notified modifications and withdrawals, together with the agreed compensatory adjustments, were incorporated into a consolidated EU GATS schedule in December 2006 (see Communication from the European Communities and Its Member States – Draft Consolidated GATS Schedule, Doc S/C/W/273, 9 October 2006). However, the Council of the EU has for a long time not been able to approve the conclusion of the agreements reached with other WTO Members as they were not ratified by the EU Member States (in the end only the French ratification was lacking, apparently because of a translation issue – the modifications had not been translated in French). The need of national ratifications, prior to Lisbon Treaty, was confirmed by the Court in Opinion 1/08. The lack of the national ratifications stopped the EU from adopting a common schedule for EU25 and also prevented it from starting the process for the incorporation of the national commitments of the three Member States that have been the last to join the Union. However, in November 2018 the Commission put forward a new proposal for a Council decision on the matter, asking the Council to approve the agreements without finishing the national ratifications (Commission Proposal for a Council Decision, COM(2018) 733 final, 8 November 2018). In light of Opinion 2/15, it now appears clear that the Council can adopt its decision based on the exclusive competence of the EU. National ratifications are therefore no longer needed.

[7] Marín Durán (2017), at 707 and 726.

responsibility for breaches of the GATS.[8] The EU Member States are WTO Members in their own right and implement a big part of trade-relevant services regulation. Other WTO Members, as well as dispute settlement panels, may understandably be willing to attribute responsibility for breaches also to the individual Member States.

When it comes to the criteria of GATS Art. V and notably the fulfilment of the criteria of eliminating 'substantially all discrimination', we would nevertheless propose that the EU should be observed as a whole. This is because of the particular nature of the provision. In a federal-type entity, which the EU arguably is in the area of trade, it can be accepted that not all sub-central actors are behind every market opening. This is evident also in the practice of the USA and Canada, as shown in Part II of the book. The removal of discrimination does not need to be perfect, but it can neither be accepted that measures by sub-central actors would be completely disregarded. Binding commitments from all EU Member States are not necessarily needed to conclude that a specific service sector has been liberalized in accordance with the criteria of Art. V. However, the higher the number of Member States without binding commitments, the higher the chance that the relevant sector cannot be considered liberalized by the EU. The same approach should be applied to all federal entities. Liberalization undertaken by the central government is of little value when it is undermined by market access barriers and discriminatory treatment undertaken by the various constituent parts of the state. This book has proposed a specific methodology that can be used to analyze to what extent federal states and entities liberalize services trade across their different levels of government. Even if various adjustments may be needed to count for the economic significance of various sub-central actors and covered service sectors, the proposed methodology is the first step in the vast task which is to understand the effects that federalism has on international liberalization of services.

---

[8] There is no WTO case law on the matter regarding the GATS. The case law on other WTO agreements is not entirely consistent. Whereas in a couple of cases the panels have attributed responsibility on the Union even when joint responsibility was invoked, the panel in *EC and Certain Member States – Large Civil Aircraft* held both the EU and its Member States jointly responsible for breaches of the SCM Agreement. See Marín Durán (2017), at 715–16.

Conclusion

There is a certain paradox in the liberalization of trade today. The most central issues on the table involve at least some regulatory reform in the domestic setting. This applies to investment, public procurement, competition rules and, of course, services. Agreeing over market-opening regulatory reforms, and related regulatory cooperation, is nevertheless extremely challenging in a multilateral organization with over 160 members. Countries are therefore entering smaller clubs with similarly thinking or otherwise willing partners. The paradox lies in the fact that regulatory reforms are nevertheless ideally implemented in a non-discriminatory manner. This is clearly the case in services. New market opening in services is likely to benefit outsiders as well. The incentives for negotiating preferential deals on services are therefore different to preferential deals in goods where tariff liberalization can be easily implemented on a discriminatory basis.

This is maybe partly behind the modest liberalization levels of EIAs so far. Countries lack incentive to commit to genuine market opening when they know that what they get from their partner is likely to benefit outsiders as well. Most EIAs go deeper than the same countries' GATS commitments, but the GATS was over twenty years ago. In practice, EIA commitments typically do not provide for much new market opening but by committing to status quo they simply guarantee that the situation does not get worse.

At the same time, the significant economic advantages of services liberalization are of course well understood. That is why the so-called 'Really Good Friends of Services', composed of a selected Members of the

WTO, including the EU and the USA, a few years ago moved to negotiate a new trade agreement in services, the TiSA. What is essential is that together, the countries account for about 70 per cent of world trade in services. Even if some important Members, such as China, were not included in the negotiations, the wide coverage alleviates concerns of significant free riding. From the outsiders' point of view, it would be important that the agreement was implemented on an MFN basis. Some more participants are possibly needed for that to happen but if the agreement finally succeeds, that is a possible scenario. As we have discussed in this book, discriminatory application of service regulation is unpractical and risks being welfare-reducing as a whole. At the moment, the talks for TiSA are, however, at halt. The difficulties in going ahead reflect the sensitivities relating to trade liberalization especially in the current political climate. Moreover, deep services liberalization can be considered especially challenging to achieve as it touches upon key societal interests and requires significant trust between regulators.

The EU is a rare example of a region that has managed to engage in deep services liberalization. Even if the EU's single market for services remains incomplete, it has liberalized services trade to a far greater extent than any other free trade area. In some sectors, trade in services between the EU Member States is freer than between the federal states of the US.[1] The EU's external trade liberalization is much weaker than the conditions that apply in the single market. As our results have shown, discriminatory measures are abundant especially under Mode 1. International services firms often need to rely on offices that are based in the country to which they wish to sell their services. This has serious implications for the UK if it goes through with Brexit. The UK services trade with the rest of the EU is in several sectors heavily reliant on cross-border supply.[2]

In our view, the core conditions of Art. V relate to the overall positive spillover effects that EIAs can have. Instead of focusing on market access (in the sense of Art. XVI GATS), Art. V:1 requires a wide sectoral coverage and deep liberalization through elimination of substantially all

---

[1] Lowe, S. (2018) Brexit and Services: How Deep Can the UK–EU Relationship Go? Policy Brief, Centre for European Reform, December 2018. Available at: www.cer.eu/publica tions/archive/policy-brief/2018/brexit-and-services-how-deep-can-uk-eu-relationship-go (last accessed on 25 February 2019).

[2] Ibid. At the time of writing it was not yet clear if the UK was going to implement Brexit and on what conditions.

discrimination. This approach facilitates non-discriminatory effects of preferential services liberalization. A focus on quotas and other quantitative restrictions could, on the other hand, lead to discriminatory results if improvements were directed towards preferential partners only. Another positive element is Art. V:6 that requires the application of very liberal rules of origin. Furthermore, the provision of 'wider process of economic integration or trade liberalization' (Art. V:2) allows some flexibility in the elimination of discrimination for the overall objective of creating a more integrated market. Such a development is likely to benefit outsiders as well. The EU is a case in point. The creation of a single market in goods has made it possible for third-country importers to sell their products on similar conditions anywhere in the EU. In the field of services, such a situation is not yet a reality but a single market in services is progressing step by step. A highly integrated services market would fuel economic growth and provide attractive trading opportunities also for service suppliers from third countries. We consider that to be the objective of Art. V GATS as well.

When analyzing the discipline for EIAs under Art. V GATS, the book has paid particular attention to the way in which federal states, and federal-type entities such as the EU, engage in services liberalization. As seen in Part II of the book, NAFTA and the FTAs concluded by the USA and Canada with Korea as well as with many other countries exempt measures applied by sub-central levels of government. With Korea, both countries have only provided an illustrative list of such measures. Based on this practice it is clear to see why the listing of sub-central measures in CETA by Canada is such a big step forward.

In CETA Canada has included in its schedule separate federal, and provincial and territorial annexes, which together form the entirety of its commitments. Canada's two annexes with federal measures take approximately fifty pages of the agreement, whereas the two annexes with provincial and territorial restrictions occupy over 200 pages. This success is related to the unprecedented participation of the Canadian sub-central entities in the CETA negotiations.

The EU follows a scheduling practice of its own. It is still far from putting forward a common EU offer but instead describes Member State-specific limitations in cases where they exist. This goes further than what can be observed in the case of the USA that has not yet engaged in extensive state-specific liberalization in its EIAs. Meaningful services liberalization in any federal entity, whether a state or a structure such as the EU, should encompass sub-central measures.

In the case of the EU, the same issue can be put forward with regard to the Member States' own sub-national measures. There are some but in general very few appearances of sub-national entities, such as the German or Austrian Länder in the EU's services schedules. This may mean that such sub-central limitations do not exist, or that the liberalization level of the agreement does not reveal all of them. In any case, truly deeper service liberalization calls for a more extensive inclusion of sub-central entities in international services negotiations through legally binding commitments.

When assessing WTO Members' compliance with the requirements of GATS Art. V, it may be difficult, or practically impossible, to map all existing non-conforming measures by sub-central entities in different countries and thus understand to what extent they do away with the amount of non-discriminatory treatment granted on the central level. That is the case especially when sub-central restrictions are not listed in a specific EIA. Sometimes the mapping may be possible. This is the situation in CETA. The inclusion of sub-central measures should thus be encouraged also in order to analyze services PTAs in light of the Art. V criteria.

Services liberalization is likely to be weak in such federal states that liberalize services trade only on the level of the central government. The same applies to some other areas of trade liberalization, especially to commitments taken with regard to public procurement. Investment liberalization can be similarly affected. The general scarcity of sub-central commitments in trade agreements is noteworthy considering that many of the purported gains of modern trade agreements relate to the liberalization of behind-the-border barriers, such as discrimination against foreign service suppliers. Therefore, true and deep liberalization of services should not neglect sub-national actors but demand their greater engagement with international services trade negotiations.

The results of the empirical analysis have shown that the four analyzed EU's EIAs provide for relatively similar levels of non-discrimination across the EU party. This is in contrast with the assumption that was made when choosing these EIAs for review. The four agreements represent very different types of EU's external agreements, with varying objectives. We would have therefore expected those different goals, whether more development-oriented or more commercially driven, to be reflected in the results. However, there are surprisingly small differences in the EU's average liberalization levels across the studied agreements. We have refrained from making any ultimate determination as to the compliance of the EU with GATS Art. V. Certain proposals to this effect can nevertheless be made. The results of the empirical analysis show that in average about 70 per cent of the EU Member States have provided for non-discrimination across Modes 2 and 3. For Mode 1, the results show more moderate levels of non-discrimination, staying below 50 per cent in average in all of the reviewed EIAs. For Mode 4, the otherwise high score is undermined by the numerous sectoral exclusions that the EU has applied. As Art. V GATS requires elimination of substantially all discrimination across all four modes, it would appear that the EU falls short of this requirement with regard to Mode 1 and possibly also with regard to Mode 4 (because of the high number of sectoral exclusions). Also, in certain important services sectors, such as banking and insurance services, in average only about 50 per cent of the Member States provide for non-discrimination also under Mode 3. However, it should be kept in mind that the results are averages and reflect the internal diversity that exists in the EU Member States' commitments. Some of the Member States are more liberal than others and can therefore individually match the requirements of Art. V to a higher or lower degree. To get a complete picture as to what extent discrimination is eliminated in the studied EIAs, one must look at the numbers on the sectoral level. The detailed results sheets in Appendix 3 can be used for this purpose.

As services are now occupying a central place in trade negotiations, individual Member States may in the future face an increasing number of bilateral requests to open up their national service markets, especially in the economically most relevant sectors. A higher level of homogeneity within the EU, whether through internal harmonization or by simple coordination of the EU Member States' positions, would provide for more clarity and predictability for third-country service suppliers. The ultimate goal for the EU should be the creation of a more coherent internal services market. Such a development would reduce barriers in intra-EU provision of services. At the same time it would enhance the EU's international negotiation position. The dismantling of barriers within the EU would make it possible to extend similar treatment also to third country partners. Such a development is desirable as the reduction of trade barriers towards service suppliers from certain countries only is likely to create economic distortions that result in general productivity losses. However, it is realistic to anticipate that due to the numerous political and cultural sensitivities relating to the cross-border liberalization of services, significant advancement in the most sensitive areas, such as mutual recognition, is most likely to take place only in relatively closed groups of like-minded countries. An openly implemented, integrated services market along the lines of Art. V GATS is, nevertheless, an objective that should rather be encouraged than prevented.

Appendix 1 *Preferential Trade Agreements Notified by the EU to the WTO (excl. inactive PTAs)*

RTA Name	Coverage	Type	Date of notification	Notification	Date of entry into force	Status
EU – Albania	Goods & Services	FTA & EIA	07-Mar-2007(G) / 07-Oct-2009(S)	GATT Art. XXIV & GATS Art. V	01-Dec-2006(G) / 01-Apr-2009(S)	In Force
EU – Algeria	Goods	FTA	24-Jul-06	GATT Art. XXIV	01-Sep-05	In Force
EU – Andorra	Goods	CU	23-Feb-98	GATT Art. XXIV	01-Jul-91	In Force
EU – Bosnia and Herzegovina	Goods & Services	FTA & EIA	11-Jul-2008(G) / 12-Jan-2016(S)	GATT Art. XXIV & GATS Art. V	01-Jul-2008(G) / 01-Jun-2015(S)	In Force
EU – Cameroon	Goods	FTA	24-Sep-09	GATT Art. XXIV	04-Aug-2014	In Force
EU – Canada	Goods & Services	FTA & EIA	19-Sep-17	GATT Art. XXIV & GATS Art. V	21-Sep-17	In Force
EU – CARIFORUM States EPA	Goods & Services	FTA & EIA	16-Oct-08	GATT Art. XXIV & GATS Art. V	29-Dec-2008	In Force
EU – Central America	Goods & Services	FTA & EIA	26-Feb-13	GATT Art. XXIV & GATS Art. V	01-Aug-2013	In Force
EU – Chile	Goods & Services	FTA & EIA	03-Feb-2004(G) / 28-Oct-2005(S)	GATT Art. XXIV & GATS Art. V	01-Feb-2003(G) / 01-Mar-2005(S)	In Force
EU – Colombia and Peru	Goods & Services	FTA & EIA	26-Feb-13	GATT Art. XXIV & GATS Art. V	01-Mar-13	In Force

Appendix 1 (*cont.*)

RTA Name	Coverage	Type	Date of notification	Notification	Date of entry into force	Status
EU – Colombia and Peru – Accession of Ecuador	Goods & Services	FTA & EIA	02-Mar-17	GATT Art. XXIV & GATS Art. V	01-Jan-2017	In Force
EU – Côte d'Ivoire	Goods	FTA	11-Dec-2008	GATT Art. XXIV	03-Sep-16	In Force
EU – Eastern African Community (EAC) EPA						Early announcement- Under negotiation
EU – Eastern and Southern Africa States Interim EPA	Goods	FTA	09-Feb-12	GATT Art. XXIV	14-May-12	In Force
EU – Egypt	Goods	FTA	03-Sep-04	GATT Art. XXIV	01-Jun-04	In Force
EU – Faroe Islands	Goods	FTA	17-Feb-97	GATT Art. XXIV	01-Jan-1997	In Force
EU – Georgia	Goods & Services	FTA & EIA	02-Jul-14	GATT Art. XXIV & GATS Art. V	01-Sep-14	In Force
EU – Ghana	Goods	FTA	03-Apr-2017	GATT Art. XXIV	15-Dec-2016	In Force
EU – Iceland	Goods	FTA	24-Nov-72	GATT Art. XXIV	01-Apr-1973	In Force

Agreement	Coverage	Type	Date signed	Legal basis	Date in force	Status
EU – India						Early announcement-Under negotiation
EU – Indonesia						Early announcement-Under negotiation
EU – Israel	Goods	FTA	20-Sep-00	GATT Art. XXIV	01-Jun-00	In Force
EU – Japan	Goods & Services	FTA & EIA	14-Jan-19	GATT Art. XXIV & GATS Art. V	01-Feb-19	In Force
EU – Jordan	Goods	FTA	17-Dec-02	GATT Art. XXIV	01-May-02	In Force
EU – Korea, Republic of	Goods & Services	FTA & EIA	07-Jul-11	GATT Art. XXIV & GATS Art. V	01-Jul-11	In Force
EU – Lebanon	Goods	FTA	26-May-03	GATT Art. XXIV	01-Mar-03	In Force
EU – Malaysia						Early announcement-Under negotiation
EU – Mexico	Goods & Services	FTA & EIA	25-Jul-00(G) / 21-Jun-02(S)	GATT Art. XXIV & GATS Art. V	01-Jul-00(G) / 01-Oct-00(S)	In Force
EU – Moldova, Republic of	Goods & Services	FTA & EIA	30-Jun-14	GATT Art. XXIV & GATS Art. V	01-Sep-14	In Force

Appendix 1 (*cont.*)

RTA Name	Coverage	Type	Date of notification	Notification	Date of entry into force	Status
EU – Montenegro	Goods & Services	FTA & EIA	16-Jan-2008(G) / 18-Jun-10(S)	GATT Art. XXIV & GATS Art. V	01-Jan-08(G) / 01-May-10(S)	In Force
EU – Morocco	Goods	FTA	13-Oct-00	GATT Art. XXIV	01-Mar-00	In Force
EU – Morocco						Early announcement-Under negotiation
EU – North Macedonia	Goods & Services	FTA & EIA	23-Oct-01(G) / 02-Oct-09(S)	GATT Art. XXIV & GATS Art. V	01-Jun-01(G) / 01-Apr-04(S)	In Force
EU – Norway	Goods	FTA	13-Jul-73	GATT Art. XXIV	01-Jul-73	In Force
EU – Overseas Countries and Territories (OCT)	Goods	FTA	14-Dec-70	GATT Art. XXIV	01-Jan-71	In Force
EU – Palestinian Authority	Goods	FTA	29-May-97	GATT Art. XXIV	01-Jul-97	In Force
EU – Papua New Guinea / Fiji	Goods	FTA	18-Oct-11	GATT Art. XXIV	20-Dec-09	In Force
EU – Philippines						Early announcement-Under negotiation

Agreement	Coverage	Type	Notification	Legal Basis	Entry into Force	Status
EU – SADC	Goods	FTA	03-Apr-17	GATT Art. XXIV	10-Oct-16	In Force
EU – San Marino	Goods	CU	24-Feb-10	GATT Art. XXIV	01-Apr-02	In Force
EU – Serbia	Goods & Services	FTA & EIA	31-May-10(G) / 20-Dec-13(S)	GATT Art. XXIV & GATS Art. V	01-Feb-10(G) / 01-Sep-13(S)	In Force
EU – Singapore						Early announcement- Under negotiation
EU – South Africa	Goods	FTA	02-Nov-00	GATT Art. XXIV	01-Jan-00	In Force
EU – Switzerland – Liechtenstein	Goods	FTA	27-Oct-72	GATT Art. XXIV	01-Jan-73	In Force
EU – Syria	Goods	FTA	15-Jul-77	GATT Art. XXIV	01-Jul-77	In Force
EU – Thailand						Early announcement- Under negotiation
EU – Tunisia	Goods	FTA	15-Jan-99	GATT Art. XXIV	01-Mar-98	In Force
EU – Tunisia						Early announcement- Under negotiation

Appendix 1 (*cont.*)

RTA Name	Coverage	Type	Date of notification	Notification	Date of entry into force	Status
EU – Turkey	Goods	CU	22-Dec-95	GATT Art. XXIV	01-Jan-96	In Force
EU – Ukraine	Goods & Services	FTA & EIA	01-Jul-14	GATT Art. XXIV & GATS Art. V	23-Apr-14	In Force
EU – US TTIP						Early announcement- Under negotiation
EU – Viet Nam						Early announcement- Under negotiation
EU – West Africa EPA						Early announcement- Under negotiation
European Economic Area (EEA)	Services	EIA	13-Sep-96	GATS Art. V	01-Jan-94	In Force

Source: WTO (RTA Information System, available at http://rtais.wto.org), 28 February 2019.

The Agreements Reviewed in the Empirical Study

EU–CARIFORUM Economic Partnership Agreement 2008

Economic Partnership Agreement between the CARIFORUM States, of the one part, and the European Community and its Member States, of the other part
Official Journal of the European Union L 289, 30.10.2008
The CARIFORUM parties: Antigua and Barbuda, The Bahamas, Barbados, Belize, Dominica, Grenada, Guyana, Haiti, Jamaica, Saint Lucia, Saint Vincent and the Grenadines, Saint Kitts and Nevis, Surinam, Trinidad, Tobago, and the Dominican Republic.

EU–South Korea Free Trade Agreement 2011

Free Trade Agreement between the European Union and its Member States, of the one part, and the Republic of Korea
Official Journal of the European Union L 127, 14.05.2011

EU–Central America Association Agreement 2013

Agreement Establishing an Association between Central America, on the one hand, and the European Community and its Member States, on the other
Official Journal of the European Union L 346, 15.12.2012
The Central America parties: Costa Rica, El Salvador, Guatemala, Honduras, Nicaragua and Panama.

EU–Georgia Association Agreement 2014

Association Agreement between the European Union and the European Atomic Energy Community and their Member States, of the one part, and Georgia, of the other part
Official Journal of the European Union L 216, 30.08.2014

APPENDIX 3 The Result Sheets of the Empirical Analysis

EU–CARIFORUM EPA

NAME OF AGREEMENT: Economic Partnership Agreement

PARTIES: CARIFORUM states, of the one part, and the European Community and its Member States, of the other part

Type

Bilateral	Regional		Number of EU Member State parties:	27
	x			

Development level of the non-EU party

Developed	Developing
	x

STATUS OF THE AGREEMENT

	Signature	In Force	Notification
	15/10/2008	Provisional	16/10/2008

Haiti signed on 11/12/2009, pending ratification. For the EU side, provisional application as from 29/12/2008

ELEMENTS RELATED TO NON-DISCRIMINATION	Yes	No	Explanation
MFN	x		Under Modes 1–3, subject to exceptions
Standstill (prohibition of new or more discriminatory measures)		x	Applies only to the CARIFORUM states with respect to Modes 1, 2 and 3
WIDER PROCESS OF ECONOMIC INTEGRATION	Yes	No	Explanation
Progressive liberalization		x	
Art. XXIV GATT agreement	x		
Art. V bis GATS agreement		x	
Mode 3 relating also to goods	x		Establishment covers certain goods-related economic activities
Harmonization		x	
Mutual recognition	x		Services: non-binding, encourages relevant professional bodies to develop recommendations (Art. 85)
Domestic regulation discipline(s)	x		Financial services (Art. 105), concerning certain procedures (Art. 87), regulatory bodies & authorities (Arts. 93 & 95)
Regulatory cooperation		x	Regulatory dialogues only
Transparency	x		Generally (Art. 235) and specifically regarding services (Art. 86)
Intellectual property	x		
Public procurement	x		

	Yes	No	Explanation
Competition policy	x		
Investment protection		x	
Labour mobility (labour market access)		x	Commitment to basic ILO conventions; upholding levels of protection in domestic legislation (Art. 193)
Labour protection	x		
Consumer protection		x	Upholding levels of protection in domestic legislation (Art. 188)
Environment	x		
Cultural cooperation	x		
Sustainable development	x		Specifically in Art. 3

OTHER ELEMENTS (related to services only)	Yes	No	Explanation
Time-frame for implementation	x		Some EU states apply transitional periods for Mode 4 commitments for CSSs and IPs (expired in 2011 and 2014)
Ratchet clause (autonomous liberalization included)		x	
Safeguards		x	
Subsidies		x	
Exceptions			GATS Art: XII XVI XIVbis / x x x
Compatibility clause (relationship to Art. V GATS)		x	

Categories of Mode 4 covered	Yes	No	Includes business visitors (responsible for setting up a commercial presence) and intra-corporate transfers
Cat. 1 Key personnel	x		
Cat. 1 Graduate trainees	x		
Cat. 2 Contractual service suppliers	x		
Cat. 2 Independent professionals	x		
Short term visitors for business purposes	x		Endeavour to facilitate short-term business visits for specific purposes (Art. 84)
Business services sellers	x		Temporary entry and stay for a period of up to 90 days in any 12-month period (Art. 82)

SECTORS	CPC	MODE 1		MODE 2		MODE 3		MODE 4: Cat. 1		Mode 4: Cat. 2	
		SC	NT	SC	NT	SC	NT	SC	NT	SC	NT
AVERAGE FOR MODE		**0.40**	**0.43**	**0.70**	**0.76**	**0.78**	**0.72**	**0.51**	**0.82**	**0.22**	**0.33**
1. BUSINESS SERVICES		0.72	0.71	0.94	0.93	0.95	0.92	0.44	0.54	0.51	0.31
A. Professional Services		0.51	0.44	1.00	0.95	0.97	0.85	1.00	0.66	0.73	0.31
a. Legal Services	861	1.00	0.48	1.00	0.48	1.00	0.81	1.00	0.44	0.00	
b. Accounting, auditing and bookkeeping services	862	0.33	0.22	1.00	1.00	1.00	0.70	1.00	0.74	0.00	
c. Taxation Services	863	0.85	0.78	1.00	1.00	1.00	0.93	1.00	0.85	1.00	0.44
d. Architectural services	8671	0.56	0.56	1.00	1.00	1.00	0.93	1.00	0.81	1.00	0.48
e. Engineering services	8672	0.70	0.70	1.00	1.00	1.00	0.96	1.00	0.81	1.00	0.52
f. Integrated engineering services	8673	0.70	0.70	1.00	1.00	1.00	0.96	1.00	0.81	1.00	0.52
g. Urban planning and landscape architectural services	8674	0.56	0.56	1.00	1.00	1.00	0.93	1.00	0.81	1.00	0.48
h. Medical and dental services	9312	0.22	0.22	1.00	1.00	0.89	0.70	1.00	0.41	0.67	0.04
i. Veterinary services	932	0.15	0.15	1.00	1.00	0.96	0.89	1.00	0.52	0.78	0.00
j. Services provided by midwives, nurses, physiotherapists and para-medical personnel	93191	0.04	0.04	1.00	1.00	0.85	0.70	1.00	0.41	0.81	0.00
k. Other											

	Code										
B.	Computer and Related Services	1.00	1.00	1.00	1.00	1.00	1.00		0.00	1.00	0.44
C.	Research and Development Services	1.00	1.00	1.00	1.00	1.00	1.00		0.00	1.00	0.00
D.	Real Estate Services	0.52	0.52	1.00	1.00	1.00	1.00	1.00	0.72	0.00	0.00
a.	Involving own or leased property	821	0.52	0.52	1.00	1.00			1.00	0.74	0.00
b.	On a fee or contract basis	822	0.52	0.52	1.00	1.00			1.00	0.70	0.00
E.	Rental/Leasing Services without Operators	0.59	0.58	0.75	0.75	0.83	0.82	0.20	0.00	0.00	0.00
a.	Relating to ships	83103	0.78	0.78	1.00	1.00	1.00	0.93	0.00		0.00
b.	Relating to aircraft	83104	0.67	0.67	0.67	0.67	1.00	1.00	0.00		0.00
c.	Relating to other transport equipment	83101+ 83102+	0.70	0.70	1.00	1.00	1.00	1.00	0.00		0.00
d.	Relating to other machinery and equipment	83106–83109	0.70	0.70	1.00	1.00	1.00	1.00	0.00		0.00
e.	Other	832	0.07	0.07	0.07	0.07	0.15	0.15	1.00	0.00	0.00
F.	Other Business Services	0.72	0.72	0.88	0.88	0.87	0.86	0.42	0.79	0.36	0.49
a.	Advertising services	871	1.00	1.00	1.00	1.00	1.00	1.00	0.00		1.00	0.52
b.	Market research and public opinion polling services	864	1.00	1.00	1.00	1.00	1.00	1.00	0.00		0.89	0.33
c.	Management consulting service	865	1.00	1.00	1.00	1.00	1.00	1.00	0.00		1.00	0.52

	Service	Code	1	2	3	4	5	6	7	8	9	10
d.	Services related to man. consulting	866	0.96	0.96	0.96	0.96	0.96	0.96	0.00	0.00	1.00	0.52
e.	Technical testing and analysis serv.	8676	0.67	0.67	0.67	0.67	1.00	1.00	1.00	0.93	1.00	0.52
f.	Services incidental to agriculture, hunting and forestry	881	0.81	0.81	1.00	1.00	1.00	1.00	1.00	0.96	0.00	
g.	Services incidental to fishing	882	0.85	0.85	1.00	1.00	1.00	1.00	0.00		0.00	
h.	Services incidental to mining	883+5115	1.00	1.00	1.00	1.00	1.00	1.00	0.00		0.00	
i.	Services incidental to manufacturing	884+885 (except for 88442)	1.00	1.00	1.00	1.00	1.00	1.00	0.00		0.00	
j.	Services incidental to energy distribution	887	0.00	0.00	1.00	1.00	0.04	0.04	0.00		0.00	
k.	Placement and supply services of personnel	872	0.04	0.04	0.11	0.11	0.44	0.37	0.00		0.00	
l.	Investigation and security	873	0.07	0.07	0.07	0.07	0.19	0.19	0.00		0.00	
m.	Related scientific and technical consulting services	8675	0.33	0.33	1.00	1.00	0.96	0.96	1.00	0.81	0.93	0.44
n.	Maintenance and repair of equipment (not including maritime vessels, aircraft or other transport equipment)	633+ 8861-8866	1.00	1.00	1.00	1.00	1.00	1.00	1.00	0.00	1.00	0.56
o.	Building-cleaning services	874	0.07	0.07	1.00	1.00	1.00	1.00	1.00	0.78	0.00	
p.	Photographic services	875	0.81	0.81	1.00	1.00	1.00	1.00	1.00	0.93	0.00	
q.	Packaging services	876	1.00	1.00	1.00	1.00	1.00	1.00	1.00		0.00	
r.	Printing, publishing	88442	1.00	1.00	1.00	1.00	1.00	0.89	0.00	0.96	0.00	
s.	Convention services	87909	1.00	1.00	1.00	1.00	1.00	1.00	1.00	0.96	0.00	
t.	Other	8790	1.00	1.00	1.00	1.00	1.00	1.00	1.00			

No.	Sector	CPC										
2.	**COMMUNICATION SERVICES**		0.75	1.00	0.75	1.00	0.75	1.00	1.00	0.00		0.00
A.	Postal services	7511	1.00	1.00	1.00	1.00	1.00	1.00	1.00	0.00	0.00	0.00
B.	Courier services	7512	1.00	1.00	1.00	1.00	1.00	1.00	1.00	0.00	0.00	0.00
C.	Telecommunication services		1.00	1.00	1.00	1.00	1.00	1.00	1.00	0.00	0.00	0.00
D.	Audiovisual services		0.00	0.00	0.00	0.00	0.00	0.00	0.00	0.00	0.93	**0.00**
3.	**CONSTRUCTION AND RELATED ENGINEERING SERVICES**		1.00	1.00	1.00	1.00	1.00	1.00	0.96	1.00	0.96	0.00
4.	**DISTRIBUTION SERVICES**		0.00	0.00	0.00	0.94	0.00	0.88	0.25	0.00	0.96	**0.00**
A.	Commission agents' services	621	0.00	0.00	0.00	1.00	0.00	1.00	0.00	0.00	0.00	0.00
B.	Wholesale trade services	622	0.00	0.00	0.00	0.93	0.00	0.93	0.00	0.00	0.00	0.00
C.	Retailing services	631+632 / 6111+6113+6121	0.00	0.00	0.00	0.85	1.00	0.59	1.00	0.00	0.96	0.00
D.	Franchising	8929	0.00	0.00	0.00	1.00	0.00	1.00	0.00	0.00	0.00	0.00
E.	Other											
5.	**EDUCATIONAL SERVICES**		0.56	0.56	0.61	0.61	0.55	0.01	0.60		0.86	**0.00**
A.	Primary education services	921	0.67	0.67	0.78	0.78	0.67	0.00	1.00		0.89	0.00

	(1)	(2)	(3)	(4)	(5)	(6)	(7)	(8)	(9)	(10)
B. Secondary education services — 922	0.67	0.67	0.78	0.78	0.67	0.00	1.00	0.85	0.00	
C. Higher education services — 923	0.59	0.59	0.67	0.67	0.67	0.00	1.00	0.85	0.00	
D. Adult education — 924	0.78	0.78	0.78	0.78	0.67	0.00	0.00		0.00	
E. Other education services — 929	0.07	0.07	0.07	0.07	0.07	0.07	0.00		0.00	
6. ENVIRONMENTAL SERVICES	0.00	0.00	1.00	1.00	1.00	1.00	0.00	0.81	1.00	0.52
7. FINANCIAL SERVICES	0.02	0.02	0.50	0.50	0.98	0.57	1.00	0.81	0.00	
A. All insurance and insurance-related services — 812	0.04	0.04	0.07	0.07	1.00	0.63	1.00	0.81	0.00	
B. Banking and other financial services (excl. insurance)	0.00	0.00	0.93	0.93	0.96	0.52	1.00		0.00	
8. HEALTH RELATED AND SOCIAL SERVICES (other than those listed under 1.A.h-j.)	0.04	0.06	0.65	0.98	0.32	0.48	0.67	0.89	0.00	
A. Hospital services — 9311	0.04	0.04	1.00	1.00	0.48	0.48	1.00	0.89	0.00	
B. Other Human Health Services — 9319 (other than 93191)	0.00		0.00		0.00		0.00			
C. Social Services — 933	0.07	0.07	0.96	0.96	0.48	0.48	1.00	0.89	0.00	
D. Other										
9. TOURISM AND TRAVEL RELATED SERVICES	0.56	0.56	1.00	1.00	0.99	0.95	1.00	0.83	0.59	0.28

	Code	1	2	3	4	5	6	7	8	9	10
A. Hotels and restaurants (incl. catering)	641-643	0.11	0.11	1.00	1.00	1.00	0.93	1.00	0.96	0.00	
B. Travel agencies and tour operators services	7471	0.93	0.93	1.00	1.00	0.96	0.93	1.00	0.96	0.96	0.52
C. Tourist guides services	7472	0.63	0.63	1.00	1.00	1.00	1.00	1.00	0.56	0.81	0.04
D. Other											
10. RECREATIONAL, CULTURAL AND SPORTING SERVICES		0.44	0.44	0.58	0.58	0.56	0.54	0.25	0.96	0.24	0.00
(other than audiovisual services)											
A. Entertainment services (incl. theatre, live bands and circus services)	9619	0.07	0.07	0.56	0.56	0.59	0.59	1.00	0.96	0.96	0.00
B. News agency services	962	1.00	1.00	1.00	1.00	1.00	0.96	0.00	0.00		
C. Libraries, archives, museums and other cultural services	963	0.04	0.04	0.07	0.07	0.07	0.00	0.00	0.00		
D. Sporting and other recreational services	964	0.63	0.63	0.70	0.70	0.59	0.59	0.00	0.00		
E. Other											
11. TRANSPORT SERVICES		0.34	0.40	0.71	0.79	0.50	0.62	0.35	0.64	0.10	0.53
A. Maritime Transport Services		0.66	0.45	1.00	0.79	0.20	0.20	1.00	0.62	0.20	0.52
a. Passenger transportation	7211	1.00	0.37	1.00	0.37	0.04	0.04	1.00	0.93	0.00	
b. Freight transportation	7212	1.00	0.37	1.00	0.37	0.04	0.04	1.00	0.93	0.00	

	Code											
c. Rental of vessels with crew	7213	0.00	0.00	1.00	1.00	0.04	0.04	1.00	1.00	0.89	0.00	
d. Maintenance and repair of vessels	8868	0.26	0.26	1.00	1.00	1.00	1.00	1.00	0.96	1.00	0.52	
e. Pushing and towing services	7214	0.70	0.70	1.00	1.00	0.04	0.04	1.00	0.00	0.00		
f. Supporting services for maritime transport	745	1.00	1.00	1.00	1.00	0.04	0.04	1.00	0.00	0.00		
B. Internal Waterways Transport		**0.43**	**0.41**	**0.69**	**0.67**	**0.20**	**0.20**	**0.33**	**0.00**	**0.00**	**0.00**	
a. Passenger transportation	7221	0.56	0.52	0.56	0.52	0.04	0.04	0.00	0.00		0.00	
b. Freight transportation	7222	0.56	0.52	0.56	0.52	0.04	0.04	0.00	0.00		0.00	
c. Rental of vessels with crew	7223	0.44	0.44	1.00	1.00	0.04	0.04	0.00	0.00	0.00	0.00	
d. Maintenance and repair of vessels	8868	0.00	0.00	1.00	1.00	1.00	1.00	0.00	0.00	0.00	0.00	
e. Pushing and towing services	7224	0.00	0.00	0.00	0.00	0.04	0.04	1.00	1.00	0.00	0.00	
f. Supporting services for internal waterway transport	745	1.00	1.00	1.00	1.00	0.04	0.04	1.00	1.00	0.00	0.00	
C. Air Transport Services		**0.24**	**0.60**	**0.40**	**1.00**	**0.39**	**0.98**	**0.00**	**0.00**	**0.20**	**0.56**	
a. Passenger transportation	731	0.00	0.00	0.00	0.00	0.00	0.00	0.00	0.00	0.00	0.00	
b. Freight transportation	732	0.00	0.00	0.00	0.00	0.00	0.00	0.00	0.00	0.00	0.00	

Item		Code	1	2	3	4	5	6	7	8	9	10	11
c.	Rental of aircraft with crew	734	1.00	1.00	1.00	0.96	0.96	0.00	0.00				
d.	Maintenance and repair of aircraft	8868	0.19	0.19	1.00	1.00	1.00	0.00	1.00				0.56
e.	Supporting services for air transport	746	0.00	0.00	0.00	0.00	0.00	0.00	0.00				
D.	**Space Transport**	733	**0.00**	**0.00**	**0.00**	**0.00**	**0.00**	**0.00**	**0.00**				
E.	**Rail Transport Services**		**0.21**	**0.21**	**0.80**	**0.80**	**0.96**	**0.96**	**0.94**	**0.20**	**0.20**		**0.56**
a.	Passenger transportation	7111	0.00	0.00	1.00	1.00	0.96	0.96	0.96	0.00	0.00		
b.	Freight transportation	7112	0.00	0.00	1.00	1.00	0.96	0.96	0.96	0.00	0.00		
c.	Pushing and towing services	7113	0.00	0.00	0.00	0.00	0.96	0.96	0.93	0.00	0.00		
d.	Maintenance and repair of rail transport equipment	8868	0.07	0.07	1.00	1.00	0.96	0.96	0.93	1.00	1.00		0.56
e.	Supporting services for rail transport services	743	1.00	1.00	1.00	1.00	0.96	0.96	0.93	0.00	0.00		
F.	**Road Transport Services**		**0.50**	**0.50**	**1.00**	**1.00**	**0.78**	**0.78**	**0.68**	**0.80**	**0.80**	**0.66**	**0.48**
a.	Passenger transportation	7121+7122	0.00	0.00	1.00	1.00	0.00	0.00	0.00	1.00	1.00	0.85	0.00
b.	Freight transportation	7123	0.00	0.00	1.00	1.00	0.96	0.96	0.74	1.00	1.00	0.89	0.00
c.	Rental of commercial vehicles with operator	7124	0.48	0.48	1.00	1.00	0.96	0.96	0.85	1.00	1.00	0.89	0.00

	Code									
d. Maintenance and repair of road transport equipment	6112+8867	1.00	1.00	1.00	1.00	1.00	0.96	1.00	0.00	0.48
e. Supporting services for road transport services	744	1.00	1.00	1.00	1.00	0.96	0.85	0.00	0.00	0.00
G. Pipeline Transport		**0.00**	**0.00**	**0.07**	**0.07**	**0.54**	**0.52**	**0.50**	**0.00**	**0.00**
a. Transportation of fuels	7131	0.00	0.00	0.07	0.07	0.07	0.07	0.00	0.00	0.00
b. Transportation of other goods	7139	0.00	0.00	0.07	0.07	1.00	0.96	1.00	0.96	0.00
H. Services auxiliary to all modes of transport		**0.65**	**0.65**	**1.00**	**1.00**	**0.96**	**0.85**	**0.00**	**0.00**	**0.00**
a. Cargo-handling services	741	0.07	0.07	1.00	1.00	0.96	0.85	0.00	0.00	0.00
b. Storage and warehouse services	742	0.89	0.89	1.00	1.00	0.96	0.85	0.00	0.00	0.00
c. Freight transport agency services	748	1.00	1.00	1.00	1.00	0.96	0.85	0.00	0.00	0.00
d. Other	749									

EU–Central America AA

NAME OF AGREEMENT	**Association Agreement**		
PARTIES	Central America, on the on hand, and the European Union and its Member States, on the other		
Type	Bilateral	Regional x	Number of EU Member State parties: 27
Development level of the non-EU party	Developed	Developing x	
	Signature	In Force	Notification
STATUS OF THE AGREEMENT	29/6/2012	Provisional x	Provisional application since Aug-Dec-13 depending on the partner

ELEMENTS RELATED TO NON-DISCRIMINATION	Yes	No	Explanation
MFN		x	A MFN clause only in relation to intellectual property
Standstill (prohibition of new or more discriminatory measures)		x	

WIDER PROCESS OF ECONOMIC INTEGRATION	Yes	No	Explanation
Progressive liberalization		x	
Art. XXIV GATT agreement	x		
Art. V bis GATS agreement		x	
Mode 3 relating also to goods	x		Certain non-service sectors covered under Mode 3 (Establishment)
Harmonization		x	
Mutual recognition	x		Services: non-binding, encourages relevant professional bodies to develop recommendations
Domestic regulation discipline(s)	x		Financial services (Art. 196), certain procedures Art. 179 & regulatory authorities (Arts. 184, 186)
Regulatory cooperation		x	
Transparency	x		
Intellectual property	x		
Public procurement	x		

	Yes	No	Explanation
Competition policy	x		
Investment protection		x	
Labour mobility (labour market access)		x	
Labour protection	x		Commitment to basic ILO treaties; upholding levels of protection in domestic legislation (Art. 291)
Consumer protection		x	
Environment	x		Reaffirming commitment to multilateral environmental agreements; upholding levels of protection
Cultural cooperation	x		
Sustainable development	x		Specifically in Art. 284

OTHER ELEMENTS (related to services only)	Yes	No	Explanation
Time-frame for implementation		x	No phase-out periods on the EU side in services
Ratchet clause (autonomous liberalization included)		x	
Safeguards		x	
Subsidies		x	Only the possibility to exchange information upon request (Art. 344)
Exceptions			GATS Art: XII XVI XIVbis
			x x
Compatibility clause (relationship to Art. V GATS)	x		

Categories of Mode 4 covered	Yes	No	
Key personnel	x		Incl. business visitors responsible for setting up an establishment and intra-corporate transferees
Graduate trainees	x		
Business service sellers	x		No sector specific commitments, Art. 175: entry/stay for a period up to 90 days in any 12-month period
Contractual service suppliers	x		Both parties reaffirm obligations resulting from their GATS commitments.
Independent professionals		x	The same as for contractual service suppliers
Short term visitors for business purposes		x	

SECTORS		CPC	MODE 1		MODE 2		MODE 3		MODE 4	
			SC	NT	SC	NT	SC	NT	SC	NT
	AVERAGE FOR MODE		**0.41**	**0.44**	**0.77**	**0.83**	**0.77**	**0.67**	**0.51**	**0.84**
1.	BUSINESS SERVICES		**0.72**	**0.71**	**0.98**	**0.97**	**0.95**	**0.89**	**0.44**	**0.54**
A.	Professional Services		**0.51**	**0.44**	**1.00**	**0.94**	**0.97**	**0.85**	**1.00**	**0.67**
a.	Legal Services	861	1.00	0.44	1.00	0.44	1.00	0.81	1.00	0.37
b.	Accounting, auditing and bookkeeping services	862	0.33	0.22	1.00	1.00	1.00	0.74	1.00	0.78
c.	Taxation Services	863	0.85	0.78	1.00	1.00	1.00	0.93	1.00	0.85
d.	Architectural services	8671	0.56	0.56	1.00	1.00	1.00	0.93	1.00	0.81
e.	Engineering services	8672	0.70	0.70	1.00	1.00	1.00	0.96	1.00	0.81
f.	Integrated engineering services	8673	0.70	0.70	1.00	1.00	1.00	0.96	1.00	0.81
g.	Urban planning and landscape architectural services	8674	0.56	0.56	1.00	1.00	1.00	0.93	1.00	0.81
h.	Medical and dental services	9312	0.22	0.22	1.00	1.00	0.89	0.70	1.00	0.41
i.	Veterinary services	932	0.15	0.15	1.00	1.00	0.96	0.85	1.00	0.52

	Sector	Code								
j.	Services provided by midwives, nurses, physiotherapists and para-medical personnel	93191	0.04	0.04	1.00	1.00	0.81	0.70	1.00	0.48
k.	Other									
B.	Computer and Related Services		1.00	1.00	1.00	1.00	1.00	1.00	0.00	
C.	Research and Development Services		1.00	1.00	1.00	1.00	1.00	1.00	0.00	
D.	Real Estate Services		0.52	0.52	1.00	1.00	1.00	1.00	1.00	0.72
a.	Involving own or leased property	821	0.52	0.52	1.00	1.00	1.00	1.00	1.00	0.74
b.	On a fee or contract basis	822	0.52	0.52	1.00	1.00	1.00	1.00	1.00	0.70
E.	Rental/Leasing Services without Operators		0.59	0.59	1.00	1.00	0.83	0.62	0.20	0.00
a.	Relating to ships	83103	0.78	0.78	1.00	1.00	1.00	0.93	0.00	0.00
b.	Relating to aircraft	83104	0.67	0.67	1.00	1.00	1.00	0.00	0.00	0.00
c.	Relating to other transport equipment	83101+ 83102+	0.70	0.70	1.00	1.00	1.00	1.00	0.00	0.00
d.	Relating to other machinery and equipment	83106–83109	0.70	0.70	1.00	1.00	1.00	1.00	0.00	0.00

	Description	Code								
e.	Other	832	0.07	0.07	1.00	1.00	0.15	0.15	1.00	0.00
F.	**Other Business Services**		**0.72**	**0.72**	**0.89**	**0.89**	**0.88**	**0.87**	**0.42**	**0.79**
a.	Advertising services	871	1.00	1.00	1.00	1.00	1.00	1.00	0.00	
b.	Market research and public opinion polling services	864	1.00	1.00	1.00	1.00	1.00	1.00	0.00	
c.	Management consulting service	865	1.00	1.00	1.00	1.00	1.00	1.00	0.00	
d.	Services related to man. consulting	866	0.96	0.96	0.96	0.96	0.96	0.96	0.00	
e.	Technical testing and analysis serv.	8676	0.67	0.67	0.70	0.70	1.00	1.00	1.00	0.93
f.	Services incidental to agriculture, hunting and forestry	881	0.81	0.81	1.00	1.00	1.00	1.00	0.00	
g.	Services incidental to fishing	882	0.85	0.85	1.00	1.00	1.00	1.00	0.00	
h.	Services incidental to mining	883+5115	1.00	1.00	1.00	1.00	1.00	1.00	1.00	0.96
i.	Services incidental to manufacturing	884+885 (except for 88442)	1.00	1.00	1.00	1.00	1.00	1.00	0.00	
j.	Services incidental to energy distribution	887	0.00	0.00	1.00	1.00	0.07	0.07	0.00	
k.	Placement and supply services of personnel	872	0.04	0.04	0.11	0.11	0.41	0.37	0.00	
l.	Investigation and security	873	0.07	0.07	0.07	0.07	0.19	0.19	0.00	

	Description	Code							
m.	Related scientific and technical consulting services	8675	0.33	0.33	1.00	1.00	0.96	1.00	0.81
n.	Maintenance and repair of equipment (not including maritime vessels, aircraft or other transport equipment)	633+ 8861–8866	1.00	1.00	1.00	1.00	1.00	1.00	0.00
o.	Building-cleaning services	874	0.07	0.07	1.00	1.00	1.00	1.00	0.78
p.	Photographic services	875	0.81	0.81	1.00	1.00	1.00	1.00	0.93
q.	Packaging services	876	1.00	1.00	1.00	1.00	1.00	0.00	
r.	Printing, publishing	88442	1.00	1.00	1.00	1.00	0.89	1.00	0.96
s.	Convention services	87909	1.00	1.00	1.00	1.00	1.00	1.00	0.96
t.	Other	8790							
2.	COMMUNICATION SERVICES		0.75	0.75	1.00	0.75	1.00	0.00	
A.	Postal services	7511	1.00	1.00	1.00	1.00	1.00	0.00	
B.	Courier services	7512	1.00	1.00	1.00	1.00	1.00	0.00	
C.	Telecommunication services		1.00	1.00	1.00	1.00	1.00	0.00	
D.	Audiovisual services		0.00	0.00		0.00		0.00	

	Code								
3. CONSTRUCTION AND RELATED ENGINEERING SERVICES		**1.00**	**1.00**	**1.00**	**1.00**	**1.00**	**1.00**	**1.00**	**0.96**
4. DISTRIBUTION SERVICES		**0.17**	**0.17**	**0.75**	**0.75**	**0.92**	**0.86**	**0.25**	**0.96**
A. Commission agents' services	621	0.00	0.00	0.00	0.00	0.93	0.93	0.00	
B. Wholesale trade services	622	0.22	0.22	1.00	1.00	0.89	0.89	0.00	
C. Retailing services	631+632 6111+6113+6121	0.22	0.22	1.00	1.00	0.85	0.63	1.00	0.96
D. Franchising	8929	0.22	0.22	1.00	1.00	1.00	1.00	0.00	
E. Other									
5. EDUCATIONAL SERVICES		**0.56**	**0.56**	**0.61**	**0.61**	**0.46**	**0.33**	**0.60**	**0.85**
A. Primary education services	921	0.67	0.67	0.78	0.78	0.56	0.41	1.00	0.89
B. Secondary education services	922	0.67	0.67	0.78	0.78	0.56	0.41	1.00	0.85
C. Higher education services	923	0.59	0.59	0.67	0.67	0.56	0.41	1.00	0.81
D. Adult education	924	0.78	0.78	0.78	0.78	0.56	0.41	0.00	
E. Other education services	929	0.07	0.07	0.07	0.07	0.07	0.00	0.00	
6. ENVIRONMENTAL SERVICES		**0.00**	**0.00**	**1.00**	**1.00**	**1.00**	**1.00**	**0.00**	

No.	Sector	CPC								
7.	FINANCIAL SERVICES		0.00	0.00	0.54	0.54	0.98	0.28	1.00	0.81
A.	All insurance and insurance-related services	812	0.00	0.00	0.11	0.11	1.00	0.56	1.00	0.81
B.	Banking and other financial services (excl. insurance)		0.00	0.00	0.96	0.96	0.96	0.00	1.00	0.81
8.	HEALTH RELATED AND SOCIAL SERVICES (other than those listed under 1.A.h–j.)		0.04	0.06	0.65	0.98	0.32	0.00	0.67	0.89
A.	Hospital services	9311	0.04	0.04	1.00	1.00	0.48	0.00	1.00	0.89
B.	Other Human Health Services	9319 (other than 93191)	0.00	0.00	0.00	0.00	0.00	0.00	0.00	
C.	Social Services	933	0.07	0.07	0.96	0.96	0.48	0.00	1.00	0.89
D.	Other									
9.	TOURISM AND TRAVEL RELATED SERVICES		0.56	0.56	1.00	1.00	0.99	0.95	1.00	0.83
A.	Hotels and restaurants (incl. catering)	641–643	0.11	0.11	1.00	1.00	1.00	0.93	1.00	0.96

	Code								
B. Travel agencies and tour operators services	7471	0.96	1.00	0.93	0.96	1.00	1.00	0.93	0.93
C. Tourist guides services	7472	0.56	1.00	1.00	1.00	1.00	1.00	0.63	0.63
D. Other									
10. RECREATIONAL, CULTURAL AND SPORTING SERVICES		0.96	0.25	0.55	0.55	0.59	0.59	0.44	0.44
(other than audiovisual services)									
A. Entertainment services (incl. theatre, live bands and circus services)	9619	0.96	1.00	0.59	0.59	0.59	0.59	0.07	0.07
B. News agency services	962		0.00	0.96	0.96	1.00	1.00	1.00	1.00
C. Libraries, archives, museums and other cultural services	963		0.00	0.07	0.07	0.07	0.07	0.04	0.04
D. Sporting and other recreational services	964		0.00	0.59	0.59	0.70	0.70	0.63	0.63
E. Other									
11. TRANSPORT SERVICES		0.80	0.42	0.56	0.54	0.74	0.57	0.38	0.28
A. Maritime Transport Services		0.30	1.00	0.34	0.34	0.79	0.79	0.41	0.41
a. Passenger transportation	7211	0.00	1.00	0.00	0.00	0.37	0.37	0.37	0.37
b. Freight transportation	7212	0.00	1.00	0.00	0.00	0.37	0.37	0.37	0.37

	Description	Code								
c.	Rental of vessels with crew	7213	0.48	0.48	1.00	1.00	0.96	0.96	1.00	0.85
d.	Maintenance and repair of vessels	8868	0.00	0.00	1.00	1.00	1.00	1.00	1.00	0.96
e.	Pushing and towing services	7214	0.26	0.26	1.00	1.00	0.04	0.04	1.00	0.00
f.	Supporting services for maritime transport	745	1.00	1.00	1.00	1.00	0.04	0.04	1.00	0.00
B.	Internal Waterways Transport		0.58	0.58	0.67	0.67	0.34	0.34	0.50	0.96
a.	Passenger transportation	7221	0.52	0.52	0.52	0.52	0.04	0.04	0.00	
b.	Freight transportation	7222	0.52	0.52	0.52	0.52	0.04	0.04	0.00	
c.	Rental of vessels with crew	7223	0.44	0.44	1.00	1.00	0.89	0.89	0.00	
d.	Maintenance and repair of vessels	8868	1.00	1.00	1.00	1.00	1.00	1.00	1.00	0.96
e.	Pushing and towing services	7224	0.00	0.00	0.00	0.00	0.04	0.04	1.00	0.00
f.	Supporting services for internal waterway transport	745	1.00	1.00	1.00	1.00	0.04	0.04	1.00	0.00
C.	Air Transport Services		0.20	0.56	0.40	1.00	0.40	0.50	0.00	
a.	Passenger transportation	731	0.00	0.00	0.00	0.00	0.00	0.00	0.00	
b.	Freight transportation	732	0.00	0.00	0.00	0.00	0.00	0.00	0.00	

	Code	Service								
c.	734	Rental of aircraft with crew	0.96	0.00	0.00	1.00	1.00	1.00	1.00	1.00
d.	8868	Maintenance and repair of aircraft	0.00	1.00	1.00	1.00	1.00	0.12	0.19	0.00
e.	746	Supporting services for air transport	0.00	0.00	0.00	0.00	0.00	0.00	0.00	0.00
D.	733	**Space Transport**	**0.00**	0.00	0.00	1.00	1.00	0.00	0.00	**0.00**
E.		**Rail Transport Services**	**0.96**	0.95	0.95	1.00	1.00	0.21	0.21	**0.20**
a.	7111	Passenger transportation	0.96	0.96	0.96	1.00	1.00	0.00	0.00	0.00
b.	7112	Freight transportation	0.96	0.96	0.96	1.00	1.00	0.00	0.00	0.00
c.	7113	Pushing and towing services	0.96	0.96	0.96	1.00	1.00	0.00	0.00	0.00
d.	8868	Maintenance and repair of rail transport equipment	0.96	0.93	0.93	1.00	1.00	0.07	0.07	1.00
e.	743	Supporting services for rail transport services	0.96	0.93	0.93	1.00	1.00	1.00	1.00	0.00
F.		**Road Transport Services**	**0.66**	0.69	0.78	1.00	1.00	0.50	0.50	**0.80**
a.	7121+7122	Passenger transportation	0.85	0.00	0.00	1.00	1.00	0.00	0.00	1.00
b.	7123	Freight transportation	0.89	0.67	0.96	1.00	1.00	0.00	0.00	1.00

c.	Rental of commercial vehicles with operator	7124	0.48	0.48	1.00	1.00	0.96	0.89	1.00	0.89
d.	Maintenance and repair of road transport equipment	6112+8867	1.00	1.00	1.00	1.00	1.00	0.96	1.00	0.00
e.	Supporting services for road transport services	744	1.00	1.00	1.00	1.00	0.96	0.93	0.00	
G.	Pipeline Transport		0.00	0.00	0.07	0.07	0.54	0.52	0.50	0.96
a.	Transportation of fuels	7131	0.00	0.00	0.07	0.07	0.07	0.07	0.00	
b.	Transportation of other goods	7139	0.00	0.00	0.07	0.07	1.00	0.96	1.00	0.96
H.	Services auxiliary to all modes of transport		0.37	0.37	0.67	0.67	0.95	0.59	0.33	0.96
a.	Cargo-handling services	741	0.00	0.00	0.00	0.00	0.96	0.00	0.00	
b.	Storage and warehouse services	742	0.11	0.11	1.00	1.00	0.96	0.89	1.00	0.96
c.	Freight transport agency services	748	1.00	1.00	1.00	1.00	0.93	0.89	0.00	
d.	Other	749								

EU–GEORGIA AA

NAME OF AGREEMENT: Association Agreement

PARTIES	The European Union and the European Atomic Energy Community and their Member States, of the one part, and Georgia, of the other part		

Type	Bilateral	Regional	Number of EU Member State parties: 28
	x		

Development level of the non-EU party	Developed	Developing
		x

STATUS OF THE AGREEMENT	Signature	In Force	Notification
	27/6/2014	1/7/2016	2/7/2014

ELEMENTS RELATED TO NON-DISCRIMINATION	Yes	No	Explanation
MFN		x	MFN limited to establishment (Art. 79(1) and 79(2)), subject to reservations in Annex XIV-A and XIV-E)
Standstill (prohibition of new or more discriminatory measures)		x	Limited to establishment (Art. 79(3))

WIDER PROCESS OF ECONOMIC INTEGRATION	Yes	No	Explanation
Progressive liberalization	x		Establishment (Art. 80) and Cross-border supply of services (Art. 87)
Art. XXIV GATT agreement	x		
Art. V bis GATS agreement		x	
Mode 3 relating also to goods	x		
Harmonization	x		Georgia under obligation to approximate a significant part of its trade-relevant legislation with the EU's
Mutual recognition		x	Services: non-binding, encourages relevant professional bodies to develop recommendations
Domestic regulation discipline(s)	x		Articles 93–95 set out disciplines on domestic regulation as affecting trade in services
Regulatory cooperation	x		
Transparency	x		Generally and also more specifically in the field of services
Intellectual property	x		

Element	Yes	No	Explanation
Public procurement	x		Gradual approximation of the public procurement legislation of Georgia with the EU's *acquis*
Competition policy	x		
Investment protection		x	
Labour mobility (labour market access)		x	
Labour protection	x		Commitment to basic ILO conventions, upholding their level of protection
Consumer protection	x		Georgia undertakes to approximate its consumer protection laws to the EU legislation
Environment	x		Cooperation on trade-related environmental issues & commitment to implement multilateral agreements
Cultural cooperation	x		
Sustainable development	x		Reaffirming commitment to sustainable development

OTHER ELEMENTS (related to services only)

Element	Yes	No	Explanation
Time-frame for implementation	x		Full implementation to be attained through gradual legislative approximation with EU laws
Ratchet clause (autonomous liberalization included)		x	
Safeguards		x	
Subsidies	x		A transparency and information obligation under Art. 206
Exceptions	x		GATS Art: XII XVI XIVbis x x x
Compatibility clause (relationship to Art. V GATS)		x	

Categories of Mode 4 covered

Category	Yes	No	Explanation
Cat. 1 Key personnel	x		Includes business visitors for establishment purposes and intra-corporate transferees
Cat. 1 Graduate trainees	x		
Cat. 1 Business sellers	x		Scheduled with key personnel & graduate trainees. Art. 90: incl. sellers of services & goods
Cat. 2 Contractual service suppliers	x		
Cat. 2 Independent professionals	x		
Cat. 2 Short term visitors for business purposes		x	

SECTORS	CPC	MODE 1		MODE 2		MODE 3		MODE 4: Cat.1		Mode 4: Cat. 2	
		SC	NT	SC	NT	SC	NT	SC	NT	SC	NT
AVERAGE FOR MODE		**0.44**	**0.46**	**0.77**	**0.83**	**0.93**	**0.74**	**0.50**	**0.84**	**0.19**	**0.40**
1. BUSINESS SERVICES		**0.73**	**0.72**	**0.95**	**0.94**	**1.00**	**0.90**	**0.44**	**0.57**	**0.46**	**0.49**
A. Professional Services		**0.54**	**0.45**	**1.00**	**0.95**	**1.00**	**0.79**	**0.99**	**0.66**	**0.59**	**0.43**
a. Legal Services	861	0.96	0.50	1.00	0.54	1.00	0.00	1.00	0.39	1.00	0.39
b. Accounting, auditing and bookkeeping services	862	0.36	0.25	1.00	1.00	1.00	0.68	1.00	0.71	0.00	0.46
c. Taxation Services	863	0.86	0.79	1.00	1.00	1.00	1.00	1.00	0.86	0.93	0.43
d. Architectural services	8671	0.68	0.54	1.00	1.00	1.00	0.89	1.00	0.79	1.00	0.43
e. Engineering services	8672	0.75	0.71	1.00	1.00	1.00	0.93	1.00	0.75	1.00	0.43
f. Integrated engineering services	8673	0.75	0.71	1.00	1.00	1.00	0.93	1.00	0.75	1.00	0.43
g. Urban planning and landscape architectural services	8674	0.61	0.54	1.00	1.00	1.00	0.89	1.00	0.79	1.00	0.43
h. Medical and dental services	9312	0.21	0.21	1.00	1.00	1.00	0.86	1.00	0.46	0.00	
i. Veterinary services	932	0.21	0.21	1.00	1.00	1.00	0.82	1.00	0.64	0.00	

Description	Code									
j. Services provided by midwives, nurses, physiotherapists and para-medical personnel	93191	0.04	0.04	1.00	1.00	1.00	0.93	0.93	0.43	0.00
k. Other										
B. Computer and Related Services		1.00	1.00	1.00	1.00	1.00	0.00	0.00	0.96	1.00
C. Research and Development Services		1.00	1.00	1.00	1.00	1.00	0.00	0.00	0.93	0.00
D. Real Estate Services		0.52	0.52	1.00	1.00	1.00	1.00	0.00	0.73	0.00
a. Involving own or leased property	821	0.50	0.50	1.00	1.00	1.00	1.00	0.00	0.75	0.00
b. On a fee or contract basis	822	0.54	0.54	1.00	1.00	1.00	1.00	0.00	0.71	0.00
E. Rental/Leasing Services without Operators		0.61	0.61	0.77	0.77	1.00	0.79	0.20	0.00	0.00
a. Relating to ships	83103	0.79	0.79	1.00	1.00	1.00	0.93	0.00	0.00	0.00
b. Relating to aircraft	83104	0.68	0.68	0.71	0.71	1.00	0.00	0.00	0.00	0.00
c. Relating to other transport equipment	83101+ 83102+	0.71	0.71	1.00	1.00	1.00	1.00	0.00	0.00	0.00
d. Relating to other machinery and equipment	83106–83109	0.71	0.71	1.00	1.00	1.00	1.00	0.00	0.00	0.00
e. Other	832	0.14	0.14	0.14	0.14	1.00	1.00	1.00	0.00	0.00

			0.72	0.72	0.91	0.91	1.00	0.83	0.47	0.88	0.31	0.52
F.	**Other Business Services**											
a.	Advertising services	871	1.00	1.00	1.00	1.00	1.00	1.00	0.00		1.00	0.57
b.	Market research and public opinion polling services	864	1.00	1.00	1.00	1.00	1.00	1.00	0.00		0.00	
c.	Management consulting service	865	1.00	1.00	1.00	1.00	1.00	1.00	0.00		1.00	0.50
d.	Services related to man. consulting	866	0.96	0.96	0.96	0.96	1.00	1.00	0.00		0.96	0.50
e.	Technical testing and analysis services	8676	0.68	0.68	0.75	0.75	1.00	0.96	1.00	0.93	1.00	0.54
f.	Services incidental to agriculture, hunting and forestry	881	0.82	0.82	1.00	1.00	1.00	1.00	1.00	0.96	0.00	
g.	Services incidental to fishing	882	0.86	0.86	1.00	1.00	1.00	1.00	0.00		0.00	
h.	Services incidental to mining	883+5115	1.00	1.00	1.00	1.00	1.00	1.00	1.00	0.96	0.00	
i.	Services incidental to manufacturing	884+885 (except for 88442)	1.00	1.00	1.00	1.00	1.00	1.00	0.00		0.00	
j.	Services incidental to energy distribution	887	0.00	0.00	1.00	1.00	1.00	0.04	0.00		0.00	
k.	Placement and supply services of personnel	872	0.04	0.04	0.50	0.50	1.00	0.07	0.00		0.00	
l.	Investigation and security	873	0.07	0.07	0.07	0.07	1.00	0.07	0.00		0.00	
m.	Related scientific and technical consulting services	8675	0.36	0.32	1.00	1.00	1.00	0.96	1.00	0.79	0.89	0.46
n.	Maintenance and repair of equipment (not including maritime vessels, aircraft or other transport equipment)	633+ 8861–8866	1.00	1.00	1.00	1.00	1.00	0.96	1.00	0.82	1.00	0.57

	Code									
o. Building-cleaning services	874	0.07	0.07	1.00	1.00	1.00	1.00	1.00	0.75	0.00
p. Photographic services	875	0.79	0.79	1.00	1.00	0.93	1.00	1.00	0.86	0.00
q. Packaging services	876	1.00	1.00	1.00	1.00	1.00	0.00	0.00		0.00
r. Printing, publishing	88442	1.00	1.00	1.00	1.00	0.86	1.00	1.00	0.89	0.00
s. Convention services	87909	1.00	1.00	1.00	1.00	1.00	1.00	1.00	0.96	0.00
t. Other	8790									
2. COMMUNICATION SERVICES		**0.75**	**1.00**	**1.00**	**0.75**	**1.00**	**0.00**	**1.00**	**0.96**	**0.00**
A. Postal services	7511	1.00	1.00	1.00	1.00	1.00	0.00	0.00		0.00
B. Courier services	7512	1.00	1.00	1.00	1.00	1.00	0.00	0.00		0.00
C. Telecommunication services		1.00	1.00	1.00	1.00	1.00	0.00	0.00		0.00
D. Audiovisual services		0.00	0.00	0.00	0.00	0.00	0.00	0.00		0.00
3. CONSTRUCTION AND RELATED ENGINEERING SERVICES		**1.00**	**1.00**	**1.00**	**1.00**	**1.00**	**1.00**	**1.00**	**0.96**	**0.00**
4. DISTRIBUTION SERVICES		**0.36**	**0.36**	**0.75**	**0.75**	**0.79**	**0.25**	**1.00**	**0.96**	**0.00**
A. Commission agents' services	621	0.11	0.11	0.11	0.11		0.00	0.00		0.00
B. Wholesale trade services	622	0.61	0.61	0.89	0.89		0.00	0.00		0.00
C. Retailing services	631+632 6111+6113+6121	0.36	0.36	1.00	1.00		1.00	1.00	0.96	0.00
D. Franchising	8929	0.36	0.36	1.00	1.00		0.00	0.00		0.00
E. Other										

	Code									
5.	**EDUCATIONAL SERVICES**		0.60	0.56	0.62	0.62	1.00	0.72	0.60	0.86	0.00
A.	Primary education services	921	0.71	0.64	0.75	0.75	1.00	0.86	1.00	0.89	0.00
B.	Secondary education services	922	0.71	0.64	0.79	0.79	1.00	0.86	1.00	0.86	0.00
C.	Higher education services	923	0.68	0.61	0.68	0.68	1.00	0.89	1.00	0.82	0.00
D.	Adult education	924	0.79	0.79	0.79	0.79	1.00	0.89	0.00		0.00
E.	Other education services	929	0.11	0.11	0.11	0.11	1.00	0.11	0.00		0.00
6.	**ENVIRONMENTAL SERVICES**		0.10	0.10	1.00	1.00	1.00	0.00	0.00	1.00	0.54
A.	Sewage services	9401	0.11	0.11	1.00	1.00			0.00	0.79	0.00
B.	Refuse disposal services	9402	0.07	0.07	1.00	1.00			0.00	0.79	0.00
C.	Sanitation and similar services	9403	0.11	0.11	1.00	1.00			0.00	0.89	0.00
D.	Other										
7.	**FINANCIAL SERVICES**		0.00	0.00	0.52	0.52	1.00	0.54	1.00	0.79	0.00
A.	All insurance and insurance-related services	812	0.00	0.00	0.11	0.11	1.00	0.54	1.00	0.79	0.00
B.	Banking and other financial services (excl. insurance)		0.00	0.00	0.93	0.93	1.00	0.54	1.00	0.79	0.00
8.	**HEALTH RELTED AND SOCIAL SERVICES**		0.04	0.06	0.65	0.98	0.67	0.75	0.67	0.89	0.00

Service	Code	1	2	3	4	5	6	7	8	9
(other than those listed under 1.A.h.–j.)										
A. Hospital services	9311	0.04	0.04	1.00	1.00	0.96	1.00	0.89	0.00	
B. Other Human Health Services	9319 (other than 93191)	0.00	0.00	0.00	0.00	0.00	0.00	0.89	0.00	
C. Social Services	933	0.07	0.07	0.96	0.96	0.54	1.00	0.89	0.00	
D. Other										
9. TOURISM AND TRAVEL RELATED SERVICES		0.56	0.56	1.00	1.00	0.90	1.00	0.80	0.26	0.43
A. Hotels and restaurants (incl. catering)	641–643	0.11	0.11	1.00	1.00	0.96	1.00	0.93	0.00	
B. Travel agencies and tour operators services	7471	0.93	0.93	1.00	1.00	1.00	1.00	0.93	0.79	0.43
C. Tourist guides services	7472	0.64	0.64	1.00	1.00	0.75	1.00	0.54	0.00	
D. Other										
10. RECREATIONAL, CULTURAL AND SPORTING SERVICES (other than audiovisual services)		0.43	0.43	0.62	0.62	0.70	0.25	0.96	0.22	0.00
A. Entertainment services (incl. theatre, live bands and circus services)	9619	0.07	0.07	0.68	0.68	1.00	1.00	0.96	0.89	0.00
B. News agency services	962	1.00	1.00	1.00	1.00	0.96	0.00	0.00	0.00	
C. Libraries, archives, museums and other cultural services	963	0.04	0.04	0.07	0.07	0.86	0.00	0.00	0.00	

Description	Code										
D. Sporting and other recreational services	964	0.61	0.61	0.71	0.71	1.00	0.00	0.00	0.00	0.00	
E. Other											
11. TRANSPORT SERVICES											
A. Maritime Transport Services		**0.27**	**0.29**	**0.60**	**0.70**	**0.80**	**0.86**	**0.31**	**0.79**	**0.12**	**0.54**
a. Passenger transportation	7211	0.46	0.46	0.82	0.82	1.00	0.67	1.00	0.62	0.19	0.54
b. Freight transportation	7212	0.46	0.46	0.46	0.46	1.00	0.00	1.00	0.00	0.00	
c. Rental of vessels with crew	7213	0.50	0.50	1.00	1.00	1.00	0.00	1.00	0.89	0.00	0.54
d. Maintenance and repair of vessels	8868	0.43	0.43	1.00	1.00	1.00	1.00	1.00	0.96	0.96	0.54
e. Pushing and towing services	7214	0.00	0.00	1.00	1.00	1.00	1.00	1.00	0.89	0.00	
f. Supporting services for maritime transport	745	0.93	0.93	1.00	1.00	1.00	1.00	1.00	1.00	0.00	
B. Internal Waterways Transport		**0.43**	**0.42**	**0.71**	**0.70**	**1.00**	**0.96**	**0.17**	**0.96**	**0.16**	**0.54**
a. Passenger transportation	7221	0.54	0.50	0.61	0.57	1.00	0.89	0.00	0.00	0.00	
b. Freight transportation	7222	0.54	0.50	0.61	0.57	1.00	0.89	0.00	0.00	0.00	
c. Rental of vessels with crew	7223	0.43	0.43	0.96	0.96	1.00	1.00	0.00	0.00	0.00	
d. Maintenance and repair of vessels	8868	0.14	0.14	1.00	1.00	1.00	1.00	1.00	0.96	0.96	0.54
e. Pushing and towing services	7224	0.00	0.00	0.11	0.11	1.00	1.00	0.00	0.00	0.00	
f. Supporting services for internal waterway transport	745	0.96	0.96	0.96	0.96	1.00	1.00	0.00	0.00	0.00	

		Col1	Col2	Col3	Col4	Col5	Col6	Col7	Col8	Col9	Col10
C.	**Air Transport Services**	0.24	0.09	0.40	0.50	0.40	1.00	0.00		0.19	0.57
a.	Passenger transportation	731	0.00	0.00	0.00	0.00	0.00	0.00	0.00		0.00	0.00
b.	Freight transportation	732	0.00	0.00	0.00	0.00	0.00	0.00	0.00		0.00	0.00
c.	Rental of aircraft with crew	734	1.00	0.00	1.00	0.00	1.00	1.00	0.00		0.00	0.00
d.	Maintenance and repair of aircraft	8868	0.18	0.18	1.00	1.00	1.00	1.00	0.00		0.96	0.57
e.	Supporting services for air transport	746	0.00	0.00	0.00	0.00	0.00	0.00	0.00		0.00	0.00
D.	**Space Transport**	733	0.00	0.00	0.00	0.00	0.00	0.00	0.00		0.00	
E.	**Rail Transport Services**	0.21	0.21	0.80	0.80	1.00	0.98	0.00		0.19	0.57
a.	Passenger transportation	7111	0.00	0.00	1.00	1.00	1.00	0.96	0.00		0.00	0.00
b.	Freight transportation	7112	0.00	0.00	1.00	1.00	1.00	0.96	0.00		0.00	0.00
c.	Pushing and towing services	7113	0.00	0.00	0.00	0.00	1.00	0.96	0.00		0.00	0.00
d.	Maintenance and repair of rail transport equipment	8868	0.07	0.07	1.00	1.00	1.00	1.00	0.00		0.96	0.57
e.	Supporting services for rail transport services	743	0.96	0.96	1.00	1.00	1.00	1.00	0.00		0.00	0.00
F.	**Road Transport Services**	0.48	0.48	1.00	1.00	1.00	0.90	0.80	0.63	0.19	0.50

	Code										
a. Passenger transportation	7121+7122	0.00	0.00	1.00	1.00	1.00	0.75	1.00	0.82	0.00	
b. Freight transportation	7123	0.00	0.00	1.00	1.00	1.00	0.75	1.00	0.82	0.00	
c. Rental of commercial vehicles with operator	7124	0.46	0.46	1.00	1.00	1.00	1.00	1.00	0.89	0.00	0.50
d. Maintenance and repair of road transport equipment	6112+8867	1.00	1.00	1.00	1.00	1.00	1.00	1.00	0.00	0.96	
e. Supporting services for road transport services	744	0.96	0.96	1.00	1.00	1.00	1.00	0.00		0.00	
G. Pipeline Transport		0.00	0.00	0.11	0.11	1.00	0.52	0.50	0.96	0.00	
a. Transportation of fuels	7131	0.00	0.00	0.11	0.11	1.00	0.07	0.00	0.00	0.00	
b. Transportation of other goods	7139	0.00	0.00	0.11	0.11	1.00	0.96	1.00	0.96	0.00	
H. Services auxiliary to all modes of transport		0.36	0.36	0.99	0.99	1.00	1.00	0.00	0.00	0.00	
a. Cargo-handling services	741	0.00	0.00	0.96	0.96	1.00	1.00	0.00	0.00	0.00	
b. Storage and warehouse services	742	0.11	0.11	1.00	1.00	1.00	1.00	1.00	0.00	0.00	
c. Freight transport agency services	748	0.96	0.96	1.00	1.00	1.00	1.00	0.00	0.00	0.00	
d. Other	749										

EU–SOUTH KOREA FTA

NAME OF AGREEMENT — **Free Trade Agreement**

PARTIES — The European Union and its Member States, of the one part, and the Republic of Korea, of the other part

Type	Bilateral	Regional	Number of EU Member State parties:	27
	x			

Development level of non-EU party	Developed	Developing
	x	

STATUS OF THE AGREEMENT	Signature	In Force	Notification
	6/10/2010	1/7/2011	7/7/2011

ELEMENTS RELATED TO NON-DISCRIMINATION	Yes	No	Explanation
MFN	x		Limited to Modes 1 and 2 (Art. 7.8) and Mode 3 (Art. 7.14), subject to exceptions
Standstill (prohibition of new or more discriminatory measures)	x		Only in relation to the scheduled commitments (Art. 7.7)

WIDER PROCESS OF ECONOMIC INTEGRATION	Yes	No	Explanation
Progressive liberalization		x	
Art. XXIV GATT agreement	x		
Art. V bis GATS agreement		x	
Mode 3 relating also to goods	x		Regarding Modes 3 and 4, the EU has commitments also on certain non-service sectors
Harmonization		x	
Mutual recognition	x		Non-binding, encourages relevant bodies to develop recommendations + working group (Art. 7.21)
Domestic regulation discipline(s)	x		Non-binding, procedural requirements & endeavour to ensure objective criteria in different measures
Regulatory cooperation	x		Bilateral regulatory cooperation through various committees and sectoral working groups
Transparency	x		Generally and also more specifically in the field of services

	Yes	No	Explanation
Intellectual property	x		
Public procurement	x		
Competition policy	x		Chapter 11: covers goods, services, establishment. Competitive safeguards in telecomm's services.
Investment protection		x	
Labour mobility (labour market access)		x	
Labour protection	x		Commitment to basic ILO conventions, upholding their level of protection
Consumer protection		x	
Environment	x		Reaffirming commitment to multilateral environmental agreements, upholding level of protection
Cultural cooperation	x		Non-binding protocol
Sustainable development	x		Non-binding: economic development, social development and environmental protection

OTHER ELEMENTS (related to services only)	Yes	No	Explanation
Time frame for implementation		x	No phase-out periods on the EU side in services
Ratchet clause (autonomous liberalization included)		x	
Safeguards		x	
Subsidies		x	
Exceptions	x		GATS Art: XII XIV XIVbis x x
Compatibility clause (relationship to Art. V GATS)	x		Art. 1.1 of Chapter One ("Objectives")

Categories of Mode 4 covered	Yes	No	
Key personnel	x		Includes business visitors responsible for setting up an establishment and intra-corporate transferees
Graduate trainees	x		
Business service sellers	x		Scheduled together with key personnel and graduate trainees
Contractual service suppliers		x	Reaffirm obligations resulting from GATS commitments. Further commit's depend on GATS results
Independent professionals		x	The same as for contractual service suppliers
Short term visitors for business purposes		x	

SECTORS	CPC	MODE 1		MODE 2		MODE 3		MODE 4	
		SC	NT	SC	NT	SC	NT	SC	NT
AVERAGE FOR MODE		**0.44**	**0.46**	**0.73**	**0.79**	**0.80**	**0.79**	**0.48**	**0.84**
1. BUSINESS SERVICES		0.72	0.71	0.94	0.93	0.93	0.90	0.42	0.55
A. Professional Services		0.51	0.45	1.00	0.95	0.93	0.81	1.00	0.73
a. Legal Services	861	1.00	0.48	1.00	0.48	1.00	0.81	1.00	0.37
b. Accounting, auditing and bookkeeping services	862	0.33	0.22	1.00	1.00	1.00	0.67	1.00	0.96
c. Taxation Services	863	0.85	0.78	1.00	1.00	1.00	0.93	1.00	0.89
d. Architectural services	8671	0.56	0.56	1.00	1.00	1.00	0.93	1.00	0.81
e. Engineering services	8672	0.70	0.70	1.00	1.00	1.00	0.96	1.00	0.81
f. Integrated engineering services	8673	0.70	0.70	1.00	1.00	1.00	0.96	1.00	0.81

g.	Urban planning and landscape architectural services	8674	0.81	1.00	0.93	1.00	1.00	1.00	0.56	0.56
h.	Medical and dental services	9312	0.41	1.00	0.63	0.78	1.00	1.00	0.22	0.22
i.	Veterinary services	932	0.67	1.00	0.70	0.81	1.00	1.00	0.19	0.19
j.	Services provided by midwives, nurses, physiotherapists and para-medical personnel	93191	0.74	1.00	0.63	0.74	1.00	1.00	0.04	0.04
k.	Other									
B.	Computer and Related Services			0.00	1.00	1.00	1.00	1.00	1.00	1.00
C.	Research and Development Services			0.00	1.00	1.00	1.00	1.00	1.00	1.00
D.	Real Estate Services		0.72	1.00	1.00	1.00	1.00	1.00	0.52	0.52
a.	Involving own or leased property	821	0.74	1.00	1.00	1.00	1.00	1.00	0.52	0.52
b.	On a fee or contract basis	822	0.70	1.00	1.00	1.00	1.00	1.00	0.52	0.52

	Code								
E. Rental/Leasing Services without Operators		0.59	0.59	0.76	0.76	0.79	0.77	0.20	0.00
a. Relating to ships	83103	0.78	0.78	1.00	1.00	1.00	0.93	0.00	0.00
b. Relating to aircraft	83104	0.67	0.67	0.70	0.70	0.00	0.00	0.00	0.00
c. Relating to other transport equipment	83101+ 83102+	0.70	0.70	1.00	1.00	1.00	1.00	0.00	0.00
d. Relating to other machinery and equipment	83106–83109	0.70	0.70	1.00	1.00	1.00	1.00	0.00	0.00
e. Other	832	0.11	0.11	0.11	0.11	0.93	0.93	1.00	0.00
F. Other Business Services		0.72	0.72	0.88	0.88	0.85	0.84	0.32	0.77
a. Advertising services	871	1.00	1.00	1.00	1.00	1.00	1.00	0.00	
b. Market research and public opinion polling services	864	1.00	1.00	1.00	1.00	1.00	1.00	0.00	
c. Management consulting service	865	1.00	1.00	1.00	1.00	1.00	1.00	0.00	
d. Services related to man. consulting	866	0.96	0.96	0.96	0.96	0.96	0.96	0.00	
e. Technical testing and analysis serv.	8676	0.67	0.67	0.70	0.70	1.00	1.00	1.00	0.93

	Description	CPC code								
f.	Services incidental to agriculture, hunting and forestry	881	0.81	0.81	1.00	1.00	1.00	1.00	0.00	
g.	Services incidental to fishing	882	0.85	0.85	1.00	1.00	1.00	1.00	0.00	
h.	Services incidental to mining	883+5115	1.00	1.00	1.00	1.00	1.00	1.00	0.00	
i.	Services incidental to manufacturing	884+885 (except for 88442)	1.00	1.00	1.00	1.00	1.00	1.00	0.00	
j.	Services incidental to energy distribution	887	0.00	0.00	0.04	0.04	0.04	0.04	0.00	
k.	Placement and supply services of Personnel	872	0.04	0.04	0.04	0.04	0.04	0.04	0.00	
l.	Investigation and security	873	0.07	0.07	0.07	0.07	0.15	0.11	0.00	
m.	Related scientific and technical consulting services	8675	0.33	0.33	1.00	1.00	1.00	0.96	1.00	0.81
n.	Maintenance and repair of equipment (not including maritime vessels, aircraft or other transport equipment)	633+ 8861–8866	1.00	1.00	1.00	1.00	1.00	1.00	0.00	0.00
o.	Building-cleaning services	874	0.07	0.07	1.00	1.00	1.00	1.00	1.00	0.78
p.	Photographic services	875	0.81	0.81	1.00	1.00	1.00	1.00	1.00	0.93
q.	Packaging services	876	1.00	1.00	1.00	1.00	1.00	1.00	0.00	

	Code								
r. Printing, publishing	88442	0.96	1.00	0.85	1.00	1.00	1.00	1.00	1.00
s. Convention services	87909	0.96	1.00	1.00	1.00	1.00	1.00	1.00	1.00
t. Other	8790								
2. COMMUNICATION SERVICES			**0.00**	1.00	**0.75**	1.00	**0.75**	1.00	**0.75**
A. Postal services	7511		0.00	1.00	1.00	1.00	1.00	1.00	1.00
B. Courier services	7512		0.00	1.00	1.00	1.00	1.00	1.00	1.00
C. Telecommunication services			0.00	1.00	1.00	1.00	1.00	1.00	
D. Audiovisual services			0.00		0.00	0.00	0.00		0.00
3. CONSTRUCTION AND RELATED ENGINEERING SERVICES		0.96	**1.00**	1.00	**1.00**	1.00	**1.00**	1.00	**1.00**
4. DISTRIBUTION SERVICES			**0.00**	0.95	**0.95**	0.40	**0.40**	0.40	**0.40**
A. Commission agents' services	621		0.00	1.00	1.00	0.11	0.11	0.11	0.11
B. Wholesale trade services	622		0.00	1.00	1.00	0.11	0.11	0.11	0.11

	Code								
C. Retailing services	631+632 6111+6113+6121	0.37	0.37	0.37	0.37	0.81	0.81	0.00	0.00
D. Franchising	8929	1.00	1.00	1.00	1.00	1.00	1.00	0.00	0.00
E. Other									
5. EDUCATIONAL SERVICES		0.57	0.56	0.62	0.62	0.59	0.58	0.60	0.86
A. Primary education services	921	0.67	0.67	0.78	0.78	0.67	0.67	1.00	0.89
B. Secondary education services	922	0.67	0.67	0.78	0.78	0.67	0.67	1.00	0.85
C. Higher education services	923	0.67	0.59	0.67	0.67	0.67	0.67	1.00	0.85
D. Adult education	924	0.78	0.78	0.81	0.81	0.89	0.89	0.00	
E. Other education services	929	0.07	0.07	0.07	0.07	0.07	0.00	0.00	
6. ENVIRONMENTAL SERVICES		0.00	0.00	1.00	1.00	1.00	1.00	0.00	
7. FINANCIAL SERVICES		0.04	0.04	0.52	0.52	1.00	0.30	1.00	0.81

A.	All insurance and insurance-related services	812	0.07	0.07	0.11	0.11	1.00	0.59	1.00	0.81
B.	Banking and other financial services (excl. insurance)		0.00	0.00	0.93	0.93	1.00	0.00	1.00	0.81
8.	**HEALTH RELATED AND SOCIAL SERVICES** (other than those listed under 1.A.h–j.)		**0.05**	**0.08**	**0.65**	**0.98**	**0.35**	**0.52**	**0.67**	**0.89**
A.	Hospital services	9311	0.04	0.04	1.00	1.00	0.52	0.52	1.00	0.89
B.	Other Human Health Services	9319 (other than 93191)	0.00		0.00	0.00	0.00		0.00	
C.	Social Services	933	0.11	0.11	0.96	0.96	0.52	0.52	1.00	0.89
D.	Other									
9.	**TOURISM AND TRAVEL RELATED SERVICES**		**0.56**	**0.56**	**1.00**	**1.00**	**0.98**	**0.96**	**1.00**	**0.83**
A.	Hotels and restaurants (incl. catering)	641–643	0.11	0.11	1.00	1.00	1.00	0.96	1.00	0.96
B.	Travel agencies and tour operators services	7471	0.93	0.93	1.00	1.00	0.93	0.93	1.00	0.96
C.	Tourist guides services	7472	0.63	0.63	1.00	1.00	1.00	1.00	1.00	0.56

	Code								
D. Other									
10. RECREATIONAL, CULTURAL AND SPORTING SERVICES (other than audiovisual services)		0.33	0.33	0.49	0.49	0.67	0.67	0.25	0.96
A. Entertainment services	9619	0.07	0.07	0.56	0.56	0.59	0.59	1.00	0.96
B. News agency services	962	0.59	0.59	0.63	0.63	0.56	0.56	0.00	
C. Libraries, archives, museums and other cultural services	963	0.04	0.04	0.07	0.07	0.93	0.93	0.00	
D. Sporting and other recreational services	964	0.63	0.63	0.70	0.70	0.59	0.59	0.00	
E. Other									
11. TRANSPORT SERVICES		0.39	0.43	0.64	0.75	0.60	0.76	0.31	0.83
A. Maritime Transport Services		0.75	0.75	1.00	1.00	0.98	0.94	1.00	0.72
a. Passenger transportation	7211	1.00	1.00	1.00	1.00	1.00	1.00	1.00	0.00
b. Freight transportation	7212	1.00	1.00	1.00	1.00	1.00	1.00	1.00	1.00

	Code								
c. Rental of vessels with crew	7213	0.48	0.48	1.00	1.00	0.96	0.89	1.00	0.78
d. Maintenance and repair of vessels	8868	0.26	0.26	1.00	1.00	1.00	1.00	1.00	0.96
e. Pushing and towing services	7214	*	*	1.00	1.00	0.96	0.89	1.00	0.78
f. Supporting services for maritime transport	745	1.00	1.00	1.00	1.00	0.96	0.89	1.00	0.78
B. Internal Waterways Transport		**0.43**	**0.43**	**0.67**	**0.67**	**0.94**	**0.88**	**0.00**	
a. Passenger transportation	7221	0.52	0.52	0.52	0.52	1.00	0.96	0.00	
b. Freight transportation	7222	0.52	0.52	0.52	0.52	0.96	0.89	0.00	
c. Rental of vessels with crew	7223	0.44	0.44	1.00	1.00	0.89	0.81	0.00	
d. Maintenance and repair of vessels	8868	0.11	0.11	1.00	1.00	1.00	1.00	0.00	
e. Pushing and towing services	7224	0.00	0.00	0.00	0.00	0.89	0.81	0.00	
f. Supporting services for internal waterway transport	745	1.00	1.00	1.00	1.00	0.89	0.81	0.00	

	Code	0.20	0.10	0.40	0.50	0.40	0.50	0.00	0.00
C. Air Transport Services								0.00	
a. Passenger transportation	731	0.00	0.00	0.00	0.00	0.00	0.00	0.00	
b. Freight transportation	732	0.00	0.00	0.00	0.00	0.00	0.00	0.00	
c. Rental of aircraft with crew	734	1.00	0.00	1.00	0.00	1.00	0.00	0.00	
d. Maintenance and repair of aircraft	8868	0.19	0.19	1.00	1.00	1.00	1.00	0.00	
e. Supporting services for air transport	746	0.00	0.00	0.00		0.00		0.00	
D. Space Transport	733	0.00	0.00	0.00	1.00	0.00		0.00	
E. Rail Transport Services		0.21	0.21	1.00	1.00	0.96	0.94	0.20	0.96
a. Passenger transportation	7111	0.00	0.00	1.00	1.00	0.96	0.96	0.00	
b. Freight transportation	7112	0.00	0.00	1.00	1.00	0.96	0.96	0.00	
c. Pushing and towing services	7113	0.00	0.00	1.00	1.00	0.96	0.93	0.00	
d. Maintenance and repair of rail transport equipment	8868	0.07	0.07	1.00	1.00	0.96	0.93	1.00	0.96
e. Supporting services for rail transport services	743	1.00	1.00	1.00	1.00	0.96	0.93	0.00	

F.	**Road Transport Services**		0.50	0.49	1.00	1.00	0.96	0.68	0.80	0.69
a.	Passenger transportation	7121+7122	0.00	0.00	1.00	1.00	0.93	0.00	1.00	0.85
b.	Freight transportation	7123	0.00	0.00	1.00	1.00	0.96	0.74	1.00	0.89
c.	Rental of commercial vehicles with operator	7124	0.48	0.46	1.00	1.00	0.96	0.85	1.00	1.00
d.	Maintenance and repair of road transport equipment	6112+8867	1.00	1.00	1.00	1.00	1.00	0.96	1.00	0.00
e.	Supporting services for road transport services	744	1.00	1.00	1.00	1.00	0.96	0.85	0.00	
G.	**Pipeline Transport**		0.00	0.00	0.07	0.07	0.54	0.52	0.50	0.96
a.	Transportation of fuels	7131	0.00	0.00	0.07	0.07	0.07	0.07	0.00	
b.	Transportation of other goods	7139	0.00	0.00	0.07	0.07	1.00	0.96	1.00	0.96
H.	**Services auxiliary to all modes of transport**		1.00	1.00	1.00	1.00	0.00	0.89	0.00	
a.	Cargo-handling services	741	*	*	1.00	1.00	0.00	0.89	0.00	
b.	Storage and warehouse services	742	1.00	1.00	1.00	1.00	0.00	0.89	0.00	
c.	Freight transport agency services	748	1.00	1.00	1.00	1.00	0.00	0.89	0.00	
d.	Other	749								

* Unbound due to lack of technical feasibility

INDEX

Lightning Source UK Ltd.
Milton Keynes UK
UKHW020133150622
404450UK00009B/100